Wheaton Public Library
225 N. Cross
Wheaton, Illinois 60187

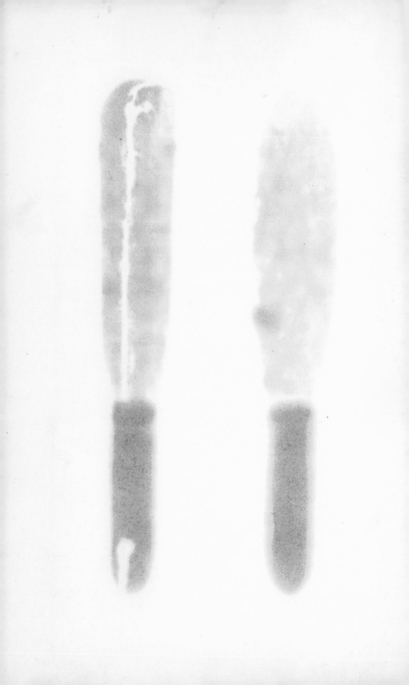

THE PHILOSOPHY
OF KANT

IMMANUEL KANT'S
MORAL AND POLITICAL
WRITINGS

THE PHILOSOPHY OF
KANT

IMMANUEL KANT'S MORAL
AND POLITICAL WRITINGS

Edited, with an Introduction, by

CARL J. FRIEDRICH

THE MODERN LIBRARY · NEW YORK

To my brother

O T T O

Sapere Auàe

PREFACE

Ever since I sat at the feet of the neo-Kantians, especially Natorp and Rickert, philosophy in general, and Kant's critical approach to it in particular, has been close to me, even though my professional concern was largely with its legal, political and critical aspects. Having experienced in my youth the "Copernican revolution" of which Kant speaks in the Preface to the second edition of the *Critique of Pure Reason*, I have often been impatient with what have seemed to me the rather naive discussions on methodology in the contemporary social sciences. At the present time, these problems are challenging the general interest in connection with the arguments over academic freedom. It therefore seems well to present to all interested Americans the thought of him who believed that of all freedoms that of speaking and writing with complete liberty on philosophical and scientific matters was the most important, and that of all values that of personal integrity was the most nearly fundamental. To make *that personal* freedom secure was the meaning and significance of laboring for constitutional government; i.e., for government under and according to law throughout the world. It is the heart of the belief in the common man for which Kant was the most outspoken advocate.

The study here presented is based upon the conviction that philosophers, like all of us, should be judged by their "fruit." Peace is the most urgent objective of foreign and domestic policy. Kant is the one great philosopher of the golden age of European philosophy who never wavered in his attachment to this task. Indeed, every one of his major works returns to the problem, and he is author of the well-known remark that one of the basic moral truths (categorical imperatives) is: "There shall not be war." Hence the selections presented here build up to that final culmination of Kantian philosophy, the essay "On Eternal Peace." Anyone who undertakes to evaluate critically the particular omissions, and the inclusion of the *Prolegomena* rather than the *Critique of Pure Reason*, ought to bear in mind that our view is that Kant's philosophy, existentially

vii

speaking, revolves around "peace" and *not* around "cognition."
The interested layman should not begin, but should *end* with
the *Critique of Pure Reason,* which ought to be read entire. The
author's *Inevitable Peace* will provide a more detailed argument
and interpretation for him who desires to probe more deeply.

Thanks are due to all the able men who have labored in the
vineyard of Kant's works, trying to render them in clear and
adequate English, especially Abbot, Bax, Bernard, Hastie, Mere-
dith, Müller, Paton, Norman K. Smith and now Beck. Great
help has been derived from their work, but each of them had, of
course, his own interpretation of Kant's "meaning" to guide him.
As the German original, Ernst Cassirer's edition, *Immanuel
Kant's Werke* (1922 ff.) has been used, and is referred to as
Works throughout. The *Akademieausgabe,* while preferred by
some, is more cumbersome to use, and the differences are not important for the work here in hand. Besides, Cassirer has, in Vol.
XI, given the perhaps most searching modern interpretation of
Kant's life and teachings.

I have had the devoted assistance of Jocelyn Kingsbury
throughout these editorial labors, as well as some initial help
from Dorothy Smith. Among the many friends who have helped
through argument and discussion, I must mention especially
Richard McKeon who first encouraged me to undertake this
task.

I am dedicating this book to my brother Otto, because he is
one of the few persons I have known who has tried to live up to
Kant's dictum never to use himself or another merely as a means,
but always to consider man as an end in himself—the core of
true humanism.

Carl J. Friedrich

Concord, Massachusetts
October, 1949

CONTENTS

* Translated by CARL J. FRIEDRICH

INTRODUCTION

by CARL J. FRIEDRICH

I

Immanuel Kant was born on April 22, 1724, and he died on February 12, 1804. He was therefore a child of the Age of Enlightenment and a witness of the French and American Revolutions. He grew up in "the heavenly city of the eighteenth-century philosophers" and lived in it until his fifty-seventh year, at which time he delivered the mortal blow against his century's unbounded faith in the limitless potentialities of reason. No one who has fully grasped the meaning of the *Critique of Pure Reason,* which appeared in 1781, has been able again to use reason as the uncritical philosophers of the Age of Reason used it. In agony, Kant's friend Moses Mendelssohn called him "the smasher of everything." Thus Kant dethroned the "Goddess Reason" even before the French revolutionaries erected altars to her. In doing this he once more vindicated the autonomy of the mind and so was not fifty years behind the actual events, as the man of affairs Edmund Burke then alleged, but fifty years ahead of them. Admittedly, Burke would not have understood what Kant was talking about, any more than he could sympathize with the Revolution the way Kant did. The message of Jean-Jacques Rousseau, whom Kant called the Newton of the moral world, was lost upon the English orator and traditionalist to whom all was sacred that bore the imprint of time, even the poorhouse and rotten borough. But if the critique of reason was lost on Burke, it was equally lost on Bentham and the utilitarians whose crude rationalism startles the modern reader. Finally, and perhaps most important, Kant's penetrating analysis of the limits of the speculative reason was entirely ineffectual in curbing the boundless enthusiasm of the Romantics and their transcendental idealism, from Fichte to Hegel. They immediately set to work to "round out" the Kantian system by providing that "missing" primary cause or basic principle which Kant had labored so hard to prove was beyond the limits of reason. It is as though the mathematicians, when the impossibility of squaring the circle had at last been established, had nevertheless set to work and proclaimed a new answer to this ancient problem.

It has been the misfortune of much American comment on Kant's philosophy that Kant has so frequently been viewed through the eyes of later German philosophers, especially Hegel. A striking instance is provided by John Dewey who comments upon Kant in terms suggesting that he thought that Kant expounded the very uncritical rationalism against which Kant's entire philosophizing is directed.[1] No one was more clearly aware than Kant of the tentative, hypothetical nature of all experiments and of the necessity for testing such hypothetical judgments by experience. Likewise, in matters of human nature, he insisted upon testing one's hypotheses by reference to one's actions.[2] Another instance of current misinterpretation is George Santayana's glib generalizations about the subjectivism of Kant's philosophy. These gibes were occasioned by a war-born desire to prove a thesis and are virtually the reverse of the truth. Actually, Kant's philosophy is among the most rigidly "objective" systems; it is inspired by a profound sense of the reality of existence as distinct from the mind of man. We shall point out presently that Kant sees the mind as essentially an instrument or tool having definite limits which it is the task of philosophy to ascertain.[3]

Kant's is a systematic philosophy par excellence. In striking contrast to philosophers like David Hume, only twelve years his senior, his basic work was completed at a time of life when most men consider their creative labors finished. Among great modern philosophers, only one can be compared with Kant in this respect; the philosopher of Malmesbury, Thomas Hobbes. He, too, was past his middle fifties when his first major work, De Cive, appeared, and he was even sixty-three when the Leviathan fully presented his philosophy. In many respects the two philosophers were poles apart, but they also had some strik-

---

[1] The Quest for Certainty (1928), pp. 58–62, 287–291.
[2] See e.g. below, pp. 154 ff.   [3] See below, pp. XXV ff.

ing characteristics in common. They shared the qualities of timidity paired with delight in conversation, a lack of erotic interest combined with a touch of misanthropy, and great moderation and self-discipline offset by tremendous intellectual enthusiasm. These two most systematic philosophers both experienced a curious philosophical fate; they philosophized in constant juxtaposition to a fellow philosopher who, unlike themselves, was an inspirational genius: Descartes in the case of Hobbes, Hume in the case of Kant. Yet Hobbes at the beginning of modern scientific rationalism and Kant at its zenith are both in the end preoccupied with the problem of government, of power and law, of how to preserve peace among bellicose and nasty men; but whereas Hobbes opted for power, Kant opted for law, and whereas Hobbes opted for determinism, Kant opted for freedom.

Indeed, the problem of freedom, the freedom of the human personality to unfold and fulfill its higher destiny, is the central issue of all of Kant's philosophizing. It is my conviction that he sought to restrict and limit the belief in the boundless potentialities of reason because, from Hobbes to Voltaire, that view was part of the philosophy of enlightened despotism, with its contempt for the common man who may possess a "sense of right," but who has no insight into the vast complexities of the laws of nature and the processes of history. Kant thus became *the* philosopher of the American and French revolutions, of liberalism and constitutionalism, and of the bourgeoisie who carried them to victory. But, like all philosophers of the first magnitude—like Plato and Aristotle, St. Thomas and Confucius, Descartes and Hobbes—Kant's philosophy transcends his historical role. He once again succeeded in identifying a fundamental problem and "solved it" for mankind ever after. The problem is: What are the limits of the human mind, what are the forms into which all human thought is cast, what is the function of this instrument given to man as we all know him? Like other great philosophers, Kant had the capacity for wondering about that which was taken for granted by all others. In an early essay, *Einführung des Begriffs der negativen Grössen in*

die Weltweisheit (1763), he remarks toward the end: [4] "I, who
. . . usually understand that the least which all people believe
readily to understand." This Socratic capacity to wonder at the
"obvious" found poetical expression in Kant's most famous saying wherein at the height of his ethical philosophy he proclaimed the famous cosmic awe: "Two matters fill me with
ever renewed wonder: the starred heaven above me and the
moral law within me."

II

Kant was the son of a poor saddle-maker who was a master-
craftsman, but definitely a man of the people. Kant's unshakable
faith in the common man, in the common humanity of all men,
probably had its foundation in this simple family background.
He was deeply attached to his mother, a woman of strong religious convictions, who reared him in the strict Lutheran
creed, but in its pietistic, that is to say, puritanical form. The
Pietists were a sect which, like the Methodists, sprang up in the
eighteenth century as a revivalist movement within the Lutheran church. While outwardly conformist and lacking in rad-
icalism, pietism was nevertheless radical in its insistence upon
individual piety. The strong humanitarian impulses which
pietism fostered inclined its adherents toward a support of the
democratic movement. There can be no question but that these
basic attitudes remained with Kant throughout his life, even
though as a mature man he showed no interest in participating
in church services and his theological views were broadly those
of the enlightenment. He laid stress upon the ethical aspect of
a "rational religion" as contrasted with the revelation of specific
creeds,[5] but also saw this "religion" as historically evolving
through these creeds, rather than unrelated to them.

In maintaining this "rational religion," Kant was, of course,
diametrically opposed to a central tenet of pietism which in part
constituted a revolt against such rationalism. The drama of this
situation is illuminated by an anecdote which occurred when

---

[4] *Works*, II, p. 240.
[5] See Ernst Troeltsch, *Das Historische in Kant's Religionsphilosophie*
(1904)

Kant sought the help of his former preacher, F. A. Schultz
(1692–1793), in applying for a professorship at Koenigsberg
University in 1758. Schultz asked him gravely: "Do you fear
God from the bottom of your heart?" "Yes," said Kant, and old
Schultz was satisfied. This Kant could say later, as well as in
1758, in spite of his "rationalism," because for him the word
"rational" had a limited meaning, different from the prevailing
eighteenth-century mood. This limitation put God and the faith
in Him beyond the sharp attacks of a Thomas Paine. Yet Kant
partly sympathized with the attack on revelation, for he stood
between Paine and those Paine sought to prove wrong in his
Age of Reason. We can catch here a glimpse of the root issue
from which Kant's critical analysis of reason evolved. It is as if
he had sought to mediate between pietism and rationalism, between mysticism and science, by restricting both to their respective spheres in the mind of man. Kant himself once expressed very well his regard for what was good in pietism when
he told a friend: "The religious views of that time (his youth)
and the notions of what was called virtue and piety may have
been anything but clear and satisfactory, yet the thing itself had
been found. One may say of pietism what he will. Just the
same, the people who took it seriously excelled in a venerable
way. They possessed the highest (quality) which man can
possess, that repose, that serenity, that inner peace which is not
disturbed by passions. No want, no persecution put them into
ill-humor; no controversy was able to provoke them to anger or
enmity. In a word, even the mere observer was involuntarily
compelled to respect. I still remember once how disputes arose
between the guilds of the harness-makers and the saddlers over
their respective privileges which caused my father rather considerable trouble. Nevertheless, even in conversations at home,
this quarrel was treated by my parents with such forbearance
and charity toward their opponents, and with so much trust in
Providence, that the memory of it will never leave me, even
though I was then merely a boy." [6]

---

[6] Rink, *Ansichten aus Immanuel Kant's Leben,* Koenigsberg, 1805,
p. 22 ff, as quoted by Cassirer, Works XI, p. 15.

At the same time, Kant detested the rigorous regulation and mechanization of religion and this feeling carried him to the point where he rejected all prayer. His later insistence upon religion as the basis for doing good for its own sake, as contrasted with all systems of morality which relate the doing of good to the securing of some reward, has its root in this deeply felt difference between the piety of his parents and the severe discipline of his school years. He often in later life commented upon the evils of such strict discipline. To be sure, during the eight years he spent at the *Gymnasium Fridericianum* in Koenigsberg, he acquired his thorough knowledge of Latin and Greek, yet "terror and fear seized him, when he recalled the 'slavery' of his youth." [7] And one of Kant's fellow students, the philosopher David Ruhnken, recalled thirty years later "the pedantic and somber discipline of the fanatics" at the *Fridericianum.*

At sixteen, in 1740, Kant entered "college," that is to say, he commenced the general studies in the philosophical faculty which preceded the work in one of the three professional schools of theology, law and medicine that together composed the University of Koenigsberg. During this period, Kant was primarily attracted by the study of the natural sciences, and for thirty years thereafter he devoted a considerable part of his energies to work in these fields. Newtonian physics and its astronomical ramifications especially aroused his interest. His first elaborated piece of work, presented to the dean of the philosophical faculty in 1746, was concerned with the problem of living forces as presented in the philosophies of Leibnitz, Newton, Wolff and others. His first major work, published in 1755, was *A General Natural History and Theory of the Heavens or an Essay concerning the constitution and the mechanical origin of the entire universe, treated according to Newtonian principles.* This much-neglected work seeks to develop a secular theory of cosmology in place of Newton's own deistic doctrine. Kant states: "However, the very difficulty which deprived Newton of the hope of explaining from forces of nature the motor force of the celestial

---

[7] Karl Vorlender, *Immanuel Kant's Leben* (1921), p. 10.

bodies, whose direction and determinations constitute the systematic edifice of the universe, has been the source of the doctrine we have expounded. This doctrine establishes a mechanical explanation: but one which is far removed from the one Newton found inadequate." His theory, which resembles that of Laplace (though not as much as is often claimed), still bears strong resemblances to some aspects of the view prevailing at the present time.[8] It is not necessary to concern oneself with the place Kant's view occupies in the history of science, for it is limited indeed. But it is worth bearing in mind that his first major effort was directed toward extending the realm of science and restricting the realm of theology. To him who is interested in Kant's philosophy of man and morals, it is especially striking that this general natural history and theory of the heavens concludes with an attempt to "compare" the inhabitants of different planets. This attempt was grounded in his general concept of nature. The concept is of such lasting significance for his philosophy that it is worth quoting. "Nature, although it has an essential determination (Bestimmung) toward perfection and order, comprises within its manifold sphere all possible variations, even faults and deviations. This same unlimited fertility of nature has created the inhabited celestial spheres and the comets, the useful mountains and the noxious riffs, the inhabitable regions and the desolate wastelands, the virtues and vices." It seems most significant that, from the beginning, Kant saw man as a part of nature and shaped by its forces as long as man is considered "from the outside," as a phenomenon.[9] After having argued that there must be living beings on other planets and that they will in part be superior, in part inferior, to man, Kant quotes Pope as imagining a planet where Newton would be looked upon as no better than a monkey seems to us, he stresses the inherent reasonableness of progress. He concludes with a panegyric on the inspiration which the sublime majesty of nature provides for a sensitive beholder. "Indeed, when one has filled one's mind with such reflections as the foregoing, the sight

---

[8] Cf, e.g., Sir James Jeans, The Universe Around Us, Ch. VI, "Beginnings and Endings."
[9] See below, pp. 116 f.

of a starred heaven on a fair evening gives a kind of pleasure which only noble souls can feel."

The year that this work appeared Kant had become a lecturer at the University of Koenigsberg, after nine years as a private tutor in several homes in the province of East Prussia. We know little of these intervening years; they evidently served to provide Kant with time to mature. His quiet, gay, sociable nature no doubt made him a pleasant companion. During the first few years at the university, Kant, in addition to his cosmology, published a number of smaller studies in the field of natural science, including some in physical geography, which he was the first to teach at Koenigsberg.

"In the sixties, a transformation begins to be apparent in Kant's thought at the expense of the mathematico-scientific, and even the scholastico-metaphysical." [10] This transformation was, in a sense, a return to earlier influences. Having fully explored the realm of science with its necessary laws and having perceived its limits, Kant became concerned with the realm of freedom—that other primary experience of man: will. During these years, he was profoundly stirred by the writings of Jean-Jacques Rousseau. To the uncomprehending neighbors who had long been amused by the clock-like regularity of the professor's daily life—they set their clocks by the time Magister Kant passed their windows on his afternoon walk—this inner drama was reflected by Kant not appearing one day. He had forgotten his walk over the reading of Rousseau's *Emile* (1762). Kant's devotion to Rousseau remained strong throughout his life; a bust of Rousseau became the only adornment of his simple study. This increasing concern with the moral and spiritual world produced two works of considerable significance, sketching as they do basic elements of Kant's moral philosophy. They appeared in 1763 and are entitled, *The One Possible Proof for Demonstrating the Existence of God*, and *Inquiry into the Clearness of the Principles of Natural Theology and Morals*. In both, the typical Kantian mode of thinking appears: the determina-

---

[10] Paulsen, Friedrich, *Immanuel Kant, His Life and Doctrine*, translated from the revised German edition by J. E. Creighton and Albert Lefevre (1902), p. 38.

tion to restrict all mental operations to their proper sphere, and not to claim greater results than are warranted by the intellectual tools available to finite man and finite minds. In the first work, he undertook to modify the traditional view, which attempted to prove the existence of God from the essence of *things,* by stressing the necessary laws. Identifying God with "absolute existence," Kant asks: can we arrive at certain proof of the existence of God if we do not posit anything but the certainty of eternal laws which constitute "general possibilities?" Kant answers this question in the affirmative and declares: "If all existence is suspended, nothing is posited, and nothing is given as material for any kind of thought and all possibility whatever is completely eliminated. . . ." To say that there exists a possibility, but nothing real, is a contradiction in itself, because if nothing exists, nothing "thinkable" is given. . . .[11] Having thus established that we have certainty of an absolutely necessary existence, he proceeds to show that such existence posits an absolutely necessary being which is one and simple, which comprises all reality within itself, and which is of a purely spiritual nature.[12] These are the predicates which together constitute the concept of God.

We have in this argument a curious anticipation of Kant's transcendental method: the justification for positing existence is found in the fact that without thus positing existence we cannot understand the possibility of any understanding or cognition whatsoever. However, as Cassirer has rightly pointed out, such a position is not absolute, in terms of the later critical system, but is relative, since the laws remain limited to the realm of the experience which they make possible. This issue, which remained hidden in *The One Possible Proof* . . . , was brought forward in the second essay, *Inquiry* . . . , which Kant wrote in response to a contest the Prussian Academy of Science had announced in 1761. In this latter work the relative certainty of

[11] *Einzig Möglicher Beweisgrund,* 1. Abt., 2. Betrachtung, *Works,* II, p. 83.
[12] Loc. cit., pp. 86–92 (I. *Abt.* 3. *Betrachtung*). The comment of Cassirer, *Works,* XI, p. 65, is misleading because he fails to distinguish between "existence" and "being."

different kinds of evidence is made the central concern. Kant begins by pointing out the difference between the method of modern natural science which first gathers the data as offered by experience and then seeks to discover the regularities which are contained in their sequence. Thus gravitation, planetary motions and the like are first of all ascertained in their quantitative relationships, and then a search is made for an analytical formula, a mathematical equation, a law. In former times, such as those of Aristotle and in the Middle Ages, reasoning on these matters had started from some preconceived force or some other *a priori* premise of that kind. Kant proposes that the modern method be employed in metaphysics. However, metaphysics is concerned with another set of "data." Its realm is "inner" experience as contrasted with the "outer" experience of the natural sciences. Metaphysics is nevertheless concerned with something very real, because these inner experiences are "real" *to* just as great an extent as the outer ones. "The true method of metaphysics," Kant concluded, "is basically the same as the one Newton introduced into natural science and which has brought such great results. We should, according to him, seek to discover the rules according to which certain phenomena occur in nature, possibly with the aid of geometry. Even though we do not understand the primary cause (located) within such bodies, it is nevertheless certain that they operate according to this law and we can explain the complicated occurrences in nature by showing clearly how they are contained within these well-proved rules. It is just the same in metaphysics: we must try to discover by way of inner experience, that is, an immediate, evident consciousness, those attributes which are certainly given in the concept of some general quality, and even though you do not know the complete essence of the thing, still you can use it securely, in order to deduce a good deal concerning the thing in hand." In short, metaphysics, like physics, cannot invent; it is her task to discover the regularities in ascertainable experience. "Such a metaphysic has, however, never yet been written," Kant exclaimed at that time.[13] He thus set the stage for his own monumental work.

---

[13] *Works*, II, p. 183.

It may, of course, be objected here that such an undertaking is incorrectly called a metaphysics, that such a critical evaluation of the mental operations which lead to so-called metaphysical questions is actually a denial of metaphysics as understood before or since. To put it another way, Kant's critical approach is a scientific and systematic elaboration of the anti-metaphysical sentiments of a man like Benjamin Franklin—another striking figure of the revolutionary age and closely paralleling Kant's own life-span. When Franklin gathered his *Junto* in Philadelphia, he laid down rules which are closely akin to Kant's philosophizing: no one must talk dogmatically, for truth is in the finding, not a given, fixed thing; moderation and a readiness to be tolerant of another's view, because it may turn out to contain valuable correctives for one's own: all these are principles which Kant would have applauded. Indeed, Franklin in turn would have been happy, no doubt, about the basic idea of Kant's late and slightly humorous essay: *On an impending eternal peace in philosophy* (1796) in which he suggested that as soon as all philosophers adopt the anti-dogmatic position of criticism, and hence the realization that truth is not given, but a task to be achieved, there will be peace among them forever after.

But before Kant fulfilled the promise of a new method of philosophizing and produced the basis of the Copernican revolution in metaphysics—a fulfillment that was as yet almost twenty years away—Kant surprised his contemporaries by two works which seemed to point in quite a different direction: *Observations concerning the Sense of the Beautiful and the Sublime* (1764), and *Dreams of a Visionary* (1766).[14] These two works are distinguished by a more pleasing style, by a rather playful tossing about of various ideas in the spirit of the eighteenth-century essayist. They no doubt reflect to some extent the gay social life which Kant was leading at that time when he was a much sought-after guest at the tables of the local gentry in Koenigsberg and was highly esteemed as a pleasing companion and a conversationalist of wit and charm. They also reflect the influence, which we have already mentioned, of Jean-Jacques Rousseau. Rousseau's stylistic brilliance so impressed Kant that

[14] See below, pp. 3 ff. and pp. 14 ff. for short selections.

he told himself: "I must read Rousseau until the beauty of his expression does no longer disturb me, and I can then get a rational over-all view." [15] This is the period during which Kant was perhaps most admired by his students, one of whom, the philosopher J. G. Herder, has left us an unforgettable portrait of Kant, the man. "I have had the good fortune to know a philosopher who was my teacher. He in his most vigorous manhood had the gay liveliness of a youth which will, I believe, accompany him into his old age. His forehead, built for thinking, was the seat of indestructible serenity and joy, talk rich in ideas issued from his lips, joking, humor and wit were at his disposal, and his teaching lectures were the most amusing concourse. He examined with as much spirit Leibnitz, Wolff, Baumgarten, and Hume, as he followed the development of physics, the laws of nature as expounded by Kepler and Newton, and as he responded to the writings of Rousseau which were then appearing, his *Emile* and his *Heloise,* and every new discovery he assessed, and he always returned to the genuine knowledge of nature and to the moral value of man. The history of man, of peoples, and of nature, mathematics and experience were the founts from which he enlivened his lectures and his conversation; nothing worth knowing left him indifferent, no cabal, no sect, no personal gain, no vain ambition had the least attraction for him as contrasted with the expansion and elucidation of truth. He encouraged and forced one agreeably to think for oneself. Domineering was alien to his nature. This man whom I name with the greatest gratitude and respect is Immanuel Kant." [16] And at a later time, Herder again spoke of the "live teaching" and of the "human philosophy" of Kant.

Kant himself has vividly expressed his admiration for and indebtedness to Rousseau. It is to Rousseau that Kant owed his "belief in the common man." In a marginal note to the essay on the beautiful and sublime, he noted during this period: "I am myself by inclination a seeker after truth. I feel a consuming thirst for knowledge and a restless passion to advance in it, as well as a satisfaction in every forward step. There was a time

---

[15] Cassirer, XI, p. 92.
[16] Herder, J. G., *Briefe zur Beförderung der Humanität,* 79. Brief.

when I thought that this alone could constitute the honor of mankind, and I despised the common man who knows nothing. Rousseau set me right. This blind prejudice vanished; I learned to respect human nature, and I should consider myself far more useless than the ordinary working man if I did not believe that this view could give worth to all others to establish the rights of man."[17] *I learned to respect human nature:* this central fact constituted the inspiration for that central concern with ethics which stands at the heart of Kant's fully developed system. Too frequently has Kant been considered primarily from an epistemological viewpoint, and his *Critique of Pure Reason* has been put into the center of things. The re-establishment of ethics as the central human concern is the real core of Kant's philosophy. This, in turn, explains why Kant could become the philosopher of peace *par excellence.* Rousseau stimulated Kant's thought immeasurably by directing the sharp scalpel of his analysis to the realm of the "inner experience." That is the meaning of Rousseau's challenge to the "age of reason."[18] Stirred by his sensitivity, urged on by his colorful imagination, and sustained by the depth of his feeling, Rousseau revolted against the conceit and self-satisfied smugness of the *philosophes* and their goddess, reason. One cannot read his *Confessions* without being struck by this cardinal concern for the "inner man," however much one may object to Rousseau's exhibitionism.

Along with this insistence upon the "given" of inner experience went the conviction of Rousseau that there must be a peculiar "law" to which the inner life responds, or, at any rate, that is Rousseau's view in Kant's opinion. Kant contrasts him with Newton who discovered the order and regularity, the objective rule in the universe around us, and maintains that Rousseau first "discovered universal human nature beneath the multiplicity of adopted human forms, and the hidden law. . . ." This hidden law is the autonomous ethical law in its pure and unalterable validity. The firm establishment of such an autono-

---

[17] *Fragmente* (ed. Hartenstein, Bd. VIII), p. 624. This translation is Cassirer's as presented in *Rousseau, Kant, Goethe* (1945).
[18] The analysis here follows that given in the author's *Inevitable Peace* (1948), Chapter VI.

mous ethic became Kant's primary concern. It is the main task
of metaphysics. After having made fun of a lot of metaphysical
clap-trap in the *Dreams of a Visionary,* he puts the elementary
question: "What? Is it only good to be virtuous, because there is
another world, or will actions be rewarded yonder, because they
were good and virtuous in themselves?" Kant's essay, concerned
as it is with the doctrines of the Swedenborgians, seems at first
sight a strange enterprise for a man of his interests. But, as
Cassirer has suggested, in dealing with these fantastic doctrines,
Kant was caricaturing the "synthetic" metaphysics of the
schools. It is a matter of establishing limits to what we can know
by showing that "the different phenomena of life in nature and
their laws are all that we can know. . . ." [19] The conclusion of
the first part which we include shows clearly Kant's conscious
determination to restrict himself to what is possible to finite
minds, to be moderate and to limit his (the metaphysician's)
enterprise to man's intellectual resources. These points are so
vividly made in the excerpt we reprint that there seems little
need to paraphrase them here. Only one further comment: the
clear recognition of the limits of man's reason highlights the
importance of *practice,* and the essay concludes with quoting
Voltaire's Candide: "Let us take care of our happiness, go into
the garden and work."

III

Ernst Cassirer has insisted upon the importance of the last
of Kant's pre-critical works, his inaugural dissertation, *De mundi
sensibilis atque intelligibilis forma et principiis,* which appeared
in 1770. Its central theme, as expressed in the title, is the distinction beween two worlds: that of the senses and that of the
mind. The dogmatic dualism expressed in this dichotomy might
well have been considered a final achievement. As a matter of
fact, this work soon appeared to Kant in a very dubious light,
and the next ten years were occupied in the most intense intellectual effort, at the end of which Kant had reached an entirely
new position, and had achieved the Copernican revolution in

---

[19] See chapter II, below, pp. 18 ff.

philosophy which he believed the *Critique of Pure Reason* to constitute.

The discovery of its central problem is connected with Kant's efforts to spell out the inherent implications of the thesis of 1770. How strange it is that, as early as 1772, he should have thought himself to be on the threshold of completing this new work. In a letter to his good friend Marcus Herz, dated February 21, 1772, Kant described what has often been considered the birth of his critical philosophy. This letter is so illuminating that it deserves to be quoted at length. After excusing himself for not having written because of his slow and deliberate nature, and his need for rest, Kant wrote: ". . . I once again looked over the plan which you and I discussed, in order to fit it to all philosophy and other knowledge and to comprehend the extent and limits of this plan. In distinguishing matters of sense from those of the mind as regards morals and the principles to be derived therefrom, I had previously gotten fairly far. The principles of sentiment, taste and judgment, together with their effects, the pleasant, the beautiful and the bad, I likewise had already previously sketched to my near satisfaction. I now drew up a plan for a work which might have the title: *The limits of the senses and of reason.* I thought of two parts, one pertaining to theory, the other to action or practice. The first contained two sections: 1. phenomenology in its entirety, 2. metaphysics, but only regarding its method. The second part was to have again two sections: 1. general principles of sentiment, taste, and of sensual desire, 2. the first basis of morality. As I explored in thought the first part in its entire range and in the mutual relations of all its parts, I noticed that something essential was lacking. This something I, like others, had overlooked in my extended metaphysical researches, and yet this something constitutes the key to the secret of metaphysics which had hitherto been hidden to metaphysics itself. I asked myself: Upon what basis or ground rests the relation of what we in ourselves call image or representation (*Vorstellung*) to the object?" After rejecting the older, familiar answers in terms of either realism or idealism, Kant continues: "The pure concepts of the intellect (*Verstandsbegriffe*) need not be abstracted from the reactions of the senses . . . but they must have their origin in the nature of the mind, but this origin need neither be due to the impact of the object, nor need it imply the creation of the object itself [by the mind]. In the Dissertation, I had restricted myself to stating merely a negation regarding the nature of representations in the intellect: namely, [to say] that these representations are not modifications of the mind by the object. But I passed over in silence how a representation or image which relates to an object could be possible without such an image being affected by the object. I had said: the sense images represent things as they appear, the mental or intellectual images [represent things] as they are. By what, however, are these things given to us, if such intellectual images rest upon our inner activity; wherefrom comes the concordance with things which they presumably posses?" All previous explanations, such as Plato's, amount to introducing something completely unknown in order to explain something partially known. Therefore the basic question regarding the objective validity of knowledge in its relation to objects must—this is the key to Kant's philosophy—be solved in terms of the process of knowing; i.e., through recognizing the peculiar conditions and limitations of the human mind and its reasoning processes." [20]

All previous metaphysics had started with the object of knowledge; Kant asks about the judgment regarding such objects. The ancient controversy in metaphysics as to the relationship of the mind and the objects of the surrounding universe had given rise to many different schools of "idealists" and "realists," of "rationalists" and "empiricists." Kant undertook to eliminate the entire controversy at one throw by declaring it a mistaken problem. This is the "Copernican revolution" in philosophy which he stated so dramatically as the philosophical culmination of the method of modern physics. In the preface to the second edition of the *Critique of Pure Reason,* he put it thus: "Until now it was assumed that all our knowledge must conform or be adjusted toward objects. But upon this assumption all attempts to figure out *a priori* by concepts anything re-

---

[20] See for this letter *Works,* IX, 102 ff.

garding such objects, that is, anything which would enlarge our knowledge, were failures. Therefore let us try to see whether we can get ahead better with the tasks of metaphysics, if we assume that the objects should conform or be adjusted to our knowledge. This [approach] would harmonize better with the desired possibility of *a priori* knowledge of objects which shall determine something regarding objects prior to their being given us. It is like the first thought of Copernicus who, when he could not get ahead with explaining the motions of the heavenly bodies as long as he assumed that the stars revolved around the observer, tried whether he might not be more successful if he let the observer revolve and allowed the stars to remain stationary." In short, Kant emphasizes the importance of asking of nature the right question, of establishing the sound working hypothesis. In that same preface he reverted, in a famous passage, to the starting point of modern physics: the conscious linking of theory and experiment. "When Galileo let balls of a certain, predetermined weight roll down an inclined plane, or when Torricelli let the air carry a weight which he had calculated before hand to be equal to a known volume of water, a new light was seen by all students of nature. They realized that reason comprehends only what it considers according to its own plan; that reason must progress in [formulating] the principles of its judgments according to fixed laws and that it must compel nature to answer the questions rather than let itself be led around by nature, as if on leading strings. Otherwise, accidental observations made without reference to any preconceived plan fail to be linked by a necessary law which, after all, is what reason seeks and requires. Reason must approach nature holding in one hand its principles according to which alone recurrent phenomena may be valid as laws [of nature], and holding in the other hand the experiment which reason has devised according to those principles in order to be informed by nature. But reason must not approach nature like a pupil who lets the teacher recite what he will, but like a duly appointed judge who compels the witnesses to answer the questions he puts to them. Thus physics owes its advantageous intellectual revolution to the idea of seeking, in accordance with what reason projects into nature, what reason must learn from nature (not just dream up about it). By this method, natural science was first brought to pursue the certain paths of a science, after having been merely groping about for many centuries." [21] These striking passages show that Kant's central problem was methodological. When he asked the startling question: "How are synthetic *a priori* propositions possible?" he meant to raise the problem of the validity of all scientific knowledge.

We cannot undertake here even to sketch the outlines of Kant's critique of man's reasoning faculties. However, a few remarks may be in order concerning the decision *not* to include the *Critique of Pure Reason* in this series of selections, but to use large parts of the *Prolegomena* instead. The *Critique of Pure Reason* is so closely reasoned, its architectonic system is so intricate, that making any relatively limited selection from it seemed like tearing a vault out of a Gothic cathedral. Surely the model of a whole chapel would be considered a better method of conveying the essence of so elaborately interrelated a configuration. What is more, Kant himself looked upon the *Prolegomena* in this light. He wrote them soon after the *Critique of Pure Reason* had appeared, because of some hostile and uncomprehending criticism and as an *introduction* to his Copernican revolution in philosophical reasoning. For the reader who is stimulated into pursuing Kant's fascinating thought processes further, the references to the *Critique of Pure Reason* in the *Prolegomena* will enable him to do so; indeed, he should first complete the *Prolegomena* itself.[22]

Kant made it rather difficult for the modern reader to orient himself regarding Kant's basic approach which is neither idealist nor realist, neither rationalist nor empiricist in the conventional sense. These difficulties arise from: (1) Kant's puzzling use of certain key concepts, especially idealism, subjectivism and tran-

---

[21] *Works,* III, pp. 16 f.

[22] Among the several translations of the *Critique of Pure Reason,* that by Norman Kemp Smith deserves to be especially recommended, and that by Meiklejohn to be warned against. It is impossible to understand Kant in the latter. Cf. also Norman Kemp Smith's *Commentary on Kant's Critique of Pure Reason* (1918).

scendentalism; (2) the problems resulting from the non-existence of certain terms in English.

As for the first of these difficulties, it is not too much to say
that Kant's use of the words idealism, subjectivism and transcendentalism is just about the opposite of their current, conventional use. With reference to idealism, Kant makes this
abundantly clear.[23] He rejects the idealism of Plato, Descartes
and Berkeley (as he does, in fact, reject the German idealists
like Fichte and Hegel). Neither ideas nor ideals are the ultimate
reality; it is man's capacity to experience the world through sensations, thoughts and actions. To deny the existence of objects
outside ourselves is absurd; that we cannot know what they are
in themselves does not justify us in denying their *being*. Nor
would we be justified in laying claim to knowing what this
"being" is like in itself and is like beyond what we experience
in the world of phenomena.[24] For Kant, the term "idealism" denoted a critical recognition of the conditions and limits of all
rational knowledge, compounded of hypothesis and verification;
in short a kind of "hypotheticism" or experimentalism. Closely
related to this strange connotation of "idealism" is that of "subjectivism." It does not mean the psychological "subjectivism"
of an emphasis upon the *ego* aspect, the subjective relativity of
judgments. Quite the contrary, Kant's concept denotes an "objective" condition of all knowledge, as he sees it, as patterned
by the *subject* of knowing: man's mind as the source of all
objectively valid judgments about a reality not knowable as it
is, in and by itself. Kant's insistence upon the *objective* core of
the subject's knowing: man's intellectual concepts or necessary
patterns of all experiencing might be called "relationism," rather
than "subjectivism," since it stresses the relation between subject and object in all knowing. Finally, the term "transcendental" is perhaps the most unfortunate of all, since it suggests
an other-worldly emphasis in a philosophy whose primary characteristic is its humanistic emphasis upon man's earthly, finite
existence. What Kant has in mind, primarily, is that he is ex-
pounding a *method* which transcends the customary dichotomies

---

[23] See *Works*, III, 200 ff.
[24] Cf. e.g., the beginning of the *Prolegomena*, § 17, below, p. 69.

by stressing the *mode* of knowing rather than what is known; it
is the core of his much disputed "formalism."

The reason for such a strange use of terms must be sought at
least partly in the fact that German philosophers were just
starting to use their own language in non-popular writings;
Leibnitz and Wolf had still written in Latin. Kant could therefore feel freer in *coining* words in the hope of investing them
with the new meaning he desired.

The resulting difficulties are enhanced by the translating of
certain German terms, for it has been the tendency to translate
in accordance with the Latin roots, so that *Idealismus* becomes
"idealism" and so forth. We have been obliged to follow this
custom, although the usage of these words in the English language is more fully established in a sense contrary to the meaning Kant attached to them. It would really be excusable to use
entirely different words which would be more nearly apt to
render Kant's meaning: methodological for transcendental,
humanist for subjectivist, and experimentalist for idealist. However, it was feared that too much objection would be raised to
such an approach. A related difficulty of greater ramification
results from the fact that certain key German terms have no
true, *single* equivalent in English, and one is confronted with
the problem of whether to adopt some one word and then me-
chanically use it wherever the corresponding German term occurs, or whether to shift the terms as the context seems to
require. The former alternative is the one more frequently
adopted; in fact, it seems to preserve the "system." But the
resulting artificialities in expression are so serious for the modern
lay reader as to make it advisable to sacrifice "system" and adopt
the second alternative. This is the more excusable in view of
Kant's "truly sovereign indifference" toward terminological consistency.[25] A few of these key terms especially call for comment.
The German word *Anschauung* is commonly rendered as intuition. This, along with "transcendental" and "idealism," is the
term most responsible for the frequent failure to appreciate
Kant's key contribution, and for the tendency to attribute to

---

[25] Works, XI, p. 147 (Cassirer).

him an inclination toward the sort of philosophizing characteristic of Hegel and the German "idealists." There are occasionally
places where the term "intuition" may possibly be right. But
most of the time it is not, for it refers to a mental act that is
generated inside a human being and not by the outside world,
whereas *Anschauung* means the exact opposite. The verb *anschauen* means to look at, to visualize and the substantive
derived therefrom means: (a) the act of looking-at something,
(b) the thing-looked-at, (c) the impression or image in the
mind resulting from this. To complicate matters further, the
word *Anschauung*, while primarily related to the sense of
sight,[26] is often used by Kant and others in a more comprehensive meaning to cover the other senses as well, so that it might
mean not only looking-at, but also hearing, smelling, etc. Under
these circumstances, it seemed possible to use only whatever
terms appeared to fit the context, including, besides those mentioned, perception,[27] envisage, observe and observation.

The last two terms must, however, also be employed at times
to render *Wahrnehmung*. Other interpreters have tried to restrict *Wahrnehmung* to the term perception, or apperception,
but it is quite certain that the more usual expression, "observation," especially in connection with scientific work, is intended
by Kant, even though still another term, *Beobachtung*, is likewise employed. The latter carries with it more of an implication
of conscious intent to watch something, than does the term
"observe."

Even more perplexing is the term *Vorstellung*. Another substantive with a distinct "verbal" connotation, the term is often
translated as "representation" or "presentation." But this usage
is often misleading as the verb *vorstellen* means primarily "to
imagine," and as noted before, the derivative noun may mean:
(a) the act of imagining, (b) the thing imagined, and (c) the
image in the mind. It is clear that (c) overlaps with the third
meaning of *Anschauung* and the resulting confusion is consid-

[26] Carus, in his introduction to the *Prolegomena,* makes the interesting
suggestion that we need a new word, "at-sight," for *anschauen.*
[27] This is the term used by Lord Lindsay (A. D. Lindsay) in his admir-
able study *Kant* (1934).

erable. But it seemed best to try and deal with each statement according to the requirements of the context and to add the German occasionally to assist the reader.

Two other basic terminological problems of the *Prolegomena* and the other writings under review here deserve special mention. One is the Kantian concept of *Erfahrung* or experience.[28] Experience in the sense of *Erfahrung* is not merely sensory experience, but is the sense impressions and other observations of phenomena as ordered by the reasoning processes. Kant therefore distinguishes, as will be seen, between judgments based on perceptions and observation (sense impressions) and judgments based on experience. But, since he uses the adjective *empirisch* as denoting "empirical" in the narrower sensory meaning, the translator is faced with the task of making a distinction in English where no differentiation exists corresponding to that between the German and the "foreign" term. Experience, in the sense of *Erfahrung* then, is solidly based upon sense perceptions and similar basic data, but only as these are related and given meaning through an activity of the mind.[29]

The other basic difficulty results from Kant placing in juxtaposition the terms *Verstand* and *Vernunft*. Many interpreters have rendered *Verstand* as "understanding," in keeping with Hume's celebrated treatise. But if this is done, it becomes very difficult to grasp the relation between *Verstand* and *Vernunft*, for both are parts of "human understanding" and are directed toward such understanding. Actually, the English verbal noun "understanding" corresponds to the German noun *Verstehen*, whereas *Verstand* is intellect, or lower reason as contrasted with *Vernunft*, or higher reason. It is necessary, I believe, to render the Kantian terms accordingly and to speak of the *Verstandesbegriffe* as "intellectual" concepts, in contrast to the *Vernunftbegriffe*, or "rational" concepts. Both "intellect" and "reason" produce "understanding." "Intellect" is the capacity to give unity to phenomena with the aid of rules. Reason, in the strict sense, is "the capacity to give unity to these rules of the intellect

---

[28] The decisive work is H. Cohen, *Kant's Theorie der Erfahrung,* 2nd edition.

[29] Cf., e.g., § 18, *Prolegomena.*

under principles." [30] Thus the intellectual concepts are concerned with matters relating to *a posteriori* judgments, while the rational concepts are strictly *a priori;* however, Kant's thought is not always consistent in this matter.

IV

Without making any attempt at outlining the *Critique of Pure Reason*, considering that Kant himself has done this superbly in the *Prolegomena*, it is only necessary to call the reader's attention to the often-overlooked fact that Kant should, in order to be precise, have called the first great *Critique* that of pure theoretical reason, so as to contrast it with the second which deals with pure practical reason. The true contrast between the two is not that one deals with pure reason and the other with applied reason, though the conventional titles seem to imply this. Practical and theoretical reason .can both be pure, if they are directed toward *a priori* judgments. But, while "theoretical" reason focuses attention upon what man experiences as he looks at the world and observes it rolling by, in the true sense of the Greek *theorein* or contemplate, practical reason is concerned with what man experiences when he acts, with the freedom and the "ought" of man-in-action—the normative realm of what is right.

Before Kant came to compose the *Critique of Practical Reason*, he sketched his view of history in philosophical terms. These essays, of which we have included the "Idea for a Universal History" (1784) and "What is Enlightenment?" (1784), are among Kant's most readable and suggestive works. The former essay opens up the imposing line of works on the philosophy of history from Condorcet to Toynbee; the latter goes to the heart of the issues of academic freedom which plague us again today. The sketch on universal history suggests that history too is not a collection of events-in-themselves, but a result of man's viewing these events in terms meaningful to himself. Kant does not, of course, wish to imply the extreme subjectivism of Carl Becker's "Everyman his own Historian," nor yet Lessing's cynical *Geschichte als Sinngebung des Sinnlosen* (1925).

---

[30] *Works*, III, p. 250.

But he does insist that man's life on this planet is part of nature and that, like all study of nature or experience, it is limited by man's intellectual capacity and tools, such as the law of causation. And since nothing can be demonstrated regarding the thing-in-itself, called history, man is not only entitled, but is bound, to interpret it in terms consonant with what he knows to be his moral nature. Thus the inquiry into the meaning of history of man leads straight into the heart of the problem of man-in-action: the practical reason. For history derives its intrinsic interest from the interplay of the ideas of freedom, causal necessity, and determinism: "suppose Washington had surrendered at Valley Forge . . ."

If the *Critique of Pure* [Theoretical] *Reason* and the *Prolegomena* were preoccupied with the validity of judgments in the realm of nature and nature's laws, then the *Critique of* [Pure] *Practical Reason* is similarly concerned with the validity of judgments in the realm of norms and normative laws. We have already quoted the famous statement of the dual problem, where Kant contrasted "the starred heavens above us," as the quintessence of nature under law, and "the moral law within us," as being the "two things which fill one with ever renewed wonder. . . ." How is it comprehensible that man should acknowledge some obligation as universally binding? In raising this question, Kant transcends once again all preceding philosophic speculation. For, while the elaborate hedonistic calculations of the Scotch enlightenment and the Utilitarians, with subtle inquiries into moral sentiment and into pleasure and pain as related to action, had produced many useful insights into what "ought to be done" when the end is given, they had failed to elucidate why man ever acknowledges the existence of a norm as absolute and unrelated to any further end. How does man come to acknowledge value judgments as valid *a priori* is the question which Kant undertook to answer in both the *Foundations of the Metaphysics of Morals* (1785), and the *Critique of Practical Reason* (1788). These works must not be seen, as has happened sometimes, as "additions" to the systematic edifice of the *Critique of Pure Reason* but must be seen as integral parts of the whole of Kant's philosophy. Indeed, the theory of "theoretical" knowledge makes no sense, except in terms of this theory of "practical" knowledge. Only when combined with the inquiry into the validity of esthetic and teleological judgments, they both together constitute the whole systematic edifice of Kant's inquiry into how the human mind comes to formulate judgments believed to be valid *a priori*. As a matter of fact, if any one problem had to be picked as vital to Kant in the original sense of that Greek word—a rock thrown in his path—it would be the question of how human freedom, as implied in normative judgments, could for a rational mind be made compatible with the processes of nature as observed and analyzed by science and built upon the law of causation. It is this dichotomy which was at the bottom of his inaugural dissertation on the sensible and intelligible world. Everything that one may say regarding the phenomenal world of the senses is hypothetical and subject to review, and definitive, *a priori* judgments are possible only with reference to the methods of all experiencing, the intellectual "tools" of all observing and generalizing. But in the world of action, that is to say, in the world of freedom, categorical judgment is possible. Basically, there is only *one* such judgment which Kant calls the categorical imperative and he gives it several different formulations.[31] But from this one imperative others are readily derived, and among them Kant emphasizes again and again the one which says that "there shall not be war." Indeed, so frequent are Kant's references to this particular categorical imperative, that one is inclined to conclude that it occupies, from a strictly existential viewpoint, a particularly important position in Kant's mind.

The writer has gradually come to the conclusion that Kant's whole system is more closely related to his basic political outlook and his sense of the broad revolutionary developments of his time than has commonly been assumed. Heine's jocular remark that Kant's work on ethics, his *Critique of Practical Reason,* was an afterthought, has been generally rejected. But the more widely held notion that Kant's views on law and government, and more especially his ideas of peace and war, are

---

[31] See H. J. Paton, *The Categorical Imperative* (1947) for an interesting re-evaluation.

peripheral to this thought, is untenable in the light of our broader insight into what *mattered* to Kant. For it was peace and freedom, in the most personal sense, that occupied the center of his hopes and fears; and peace and freedom were the themes to which his philosophizing returned again and again. Since the Prussia of Frederick the Great—perhaps even a bit more than the enlightened despotism of mid-eighteenth-century Europe generally—was built upon an explicit (and in fact cynically frank) denial of both peace and freedom, Immanuel Kant was indeed confronted with the task of lifting the entire world of enlightened despotism off its axles.

The result was not only a devastating critique of reason, the heavenly city of the eighteenth-century philosophers, but was at the same time the construction of the most profound philosophical foundation for a regime of freedom under law for all men that the bourgeois age produced.[32] It is confusing to the lay reader that professional philosophers have kept the Kantian term "practical" in spite of the fact that Kant's notion does not mean to imply what "practical" usually means, namely something useful, expedient and prudential, but something decidedly more general, and in some ways even antithetical to "practical." For the norms of "practical reason" are, as categorical imperatives, opposed to those rules of prudence and expediency which are related to ends. "Practical," for Kant, is what is related to *autonomous* action. Kant himself says: "Being an object of practical knowledge as such signifies only the relation of the will to the action by which the object or its opposite would be realized."[33]

Hence the idea of *autonomy* is central to Kant's problem of freedom and obligation. Autonomous, or self-legislative, is a will which is not subject to any restraining set of external "laws." Hence all ends which depend upon the workings of the phenomenal world for their realization, such as happiness or power

---

[32] *Inevitable Peace* (1948), p. 34. Cf. especially Chaps. VI and VII. In this connection, the study by K. Borries, *Kant als Politiker* (1928) deserves mention.

[33] W. T. Jones, *Morality and Freedom in the Philosophy of Immanuel Kant* (1940).

or even peace, must not be involved in true autonomy. The only free will is that which acts according to "moral laws" derived from the basic moral law embodied in the categorical imperative. If anyone should ask how this obedience is to be "explained," he should be answered: it cannot be done. Any attempt to do so would bring us back into the phenomenal world of causal explanations. Kant's underlying notion is that man, as an autonomous free being, fills the vacuum left by the analysis of pure theoretical reason and that this freedom offers a vista into the world of *noumena,* in which the things-in-themselves exist. Action, in other words, is just as much a primary experience as observation, and the only way in which man can resolve the apparent antinomy of the premises upon which the judgments rest, through which action and observation become ordered into experience, is to analyze and comprehend critically the limits of each kind of judgment. When viewed from this vantage point, it becomes clear why Kant's philosophy is "idealism" in a peculiarly poignant *Western* sense: it shows the way in which *ideals* may be considered the true core of existence, rather than the *ideas* of Plato, Berkeley and Hegel. That is, *ideals* in the sense of programs of action, related to moral laws.

The true significance of these views is easy to misunderstand and has often been misinterpreted. Kant, seeking to account for the validity of normative judgments, i.e., the intrinsic meaning of normativity, by no means wishes to imply that the search for happiness is unjustified or unreal. On the contrary, he insists that this search is inherent in the make-up of human beings. He even goes so far as to assert that it is man's duty to seek his own happiness. Nor does Kant deny the importance of studying man as a phenomenon of the observed world. He urges that such inquiries be pushed forward as should all scientific inquiry. Indeed, Kant had an intense interest in such fields as human geography and anthropology, and never wearied of hearing about all kinds of human habits and beliefs.[34] His very last work was an elaborate anthropology and social psychology, entitled *Anthropologie,* published in 1798. But Kant does insist that all such inquiries about what men *usually* do, or do under certain

---

[34] Cf. Kant's remarks on national character below, pp. 5 ff.

circumstances, do not throw any light upon the intrinsic meaning of normativity; upon what is implied in a judgment that states that something "ought to be done," when that "ought" does not relate to any ulterior end. The mind, in short, is engaged in a different kind of mental process. What is implied here is not merely the difference between existential and value judgments which Socrates had first stressed. Granting that difference, the question arises: Upon what ground rests the validity of a judgment concerning the "ought"? Kant points out that this *validity* of the normative judgment is based upon the self-evidence of the premise of man-in-action that man can, disregarding all considerations of prudence, act in accordance with his conscience: "Here I stand, I cannot do otherwise, God help me, Amen." (Luther) In these reflections, the concept of duty is rooted. Duty, for Kant, is essentially the claim of the moral law considered in relation to the man-in-action. "The moral law is thought of as objectively necessary only because it is valid for everybody who possesses reason and will." To argue, as many have done, that Kant expounds his concept of duty as a theory for explaining human conduct is to misunderstand his basic dualism. In fact, in a strict sense, neither duty nor the moral law nor freedom *explain anything* in the world of phenomena. They are entirely beyond that world, except when we humans in acting observe the impact of our action on the phenomenal world. It is man-in-action who thus transforms the norm and its "ought" into the fact and its "is."

So far so good. But besides the judgments involved in theoretical, scientific reasoning, and those made when value and norm are determined, there is another class of judgments entirely, namely, those judgments involved in bridging the gap of nature and freedom, or "is" and "ought." It is the "power of judgment" by which we assess a given situation by relating its various aspects to a given end or purpose. When Kant comes to define the power of judgment, taken generally, he explains it to be the capacity to think the specific or particular as contained within the general. If the general (the rule, the principle, the law) is given, the power of judgment which subsumes the particular thereunder is called by Kant a "determining power of judgment. If, on the other hand, only the particular is given, and the power of judgment has to infer the general from it, then Kant would have us call this power of judgment "reflecting." [35] But regardless of this distinction, if this were all, the "power of judgment" would be concerned with the problem of conceptualization. But this surface aspect hides much broader and deeper problems. From the time of Socrates, whom Plato considered the discoverer of abstract concepts, down to Descartes and Spinoza conceptualization had been intimately related to the problems of form and substance, of essence and being. All judgments which involve an answer to the question as to whether a given something is end-related, that is to say, can be understood in terms of a given end, involve this problem of "form." There are two primary "forms" which are end-related in the thinking of man: the form of the work of art which is called beautiful because all its constituent parts are harmoniously blended into a whole that has unity, and the form of living beings which is called organic because all its constituent parts, too, are harmoniously blended into a whole that has unity. By a species of analogical reasoning we look upon such organic entities *as if* they were directed toward their inherent end by some kind of (to us unknown) creator.[36]

Basically, Kant's problem is again that "critical" inquiry into the validity of a new kind of *a priori* judgments which the human mind appears to indulge in. From this vantage point, it is possible to describe the third critique as "the crowning phase," [37] although truly all three critiques are concerned with the "power of judgment, generally speaking"—the first with scientific judgments (of the pure theoretical reason), the second critique with normative judgments (of the pure practical reason), and the third critique with esthetic and teleological judgments (linking theoretical and practical reason). From this over-all view it can be seen that Kant's position is not truly

[35] *Works,* V, p. 248.
[36] For the development of these ideas, see the selections from the *Critique of (the Power of) Judgment,* below, pp. 307 ff.
[37] See R. A. C. Macmillan, *The Crowning Phase of Critical Philosophy* (1912).

dualistic, that he does not in the last analysis divide the "world," ontologically speaking, into a realm of being and a realm of norms, as has repeatedly been done by "Kantians" and "Neo-kantians." In one sense, Kant's position must be stated as inde-terminate in this respect: he urges us to realize that we simply *cannot know* whether the world as it is *in itself* is one, since our judgments proceed upon contradictory assumptions in making our scientific and normative judgments. But since our free actions do in fact become part of the world around us which we observe and analyze scientifically, and since more specifically the artisan and the artist when they freely create their works add to the sum total of the things which constitute the world around us, it is presumably justifiable to proceed upon the assumption that the world *is one in itself,* even though such an assumption implies the further idea of an *"intellectus arche-typus,"* that is to say of a "creative mind" to which this one world may be related as a preconceived end. We would there-fore be justified in speaking of Kant's position as in the last analysis monistic, if considered in relation to the world, but at the same as "trialistic," if considered in relation to the human mind and its judgments.

The *Critique of (the Power of) Judgment,* being the most read-able of the three great critiques, exerted the widest influence among contemporaries. Goethe no less than succeeding philos-ophers, especially Fichte and Schelling, were unanimous in praising its profundity and wealth of ideas. Goethe's well-known remark that upon reading a page of Kant he had the feeling of having entered a bright and well-lighted room is particularly striking in view of Goethe's well-known dislike for abstract, philosophical speculations. Yet, in spite of these accolades of praise, it is the *Critique of (the Power of) Judgment* which has given rise to the greatest misunderstandings. Readers unable to maintain the Kantian "critical" detachment which stressed the "transcendental" nature of all human knowledge, his rejection of all dogmatism, seized upon this discussion of the judgments involved in how things may be related to ends, deemed beau-tiful, sublime or organic, to construct new metaphysical systems of an uncritical kind. Thus the "transcendentalism" of the New

England renaissance which shaped the meaning of the word
"transcendental" in a strictly intuitive sense diametrically opposed to Kant's critical method echoed misunderstandings which
have characterized philosophizing throughout the West.

It is impossible to assess the "influence" of Kant on succeeding
generations precisely because it is so vast. Any atttempt to describe Kant's influence must end up in being a history of philosophy after 1800. Not only the German idealists, but Schopen-
hauer and Nietzsche, Marx and the positivists, T. H. Green and
Bosanquet and Hobhouse, as well as the numerous schools of
Neo-Kantians down to Vaihinger's Philosophy of the As-If and
the "Existentialists" and "Phenomenologists" testify to the all-
pervading impact of Kant's thought.[38] But in spite of the wide
ramifications, the fierce controversies over what Kant "meant"
have not been settled. Indeed it looks as if only now that the
theory of relativity and related developments in mathematics, as
well as the startling advances in the biological and social sciences concerned with "life," have laid bare the narrow frame-
work of the Newtonian cosmos, Kant's philosophy can be seen
in true perspective. For the student of man and society, there
is deeper insight to be gathered from Kant's balanced recognition of the relative importance of the triad of human judgments involved in "scientific" inquiry, "norm-related" action,
and the understanding of end-related configurations in art and
life, than from the more dogmatic positions of philosophers
stressing either one or another of these several realms of the
mind to the exclusion of the others as basic for valid knowledge.

It is for this reason that we are presenting three extensive
selections to round out the material on Kant's philosophy to show
how he himself applied his critical insights to three of man's

---

[38] Only the utilitarians among major schools show no relation to Kant's
critical evaluation of man's rational faculties. Since their approach rested
upon an uncritical "rationalism" of the crudest kind, this lack of contact should surprise no one. Much more difficult is the assessment of the
relation between Kant and the pragmatists, more especially Pierce's inquiries. John Dewey has stated his position as sharply antithetical to
Kant, e.g. in The Quest for Certainty, pp. 58–62 and 287–91, but I
doubt the adequacy of this treatment. Cf. my remarks regarding this in
Inevitable Peace (1948), pp. 52 ff.

most insistent practical problems: religion, government and peace. It had been originally our hope to add Kant's discussion of law from the *Metaphysics of Morals,* as well as the reflections on jurisprudence contained in his half-humorous *Argument of the Faculties.* But for various reasons including their considerable length,[39] it has seemed wiser to include large sections of his *Religion within the Limits of Reason Alone.* In any case, his basic approach to the importance of law in relation to freedom is clear from his discussion in the *Foundation of the Metaphysics of Morals,* as well as his argument against Hobbes in *Theory and Practice* and *On Eternal Peace.*

As has been remarked before, Kant's concern with the problem of peace was continuous throughout his life. In every one of his major works he returns to it as a central testing ground. The discussion of law in the *Metaphysics of Morals* culminates in a statement on peace; it is a summary of *On Eternal Peace.* Since "there ought not to be war" is one of the basic norms, directly to be derived from the categorical imperative, it is man's moral duty to work for the establishment and maintenance of peace in all human relations, in groups large and small. But man's combative and competitive instincts being what they are, is there any hope of eventually eliminating war and arriving at a lasting order of freedom under law, a world-wide constitutional system which makes peace secure? Kant does not answer this question in the affirmative, but he undertakes to prove that no one can prove such an order to be impossible. Constitutional order has been established in more limited, but ever-widening groups; a world-wide organization must therefore be held possible. This is crucial; but no one has a duty to work for what is demonstrably impossible.

It is touching to see how in his very last work, Kant at the end of his *Anthropology, Pragmatically Considered,* once again returns to this theme, at the very end. "Man is his own last end" is the humanist thought with which Kant had started the *Anthropology.* In conclusion, he once more asserts that free-

---

[39] Immanuel Kant, *Critique of Practical Reason and Other Writings in Moral Philosophy* (1949), edited and translated by Lewis White Beck contains several other valuable essays in very commendable form.

dom and law are the two axes of civil legislation. Freedom and
law must be combined with force in order to achieve a constitutional order. The alternatives are law and freedom without
force resulting in anarchism; law and force without freedom
making for despotism, force without freedom and law constituting barbarism. Only force combined with freedom and law
will provide the basis for a republic or commonwealth in which
the old saying prevails *salus civitatis suprema lex esto*. The
principle of the general good involved leads on to a world-wide
community, even though the threat of conflict remains, since
men cannot help being antagonistic to each other, even while
they crave each other's company. Kant then mentions once
again man's inclination to lie and cheat, and contrasts it with
that same man's moral condemnation of these evils. Hence
we may ". . . describe human kind not as evil, but as a species
of rational beings who are steadily progressing from the evil
to the good, striving against hindrances. Thus mankind's intentions *(Wollen)* are generally good, but the carrying out [of
these intentions] is made hard by the fact that the achievement
of the purpose does not depend upon the free agreement of
individuals, but upon the progressive organization of the world
citizens into a system of cosmopolitan scope." [40] These were
Kant's last words, and they are apt to strike an American or
any other freedom-loving individual throughout the world
with peculiar poignancy in these years after the Second World
War. Will we succeed, will we fail in organizing the world
community?

The world-wide sympathies and the breadth of Kant's pan-
human hopes are in strange contrast to his personal life. He
never left his native city of Koenigsberg. Toward the end of
his life, and upon the urgings of friends, he once made ready
to visit Berlin. He got all packed up, and he set out from
Koenigsberg in the horse-drawn mail-coach of his day. But he
had not gone many miles, before he decided to return. It was
too late. . . . After his appointment to his professorship, there
were no more "events" in Kant's life, apart from the great works
he published year after year, beginning with *The Critique of*

---

[40] See *Works*, VIII, pp. 225–228.

Pure Reason. We have spoken of his keen interest in the French Revolution which he maintained to the end of his life. The publication of *Religion within the Limits of Reason Alone* in 1793 aroused the ire of the Prussian authorities, since its spirit was that of the revolution. He apologized to, rather than defied, the authorities, and some have taken this for an occasion to contrast Kant with Socrates. But they forget that the Prussian authorities did not propose to kill Kant, nor did they command his unquestioning loyalty in a manner comparable to Socrates' attachment to the Athenian *polis*. What is more, Kant re-iterated the views that had been objected to in *Argument of the Faculties* rather explicitly, after having stated even more unorthodox views in his *Eternal Peace*. It is clear from the testimony of contemporaries who knew Kant well that he was rather more outspoken than most. One Metzger, a medical colleague, and no friend of his at that, spoke after Kant's death of his "frankness and intrepidness" in defending his principles which were favorable to the French Revolution to the end. "It was a time in Koenigsberg when anyone who judged the revolution even just mildly, let alone favorably, was put on a black list as a Jacobin. Kant did not allow himself by that fact to be deterred from speaking up for the revolution even at the table of noblemen." Kant's friend and publisher F. Nicolovius reported a remark Kant made in 1794: "All the terror which is happening in France is insignificant as compared to the con-tinued evil of despotism which had previously existed in France . . ." Kant, Nicolovius said, was still an avowed democrat. In all of Koenigsberg it was well known, even in 1798, that "Kant loved the French cause with all his heart, and was not swayed by the outburst of crimes in his belief that the representative system is the best form of government." [41]

This sympathy for the *esprit revolutionaire* was the more remarkable, since Kant was no ready defender of the "right of revolution." Revolutions, to be sure, occurred in the natural

---

[41] See *Abbeggs Tagebuch* for July 1, 1798, quoted in Karl Vorlaender, *Immanuel Kant* (1924), II, 222. It is perhaps worth noting that Kant and his follower Fichte were the only European philosophers of major stature to take this position.

history of man as it actually is. But there are many phrases in Kant—often cited with the intent to distort rather than to elucidate this difficult problem and its handling by our philosopher—which make him appear a strong authoritarian. But one must always bear in mind the sharp dichotomy between fact and norm that permeates his thought. His concept of the "state" is strongly normative: only a government which combines freedom and law with force is entitled to this designation. Once the "state" is thus made synonymous with a constitutional order in the modern sense,[42] Kant's doctrine is identical with the prevailing view in England and America. For in spite of occasional avowals of the beneficial results of "revolution" by great Americans, like Jefferson and Lincoln, the advocacy of the overthrow of the government by force and violence has been viewed askance in the United States no less than in Britain, to put it mildly. In any case, this doctrine has no application to the lawless despotism of modern totalitarian regimes. With reference to these, so infinitely worse than even the *Ancien Regime* in France, Kant would undoubtedly have cherished any and all who fought and died to overthrow it from within and from without.

---

[42] For this see *Constitutional Government and Democracy* 2. ed. (1950) and the literature cited there. See also H. Rickert, *Kant als Philosoph der Modernen Kultur* (1924). The leading works on Kant, besides Lindsay, Cassirer and Vorlaender mentioned in previous footnotes, are E. Caird, *The Critical Philosophy of Immanuel Kant* 2 vls. (2. ed. 1909); Kuno Fischer, *Immanuel Kant und Seine Lehre* 2 vls. (4. ed. 1898–99); vol. one of N. Hartmann, *Die Philosophie des Deutschen Idealismus* (1923); C. B. Renouvier, *Critique de la Doctrine de Kant* (1906); G. Simmel, *Kant,* (1904); Max Adler, *Kant und der Marxismus* (1925). Perhaps the most penetrating recent critical observations on Kant are contained in Morris Cohen's *Reason And Nature* (1931).

Kant's More Important Books, Articles and Reviews

1746 *Gedanken von der wahren Schätzung der lebendigen Kräfte* (Thoughts on the true evaluation of living forces)

1755 *Allgemeine Naturgeschichte und Theorie des Himmels* (General natural history and theory of the heavens)

*1755 Kant takes his degree with the treatise *De Igne,* and qualifies as a university lecturer with the treatise, *Principiorum primorum cognitionis metaphysicae nova dilucidatio.*

1756 Disputation on the treatise *Monadologia physica*

1757 Three small essays in the *Königsberger Nachrichten* on earthquakes (evoked by the Lisbon earthquake of 1755)

1762 *Untersuchung über die Deutlichkeit der Grundsätze der natürlichen Theologie und Moral* (Inquiry into the distinctness of the principles of natural theology and morals, Preisschrift der Berliner Akademie, printed in 1764)

1763 *Einzig möglicher Beweisgrund zu einer Demonstration des Daseins Gottes* (The only possible basis of proof for a demonstration of the existence of God)

1763 *Versuch, den Begriff der negativen Grössen in die Weltweisheit einzuführen* (Attempt to introduce the notion of negative quantities into philosophy)

1764 "Versuch über die Krankheiten des Kopfes" (Essay on the diseases of the head) *Königsberger Zeitung*

1764 *Beobachtungen über das Gefühl des Schönen und Erhabenen* (Observations on the sense of the beautiful and the sublime)

1766 *Träume eines Geistersehers, erläutert durch Träume der Metaphysik* (Dreams of a visionary, explained by dreams of metaphysics)

1768 "Von dem ersten Grunde des Unterschieds der Gegenden im Raum," (On the basic reason for the difference of locations in space) *Königsberger Nachrichten*

1770   *De mundi sensibilis atque intelligibilis forma et principiis* (The form and principles of the world of the senses and that of the mind)

1775   "Von den verschiedenen Rassen des Menschen" (On the different races of man) Appeared as a lecture announcement that year.

1781   *Kritik der reinen Vernunft* (Critique of Pure Reason)

1783   *Prolegomena zu einer jeden künftigen Metaphysik, die als Wissenschaft wird auftreten können* (Prolegomena to every future metaphysics that may be presented as a science)

1784   "Idee zu einer allgemeinen Geschichte in weltbürgerlicher Absicht" (Idea for a universal history with cosmopolitan intent) *Berliner Monatsschrift*

1784   "Beantwortung der Frage: Was ist Aufklärung?" (What is Enlightenment?) *Berlinische Monatsschrift*

1785   *Ideen zur Philosophie der Geschichte* (A critical review of J. G. Herder's Ideas for a Philosophy of History) *Jenaische Litteraturzeitung*

1785   "Über Vulkane im Monde" (On volcanoes in the moon) *Berlinische Monatsschrift*

1785   "Von der Unrechtmässigkeit des Büchernachdrucks" (On the illegality of reprinting books) *Berlinische Monatsschrift*

1785   "Bestimmung des Begriffs einer Menschenrasse" (Determination of the concept of a race of man) *Berlinische Monatsschrift*

1785   *Grundlegung zur Metaphysik der Sitten* (Foundation of the Metaphysics of Morals)

1786   "Mutmasslicher Anfang der Menschengeschichte" (Presumable origin of human history) *Berlinische Monatsschrift*

1786   *Was heisst sich im Denken orientieren?* (What does it mean to orient oneself in thinking?) *Berlinische Monatsschrift*

1786 *Metaphysische Anfangsgründe der Naturwissenschaften* (Metaphysical elements of the natural sciences)

1788 *Über den Gebrauch teleologischer Principien in der Philosophie* (On the use of teleological principles in philosophy) *Deutscher Merkur*

1788 *Kritik der Urteilskraft* (Critique of [the power of] Judgment)

1790 *Über Philosophie überhaupt (Erste Einleitung zur Kritik der Urteilskraft)* (On philosophy in general: first introduction to the Critique of Judgment)

1790 "Über eine Entdeckung nach der alle neue Kritik der reinen Vernunft durch eine ältere entbehrlich gemacht werden soll" (On a discovery by which all new criticism of pure reason may be made unnecessary, because of an older one which is already available)

1790 "Über Schwärmerei und die Mittel dagegen" (On enthusiasm and the means for its prevention) This essay was contained in a letter to L. E. Borowski that year.

1791 "Über das Misslingen aller philosophischen Versuche in der Theodicee" (On the failure of all philosophical attempts at a theodicy) *Berlinische Monatsschrift*

1792 "Vom radikalen Bösen" (On the radically evil) *Berlinische Monatsschrift*

1793 *Religion innerhalb der Grenzen der blossen Vernunft* (Religion within the limits of reason alone)

1793 *Über den Gemeinspruch: Das mag in der Theorie richtig sein, taugt aber nicht für die Praxis* (On the maxim: That may be true in theory, but does not apply to practice) *Berlinische Monatsschrift*

1794 "Etwas über den Einfluss des Mondes auf die Witterung" (On the influence of the moon on the weather) *Berlinische Monatsschrift*

1794 "Das Ende aller Dinge" (The end of all things) *Berlinische Monatsschrift*

1795 *Zum ewigen Frieden* (On eternal peace)

1796   "Von einem neuerdings erhobenen, vornehmen Ton in der Philosophie" (On a recent snobbish tone in philosophy) *Berlinische Monatsschrift*

1796   "Verkündigung des nahen Abschlusses eines Trakrats zum ewigen Frieden in der Philsophie" (Announcement of the approaching conclusion of a treaty of eternal peace in philosophy) *Berlinische Monatsschrift*

1797   *Die Metaphysik der Sitten* (The Metaphysics of Morals in two parts):
I. "Metaphysische Anfangsgründe der Rechtslehre" (Metaphysical elements of jurisprudence)
II. "Metaphysische Anfangsgründe der Tugendlehre" (Metaphysical elements of morals)

1797   "Über ein vermeintes Recht aus Menschenliebe zu lügen" (On a supposed right to lie out of charity)

1798   "Über die Buchmacherei. Zwei Briefe an Fr. Nicolai" (On publishing. Two letters to Fr. Nicolai)

1798   *Der Streit der Fakultäten* (The arguments between the faculties)

1798   *Anthropologie in pragmatischer Hinsicht* (Anthropology, pragmatically considered)

Lectures, edited by others

1800   *Vorlesungen über Logik* (*Logic*) edited by Jäsche

1802   *Physical Geography,* edited by Rink

1803   *Vorlesungen über Paedagogik* (*Pedagogy*) edited by Rink

1804   "On the Prize Question of the Berlin Academy: What real progress has metaphysics made in Germany since the times of Leibnitz and Wolff?" edited by Rink

THE PHILOSOPHY
OF KANT

IMMANUEL KANT'S
MORAL AND POLITICAL
WRITINGS

I

THE SENSE OF THE BEAUTIFUL
AND OF THE SUBLIME

[1764]

THE TWO DIFFERENT FEELINGS OF PLEASURE AND ANNOYANCE are not so much based upon the quality of the external things when exciting them as upon the sentiment, peculiar to each man, of being moved to pleasure or displeasure. . . .

The finer sentiment which we propose to consider here is primarily of two kinds: the sentiment of the *lofty* or *sublime* (*Erhabenen*) and the sentiment of the *beautiful*. Being moved by either is agreeable, but in a very different way. A view of a mountain, the snowy peaks of which rise above the clouds, a description of a raging storm or a description by Milton of the Kingdom of Hell cause pleasure, but it is mixed with awe; on the other hand, a view of flower-filled meadows, valleys with winding brooks and the herds upon them, the description of *elysium* or Homer's description of the belt of Venus cause an agreeable feeling which is gay and smiling. We must have a sense of the sublime to receive the first impression adequately, and a sense of the beautiful to enjoy the latter fully. Great oak trees and lovely spots in a sacred grove are sublime. Beds of flow-

3

ers, low hedges and trees trimmed into shape are beautiful. The night is sublime while the day is beautiful. Temperaments which have a sense for the sublime will be drawn toward elevated sentiments regarding friendship, contempt for the world and toward eternity, by the quiet silence of a summer evening when the twinkling light of the stars breaks through the shadows of the night and a lovely moon is visible. The glowing day inspires busy effort and a sense of joy. The sublime *moves;* the expression of a person experiencing the full sense of the sublime is serious, at times rigid and amazed. On the other hand, the vivid sense of the beautiful reveals itself in the shining gaiety of the eyes, by smiling and even by noisy enjoyment. The sublime, in turn, is at times accompanied by some terror or melancholia, in some cases merely by quiet admiration and in still others by the beauty which is spread over a sublime place. The first I want to call the terrible sublime, the second the noble, and the third the magnificent. Deep loneliness is sublime, but in a terrifying way.

The sublime must always be large; the beautiful may be small. The sublime must be simple; the beautiful may be decorated and adorned. A very great height is sublime as well as a very great depth; but the latter is accompanied by the sense of terror, the former by admiration. Hence the one may be terrible sublime, the other noble.

A long duration is sublime. If it concerns past time it is noble; if anticipated as an indeterminable future, it has something terrifying.

FOURTH SECTION

*Of National Character[1] in so far as it depends upon
a Sense of the Beautiful and the Sublime*

Among the peoples of our continent, in my opinion, the Italians
and the French are distinguished by their sense of the beautiful,
while the Germans, the English and the Spaniards by their sense
of the sublime. Holland may be taken for the country where
this finer taste becomes rather unnoticeable. The beautiful itself is either enchanting or touching, or radiating (*lachend*) or
enticing. The first kind has something of the sublime, and the
mind (*Gemuet*) when feeling it is deeply stirred or enthusiastic,
but when feeling the second kind it is smiling and joyful. The
first of these sentiments seems especially appropriate to the Italians, while the second is appropriate to the French. In the kind
of national character which responds to the expression of the
sublime [the sublime again may differ], it may be the terrifying
kind which inclines toward the quixotic, or it may be a sense for
the noble or for the magnificent. I believe there is good reason to
attribute the first kind of sentiment to the Spaniard; the second
sort to the English and the third to the German. The sense for
the magnificent is not original as are the other kinds of taste, and
while an imitative spirit may be linked to any other feeling too,
it is peculiar to the feeling for the sublime of shimmering lustre;
for this feeling is a mixed sentiment [compounded of the sense]
for the beautiful and the sublime. In this mixture each of the

---

[1] It is not my intention to describe these characters in detail, but merely
to sketch a few traits related to the sense of the beautiful and the sublime. It may be easily seen that such a sketch has only a passable cor-
rectness . . . and that no nation lacks minds which combine the most
excellent qualities. Hence such criticism as may be leveled at a people
at times ought not to offend anyone. Whether these differences are
accidental, or depend upon the times and the kind of government or are
the result of climate, I do not here explore.

components, considered by itself, is cooler, and hence the mind is free enough to notice examples in linking the two, while it also needs their stimulus. The German, therefore, will have less feeling when contemplating the beautiful than the Frenchman, and less of that which relates to the sublime than the Englishman, but in those cases where both ought to appear linked, [the mixed feeling] will be more in keeping with his sentiment, and he will avoid those errors which result from too far-reaching a force of each of these kinds of sentiments.

I will touch only briefly on the arts and sciences whose choice will confirm the taste of the nations which we have attributed to them. Italian genius has primarily excelled in music, painting, sculpture and architecture. All these fine arts meet an equally fine taste in France, although their beauty is less touching here. The taste in regard to poetic and oratorical perfection in France stresses beauty, while in England it stresses the lofty [sentiments]. In France, subtle wit, comedy, laughing satire, amorous play and an easy and naturally flowing diction are quite inborn (original). In England, by contrast, [we find] thoughts of deep content, tragedy, epic poetry and the heavy gold of wit which under the French hammer may be stretched into thin sheets of great surface. In Germany, wit is seen as through a foil. Formerly it was loud, but through (good) examples and the intelligence of the nation it has become more charming and noble, but charming with less naïveté, and noble with less bold inspiration than among the other two peoples. . . .

The national characters are most clearly marked in their morals, and therefore we will consider their different sense of the beautiful and the sublime from this standpoint. [2] The Spaniard is serious, discreet and truthful. There are few merchants who are more honest than the Spanish. He has a proud soul and more feeling for great than for beautiful deeds. Since in his mixture there is little of a kind and gentle goodwill, the Spaniard is often

---

[2] It is hardly necessary for me to repeat my former caution here. In every people the best part contains praiseworthy characters of every kind.

hard and sometimes cruel. The *auto da fé* is maintained not so much because of superstition, but because of the quixotic inclination of this nation which is moved by a spectacle that is venerable and terrifying and where it can witness a *San Benito* painted with figures of Satan delivered into the flames which a raging devotion has lighted. One cannot say that the Spaniard is more haughty or more amorous than someone from another people, but he is both in a quixotic, adventurous way which is strange and unusual. To leave one's plow and to parade in a long coat and sword upon one's plow-field, until the passing stranger is gone, or to greet one's beloved by a special compliment at a bull-fight where the beauties of the country can for once be seen unveiled, and then to plunge oneself into a dangerous fight with a wild animal, these are unusual and strange deeds which deviate far from what is natural.

The Italian seems to have feelings which are a mixture of the French and Spanish; more of a sense of the beautiful than the latter, and more of a sense of the sublime than the former. In this way the various traits of his moral character may be explained.

The Frenchman has a dominant sense of the morally beautiful. He is gracious, polite and obliging. He quickly becomes intimate, is gay and free in meeting others, and such an expression as "a man of *bon ton*" or "a lady of *bon ton*" has a comprehensible meaning only for him who has acquired the gracious sense of a Frenchman. Even his sublime sentiments, of which he has quite a few, are subordinated to his sense of the beautiful and they receive their intensity by their harmonizing with the sense of the beautiful. The Frenchman loves to be witty, and he will therefore readily subordinate truth to a sudden idea. But where one cannot be witty[3] he shows as thorough an insight as anyone from any other nation, e.g. in mathematics and in the other dry and

---

[3] In metaphysics, in morals and religious doctrines one has to be on one's guard in the writings of this nation. There is much beautiful illusion and vanity which does not stand cold analysis. The Frenchman loves the bold in his sayings; but to reach truth one needs caution, not boldness. In history he likes anecdotes which lack nothing but . . . truth.

deep arts and sciences. A *bon mot* does not in France have the
fleeting value it has elsewhere; it is eagerly disseminated and
preserved in books like the most important event. The Frenchman is a quiet citizen and takes revenge upon the tax collector
by satires or by remonstrances in parliament. Such acts after having given to the people's fathers a beautiful patriotic appearance
accomplish no more than being crowned by a praiseworthy re-
buke and being celebrated in ingenious paeans of praise. The
object to which the merits and capacities of this nation are
mostly related is woman.[4] Not that woman is more loved or respected than elsewhere, but because she offers the best excuse
[for men] to display the very popular talents of wit, of gracious-
ness and of good manners in their best light; for the rest a vain
person of either sex, at all times, only dallies with himself, and
the other is only his toy. Since the French do not at all lack noble
qualities (and yet these qualities can only be animated by a
sense of the beautiful), the beautiful sex could have a more
powerful influence in rousing the most noble deeds of the male
than anywhere else in the world if efforts were made to favor
this tendency of the national spirit. It is too bad that lilies won't
spin.

The shortcoming which limits this national character is the

---

[4] Woman colors all social gatherings and all conversation in France. It
cannot be denied that social gatherings without the more beautiful sex
are rather tasteless and dull. But if woman contributes the beautiful
touch (*schoenen Ton*), man should provide the noble one. Otherwise
conversation becomes equally dull, but for the opposite reason, because
nothing is more revolting than pure sweetness. According to French
taste, the question is not: is the gentleman at home? but: is Madame at
home? Madame is dressing, madame has vapours (a kind of pretty hu-
mors); in short, all entertainments are occupied with madame and center
about madame. Yet, woman is not more honored by all this. A man
who flirts is without the feeling either of true respect or of tender love.
I should not want, for any price, to have said what Rousseau so boldly
alleges: *that a woman never becomes more than a big child.* Still, the
keen Swiss wrote this in France, and presumably he, the great defender
of the beautiful sex, felt with indignation that in France the beautiful
sex is not met with great respect.

silly or insipid, or, to use a more polite expression, the light-hearted. Important matters are treated as jokes, and trivialities occasion serious effort. In his old age, the Frenchman still sings gay songs and is gallant to a lady, as much as he can be. In making these comments I have great witnesses from that nation itself on my side, and retreat behind a Montesquieu and a d'Alembert, in order to protect myself against possible indignation.

The Englishman is in the beginning of every acquaintance cold and indifferent toward a stranger. He is little inclined to offer small services; but if he becomes a friend, he is prepared to render great service. He makes little effort to be witty in conversation, but he is reasonable and dignified. He is a poor imitator, does not bother about other people's opinions, and follows only his own taste. In relation to woman he is not gracious, like a Frenchman, but he shows her greater respect and perhaps even carries this too far, since he frequently concedes to his wife unlimited regard. He is constant, at times to the point of stubbornness, bold and determined, often to the point of recklessness, and he acts according to his principles, usually being almost headstrong. He easily becomes an odd fellow, not from vanity, but because he cares little about others and because he does not readily allow his tastes to be distorted in order to be agreeable or imitative; therefore he is rarely liked as much as a Frenchman, but if he is well known, he is more highly respected.

The German has an emotional structure (*Gefuehl*) which is a mixture of the Englishman's and the Frenchman's, but it appears to be nearer the former, and the greater similarity to the latter is artificial and imitated. He has a happy mixture of the sense of the beautiful and of the sublime, and if he does not equal a Frenchman in the first, nor an Englishman in the second quality, he excels both in combining them. He shows greater grace in intercourse than an Englishman, and while he does not bring as much agreeable vivacity and wit to a social gathering as a Frenchman, he displays greater modesty and reason. He is, as in all kinds of matters of taste, as in love, rather methodical. In combining the beautiful with the sublime, he is cool enough in feeling to occupy his mind with considerations of good manners, of magnificence and of public opinion. Therefore family, title and status are matters of great importance to him both in civil life and in love affairs. He asks, much more than the other two nations, *what people may think of him,* and if there is anything in his character which would suggest the wish for a major improvement, it is this weakness, as a result of which he does not make bold to be original, although he has the necessary talents; the German concerns himself so much with the opinion of others that it deprives his moral qualities of all firmness, making them changeable and falsely artificial.

If we apply these thoughts to any particular case, for example to evaluate the sense of honor in different peoples, the following national differences appear. The sentiment of honor is in the Frenchman *vanity,* in the Spaniard *haughtiness,* in the Englishman *pride,* in the German *ostentation.* . . . These expressions seem at first sight to mean the same thing, but they signify very noticeable differences. *Vanity* seeks acclaim, is fickle and changeable, but in external conduct is *polite.* The *haughty* is filled with a sense of falsely imagined great qualities, does not compete for the acclaim of others, in conduct is stiff and arrogant. *Pride* is really only a greater consciousness of one's own value which may often be quite justified, but the conduct of the proud toward others is indifferent and cold. The ostentatious is a proud man who is also vain.[5] The acclaim which he seeks from others consists in honorary salutations. Hence he likes to shine with titles, pedigrees and display. The German is badly infected with this weakness. Words such as gracious, well-inclined, high and well-born and similar bombast make his address stiff and clumsy and prevent the beautiful simplicity which other people can give

---

[5] It is not necessary that an ostentatious man be also haughty, that is, that he has an exaggerated, false idea of his qualities; he may not esteem himself more highly than he deserves, but he shows poor taste in displaying this value.

their diction. The conduct of a ostentatious man is ceremonious in intercourse.

In love, the German and the Englishman have a pretty good stomach, a bit fine in sentiment, but of a hale and hearty taste. The Italian is in this respect moody, the Spaniard fantastic, the Frenchman inclined to enjoy forbidden fruit.

The religion of our continent is not a matter of willful taste, but has a more venerable origin. Hence only its excrescences and what is peculiar to particular kinds of men can indicate signs of different national traits. I shall list these digressions according to the following main heads: credulity, superstition, fanaticism, and indifferentism. The ignorant part of every nation is credulous, although it has no finer feeling. The persuasion results merely from hearsay and apparent authority without any kind of finer feeling providing an impulse. For examples of this kind of people one must seek in the North. The credulous, if he has a quixotic taste, becomes superstitious. This taste is in itself a reason for believing something more readily.[6] Of two people of whom one has been infected by this sentiment, while the other is of a cold and temperate disposition, the first will be more easily seduced by his dominant tendency to believe something unnatural, even though he has more intelligence than the other who has not insight but by his ordinary and phlegmatic sentiment preserves himself from such an illusion. The superstitious in religion likes to imagine as standing between himself and the highest being some powerful and astonishing persons, giants of sanctity, so to speak, whom nature obeys and whose exorcising voice opens and closes the iron gates of Tartarus—men whose heads touch the heavens while their feet still rest upon the lowly

---

[6] It has been observed that the English people, though very intelligent, may be taken in by the impudent assertion of a strange and unbelievable matter, and be made to believe if there are many examples. But a bold mind, prepared by many experiences in the course of which some strange things have turned out to be true, quickly discards small doubts which detain a weak and suspicious mind and thus preserve it from error without its having merited it.

earth. Common sense and its teaching will therefore have to surmount great obstacles in Spain, not because one would have to drive out ignorance, but because such common sense is obstructed by a curious taste which looks upon the natural as "common" and which never believes to be feeling the sublime unless the object of the sentiment is quixotic. *Enthusiasm* is so to speak a devout audacity which is caused by a certain pride and a too great self-confidence [which imagines that it can] come close to the divine nature yet rise above the ordinary and prescribed order of nature. The enthusiast talks only of direct intuition and of the contemplative life, while the superstitious makes vows before the pictures of great and miracle-performing saints and puts his faith into the imagined and inimitable superiority of other persons over himself. Even these excrescences, as we suggested above, are manifestations of national sentiment. Hence fanaticism[7] has, at least in former times, been encountered most in Germany and England. It is like the unnatural excrescence of the noble sentiment which belongs to the character of these nations. Such fanaticism is not nearly as damaging as the superstitious tendency, even though it is virulent at the start, because the excitement of a roving spirit gradually cools off and must in the end arrive at an orderly moderation. Superstition, on the other hand, gets imperceptibly deeply rooted in a quiet and suffering mind and deprives a man thus chained of the confidence that he can shake off his noxious illusion. Finally, a vain and carefree man is at all times without a strong sense of the sublime; his religion is without emotion, but is mostly a matter of fashion which he attends to with grace though remaining cold. This is the practical *indifferentism* toward which the French

---

[7] Fanaticism must at all times be distinguished from enthusiasm. The fanatic believes that he is feeling a direct and extraordinary communion with a higher nature, while enthusiasm is a state of mind when the mind has by some idea been excited beyond the proper degree, be it the maxim of patriotic virtue or of friendship or of religion, without the idea of a supernatural communion being involved.

national spirit seems most inclined; from such indifferentism to impious mockery is only a step; it means, if one considers the inner value, little more than a complete rejection [of religion]. . . .

II

DREAMS OF A VISIONARY EXPLAINED BY DREAMS OF METAPHYSICS

[1766]

Part I

FOURTH CHAPTER

Theoretical Conclusion From the Whole of the Considerations of the First Part

THE ACCURACY OF SCALES USED FOR COMMERCIAL MEASURE-ments, according to civil law, is discovered if we let the merchandize and the weights exchange pans. So the partiality of the scales of reason is revealed by the same trick, without which, in philosophical judgments, no harmonious result can be obtained from the compared weighings. I have purified my soul from prejudices; I have destroyed any blind affection which ever crept in to procure in me an entrance for much fancied knowledge. I now have nothing at heart; nothing is venerable to me but what enters by the path of sincerity into a quiet mind open to all reasons—whether thereby my former judgment is confirmed or abolished, or whether I am convinced or left in doubt. Wherever I meet with something instructive, I appropriate it. The judgment of him who refutes my reasons fashions my judgment, after I first have weighed it against the scale of self-love, and afterwards in that scale against my presumed reasons, and have found it to have a higher intrinsic value.

14

Formerly, I viewed human common sense only from the standpoint of my own; now I put myself into the position of another's reason outside of myself, and observe my judgments, together with their most secret causes, from the point of view of others. It is true that the comparison of both observations results in pronounced parallaxes, but it is the only means of preventing the optical delusion, and of putting the concept of the power of knowledge in human nature into its true place. You may say that this is very serious talk in connection with so trifling a problem as that under consideration, which deserves to be called a plaything rather than a serious occupation, and you are not exactly wrong in thus judging. But although one ought not to make a great ado about a small matter, yet one may perhaps be allowed to make use of such occasions; and unnecessary circumspection in small matters may furnish a useful example in important matters. I find that no attachment nor any other inclination has crept in before examination, depriving my mind of a readiness to be guided by any kind of reason *pro* or *con,* except one. The scale of reason after all is not quite impartial, and one of its arms, bearing the inscription, "Hope of the Future," has an advantage of construction, causing even those slight reasons which fall into its scale to outweigh the speculations of greater weight on the other side. This is the only inaccuracy which I cannot easily remove, and which, in fact, I never want to remove. I confess that all stories about apparitions of departed souls or about influences from spirits, and all theories about the presumptive nature of spirits and their connection with us, seem to have appreciable weight only in the scale of *hope,* while in the scale of speculation they seem to consist of nothing but air. If the answer to this problem were not in consonance with a prior inclination, what reasonable man would be doubtful as to whether it were more plausible to assume the existence of a kind of beings having no similarity whatever with anything taught him by his senses, or to attribute certain alleged experiences to a kind of self-deception and invention which, under certain circumstances, is by no means uncommon?

In fact this seems generally to be the main reason for crediting the ghost-stories so widely accepted. Even the first delusions about presumed apparitions of deceased people have probably arisen from the fond hope that we still exist in some way after death. And then, at the time of the shadows of night, this illusion has probably deluded the senses, and created, out of doubtful forms, phantoms corresponding to preconceived ideas. From these, finally, the philosophers have taken occasion to devise the rational idea of spirits, and to bring it into a system. You probably will recognise also in my own assumed doctrine of the communion of spirits this trend to which people commonly incline. For its propositions evidently unite only to give an idea how man's spirit leaves this world, i.e., of the state after death. But how it enters, i.e., of procreation and propagation, I make no mention. Nay, I do not even mention how it is present in this world, i.e., how an immaterial nature can be in an immaterial body and act by means of it. The very good reason for all this is that I do not understand a single thing about the whole matter, and consequently might as well have been content to remain just as ignorant as before in regard to the future state, had not the partiality to a pet notion recommended the reasons which offered themselves, however weak they were.

The same ignorance makes me so bold as to deny absolutely the truth of the various ghost stories, and yet with the common, although queer, reservation that while I doubt any one of them, still I have a certain faith in the whole of them taken together. The reader is free to judge as far as I am concerned. The scales are tipped far enough on the side containing the reasons of the second chapter to make me serious and undecided when listening to the many strange tales of this kind. But, as reasons to justify one's self are never lacking when the mind is prejudiced, I do not want to bother the reader with any further defense of such a way of thinking.

As I am now at the conclusion of the theory of spirits, I am bold enough to say that this study, if properly used by the reader, exhausts all philosophical knowledge about such beings, and that perhaps in the future many things may be thought about it, but never more known. This assumption sounds rather vainglorious. The problems offered by nature are of such multifariousness, in its smallest parts, to a reason so limited as the human, that there is certainly no object of nature known to the senses, be it only a drop of water or a grain of sand, which ever could be said to be exhausted by observation or reason. But the case is entirely different with the philosophical concept of spiritual beings. It may be complete, but in the negative sense, by fixing with assurance the limits of our knowledge, and convincing us that: all that is granted to us is to know the diverse manifestations of life in nature and its laws; but that the principle of this life, i.e., the unknown and only assumed spiritual nature, can never be thought of in a positive way, because for this purpose no data can be found in all our sensations; that therefore we have to resort to negations for the sake of thinking of something so entirely different from everything sensuous; and that the possibility of such negations rests likewise neither upon experience nor upon conclusions, but upon invention, to which a reason deprived of all other expedients finally resorts. With this understanding pneumatology may be called a doctrinal conception of man's necessary ignorance in regard to a supposed kind of beings, and as such it can easily be adequate to its task.

And now I lay aside this whole matter of spirits, a remote part of metaphysics, since I have finished and am done with it. In future it does not concern me any more. By thus making the plan of my investigation more concentrated and sparing myself some entirely useless inquiries, I hope to be able to apply to better advantage my small reasoning power upon other subjects. It is generally vain to try to extend the little strength one has over a wide range of undertakings. It is therefore a matter of policy, in this as other cases, to fit the pattern of one's plans to one's powers, and if one cannot obtain the great, to restrict oneself to the mediocre.

Second Part
THIRD CHAPTER

Practical Conclusion from the Whole Treatise

It is the zeal of a sophist to inquire into any idle proposition and to set to the craving after knowledge no other limits than impossibility. But to select from among the innumerable tasks before us the one which humanity must solve is the merit of the wise. After science has completed its course, it naturally arrives at a modest mistrust and, indignant with itself, it says: How many things there are which I do not understand! But reason, matured by experience so as to become wisdom, speaks through the mouth of Socrates when, of all the merchandise of a fair, he says serenely: "How many things there are which I do not need!" In this manner two endeavors of a dissimilar nature flow together into one, though in the beginning they set out in very different directions, the one being vain and discontented, the other staid and content.

To be able to choose rationally, one must know first even the unnecessary, yea the impossible; then at last science arrives at the definition of the limits set to human reason by nature. All hollow schemes, perhaps not unworthy in themselves but lying outside of the sphere of men, will then recede to the limbo of vanity. Then even metaphysics will become that which at present it is rather distant from, and which would seem the last thing to be expected of her—the companion of wisdom. As long as people think it is possible to attain knowledge about things so far off, wise simplicity may call out in vain that such great endeavors are unnecessary. The pleasure accompanying the extension of knowledge will easily make the latter appear a duty, and will consider deliberate and intentional contentedness to be foolish simplicity, opposed to the improvement of our nature.

The questions about the spiritual nature, about freedom and predestination, the future state, etc., at first animate all the powers of reason, and through their excellency draw man into the rivalry of a speculation which reasons and decides, teaches and refutes without discrimination, just according to the nature of the apparent knowledge in each case. But if this investigation develops into philosophy which judges its own proceedings, and which knows not only objects, but their relation to man's reason, then the lines of demarcation are drawn closer, and the boundary stones are laid which will never allow investigation to wander beyond its proper province. We had to make use of a good deal of philosophy to know the difficulties surrounding a concept generally treated as being very convenient and common. Still more philosophy moves this phantom of knowledge yet further away, and convinces us that it is entirely beyond the horizon of man. For in the relations of cause and effect, of substance and action, philosophy at first serves to dissolve the complicated phenomena, and to reduce them to simpler concepts. But when one has finally arrived at fundamental relations, philosophy has no more employment.

Questions like "How something can be a cause, or possess power," can never be decided by reason; but these relations must be taken from experience alone. For the rules of our reason are applicable only to comparison in respect to identity or contrast. But in the case of a cause something is assumed to have come from something else; one can find therefore no connection in regard to identity. In the same way, if this effect is not already implied in what preceded, a contrast can never be made out; because it is not contradictory merely to assume one thing and abolish another. Thence the fundamental concepts of causes, of forces, and of actions, if they are not taken from experience, are entirely arbitrary, and can be neither proved nor disproved. I know that will and understanding move my body, but I can never reduce this experience by analysis, and can therefore recognize it, but can not understand it. That my will moves my arm is not more intelligible to me than if somebody said to me that he could stop the moon in its orbit. The difference is only that the one I experience, but that the other has never occurred to me. I recognize in myself changes as of a living subject, namely, thoughts, power to choose, etc., and as these terms indicate things different in kind from any of those which taken together make up my body, I have good reason to conceive of an incorporeal and constant being. Whether such a being is able to think without connection with a body can never be concluded from this empirical concept of its nature. I am conjoined with beings kindred to myself by means of corporeal laws, but whether I am, or ever shall be, conjoined according to other laws which I will call spiritual, without the instrumentality of matter, I can in no way conclude from what is given to me.

All such opinions, as those concerning the manner in which the soul moves my body, or is related to other beings now or in the future can never be anything more than fictions. And they are far from having even that value which fictions of science, called hypotheses, have. For with these no fundamental powers are invented; only those already known by experience are connected according to the phenomena; their possibility, therefore, must be provable at any moment. It is different in the former case, when even new fundamental relations of cause and effect are assumed, the possibility of which can never, nor in any way, be ascertained, and which thus are only invented by creative genius or by chimera, whichever you like to call it. That several true or pretended phenomena can be comprehended by means of such assumed fundamental ideas cannot at all be quoted in their favour. For a reason may be given for everything, if one is entitled to invent at will actions and laws of operation. We must wait, therefore, perhaps until in the future world, by new experiences, we are informed about new concepts concerning powers in our thinking selves which, as yet, are hidden to us.

Thus the observations of more recent days, analyzed by mathematics, have revealed to us the power of attraction in matter, concerning the possibility of which we shall never be able to learn anything further, because it seems to be a fundamental power. Those who would have invented such a quality without first having obtained the proof from experience would rightly have deserved to be laughed at as fools. Because, in such cases, reasons are of no account whatever, neither for the sake of inventing, nor for confirming the possibility or impossibility of certain results: the right of decision must be left to experience alone. Similarly I leave to time, which brings experience, the ascertainment of something about the famous healing-powers of the magnet in cases of toothache, when experience shall have produced as many observations to the effect that magnetic rods act upon flesh and bones, as we already have proving their effect on steel and iron. But, if certain pretended experiences cannot be classified under any law of sensation that is unanimously accepted by men: if, therefore, they would only go to prove irregularity in the testimony of the senses—which, indeed, is the case with rumoured ghost-stories—then it is advisable simply to ignore them. For the lack of unanimity and uniformity makes the historic knowledge about them valueless for proving anything, and renders them unfit to serve as a basis for any law of experience within the domain of reason.

Similarly, while on the one hand, by somewhat deeper investigation, one will learn that convincing and philosophic knowledge is impossible in the case under consideration, one will have to confess, on the other hand, in a quiet and unprejudiced state of mind, that such knowledge is dispensable and unnecessary. The vanity of science likes to excuse its occupations by the pretext of importance; thus it is pretended in this case that a rational understanding of the spiritual nature of the soul is very necessary for the conviction of an existence after death; again, that this conviction is very necessary as a motive for a virtuous life. Idle curiosity adds that the fact of apparitions of departed souls even furnishes us with a proof from experience of the existence of such things. But true wisdom is the companion of simplicity, and as, with the latter, the heart rules the understanding, it generally renders unnecessary the great preparations of scholars, and its aims do not need such means as can never be at the command of all men. What? Is it good to be virtuous only because there is another world, or will not actions be rewarded rather because they were good and virtuous in themselves? Does not man's heart contain immediate moral precepts, and is it absolutely necessary to link our thought to the other world for the sake of moving man here according to his destiny? Can he be called honest, can he be called virtuous, who would like to yield to his favorite vices if only he were not frightened by future punishment? Must we not rather say that indeed he shuns the doing of wicked things, but nurtures the vicious disposition in his soul; that he loves the advantages of actions similar to virtue, but hates virtue itself? In fact, experience teaches that very many who are instructed concerning the future world, and are convinced of it, nevertheless yield to vice and corruption, and only think upon means cunningly to escape the threatening consequences of the future. But there probably never was a righteous soul who could endure the thought that with death everything would end, and whose noble mind had not elevated itself to the hope of the future. Therefore it seems to be more in accordance with human nature and the purity of morals to base the expectation of a future world upon the sentiment of a good soul, than, conversely, to base the soul's good conduct upon the hope of another world. Of a similar nature is that moral faith, the simplicity of which can do without many a subtlety of reasoning, and which alone is appropriate to man in any state, because, without deviations, it guides him to his true aims. Let us therefore leave to speculation and to the care of idle men all the noisy systems of doctrine concerning such remote subjects. They are really immaterial to us, and the reasons pro and con which, for the moment, prevail, may, perhaps, decide the applause of schools, but hardly anything about the future destiny of the righteous. Human reason was not given strong enough wings to part clouds so high above us, clouds which withhold from our eyes the secrets of the other world. The curious who inquire about it so anxiously may receive the simple but very natural reply that it would be best for them please to have patience until they get there. But as our fate in the other world probably depends very much on the manner in which we have conducted our office in the present world, I conclude with the words with which Voltaire, after so many sophistries, lets his honest Candide conclude: *"Let us look after our happiness, go into the garden, and work."*

CRITIQUE OF PURE REASON

[1780]

SELECTIONS FROM THE INTRODUCTION

INTRODUCTION

I. *The Distinction Between Pure and Empirical Knowledge*

THERE CAN BE NO DOUBT THAT ALL OUR KNOWLEDGE BEGINS with experience. For how should our faculty for knowing be awakened into action if the objects affecting our senses did not partly of themselves produce images, partly arouse the activity of our intellect to compare these images, and, by combining or separating them, work up the raw material of the sensible impressions into that knowledge of objects which is entitled experience? Therefore in the order of time we have no knowledge antecedent to experience, and with experience all our knowledge begins.

Although all our knowledge begins with experience, it does not follow that it all arises out of experience. For it may well be that even our empirical knowledge is made up of what we receive through impressions and of what our own faculty for knowing (sensible impressions serving merely as the occasion) supplies from itself. If our faculty for knowing makes any such addition, it may be that we are not in a position to distinguish it from the raw material, until with long practice of attention we have become skilled in separating it.

This, then, is a question which at least calls for closer examination, and does not permit any off-hand answer: whether there is any knowledge that is thus independent of experience and even of all impressions of the senses. Such knowledge is entitled *a priori,* and is distinguished from the *empirical,* which has its sources *a posteriori,* that is, in experience.

However, the expression *"a priori"* does not indicate with sufficient precision the full meaning of our question. For it has been customary to say, even of much knowledge that is derived from empirical sources, that we have it or are capable of having it *a priori,* meaning thereby that we do not derive it immediately from experience, but from a universal rule—a rule which is itself, however, borrowed by us from experience. Thus we would say of a man who undermined the foundations of his house, that he might have known *a priori* that it would fall, that is, that he need not have waited for the experience of its actual falling. But still he could not know this completely *a priori.* For he had first to learn through experience that bodies are heavy, and therefore fall when their supports are withdrawn.

In what follows, therefore, we shall understand by *a priori* knowledge, no knowledge independent of this or that experience, but knowledge absolutely independent of all experience. Opposed to it is empirical knowledge, which is knowledge possible only *a posteriori,* that is, through experience. *A priori* modes of knowledge are entitled pure when there is no admixture of anything empirical. Thus, for instance, the proposition, "every alteration has its cause," while an *a priori* proposition, is not a pure proposition, because alteration is a concept which can be derived only from experience.

II. We are in Possession of Certain Modes of A Priori Knowledge, and even the Common Understanding is never without Them

What we require here is a criterion by which to distinguish with certainty between pure and empirical knowledge. Experience teaches us that a thing is thus and so, but not that it cannot be otherwise. First, then, if we have a proposition which in be-ing thought is thought as *necessary*, it is an *a priori* judgment; and if, besides, it is not derived from any proposition except one which also has the validity of a necessary judgment, it is an absolutely *a priori* judgment. Secondly, experience never confers on its judgments true or strict, but only assumed and comparative *universality*, through induction. We can properly only say, there-fore, that, so far as we have hitherto observed, there is no excep-tion to this or that rule. If, then, a judgment is thought with strict universality, that is, in such a manner that no exception is allowed as possible, it is not derived from experience, but is valid absolutely *a priori*. Empirical universality is only an arbitrary extension of a validity holding in most cases to one which holds in all, for instance, in the proposition, "all bodies are heavy." When, on the other hand, strict universality is essential to a judgment, this indicates a special source of knowledge; namely, a faculty for *a priori* knowledge. Necessity and strict universality are thus sure criteria of *a priori* knowledge, and are inseparable from one another. But since in the employment of these criteria the contingency of judgments is sometimes more easily shown than their empirical limitation, or, as sometimes also happens, their unlimited universality can be more convincingly proved than their necessity, it is advisable to use the two criteria sepa-rately, each by itself being infallible.

Now it is easy to show that there actually are in human knowl-edge judgments which are necessary and in the strictest sense universal, and which are therefore pure *a priori* judgments. If an example from the sciences be desired, we have only to look to any of the propositions of mathematics; if we seek an example from the intellect in its quite ordinary employment, the proposi-tion, "every alteration must have a cause," will serve our purpose. In the latter case, indeed, the very concept of a cause so mani-festly contains the concept of a necessity of connection with an effect and of the strict universality of the rule that the concept would be altogether lost if we attempted to derive it, as

Hume has done, from a repeated association of that which happens with that which precedes, and from a custom of connecting images, a custom originating in this repeated association, and constituting therefore a merely subjective necessity. Even without appealing to such examples, it is possible to show that pure *a priori* principles are indispensable for the possibility of experience, and so to prove their existence *a priori*. For whence could experience derive its certainty, if all the rules, according to which it proceeds, were always themselves empirical, and therefore contingent? Such rules could hardly be regarded as first principles. At present, however, we may be content to have established the fact that our faculty of knowledge does have a pure employment, and to have shown what are the criteria of such an employment.

Such *a priori* origin is manifest in certain concepts, no less than in judgments. If we remove from our empirical concept of a body, one by one, every feature in it which is [merely] empirical, the color, the hardness or softness, the weight, even the impenetrability, there still remains the space which the body (now entirely vanished) occupied, and this cannot be removed. Again, if we remove from our empirical concept of any object, corporeal or incorporeal, all properties which experience has taught us, we yet cannot take away that property through which the object is thought as substance or as inhering in a substance (although this concept of substance is more determinate than that of an object in general). Owing, therefore, to the necessity with which this concept of substance forces itself upon us, we have no option save to admit that it has its seat in our faculty for *a priori* knowledge.

III. *Philosophy Stands in need of a Science which shall Determine the Possibility, the Principles, and the Extent of all* A Priori *Knowledge*

But what is still more extraordinary than all the preceding is this, that certain modes of knowledge leave the field of all possible experience and have the appearance of extending the scope of our judgments beyond all limits of experience, and this by means of concepts to which no corresponding object can ever be given in experience.

It is precisely by means of the latter modes of knowledge, in a realm beyond the world of the sense, where experience can yield neither guidance nor correction, that our reason carries on those inquiries which owing to their importance we consider to be far more excellent, and in their purpose far more lofty, than all that the intellect can learn in the field of appearances. Indeed we prefer to run every risk of error rather than desist from such urgent inquiries, on the ground of their dubious character, or from disdain and indifference. These unavoidable problems set by pure reason itself are *God, freedom* and *immortality*. The science which, with all its preparations is in its final intention directed solely to their solution is metaphysics; and its procedure is at first dogmatic, that is, it confidently sets itself to this task without any previous examination of the capacity or incapacity of reason for so great an undertaking.

Now it does indeed seem natural that, as soon as we have left the ground of experience, we should, through careful inquiries, assure ourselves as to the foundations of any building that we propose to erect, not making use of any knowledge that we possess without first determining whence it has come, and not trusting to principles without knowing their origin. It is natural, that is to say, that the question should first be considered, how the intellect can arrive at all this knowledge *a priori,* and what extent, validity, and worth it may have. Nothing, indeed, could be more natural, if by the term "natural" we mean what fittingly and reasonably ought to happen. But if we mean by "natural" what ordinarily happens, then on the contrary nothing is more natural and more intelligible than the fact that this inquiry has been so long neglected. For one part of this knowledge, the mathematical, has long been of established reliability, and so gives rise to a favorable presumption as regards the other part, which may yet be of quite different nature. Besides, once we are outside the circle of experience, we can be sure of not being contradicted by experience. The charm of extending our knowledge is so great that nothing short of encountering a direct contradiction can suffice to arrest us in our course; and this can be avoided, if we are careful in our fabrications—which none the less will remain fabrications. Mathematics gives us a shining example of how far, independently of experience, we can progress in *a priori* knowledge. It does, indeed, occupy itself with objects and with knowledge solely in so far as they allow of being exhibited in intuition. But this circumstance is easily overlooked, since the intuition, in being thought, can itself be given *a priori,* and is therefore hardly to be distinguished from a mere pure concept. Misled by such a proof of the power of reason, the demand for the extension of knowledge recognizes no limits. The light dove, cleaving the air in her free flight, and feeling its resistance, might imagine that its flight would be still easier in empty space. It was thus that Plato left the world of the senses, as setting too narrow a limit to the understanding, and ventured out beyond it on the wings of the ideas, into the empty space of the pure intellect. He did not observe that with all his efforts he made no advance—meeting no resistance that might, as it were, serve as a support upon which he could take a stand, to which he could apply his powers, and so set his intellect in motion. It is, indeed, the common fate of human reason to complete its speculative structures as speedily as may be, and only afterwards to inquire whether the foundations are reliable. All sorts of excuses will then be appealed to, in order to reassure us of their solidity, or rather indeed to enable us to dispense altogether with so late and so dangerous an inquiry. But what keeps us, during the actual building, free from all apprehension and suspicion, and flatters us with a seeming thoroughness, is this other circumstance, namely, that a great, perhaps the greatest, part of the business of our reason consists in analysis of the concepts which we already have of objects. This analysis supplies us with a considerable body of knowledge, which, while nothing but explanation or elucidation of what has already been thought in our concepts, though in a confused manner, is yet prized as being, at least as regards its form, new insight. But so far as the matter or content is concerned, there has been no extension of our previously possessed concepts, but only an analysis of them. Since this procedure yields real knowledge *a priori*, which progresses in an assured and useful fashion, reason is so far misled as surreptitiously to introduce, without itself being aware of so doing, assertions of an entirely different order, and it does so *a priori*. And yet it is not known how reason can be in a position to do this. Such a question is never so much as thought of. I shall therefore at once proceed to deal with the difference between these two kinds of knowledge.

IV. The Distinction between Analytic and Synthetic Judgments

In all judgments in which the relation of a subject to the predicate is thought (I take into consideration affirmative judgments only, the subsequent application to negative judgments being easily made), this relation is possible in two different ways. Either the predicate B belongs to the subject A, as something which is (covertly) contained in this concept A; or B lies outside the concept A, although it does indeed stand in connection with it. In the one case I entitle the judgment analytic, in the other synthetic. Analytic judgments (affirmative) are therefore those in which the connection of the predicate with the subject is thought through identity; those in which this connection is thought without identity should be entitled synthetic. The former judgments, adding nothing through the predicate to the concept of the subject, but merely breaking it up into those constituent concepts that have all along been thought in it, although confusedly, can also be entitled explicative. The latter judgments, on the other hand, add to the concept of the subject a predicate which has not been in any wise thought in it, and which no analysis could possibly extract from it; and they may therefore be entitled ampliative. If I say, for instance, "All bodies are extended," this is an analytic judgment. For I do not require to go beyond the concept which I connect with "body" in order to find extension as bound up with it. To meet with this predicate, I have merely to analyze the concept, that is, to become conscious myself of the manifold which I always think in that concept. The judgment is therefore analytic. But when I say, "All bodies are heavy," the predicate is something quite different from anything that I think in the mere concept of body in general; and the addition of such a predicate therefore yields a synthetic judgment.

Judgments of experience, as such, are one and all synthetic. For it would be absurd to found an analytic judgment on experience. Since, in framing the judgment, I must not go outside my concept, there is no need to appeal to the testimony of experience in its support. That a body is extended is a proposition that holds *a priori* and is not empirical. For, before appealing to experience, I have already in the concept of body all the conditions required for my judgment. I have only to extract from it, in accordance with the principle of contradiction, the required predicate, and in so doing can at the same time become conscious of the necessity of the judgment—and that is what experience could never have taught me. On the other hand, though I do not include in the concept of a body in general the predicate "weight," none the less this concept indicates an object of experience through one of its parts, and I can add to that part other parts of this same experience, as in this way belonging together with the concept. From the start I can apprehend the concept of body analytically through the characters of extension, impenetrability, figure, etc., all of which are thought in the concept. Now, however, looking back on the experience from which I have derived this concept of body, and finding weight to be invariably connected with the above characters, I attach it as a predicate to the concept; and in doing so I attach it synthetically, and am therefore extending my knowledge. The possibility of the synthesis of the predicate "weight" with the concept of "body" thus rests upon experience. While the one concept is not contained in the other, they yet belong to one another, though only contingently, as parts of a whole, namely, of an experience which is itself a synthetic combination of objects seen (*Anschauungen*).

But in *a priori* synthetic judgments this help is entirely lacking. [I do not here have the advantage of looking around in the field of experience.] Upon what, then, am I to rely, when I seek to go beyond the concept A, and to know that another concept B is connected with it? Through what is the synthesis made possible? Let us take the proposition, "Everything which happens has its cause." In the concept of "something which happens," I do indeed think an existence which is preceded by something in time, etc., and from this concept analytic judgments may be obtained. But the concept of a "cause" lies entirely outside the other concept, and signifies something different from "that which happens," and is not therefore in any way contained in this latter image or representation. How come I then to predicate of that which happens something quite different, and to apprehend that the concept of cause, though not contained in it, yet belongs, and indeed necessarily belongs, to it? What is here the unknown = X which gives support to the intellect when it believes that it can discover outside the concept A a predicate B foreign to this concept, which it yet at the same time considers to be connected with it? It cannot be experience, because the suggested principle has connected the second image with the first, not only with greater universality than experience can give, but also with the expression of necessity, and therefore completely *a priori* and on the basis of mere concepts. Upon such synthetic, that is, ampliative principles, all our *a priori* speculative knowledge must ultimately rest; analytic judgments are very important, and indeed necessary, but only for obtaining that clearness in the concepts which is requisite for such a sure and wide synthesis as will lead to a genuinely new addition to all previous knowledge.

V. In all Theoretical Sciences of Reason Synthetic A Priori Judgments are Contained as Principles

1. *All mathematical judgments, without exception, are synthetic.* This fact, though incontestably certain and in its consequences very important, has hitherto escaped the notice of those who are engaged in the analysis of human reason, and is, indeed, directly opposed to all their conjectures. For as it was found that all mathematical inferences proceed in accordance with the principle of contradiction (which the nature of all apodictic certainty requires), it was supposed that the fundamental propositions of the science can themselves be known to be true through that principle. This is an erroneous view. For though a synthetic proposition can indeed be discerned in accordance with the principle of contradiction, this can only be if another synthetic proposition is presupposed, and if it can then be apprehended as following from this other proposition; it can never be so discerned in and by itself.

First of all, it has to be noted that mathematical propositions, strictly so called, are always judgments *a priori,* not empirical; because they carry with them necessity, which cannot be derived from experience. If this be demurred to, I am willing to limit my statement to *pure* mathematics, the very concept of which implies that it does not contain empirical, but only pure *a priori* knowledge.

We might, indeed, at first suppose that the proposition $7 + 5 = 12$ is a merely analytic proposition, and follows by the principle of contradiction from the concept of a sum of 7 and 5. But if we look more closely we find that the concept of the sum of 7 and 5 contains nothing save the union of the two numbers into one, and in this no thought is being taken as to what that single number may be which combines both. The concept of 12 is by no means already thought in merely thinking this union of

7 and 5; and I may analyze my concept of such a possible sum as long as I please, still I shall never find the 12 in it. We have to go outside these concepts, and call in the aid of the observation which corresponds to one of them, our five fingers, for instance, or, as Segner does in his *Arithmetic,* five points, adding to the concept of 7, unit by unit, the five given as seen (*Anschauung*). For starting with the number 7, and for the concept of 5 calling in the aid of the fingers of my hand as seen, I now add one by one to the number 7 the units which I previously took together to form the number 5, and with the aid of that figure [the hand] see the number 12 come into being. That 5 should be added to 7, I have indeed already thought in the concept of a sum = 7 + 5, but not that this sum is equivalent to the number 12. Arithmetical propositions are therefore always synthetic. This is still more evident if we take larger numbers. For it is then obvious that however we might turn and twist our concepts, we could never, by the mere analysis of them, and without the aid of envisaging, discover what [the number is that] is the sum.

Just as little is any fundamental proposition of pure geometry analytic. That the straight line between two points is the shortest is a synthetic proposition. For my concept of *straight* contains nothing of quantity, but only of quality. The concept of the shortest is wholly an addition, and cannot be derived, through any process of analysis, from the concept of the straight line. Looking at these figures (*Anschauung*), therefore, must be called in; only by its aid is the synthesis possible. What here causes us commonly to believe that the predicate of such apodictic judgments is already contained in our concept, and that the judgment is therefore analytic, is merely the ambiguous character of the terms used. We are required to join in thought a certain predicate to a given concept, and this necessity is inherent in the concepts themselves. But the question is not what we *ought* to join in thought to the given concept, but what we *actually* think in it, even if only obscurely; and it is then manifest that, while the predicate is indeed attached necessarily to the concept, it is so in virtue of an observation which must be added to the concept, not because it is thought in the concept itself.

Some few fundamental propositions, presupposed by the geometrician, are, indeed, really analytic, and rest on the principle of contradiction. But, as identical propositions, they serve only as links in the chain of method and not as principles; for instance, a = a; the whole is equal to itself; or $(a + b) > a$, that is, the whole is greater than its part. And even these propositions, though they are valid according to pure concepts, are only admitted in mathematics because they can be shown in observation.

(2) *Natural science (physics) contains* a priori *synthetic judgments as principles.* I need cite only two such judgments: that in all changes of the material world the quantity of matter remains unchanged; and that in all communication of motion, action and reaction must always be equal. Both propositions, it is evident, are not only necessary, and therefore in their origin *a priori,* but also synthetic. For in the concept of matter I do not think its permanence, but only its presence in the space which it occupies. I go outside and beyond the concept of matter, joining to it *a priori* in thought something which I have not thought *in* it. The proposition is not, therefore, analytic, but synthetic, and yet is thought *a priori;* and so likewise are the other propositions, of the pure part of natural science.

(3) *Metaphysics,* even if we look upon it as having hitherto failed in all its endeavors, is yet, owing to the nature of human reason, a quite indispensable field of knowledge, and *ought to contain* a priori *synthetic knowledge.* For its business is not merely to analyze concepts which we make for ourselves *a priori* of things, and thereby to clarify them analytically, but to extend our *a priori* knowledge. And for this purpose we must employ principles which add to the given concept something that was not contained in it, and through *a priori* synthetic judgments

venture out so far that experience is quite unable to follow us, as, for instance, in the proposition, that the world must have a first beginning, and such like. Thus metaphysics consists, at least *in intention*, entirely of *a priori* synthetic propositions.

VII. The Idea and Division of a Special Science, under the Title "Critique of Pure Reason"

In view of all these considerations, we arrive at the idea of a special science which can be entitled the Critique of Pure Reason. For reason is the faculty which supplies the principles of *a priori* knowledge. Pure reason, therefore, contains the principles whereby we know anything absolutely *a priori*. An organon of pure reason would be the sum-total of those principles according to which all modes of pure *a priori* knowledge can be acquired and actually brought into being. The exhaustive application of such an organon would give rise to a system of pure reason. But as this would be asking rather much and as it is still doubtful whether and in what cases any extension of our knowledge would be possible here, we can regard a science of the mere examination of pure reason, of its sources and limits, as the *propædeutic* to the system of pure reason. As such, it should be called a critique, not a doctrine, of pure reason. Its utility, in speculation, ought properly to be only negative, not to extend, but only to clarify our reason, and keep it free from errors—which is a very great gain. I entitle *transcendental* all knowledge which is occupied not so much with objects as with the mode of our knowledge of objects in so far as this mode of knowledge is to be possible *a priori*. A system of such concepts might be entitled transcendental philosophy. But that is still, at this stage, too large an undertaking. For since such a science must contain with completeness both kinds of *a priori* knowledge, the analytic no less than the synthetic, it is, so far as our present purpose is concerned, much too comprehensive. We have to carry the analysis so far only as is indispensably necessary in order to comprehend, in their whole extent, the principles of *a priori* synthesis, with which alone we are called upon to deal. It is upon this inquiry, which should be entitled not a doctrine, but only a transcendental critique, that we are now engaged. Its purpose is not to extend knowledge, but only to correct it, and to supply a touchstone of the value, or lack of value, of all *a priori* knowledge. Such a critique is therefore a preparation, so far as may be possible, for an organon, and if this should not succeed, then at least for a canon, according to which, in due course, the complete system of the philosophy of pure reason—be it in extension or merely in limitation of its knowledge—may be carried into execution, analytically as well as synthetically. That such a system is possible, and indeed that it may not be of such great extent as to deprive us of the hope of entirely completing it, may already be gathered from the fact that what here constitutes our subject matter is not the nature of things, which is inexhaustible, but the intellect which passes judgment upon the nature of things; and this intellect, again, only in respect of its *a priori* knowledge. This body of possible *a priori* knowledge of the intellect cannot remain hidden from us, since we should not look for it outside ourselves. In all probability it is sufficiently small in extent to allow of our receiving it completely, of judging as to its value or lack of value, and so of rightly appraising it. Still less may the reader here expect a critique of books and systems of pure reason; we are concerned only with the critique of the faculty of pure reason itself. Only in so far as we build upon this foundation do we have a reliable touchstone for estimating the philosophical value of old and new works in this field. Otherwise the unqualified historian or critic is passing judgments upon the groundless assertions of others by means of his own, which are equally groundless.

Transcendental philosophy is the idea of a science for which the critique of pure reason has to lay down the complete architectonic plan. That is to say, it has to guarantee, as following from principles, the completeness and certainty of the structure in all its parts. It is the system of all principles of pure

reason. And if this critique is not itself to be entitled a transcendental philosophy, it is solely because, to be a complete system, it
would also have to contain an exhaustive analysis of the whole of
a priori human knowledge. Our critique must, indeed, supply a
complete enumeration of all the fundamental concepts that go
to constitute such pure knowledge. But it is not required to
give an exhaustive analysis of these concepts, nor a complete
review of those that can be derived from them. Such a demand
would be unreasonable, partly because this analysis would not
be appropriate to our main purpose, inasmuch as there is no
such uncertainty in regard to analysis as we encounter in the
case of synthesis, for the sake of which alone our whole critique
is undertaken; and partly because it would be inconsistent with
the unity of our plan to assume responsibility for the completeness of such an analysis and derivation, when in view of our
purpose we can be excused from doing so. The analysis of these
a priori concepts, which later we shall have to enumerate, and
the derivation of other concepts from them, can easily, however, be made complete when once they have been established
as exhausting the principles of synthesis, and if in this essential
respect nothing be lacking in them.

The critique of pure reason therefore will contain all that is
essential in transcendental philosophy. While it is the complete
idea of transcendental philosophy, it is not equivalent to that
latter science; for it carries the analysis only so far as is requisite
for the complete examination of knowledge which is *a priori*
and synthetic.

What has chiefly to be kept in view in the division of such a
science is that no concepts be allowed to enter which contain in
themselves anything empirical, or, in other words, that it consist
in knowledge wholly *a priori*. Accordingly, although the highest
principles and fundamental concepts of morality are *a priori*
knowledge, they have no place in transcendental philosophy,
because, although they do not lay at the foundation of their
precepts the concepts of pleasure and pain, of the desires and in-

clinations, etc., all of which are of empirical origin, yet in the construction of a system of pure morality these empirical concepts must necessarily be brought into the concept of duty, as representing either a hindrance, which we have to overcome, or an allurement, which must not be made into a motive. Transcendental philosophy is therefore a philosophy of pure and merely speculative reason. All that is practical, so far as it contains motives, relates to feelings, and these belong to the empirical sources of knowledge.

If we are to make a systematic division of the science which we are engaged in presenting, it must have first a *doctrine of the elements,* and secondly, a *doctrine of the method of pure reason.* Each of these chief divisions will have its subdivisions, but the grounds for these we are not yet in a position to explain. By way of introduction or anticipation we need only say that there are two stems of human knowledge, namely, *the senses* and *the intellect,* which perhaps spring from a common, but to us unknown, root. Through the former, objects are given to us; through the latter, they are thought. Now in so far as sensibility may be found to contain *a priori* images constituting the condition under which objects are given to us, it will belong to transcendental philosophy. And since the conditions under which alone the objects of human knowledge are given must precede those under which they are thought, the transcendental doctrine of sensibility will constitute the first part of the science of the elements.

PROLEGOMENA TO EVERY FUTURE METAPHYSICS THAT MAY BE PRESENTED AS A SCIENCE

[1783]

INTRODUCTION

THESE PROLEGOMENA ARE NOT DESIGNED FOR THE USE OF STU-dents, but for future teachers, and even for the latter they should serve not so much to provide the order of exposition of an already existing science as to create such a science.

There are scholars for whom the history of philosophy (ancient no less than modern) constitutes their own philosophy; for these the present *Prolegomena* are not written. These scholars must wait until the people who are endeavoring to tap the sources of reason have completed their work and then it will be the turn of the scholars to give an account to the world of what has been done by the others. Otherwise nothing can be said that, in their opinion, has not been said before. In fact, this may pass as an infallible prophecy for all future time. Since the human mind has speculated for so many centuries on countless subjects in so many ways, it is likely that for every new idea an old one can be found having some affinity with it.

My purpose is to convince all those caring to occupy themselves with metaphysics that for the present it is indispensably necessary that they suspend their work, look upon all that has gone before as non-existent and above all, first ask the question: "Whether such a thing as metaphysics is even possible at all?"

If metaphysics is a science, how does it happen that it cannot win for itself universal and lasting applause like other sciences? If it is not a science, how is it that under the semblance of a science it is ceaselessly boasting and holding out to the human mind hopes that are never extinguished and never fulfilled? Something definite must be worked out respecting the nature of this assumed science, whether it demonstrates our knowledge or our ignorance; for it is impossible that metaphysics should remain on the same footing any longer. It seems almost ridiculous that, while every other science moves forward ceaselessly, this one claiming to be wisdom itself, whose oracular pronouncements everyone consults, is continually revolving in one spot without advancing a step. Furthermore, its votaries have much decreased and we do not see that those who feel strong enough to shine in other sciences are willing to risk their fame in this one. On this science everyone, ignorant though he may be in all else, presumes to have a decided opinion just because in this sphere there is no certain weight and measure at hand by which to distinguish a thorough work from superficial chatter.

However, it is not an uncommon occurence that, after long-continued work in a science in which wonders of progress are believed to have been made, the question occurs to someone: Whether and how such a science is possible at all? For human reason is so fond of building that many times it has reared up a lofty tower and then afterwards pulled it down to see how the foundation was laid. It is never too late to become reasonable and wise; but it is always more difficult when the insight for initiating it comes late.

To ask whether a science is possible presupposes a doubt as to its existence. But such a doubt would offend all those whose whole fortune may consist of this supposed treasure; anyone who raises such a doubt must anticipate resistance on all sides. Some people, in the proud consciousness of their ancient, and therefore what they consider legitimate, possession, will, with their metaphysical textbook in hand, look down with contempt upon him who raises such a doubt. Others, who never notice anything that does not coincide with what they have previously seen elsewhere, will not understand him, and so everything will remain for some time as though nothing at all had happened that could allow one to fear or to hope for an impending change.

At the same time I confidently dare to predict that the thoughtful reader of these *Prolegomena* will not only doubt his previous science, but will be quite convinced in the end that such a science cannot exist unless the demands made here have been satisfied; for upon them rests the possibility of metaphysics. Inasmuch as this has never happened, there is as yet no such thing as metaphysics. But, since the demand for metaphysics can never disappear because the interests of universal human reason are so intimately bound up with it, the thoughtful reader will confess that a complete reform, or rather a new birth, is inevitable according to a plan hitherto quite unknown, however much this may be resisted for a time.

Since the attempts of Locke and Leibnitz, or rather since the first rise of metaphysics, no event has occurred that could be more decisive for the fortunes of this science than the attack made upon it by David Hume. He contributed no new light to this kind of knowledge, but he struck a spark by which a light might have been kindled had it encountered receptive tinder whose glimmer could have been preserved and enlarged.

Hume took for his initial starting point a single but important conception of metaphysics, namely, that of the *connection of cause and effect* (together with the derivative conceptions of force and action, etc.). He demanded that reason, which pretends to have given metaphysics birth, give a reasoned answer to the question: By what right does reason think that something is of such a quality that on its being posited something else is thereby necessarily also posited? For that is the meaning of the concept of cause. Hume proved irrefutably that it is quite impossible for reason to imagine this connection *a priori* and based on a mere concept since this connection involves necessity. It is not at all apparent how, because something exists something else must necessarily exist, and thus how the concept of such a connection can be introduced *a priori*. Hence Hume concluded that reason completely deceived itself by this concept, that reason falsely claimed this concept as its own child, while it was nothing more than a bastard of the imagination which, conceived by experience, had brought certain representations under the law of association, and had substituted a resulting subjective necessity, i.e., habit, for an objective necessity based on insight. From this he concluded that reason possessed no faculty for thinking of such connections even in general terms, because [if it did] its concepts would then be mere constructs, and all its pretended *a priori* knowledge nothing but common experiences mislabeled; which is to say that no such thing as metaphysics exists at all and that there is no possibility of its ever existing.

However hasty and incorrect Hume's conclusion was, at least it was based on investigation and this investigation would have been worthwhile if the good brains of his time could have possibly united to solve, with happier results, the problem in the sense in which he had stated it. Then a speedy and complete reform of the science would have resulted.

But fate, always unfavorable to metaphysics, willed that Hume should be understood by no one. One cannot see, without feeling a certain regret, how completely his opponents: Reid, Oswald, Beattie, and lastly Priestley, missed the point of his task; for they took for granted precisely that which Hume doubted and then they proved heatedly and mostly quite immodestly what it had never entered his head to question. As a result, they so completely misunderstood his hint at improvement that everything remained in the same state as though nothing had happened. It was not a question whether the concept of cause was correct and useful, and indispensable in regard to the whole knowledge of nature, for Hume had never doubted this. It was a question whether this concept could be thought of *a priori* by reason, and in this way the concept would have inherent truth independent of all experience, and therefore also have a more extended usefulness which would not be limited to objects of experience; it was upon this problem that Hume desired clarification. The question was as to the origin of the concept, not as to its practical indispensability in use. As soon as the origin of the concept had been ascertained, the conditions of its use and the extent to which it is valid would have been settled of themselves.

To have done the problem full justice, the opponents of this celebrated man would have had to penetrate deeply into the nature of reason, in so far as it is occupied solely with pure thought, a course which was inconvenient for them. Therefore they invented a more convenient means by which they might defy him without any insight, namely, the appeal to the *common sense of mankind*. Common sense (or, as it has recently been called, plain sense) is indeed a great natural gift to possess. But it must be proved by acts, by the thoughtfulness and reasonableness of what one thinks and says, and not by appealing to it as to an oracle when one has nothing intelligent to adduce to justify oneself. When insight and knowledge are at a low ebb, then and not before, one of the subtle inventions of modern times is to appeal to common sense, by means of which the shallowest talker may calmly confront the profoundest thinker and hold out against him. But so long as there is a small remnant of insight left, one will be hesitant to use this crutch. Seen in its true light, that argument is nothing better than an appeal to the verdict of the multitude; an applause at which the philosopher blushes, but about which the popular smart-aleck boasts scornfully. But I should think that Hume can make as good a claim to the possession of common sense as Beattie, and furthermore, to something the latter certainly did not possess, namely, critical reason, which keeps common sense from overreaching itself in speculations. If we are merely concerned with speculations, a restrained common sense will then not seek to decide them, as common sense does not know how to justify its own principles; only in this way will common sense remain healthy. Chisel and hammer are quite sufficient for working on a piece of wood, but for copper-engraving an etching needle is necessary. In the same way, the common intellect, no less than the speculative philosophical intellect, is useful in itself; the former when we have to do with judgments having an immediate bearing on experience, but the latter when we have to judge universally on the basis of mere concepts, as for instance in metaphysics where the self-appointed, healthy common sense is capable of no judgment at all.

I readily confess that the reminder [challenge] of David Hume was what first interrupted my dogmatic slumber many years ago and gave my research in the field of speculative philosophy quite a different direction. I was quite far from accepting the consequences which resulted merely from his not having faced his problem squarely, but having only attacked a part of it which could not possibly afford a solution by itself. When one starts from a well-founded, though undeveloped, idea that a predecessor has left, one may well hope that by increased reflection one can bring it further than was possible for the acute man whom one has to thank for the original sparks of its light.

First of all, I tried to see whether Hume's observation could not be made general and soon found that the concept of the connection of cause and effect was not the only one, by a great deal, by which the intellect thinks *a priori* of the connections of things, but that metaphysics consists entirely of such concepts. I endeavored to ascertain their number, and as I succeeded in doing this to my satisfaction, namely, out of a single principle, I proceeded to the deduction of these concepts, which I was now assured could not be derived from experience as Hume had pretended, but must have originated in the pure intellect. This deduction that had seemed impossible to my acute predecessor and that had not even occurred to anyone except him, although everyone unconcernedly used these concepts (without asking on what their objective validity rested); this deduction, I say, was the most difficult problem that could ever be undertaken in the interests of metaphysics. The worst of it was that metaphysics, so far as it exists at all at present, could not afford me the least help because the above deduction was needed to make metaphysics possible in the first place. Having now succeeded in the solution of Hume's problem, not only in one particular case, but in respect to the entire capacity of pure reason, I could at least determine more surely, though still only by slow steps, the whole range of pure reason in its limits as well as in its content. I could determine it completely according to the universal principles which are required for metaphysics in order to construct its system on a secure plan.

However I am afraid that [my effort to resolve] the problem of Hume to the greatest possible extent (namely, in the *Critique of Pure Reason*) will fare as the *problem* itself fared when it was first stated. My effort will be mistakenly judged because it is not understood; it will not be understood because people, though they may care to turn over the leaves of my book, will not care to think it through; and they will be unwilling to take this trouble with it because the work is dry, obscure, and, besides being diffuse, contrary to all accustomed conceptions. But I must confess that I was quite surprised to hear from a philosopher complaints as to the work not being popular, entertaining, and agreeably arranged. What is at stake is a branch of knowledge highly prized and indispensable to humanity which cannot be treated otherwise than according to the most strict rules of academic precision. Popularity may indeed follow in time but it can never be expected at the beginning. However, a grievance must be admitted as regards a certain obscurity which arises partly from the diffuseness of the plan, as a result of which the main points of the investigation are not so readily perceived. It is the task of the present *Prolegomena* to remove this difficulty.

The *Critique of Pure Reason,* which presents the capacity of pure reason in its whole range and limits, remains the foundation to which the *Prolegomena* are only preparatory. For the *Critique* must, as a science, be complete and systematic even down to the smallest detail before we can so much as think of presenting metaphysics, or of even allowing ourselves the most distant hope in this direction.

We have long been accustomed to seeing old and worn-out theories remodeled by being taken out of their former coverings and fitted to a systematic garment according to our own approved style but under new titles; the great majority of readers will expect nothing different from our *Critique.* But these *Prolegomena* will convince them that it is quite a new science of which no one had previously had the smallest conception, of which even the idea was unknown, and with reference to which all hitherto received knowledge was unavailable, with the exception of the hint afforded by Hume's doubt. But Hume never dreamt of a possible formal science of this nature, and in order to land his ship in safety, he ran it aground on the shore of scepticism where it might lie and rot. Instead of doing this, it is my purpose to furnish a pilot who, according to certain principles of seamanship derived from a knowledge of the globe, and supplied with a complete map and compass, may steer the ship with safety wherever it seems good to him. For were we not to do this we should only fancy, because the terms sound alike, that we saw everywhere what we had known already except that everything would appear misshapen, senseless and unintelligible because we would be basing our approach upon our own notions to which we have become habituated by long use, instead of basing our approach on the author's thought. But the diffuseness of the work and the ensuing unavoidable dryness and academic precision, however advantageous these may be objectively, are undoubtedly disadvantageous to the book in so far as this is a result of the nature of the science itself and not of its presentation.

Indeed, it is not given to everyone to write as subtly and at the same time as charmingly as David Hume, or as thoroughly and as elegantly as Moses Mendelssohn; but I flatter myself that I might have rendered my style popular had I only set out to sketch a plan and had left its completion to others, and if I had not had the interests of the science, with which I have been occupied so long, so much at heart. For it requires considerable persistence and not a little self-denial to choose a late but enduring fame in preference to the allure of an early and favorable reception.

Plan-making is often a luxurious and pretentious mental occupation, whereby one acquires the reputation of a creative genius by demanding what one cannot achieve oneself, by censuring what one cannot improve, and by proposing what one does not know how to find. But in a thorough plan of the general *Critique of Reason* something more is necessary that perhaps may be supposed, if the plan is not to be the usual mere declamation of pious wishes. For pure reason is so isolated, and is so closely-knit a sphere in itself, that no part of it can be touched upon without affecting the rest. Therefore, we can accomplish nothing without determining the position and influence of each part with regard to the others because there is nothing outside each part by which we can judge correctly as to anything inside. The validity and use of every part depends upon the relation in which the part stands in respect to this composition. The situation is *similar* to that of an organized body where the purpose of each member can only be deduced from a complete concept of the whole. Therefore it may be said that such a critique is never reliable unless it is quite complete down to the least of the elements of pure reason; and that in the sphere of this faculty one must determine and expound either *everything* or *nothing*.

A mere plan preceding the *Critique of Pure Reason* would be incomprehensible, unreliable and useless, but following the *Critique* it is much more useful. Then one is in a position to view the whole, to test one by one the main points upon which the science rests and to render the style better than was possible on the first execution of the work.

The following is such a plan which may be presented according to an analytical method, since the work is complete, whereas the work itself had to be constructed throughout according to synthetic method in order that the new science might exhibit all its articulations in their natural connection as the organization of a special faculty of knowledge. On the other hand, should anyone find that this plan which I am putting forward as a Prolegomena to any future system of metaphysics, is itself obscure, he must bear in mind that it is not necessary for *everyone* to study metaphysics. There is much talent which is perfectly adequate for investigating the thorough and even profound sciences which lie more in the field of observation, but this talent is apt to be unsuccessful in a species of research based solely on abstract conceptions. When this last happens, one's mental abilities should be turned in another direction. But he who undertakes to judge a system of metaphysics, or to construct one, must satisfy in every way the demands that will be made here. It may happen that he either accepts my solution or he utterly refutes it and offers another in its stead; but evade it, he cannot. Thus, the much-decried obscurity (though it is a frequent covering for indolence and stupidity) may have its uses in the end, since those who maintain a judicious silence in respect to other sciences speak masterfully and decide anew in questions of metaphysics because in this their ignorance does not contrast conspicuously with established scientific knowledge, although it certainly does with the principles of sound criticism. Of these one may claim, *Ignavum, fucos, pecus a praesepibus arcent.* (Virgil: They keep off from the hives the lazy swarm of drones.)

INTRODUCTORY REMARKS ON THE SPECIFIC QUALITY OF ALL METAPHYSICAL KNOWLEDGE

§ 1

Of the Sources of Metaphysics

In presenting a branch of knowledge as *science,* it is necessary to be able to define with precision its distinguishing characteristic, that which it possesses in common with no other branch and which is therefore specific to this science. Otherwise, the boundaries of all sciences run into one another and no one of them can be thoroughly treated according to its own nature.

Whether this specific quality consists in the distinction of its *object,* of its *sources of knowledge,* of its *kind of knowledge,* or lastly, of several if not all these points taken together, the idea of this possible science and of its sphere rests primarily upon this specific quality.

Firstly, as regards the *sources* of metaphysical knowledge, its very conception shows that these sources cannot be empirical. Its principles (which include not merely its axioms, but also its fundamental conceptions) consequently can never be taken from experience; since it is not *physical* but *metaphysical* knowledge, i.e., knowledge beyond experience, that is wanted. Thus neither external experience which is the source of physical science proper, nor internal experience which is the groundwork of empirical psychology, will constitute its foundation. Metaphysics consists, then, of *a priori* knowledge, that is, of knowledge derived from pure intellect and pure reason.

But there is nothing in this to distinguish it from pure mathematics; therefore metaphysics must be defined as *pure philosophical knowledge.* Regarding the meaning of this expression, I must refer the reader to the *Critique of Pure Reason* where the distinction between these two ways of using reason are clearly and adequately presented. So much for the sources of metaphysical knowledge.

§ 2

Of the only kind of Knowledge that can be termed Metaphysical

A. Of the difference between synthetic and analytic judgments in general

Metaphysical knowledge must only contain *a priori* judgments; that much is required by the specific quality of its sources. But all judgments, no matter what origin they may have, or how they are constructed in regard to logical form, differ according to their content, by virtue of which they are either simply *explanatory* and add nothing to the content of knowledge, or they are *extensive* and enlarge the given knowledge. The first may be termed *analytic* and the second *synthetic* judgments.

Analytic judgments say nothing in the predicate but what has already been thought of in the conception of the subject, although perhaps not so clearly, nor with the same degree of consciousness. When I say that all bodies are extended, I do not thereby in the least enlarge my concept of a body but have simply resolved it, inasmuch as extension, although not expressly stated, was already thought of in that conception; in other words the judgment is analytic. On the other hand, the proposition that some bodies are heavy contains something in the predicate which was not already thought of in the general conception of a body; that is to say, it enlarges my knowledge in so far as it adds something to my conception and therefore it must be termed a synthetic judgment.

B. The common principle of all analytic judgments is the principle of contradiction

All analytic judgments are based entirely on the principle of contradiction and are *a priori* cognitions by their nature, whether the concepts involved are empirical or not. Since the predicate of an affirmative analytic judgment is previously implied in the conception of the subject, such a predicate cannot be denied of the subject without contradiction. In the same way, and also in accordance with the principle of contradiction, the reverse of this subject must necessarily be denied in a negative analytic judgment. This is the situation with the propositions: every body is extended and no body is unextended (simple). For this reason all analytic propositions are *a priori* judgments, although their conceptions may be empirical. Let us take as an instance the proposition: gold is a yellow metal. Now in order to know this I require no further experience beyond my concept of gold which contains the propositions that this body is yellow and a metal. This precisely constitutes my concept and therefore I only have to analyze it without needing to look around for anything elsewhere.

C. Synthetic judgments demand a principle other than that of contradiction

There are synthetic *a posteriori* judgments whose origin is empirical, but there are also others which are certain and *a priori* and which spring from pure intellect and reason. Both kinds of judgments are alike in that they can never have their source solely in the principle of analysis, namely, the principle of contradiction. They require an altogether different principle in spite of the fact that no matter what principle they may be deduced from, they must always *conform to the principle of contradiction*, for nothing can be at variance with this principle, although not everything can be deduced from it. I shall now classify synthetic judgments.

(1) *Empirical judgments are always synthetic.* It would be absurd to found an analytic judgment on experience, as it is unnecessary to go beyond my own concept in order to construct the judgment, and therefore the confirmation of experience is unnecessary to it. That a body is extended is a proposition possessing *a priori* certainty; it is not an empirical judgment. For before I turn to experience I have all the conditions of my judgment already at hand in the conception from which I simply deduce the predicate in accordance with the principle of contradiction. Thereby I may, at the same time, become conscious of the *necessity* of the judgment which experience could never teach me.

(2) *All mathematical judgments are synthetic.* Up till now this truth seems to have altogether escaped those who have analyzed human reason; indeed, it seems to be directly opposed to all their guesses, although it is indisputably certain and very important in its consequences. Because it was found that the conclusions of mathematicians all proceed according to the principle of contradiction, which the nature of every apodictic certainty demands, it was concluded that the axioms were also known through the principle of contradiction. This was a great error; for although a synthetic proposition can be viewed in the light of the principle of contradiction, this can only be done by presupposing another synthetic proposition from which the first proposition is derived, but such a proposition can never be derived from the principle of contradiction.

First of all it must be remarked that genuinely mathematical propositions are always judgments *a priori* and are never empirical because they involve necessity which cannot be derived from experience. Should anyone be unwilling to admit this, I will limit my proposition to *pure mathematics,* the very conception of which implies that it contains nothing empirical but simply pure, *a priori* knowledge.

At first sight, one might be disposed to think that the proposition $7 + 5 = 12$ is merely analytic resulting from the conception of a sum of seven and five according to the principle of contradiction. But if one considers it more closely one will find that the conception of the sum of 7 and 5 comprises nothing beyond the union of two numbers in a single one, and that there is nothing whatever implied in it as to what this single number is, which comprehends both the others. The concept of twelve is by no means already thought of when I think merely of the union of seven and five, and I may dissect my concept of such a possible sum as long as I please without discovering the number twelve in it. One must go beyond these concepts and seek the assistance from observing something which corresponds to one or the other of them, as for example, one's five fingers, and so gradually add the units of the five given in observation to the conception of the seven. One's conception is therefore really enlarged by the proposition $7 + 5 = 12$; to the first conception a new one is being added which was in no way implied in the former. In other words, arithmetical propositions are always synthetic. This is more clear when we take larger numbers, for then we will be clearly convinced that, turn and twist our concept as we may, we shall never find the sum required by the mere dissection of the original concept without calling observation to our aid.

A principle of pure geometry is not any more analytic than a principle of arithmetic. That a straight line is the shortest distance between two points is a synthetic proposition. For my concept of straight has no reference to size but only to quality. Therefore the concept of the "shortest" is quite additional and cannot be drawn from any analysis of the conception of a straight line. Therefore observation must again be brought to our aid; by means of it alone the synthesis is possible.

Indeed certain other principles which are postulated by geometricians are really analytic and rest on the principle of contradiction, but they only serve as links in the chain of method like identical propositions and are not true principles. For instance a = a, the whole is equal to itself, or $(a + b) > a$, i.e., the whole is greater than its part. But even these, although they are valid according to mere conceptions, are only admitted in mathematics because they can be presented in observation. What produces the common belief that the predicate of such apodictic judgments is already unified in our conception, and that therefore the judgment is analytic, is merely the ambiguity of expression. We ought to add in one thought a certain predicate to a given concept, for this necessity is implied in the concepts themselves. But the question is not what we *ought* to think, but what we actually, though obscurely, think in connection with them. This shows us that the predicate is implied in those conceptions necessarily though not immediately, and it must be added by means of an observation.

The essential feature distinguishing pure *mathematical* * knowledge from all other *a priori* knowledge is that it does not proceed from *concepts themselves* but always from the construction of concepts. (*Critique of Pure Reason,* p. 435) Therefore, since mathematics in its propositions must go beyond the concept to that which the corresponding observation contains, these propositions never can nor ought to arise from the analysis of the concepts, that is, arise analytically; in other words, these propositions are synthetic in their entirety.

I cannot refrain from remarking on the disadvantage which the neglect of this simple and apparently insignificant observation has brought on philosophy. Hume inadvertently severed from pure knowledge an entire and indeed more important province, namely that of pure mathematics, when he cast his eye over the whole field of pure, *a priori* knowledge in which the human intellect claims such extensive possessions.

---

*Vaihinger has urged ("Eine Blattversetzung in Kant's Prolegomena" *Philosophische Monatshefte* XV (1882) that the following six paragraphs belong in this section 2, rather than where they occur in section 4. The argument is convincing and they nave therefore been shifted here.—Ed.)

He was under the impression that the nature of pure mathematics rested on totally different principles; namely, that it rested solely on the principle of contradiction. Although he did not undertake such a formal and general classification of propositions, nor in the same terms as I do here, yet what he did was like saying: pure mathematics contains merely analytic judgments, while metaphysics contains synthetic *a priori* judgments. Now he made a great mistake in this and this mistake had decidedly injurious consequences for his whole conception [of knowledge]. For if he had not made it, he would have broadened his question respecting the origin of our synthetic judgments far beyond his metaphysical concept of causality, and extended it [to include] the possibility of *a priori* mathematics; for he should have regarded this as synthetic also. But in the latter case, he could under no circumstances have based his metaphysical propositions on mere experience, as then he would have been obliged to subordinate the axioms of pure mathematics to experience, a proceeding for which he had too much insight.

The good company into which metaphysics would have thereby been brought would have ensured it against mean maltreatment; for the thrusts aimed at metaphysics would have also hit mathematics, and this neither was nor could have been Hume's opinion. Thus this keen man would have been led to reflections similar to those with which we are now occupied, but they would have gained infinitely by his inimitably beautiful style of presentation.

(3) *Metaphysical judgments proper are synthetic in their entirety.* We must distinguish between judgments belonging to *metaphysics* and metaphysical judgments. Among the former are included many that are analytic, but these only furnish the means for metaphysical judgments proper which form the entire purpose of the science and are all synthetic. For, when concepts belong to metaphysics, as does for instance that of substance, the judgments arising from the analysis of the concepts also belong

to metaphysics. For example, [we say] substance is that which only exists as a subject, etc., and [by making] several analytic judgments of this kind we seek to approach the definition of the concept. However, since the analysis of a pure intellectual concept, such as those concepts continued in metaphysics, cannot proceed differently than the analysis of any other empirical concept which does not belong to metaphysics (e.g., air is an elastic fluid, the elasticity of which is not destroyed by any known degree of coldness), [it follows that] the concept but not the analytic judgment is peculiarly metaphysical. For this science exhibits something special and peculiar in the way it produces its intellectual knowledge *a priori*. This peculiar mode of production must be distinguished from what metaphysics has in common with all other intellectual knowledge. Thus, for example, the proposition that all that is substance in things persists is a synthetic and properly metaphysical proposition.

When the *a priori* concepts constituting the structural materials of metaphysics have been collected according to certain principles, the analysis of these concepts is of great value. They can then be presented as a special part (as it were, a *philosophia definitiva*), containing solely analytic propositions relating to metaphysics and this part would be separate from the synthetic propositions which constitute metaphysics itself. Actually, these analyses have nowhere any important use except in metaphysics, that is, no use in reference to the synthetic propositions which are constructed from these analyzed concepts.

Hence the conclusion to be drawn in this section is that metaphysics is properly concerned with *a priori* synthetic propositions, and that these alone constitute its task, but that metaphysics requires for this purpose some analyses of its concept or analytic judgments, the procedure in this respect being no different than in other kinds of knowledge in which concepts are sought to be made clear by analysis. But the *generation* of *a priori* knowledge which is derived as much from observation as from concepts, together with *a priori* synthetic propositions understood philosophically, finally constitute the essential content of metaphysics.

§ 3

A Footnote on the General Classification of Judgments into Analytic and Synthetic Judgments

This classification is indispensable in regard to the critique of the human mind and therefore deserves to be *classic* in this critique, but I do not know of any other considerable use for it. I also find here the reason why dogmatic philosophers, who, looking for the sources of metaphysical judgments in metaphysics itself (rather than outside it in the laws of pure reason in general), have neglected this classification which seems to offer itself so naturally. I see why men like the celebrated Wolff, or the acute Baumgarten who followed in his steps, have sought the proof of the principle of sufficient cause, which is obviously synthetic, in the principle of contradiction. I encountered a hint of this classification in Locke's "Essay on the Human Understanding." In the third chapter of the fourth book he discusses the association of different ideas (*Vorstellungen*) in judgments and their sources. He sees one of their sources in the principles of identity and contradiction while he sees the other source in the existence of such ideas in a subject (synthetic judgments). Locke then confesses that our *a priori* knowledge of the latter judgments is very limited, amounting to almost nothing. But there is so little that is definite and reduced to rules in what he says respecting this kind of knowledge that one cannot be surprised that no one, not even Hume, has undertaken to reflect upon this class of propositions. For such general yet definite principles as these are not easily learned from other men to whom they have only been dimly discernible. One must first discover them through one's own reflection and then one will find them elsewhere in places where otherwise one certainly would not have noticed them, since the authors themselves did not know that their own remarks were based upon such an idea. Once a point has been clarified, writers who do not think for themselves nevertheless possess the acumen to hunt it up in what has previously been said though no one could see it before.

THE GENERAL QUESTION OF THE PROLEGOMENA

Is Metaphysics possible at all?

§ 4

Were metaphysics actually a viable science, one could say: here is metaphysics, you only have to learn it and it will convince you permanently and irresistibly of its truth. In that case the present question would be unnecessary and there would only remain the question: how is such metaphysics possible, and how is reason to set about attaining it? (This would be more a testing of our acuteness than a proof of the existence of metaphysics.) Unfortunately, in this case human reason is not in such a happy position. One cannot point to a single book like *Euclid* and say: this is metaphysics, in this is to be found the supreme purpose of this science, the knowledge of a supreme being and of a future world, demonstrated upon principles of pure reason. One can produce many propositions that are apodictically certain and that have never been contested. But these propositions are analytic in their entirety and concern more the materials and the elements of construction than the extension of knowledge which is our special object in the present case (§ 2, B, C above). Then there is the case of certain synthetic propositions, such as the principle of sufficient cause, which are readily conceded though they have never been proved by mere reason, that is, proved *a priori* as they ought to have been. In these cases, whenever someone attempted to make use of such propositions for the main purpose [of establishing a metaphysics], he ended up in such inadmissible and doubtful assertions that it has always happened that one system of metaphysics has contradicted another, either in respect to the assertions in it or their proofs, thus destroying all claim to a lasting recognition. Without doubt, the very attempts to establish such a science were the first cause of the scepticism that arose so soon. Scepticism is a mode of thought in which reason treats itself with such violence that this scepticism would never have arisen but for reason's utter despair of satisfying its [own] chief aspirations. For, long before man methodically began to question nature, he interrogated his own isolated reason, which had already become skilled to a certain extent by common experience, while the laws of nature must usually be laboriously discovered. So metaphysics floated to the surface like foam and also like foam no sooner was it gathered up than it dissolved, and more of it appeared on the surface which some people were always eager to gather, while others, instead of seeking to penetrate the cause of this phenomenon considered themselves wise in laughing at the futile endeavors of the former.

Wearied then of a dogmatism that teaches us nothing as well as of a scepticism that promises us nothing, not even the peace of a permissible ignorance, led on by the importance of the knowledge we need, yet rendered mistrustful by long experience regarding all knowledge that we believe ourselves to possess or that offers itself in the name of pure reason, we still face one critical question; *is metaphysics possible at all?* We shall adopt our future conduct in the light of the answer. But this question must be answered, not by sceptical objections to particular assertions of any actual system of metaphysics (for we do not admit of any at present), but from the as yet only problematical conception of such a science.

In the *Critique of Pure Reason* I went to work synthetically on this question by investigating pure reason itself and from this source I endeavored to determine according to principles the elements as well as the laws of the pure use of reason. This task is difficult and a resolute reader is needed to penetrate step by step into a system which presupposed nothing but itself and which consequently seeks to unfold knowledge from its original germs without depending upon any external fact. On the contrary the *Prolegomena* should be preparatory exercises designed to show what has to be done if possible to realize such a science, rather than to expound one. Therefore the *Prolegomena* must rely on something known as trustworthy from which we may proceed with confidence and ascend to the sources which are yet unknown to us and whose discovery will not only explain what we already know but will exhibit to us at the same time a range of many insights all arising from the same sources. Therefore the methodical procedure of the *Prolegomena* will be analytic, especially those [parts of it] destined to prepare for a future system of metaphysics.

Now it fortunately happens that, although we cannot assume metaphysics to be an actual science, we may assert with confidence that certain pure synthetic insights are *a priori,* actual and given; namely, *pure mathematics* and *pure natural science.* Both contain propositions some of which are apodictically certain through mere reason and some of which are recognized as being in general accord with experience, though completely independent of such experience. At least we now have some *uncontested, a priori,* synthetic knowledge, and since such knowledge exists we should not ask whether it is possible, but only ask; *how is it possible?* [We should do this] in order to deduce from the principle of the possibility of such existing knowledge the possibility of all other such knowledge.

GENERAL QUESTION:

How is knowledge possible from pure reason?

§ 5

We have already seen the important distinction between analytic and synthetic judgments. The possibility of analytic propositions can be conceived very easily for they are simply based on the principle of contradiction. The possibility of synthetic *a posteriori* propositions, i.e. of such as are derived from experi-

ence, requires no particular explanation, for experience is nothing more than a continual fitting together (synthesis) of perceptions (*Wahrnehmungen*). There remain only synthetic *a
priori* propositions, the possibility of which has yet to be discovered and examined because their possibility must rest on
principles other than that of contradiction.

But we do not need to inquire into the possibility of such
propositions, that is to ask whether they are possible, for there
are enough of them actually given and given with unquestion-
able certainty. As the method we are following here is analytic,
we shall assume at the outset that such synthetic but also pure
knowledge exists based on reason. But we must investigate the
grounds for this possibility and proceed to ask: how is this
knowledge possible? We must do this so that we may be in a
position to determine the conditions, scope and limits of the use
of this knowledge from the principles of its possibility. Therefore the specific task on which everything turns will be the
question, when expressed with academic precision: *How are
synthetic,* a priori *propositions possible?*

A little earlier I expressed the problem somewhat differently
for the sake of popularity; namely, as an inquiry into knowledge
derived from pure reason. I could do this on that occasion without detriment to the desired insight. For, as we are simply concerned here with metaphysics and its sources, I hope that
after the above remarks readers will constantly bear in mind that
when we speak here of knowledge derived from pure reason, we
invariably refer to synthetic and never to analytic knowledge.

The very existence of metaphysics depends upon the solution of this problem. It does not matter if anyone presents assertions however plausible with regard to this problem and
piles conclusion upon conclusion. I have a right to say that, if
he has not first been able to answer satisfactorily the above
question, this is all vain, baseless philosophy and false wisdom.
You speak through pure reason and claim to create *a priori*
knowledge inasmuch as you not only dissect given conceptions

but you pretend to establish new connections which do not rest on the principle of contradiction and which you still believe to understand quite independently of all experience. How do you arrive at the new connections and how will you justify such pretensions? You cannot be allowed to appeal to the concurrence of the general common sense of mankind for that is a witness whose reputation rests only on popular rumor. *Quodcumque ostendis mihi sic, incredulus odi.* (Horace: All that you thus show me, I unbelieving hate.)

While the answer to this question is indispensable, at the same time it is very difficult. The chief reason why men have not endeavored to answer it long before lies in the fact that it never occurred to them that anything of the kind could be asked. But a second cause is that the satisfactory answer to this one question demands a more persistent, deeper and more laborious reflection than did the most diffuse work on metaphysics that gave promise of immortal fame to its author on its first appearance. Every thoughtful reader, on attentively considering the requirements of this problem and frightened at the outset by its difficulty, would regard it as insoluble, and even as altogether impossible were it not for the actual existence of such pure, *a priori,* knowledge. This happened in the case of David Hume, although he did not place the problem before him in nearly as much generality as is done here, and as must be done if the answer is to be decisive for the whole of metaphysics. For how is it possible, said that acute man, that when I am given a concept, I can go beyond it and connect it with another which is not contained in it at all [but which is connected] in such a manner as if it necessarily belonged to it? He concluded from that difficulty which he mistook for an impossibility that only experience can present us with such associations and hence that all this presumed necessity (or what is the same thing, knowledge assumed to be *a priori*) is nothing but a long habit of believing something to be true, and therefore of believing the subjective necessity to be objective.

If the reader should complain of the difficulty and trouble I shall give him in solving this problem, then let him set about attempting to solve it in an easier way. Perhaps he will then feel obligated to one who has undertaken for him the labor of such searching inquiry. He may then show some surprise at the facility with which it has been possible to find the solution, considering the nature of the subject. It has cost years of trouble to solve this problem in a general way (taking the word "general" in the sense in which mathematicians use it, namely; sufficient for all cases), and finally to be able to present the solution in analytic form, such as the reader will find here.

Therefore all metaphysicians are solemnly and legally suspended from their business until they shall have answered adequately the question: *How is synthetic* a priori *knowledge possible?* For their answer alone can provide the credentials they must show if they have anything to present to us in the name of pure reason. In default of this, they can expect nothing else but to be rejected, without any further inquiry into their work, by sensible people who have been so often deceived.

On the other hand, should they want to carry on their business not as a *science,* but as an *art* of helpful persuasion that is suitable to the general common sense of mankind, this calling cannot in fairness be denied them. In that case they should use only the modest language of a reasonable belief, they should admit that it is not even allowed them to *conjecture,* much less to *know* anything respecting what lies beyond the boundaries of all possible experience, but merely to *assume* what is possible and even indispensable for directing the intellect and the will in life. Only in this way can they possibly acquire the reputation of wise and useful men and they will have it to a greater extent the more they renounce the title of metaphysicians. For metaphysicians want to be speculative philosophers, and, inasmuch as bare probabilities cannot be accepted, it cannot be allowed them to play with conjectures; their assertions must either be true knowledge, or they are nothing at all.

It may be said that the whole of transcendental philosophy, which necessarily precedes all metaphysics, is itself nothing more than the full solution, in systematic order and completeness, of the question propounded here. Therefore it may be said that we have no transcendental philosophy as yet. What bears its name is properly a part of metaphysics, and since transcendental philosophy is to establish the possibility of metaphysics, it must precede all metaphyics. Considering then that a complete science, entirely new in itself and lacking assistance from other sciences, is needed in order to answer a single question adequately, it is not surprising that the solving of this task is accompanied by trouble and difficulty and even perhaps by some degree of obscurity.

As we now proceed to this solution according to the analytic method, presupposing that such knowledge exists from pure reason, we can only cite two *sciences* of theoretic knowledge, (with which we are solely concerned here), namely; *pure mathematics* and *pure natural science*. Only these can present to us objects in observation and therefore if *a priori* knowledge should occur in these sciences, they could show the truth or agreement of such knowledge with the object *in concreto*. In other words, these sciences can show the existence of such objects. We can proceed analytically from this existence to the ground of its possibility. This facilitates the matter very much as the general considerations are not only applied to facts but even start from them when otherwise they would have to be deduced by synthetic procedure from concepts *in abstracto*.

But in order to ascend from these existing and well-grounded pure, *a priori* insights to a possible knowledge such as we are seeking, namely, to reach metaphysics as a science, we have to embrace that which occasions it under our main question. For what occasions metaphysical questions and forms the basis of metaphysics is given naturally, although as regards the truth in it, it is rather suspect *a priori* knowledge, the treatment of which is usually called metaphysics without any [prior] critical inquiry as to its possibility. In short we must comprise within our main question the natural propensity of mankind toward such a science [as metaphysics.] [If we do that then] the main transscendental question will be divided into four more questions which will be answered step by step.

(1) How is pure mathematics possible?
(2) How is pure natural science possible?
(3) How is metaphysics in general possible?
(4) How is metaphysics as a science possible?

It will be seen that although the solution of these problems is chiefly intended to present the essential contents of the *Critique of Pure Reason,* the solution itself has something specific [to offer]. This in itself is worthy of attention; for it is the task of discovering in reason the sources of given sciences in order to explore and measure in the process the faculty of reason for realizing something *a priori.* In this way the sciences themselves should gain, if not in their content, at least in regard to their proper use. These sciences should also gain from greater clarification of their proper nature since the consideration of these problems [the four stated above] will provide a better insight into the common origin of these sciences.

FIRST PART OF THE MAIN TRANSCEN-DENTAL QUESTION

How is pure Mathematics possible?

§6

Mathematics is a great and established branch of knowledge, already of remarkable compass and promising unlimited expansion in the future. Yet it carries with it a thoroughly apodictic certainty, i.e., an absolute necessity. Thus mathematics rests on no empirical grounds but is a pure product of reason, besides being thoroughly synthetic. "How is it possible for the human mind to create such knowledge entirely *a priori?*" Does not this capacity, since it does not and cannot rest on experience, presuppose some ground of *a priori* knowledge which lies deep-hidden, but which might manifest itself in these its effects, if only their first beginnings were diligently explored?

SECOND PART OF THE MAIN TRANSCEN-DENTAL PROBLEM

How is Pure Natural Science Possible?

§ 14

Nature is the existence of things in so far as this existence is determined by universal laws. If Nature signified the existence of *things in themselves*, we could never know it either *a priori* or *a posteriori*. Not *a priori*, for how shall we know what applies to things in themselves since this can never be done by analyzing our concepts (analytic propositions)? For what I [would then] want to know is not what is contained in my concept of a thing (for that concerns its logical essence), but what, in the reality of the thing, is added to this concept, by which the thing itself is determined in its existence outside my concept. My intellect, which is subject to the conditions under which alone it can relate the qualities of things as they exist, prescribes no rules for the things in themselves; these things do not conform to my intellect, but my intellect must conform to them. These things would therefore have to be given me previously, in order for these qualities to be discovered in them; and in this case they would not be known *a priori*.

But such a knowledge of the nature of things in themselves would be equally impossible *a posteriori*. For if experience is to teach me laws to which the existence of things is subject, these laws would, in so far as they concerned things in themselves, necessarily also apply to them outside my experience. Now experience teaches me what exists and how it exists, but never that it exists necessarily in such a manner and no other. Therefore it can never teach the nature of things in themselves.

§ 15

Nevertheless, we are actually in possession of a pure natural science, which puts forward, *a priori* and with all the necessity requisite to apodictic propositions, laws to which nature is subordinated. I only need to call to witness here that introductory field which, under the title of general natural science, precedes all physics based on empirical principles. Therein we find mathematics applied to phenomena and also to those discursive principles derived from concepts which constitute the philosophical part of pure knowledge of nature. But this knowledge also contains some matters which are not pure and are not independent of experience, such as the concept of motion, impenetrability (on which the empirical concept of matter rests), inertia, and others. These matters prevent physics from being called a perfectly pure natural science. Besides, physics is only concerned with objects of the sense and thus furnishes no example of a pure natural science in the strict meaning. For, such a science must bring nature under general laws, irrespective of whether it concerns the object of the outer or of the inner sense; that of physics or that of psychology. But, among the principles of this universal physics are to be found some that really possess the universality we require, such as the proposition: *substance continues and is permanent,* and that, according to fixed laws: *all which happens is at all times previously determined by a cause.* These are really universal natural laws, existing completely *a priori.* Therefore a pure natural science actually exists, and now the question arises: *how is it possible?*

§ 16

However, the word *nature* can take on another meaning defining the *object,* whereas in the above meaning it suggested merely that *laws* determined the qualities of things as they exist. *Nature,* when considered *materialiter,* is the *sum-total of all the objects of experience.* We are only concerned with this nature here, since anyhow things which could never be objects of an experience, if they were known according to their nature, would force us to form concepts whose meaning could never be given *in concreto* (in an example of a possible experience). Therefore we would have to form concepts of which it could never be decided whether they really referred to objects or were mere figments of thought. The knowledge of that which cannot be an object of experience would be beyond the physical and we have nothing at all to do with such matters here. We are only concerned with that knowledge of nature whose reality can be confirmed by experience, even though it is possible *a priori*, and precedes all experience.

§ 17

In this narrower meaning the *formal* in nature are the laws of nature which regulate all the objects of experience, and, in so far as they are known *a priori*, these laws constitute the necessary regularity of nature. But it has just been demonstrated that the laws of nature can never be known *a priori* in objects when these objects are considered as things in themselves. . . . Hence we are not concerned here with things in themselves, but merely with things as the objects of a possible experience. The sum-total of these is what we properly call nature. Therefore, if the question concerns the possibility of *a priori* knowledge of nature, would it not be better to formulate the problem as follows? How is it possible to know *a priori* the necessary laws regulating things as objects of experience? Or, how can the necessary laws, which regulate experience itself in respect to all its objects, be known generally and *a priori*?

Seen in its true light, the solution of the problem of pure knowledge of nature (which constitutes the real point of the question) is all the same in the end, whether imagined in one form or another. For the subjective* laws, under which alone a knowledge of things through experience is possible, are also

---

* [For the meaning of subjective see Introduction, Pp. XXIX.—Ed.]

valid for those things as objects of a possible experience. It does not matter then whether I say: No judgment based on observation can be considered experience without the law, that any event on being observed must invariably be referred to something preceding it upon which it follows according to a general rule; or whether I express myself thus: Everything that experience teaches as happening must have a cause.

However, it is advisable to choose the first statement. For we can have, *a priori* and before all given objects, a knowledge of those conditions under which alone an experience is possible. But we can never have knowledge of what laws those objects are subject to by themselves without reference to a possible experience. Therefore we shall not be able to study *a priori* the nature of things except by investigating the conditions and by investigating general, though subjective, laws, under which alone such a knowledge as experience is formally possible, and then by determining in accordance with this the possibility of things as objects of experience. Were I to choose the second mode of expression and were I to investigate the *a priori* conditions under which nature can possibly be an *object* of experience, I should easily be led into misunderstanding, and might then fancy I had to explain nature as a thing in itself, and I should then be fruitlessly involved in endless efforts to seek laws for things of which nothing is given me.

Therefore we shall simply be concerned here with experience and with the general and *a priori* given conditions of its possibility, and we shall thereby determine nature as the complete object of all possible experience. I think it will be understood that I am not referring to the rules for the *observation* of a nature already given, which [rules] presuppose experience, [nor am I referring to the procedure by which] we can arrive at the laws of nature through experience, for then these laws would not be laws *a priori* and they would give no pure science of nature. [What I do mean is to show] how the *a priori* conditions of the possibility of experience are at the same time the sources from which all the general laws of nature must be derived.

§ 18

First of all we must observe that while all judgments based on experience are empirical, (i.e., have their foundation in immediate sense perception) on the other hand empirical judgments are not judgments based solely on experience, but that beyond the empirical, and beyond the perception given by the senses generally, special concepts must come into play. These concepts have their origin entirely *a priori* in the pure intellect; every perception is first of all subsumed under them and can then be transformed into experience by means of these concepts.

Empirical judgments, in so far as they have objective validity, are JUDGMENTS BASED ON EXPERIENCE; but those which are merely *subjectively valid* I call judgments based on perception. . . .

All our judgments are at first mere judgments based on perception; they are valid simply for ourselves, as subject. Only subsequently do we give them a new reference, namely, to an object, and insist that they shall always be valid for ourselves as well as for everyone else. For, when a judgment agrees with an object, all judgments concerning the same object must agree with one another; hence the objective validity of a judgment based on experience means nothing more than its necessary general validity. Reversely, when we have to consider a judgment as necessarily and generally valid (a judgment which never rests on the perception but on the pure intellectual concept under which the perception is subsumed), we have to regard the judgment as objective, i.e., as expressing not merely the regulation of the perception to a subject but a quality of the object. For there would be no reason why the judgments of other persons must necessarily agree with mine, if it were not for the unity of the object to which they all refer, with which they agree; consequently, they must all agree with one another.

§ 19

Objective validity and necessary general validity are therefore interchangeable notions. Although we do not know the object in itself, we regard a judgment as both general and necessary when objective validity is understood thereby. We know the object through this judgment by the general and necessary linking of given perceptions, though what it is in itself remains unknown. As this is the case with all objects of sense, judgments of experience owe their objective validity not to the direct knowledge of the object, but merely to the condition of the general validity of judgments. The object in itself always remains unknown; but when the linking of the images given to our imagination is by this intellectual concept determined as generally valid through the concept that the intellect provides, the object is determined by this relation and the judgment is objective.

We will illustrate this. That the room is warm,[1] the sugar sweet, the wormwood bitter, are merely subjectively valid judgments. I do not expect that I, or every other person, will always find them as I do now. They only express a relation of two sensations to the same subject, namely, myself, and they do so only in my present state of perception and are therefore not valid of an object. I call these judgments based on perception. With judgments based on experience the case is altogether different. What experience teaches me under certain circumstances, it must teach me, and every other person as well, at all

[1] I readily admit that these instances do not present judgments of perception that could ever become judgments of experience, even if an intellectual concept came into play, because they refer to mere feeling, which everyone recognizes as merely subjective, and as such never predicable of the object, and thus never capable of becoming objective. At present I only wish to give an instance of a judgment that is subjectively valid, but that contains in itself no reason for necessary general validity and hence no reference to an object. An example of judgments of perception that become judgments of experience by the employment of an intellectual concept follows in the next footnote.

times; its validity is not limited to the subject or to the state of such a subject at a particular time. All such judgments are stated as objectively valid. For instance, when I say that the air is elastic, this judgment is first of all a judgment of perception since I only link (associate) the two sensations with one another. If I wish it to be called a judgment of experience I must demand that this link (association) be so conditioned as to make it generally valid. I wish that I, and every other person shall at all times necessarily so associate the same perceptions under the same circumstances.

§ 20

Therefore, we must analyze experience, in order to see what is contained in this product of the senses and of the intellect, and how the judgment based on experience is itself possible. Such judgment is based on the thing-looked-at [Anschauung] of which I am conscious, the perception which merely belongs to the senses. But secondly, judging which is the sole province of the intellect is also a part of it. This [act of] judgment may be twofold; firstly, I may simply compare the perceptions in a particular state of my own consciousness; or secondly, I may link (associate) them in a general consciousness. The first judgment is a simple judgment based on perception and has [as we have seen] only subjective validity. . . . No general validity and necessity of the judgment can arise therefrom. . . .

Before a judgment of perception can become a judgment of experience, it is first of all necessary that the perception be subsumed under intellectual concepts [as stated above, § 18]. For instance, air may be subsumed under the concept of cause, which determines the judgment regarding its extension, as hypothetical.[1] In this way the extension is represented not as merely belonging to my perception of air in my particular state, or in any of my states, or in a particular state of the perception of others, but as *necessarily* belonging thereto; and the judgment that the air is elastic becomes generally valid. It thereby becomes a judgment of experience, preceded by certain other judgments which subsume the thing-looked-at, air, under the concept of cause and effect. Thus these judgments determine the perceptions, not only with respect to one another in myself as subject, but with respect to the form of judgment generally (in this case an hypothetical judgment), and they thereby make the empirical judgment universally valid.

If we analyze all our synthetic judgments in so far as they are objectively valid, we shall find that they never consist of mere things-looked-at, which are linked, as is commonly believed, through comparison in a judgment, but that they would be impossible had there not been added, besides, to the concepts derived from looking at things, a pure intellectual concept under which the former concepts are subsumed and, only in this way, connected in an objectively valid judgment. Even the judgments of pure mathematics in its simplest axioms are not excepted from this condition. The axiom that the straight line is the shortest distance between two points presupposes that the line be subsumed under the concept of quantity, which is assuredly not a thing-looked-at, but which has its origin in the intellect. This concept serves to determine the thing-looked-at, the line, with respect to the judgments which may be made regarding it. Judgments about its quantity may be called *judicia plurativa*[2] inasmuch as it is understood through them that many sim-

---

[1] The following may be taken as a more readily understandable example: When the sun shines on the stone it grows warm. This judgment [that the stone is warm] is a mere judgment of perception and contains no necessity no matter how often I or others have perceived it. These perceptions usually find themselves so linked (associated). If I say that the sun warms the stone, the intellectual concept, cause, comes into play in addition to the perception. The conception of sunshine necessarily becomes causally linked to that of warmth, and thereupon the synthetic judgment of necessity becomes generally valid, and consequently becomes objective: thus a perception is transformed into experience.

[2] I would prefer to call by this name those judgments which are known in logic as *particularia*, for this expression implies the notion that they are not general. When I start with unity in individual judgments and

ilar things are comprehended under a given thing-looked-at (intuition) *[Anschauung]*.

§ 21

In order to demonstrate the possibility of experience, in so far as it rests on pure, intellectual, *a priori* concepts, we must first present in a complete table what belongs to judgments generally and the various aspects of the intellect in these [judgments]. For the pure intellectual concepts will exactly parallel them, since they are nothing but concepts of things looked at in general, in so far as these [concepts] are determined in themselves by one or another of these aspects of judgment, that is, are necessarily and universally valid. In this way, the *a priori* principles of the possibility of all experience are precisely determined as an objectively valid empirical knowledge. For they are nothing but propositions which subsume all perception under the pure intellectual concepts in accordance with certain general conditions.

LOGICAL TABLE OF THE JUDGMENTS

1 *According to Quantity*	2 *According to Quality*
General	Affirmative
Particular	Negative
Single	Indefinite

3 *According to Relation*	4 *According to Modality*
Categorical	Problematical
Hypothetical	Assertive
Disjunctive	Apodictic

---

proceed to universality, I cannot include any reference to universality; I think merely of plurality without universality, not of an exception from universality. This is necessary if the logical aspects are to be the basis of the pure intellectual concept; in logical use the matter may be left as heretofore.

TRANSCENDENTAL TABLE OF THE INTELLECTUAL CONCEPTS

I *According to Quantity*	2 *According to Quality*
Unity (the measure)	Reality
Plurality (the magnitude)	Negation
Universality (the whole)	Limitation

3 *According to Relation*	4 *According to Modality*
Substance	Possibility (potentiality)
Cause	Actuality (existence)
Togetherness (interaction)	Necessity

PURE PHYSIOLOGICAL TABLE OF THE UNIVERSAL PRINCIPLES OF NATURAL SCIENCE

I
Axioms of intuition [of looking at or envisaging things]

2 Anticipations of Perception	3 Analogies of Experience

4
Postulates of empirical thought in general

§ 22

The sum of all the above is this: the business of the senses is to look at (*anschauen*), that of the intellect to think. But to think is to bring together images in a consciousness. This bringing together is either merely related to the subject and is fortuitous and subjective, or it is necessary or objective. The bringing together of images in a consciousness is judgment. Thus thinking is the same as judging or referring images to judgments in general. Hence judgments are either merely subjective when images are referred to a single consciousness and brought together in it, or judgments are objective if they are brought together in the general consciousness. The logical aspects of all judgments are so many possible modes of bringing together images in a consciousness. But if they serve as concepts, they are concepts of the *necessary* togetherness of these images in a consciousness, and therefore are principles of objectively valid judgments. This togetherness in a consciousness is either analytic by identity, or synthetic by the combination and addition of different images to one another. Experience consists of the synthetic linking (associating) of phenomena (perceptions) in a consciousness, in so far as such association is necessary. Hence pure intellectual concepts are those under which all perceptions must be previously subsumed, before they can serve in judgments of experience.[1]

§ 23

Judgments, considered merely as the condition for bringing together given images in a consciousness, are rules. These rules, in so far as they present the togetherness as necessary, are *a priori*. In so far as there are none above these rules from which they can be derived, they are principles. Since there are no conditions of the judgments based on experience, in respect to the possibility of all experience when considered as a mere form of thought, beyond those conditions of the judgments which subsume the phenomena in their various forms under the pure intellectual concepts which make the empirical judgment objectively valid, these [principles] must be the *a priori* principles of all experience.

At the same time, the principles of possible experience are the universal laws of nature which may become known *a priori*. Thus the problem contained in our present second question (*How is pure natural science possible?*) is solved. For the systematic character required by the form of a science is completely met with here since beyond the above-named formal conditions

---

[1] As to how the perception came by this addition [of the concept], the *Critique of Pure Reason* may be consulted in the section dealing with the transcendental faculty of judgment, entitled, "Of the *Schematization* of Pure Intellectual Concepts," *Works*, vol. III, 137 ff.

of all judgments in general, that is, of all the general rules to be found in logic, there are none possible. These constitute a logical system; while the concepts founded upon them containing the *a priori* conditions of all synthetic and necessary judgments [constitute] a transcendental system, and the principles by means of which all phenomena are subsumed under the concepts, constitute a natural system preceding all empirical knowledge of nature and rendering this knowledge possible in the first place. Therefore such a system may properly be termed the general and pure science of nature.

§ 24

The first[1] of the above natural principles subsumes all phenomena, as things-looked-at in space and in time, under the conception of *quantity*, and to that extent it is a principle of the application of mathematics to experience. The second principle subsumes the sensation which is properly empirical and denotes the reality of things-looked-at, though not precisely, under the concept of *quantity* because sensation is not a looking-at-things which contains space and time although it places its corresponding object in both. But between the reality of a sensation and zero, i.e., the complete lack of anything felt, there is a quantitative difference. For between each given degree of light and darkness, between each degree of heat and complete coldness, each degree of weight and of absolute lightness, each degree of filling a space and the complete vacuum, progressively smaller degrees can be thought of, just as between consciousness and complete unconsciousness (psychological darkness) continually smaller [degrees] exist. Hence no perception is possible that would prove an absolute lack (of something); for instance, no psychological darkness which could not be viewed as a consciousness that is being surpassed by another stronger

---

[1] The three following paragraphs will hardly be understood without referring to what the *Critique of Pure Reason* says on the principles, but it may be useful to have a general view of them, and to fix the attention on the main points. Cf. *Works*, vol. III, 137–224.

consciousness, and the same in all cases of sensation. In this way the intellect can even anticipate sensations which constitute the proper quality of empirical images (phenomena) by means of the principle that all these sensations (and thus the reality of all phenomena) have degrees. This is the second application of mathematics (*mathesis intensorum*) to natural science.

§ 25

The determination of the relation of phenomena, if we consider merely their existence, is not mathematical but dynamic; it can never be objectively valid and therefore appropriate for an experience if it is not subordinated to *a priori* principles rendering their knowledge based on experience possible in the first place. Hence phenomena must be subsumed under [three concepts. Of these the first is] the concept of substance upon which is based all determination of existence as a concept of the thing itself. The second concept is that of cause and effect in so far a succession of phenomena, that is, an event, is met with. The third concept is that of reciprocal action in so far as co-existence is to be known objectively. These *a priori* principles are those upon which objectively valid, though empirical, judgments are based. These principles are the proper laws of nature which may be termed dynamic.

Finally, there belong to judgments based on experience the knowledge and insight into the agreement and connection, not so much of phenomena in experience, as of the relation of phenomena to experience generally. This relation brings together in one concept either the agreement of phenomena with the formal conditions known by the intellect or their connection with the material of the senses and of perception, or both. Thus this relation comprises potentiality, actuality and necessity, according to the general laws of nature. [This knowledge then] constitutes the natural theory of method, the distinction between truth and hypotheses, and the limits of the reliability of the latter.

§ 26

The third table, that of the principles, is derived *from the nature of the intellect itself* according to the critical method; it shows a completeness that raises it far above every other table that has been deduced in a dogmatic way from things themselves, (although to no purpose) or that may be so attempted in the future. In this table, all synthetic *a priori* principles have been set forth completely and in accordance with a [higher] principle, the general capacity of judging, which constitutes the essence of experience as far as the intellect is concerned. Thus one can be certain that there are no additional principles —a satisfaction that cannot be obtained by the dogmatic method. Yet all this is by far not the greatest service of this table.

Attention must be paid to the grounds of proof that reveal the possibility of this *a priori* knowledge, and at the same time limit all such principles by a condition that must never be overlooked if this knowledge is not to be misunderstood and not to be extended further in use than the original meaning attached to the principles by the intellect will allow. These principles only contain the conditions of possible experience in general in so far as such experience is subordinated to *a priori* laws. Thus I do not say that *things in themselves* possess quantity, that their reality contains degrees, that their existence implies a connection of accidents in a substance, etc. For no one can prove these propositions since such a synthetic connection is simply impossible when based on mere concepts, where there is wanting on the one hand all reference to things felt by the senses, and on the other all linking of the same in a possible experience. Therefore the essential limitation of the concepts in these principles is that all things are only necessarily and *a priori* subject to the above-mentioned conditions when they are *objects of experience*.

In the second place there follows from this a specific and peculiar mode of proof of these principles. They do not refer directly to phenomena and their relation, but to the possibility of experience, of which phenomena constitute the matter but not the form. In other words, these principles refer to objective and universally valid synthetic propositions which is precisely the distinction between judgments based on experience and mere judgments based on perception. This results from the fact that the phenomena, as mere things-looked-at which occupy a part of space and time, are subsumed under the concept of quantity. This concept unites the manifold of these phenomena synthetically and *a priori* in accordance with rules. . . . [Here follows a restatement of §24., Ed.] [1]

The reader must give the greatest attention to the mode of proof of the principles which go under the name of analogies of experience. For these principles do not concern the origin of impressions (*Anschauung*), like the principles of the application of mathematics to natural science generally, but they do concern the connection of their existence in an experience. Since this experience can be nothing but the ascertaining of existence in time according to necessary laws, under which alone this experience is objectively valid and hence is [true] experience, it follows that the proof is not directed toward showing the synthetic unity of the connection of *things in themselves,* but [it is directed toward showing the synthetic unity of] *perceptions.* As far as these perceptions are concerned, the proof does not do this with respect to their content but with respect to their de-

---

[1] The degree of heat, light, etc., is as great in a small space as in a large one. In the same way inward presentations (*Vorstellungen*), such as pain or consciousness in general, are not smaller in degree whether they last a long or a short time. Hence quantity is as great here at one point and at one moment as at any time or in any space however large. Therefore degrees are quantities, not in the looking at them, but only in the mere feeling of them. Degrees can only be estimated as quantity through the relation of 1 to 0, that is, by each one passing through infinitely small intermediate degrees to the point where it disappears, or by each one growing from zero through infinitely small momenta of increase to a definite feeling in a given time. *Quantitas qualitatis est gradus.* (The quantity of quality is a matter of degree.)

termination in time and to the relation of existence thereto according to universal laws. Therefore these general laws contain the necessary determination of existence in time and consequently according to an *a priori* rule of the intellect whenever the empirical determination in the relative time is to be objectively valid, that is, [whenever it is to be] experience. I cannot enter further into the matter here, in these *Prolegomena,* but I recommend that the reader, who has been long accustomed to regard experience as a mere empirical joining together of perceptions give close attention to this distinction between experience and a mere aggregate of perceptions.

§ 27

This is the place to remove Hume's doubt at its basic point. He maintained justly that we can in no way, through reason, understand the possibility of causation, that is to say, the reference of the existence of one thing to the existence of some other thing necessarily posited by the former. I may add to this that we can just as little understand the conception of subsistence [substance], i.e., the necessity for a subject lying at the basis of the existence of things which is itself no predicate of any other thing. [I would even say] that we can form no conception of the possibility of such a thing (though we can point out examples of its use in experience). In the same way, this incomprehensibility even attaches to the togetherness of things since it is not possible to see how, from the state of one thing, a consequence can be drawn as to the state of some totally different thing external to it, and vice versa; and how substances, of which each has its own separate existence, are necessarily dependent on one another. At the same time I am far from regarding these conceptions [of causation, substance and togetherness] as merely borrowed from experience, and [equally far] from regarding the necessity that is imagined through them as fictitious and mere illusion, by which we are deluded through long habit. Rather have I shown sufficiently that both they and the principles deduced from them are *a priori* certain before all experience, and that they possess indubitable objective validity, although unquestionably only in respect of experience.

§ 28

Although I do not have the slightest notion of the connection of things in themselves, or how they exist as substances, how they work as causes, or how they co-exist together as parts of a real whole, I can even less conceive of such properties in phenomena *as* phenomena because these concepts contain nothing that is inherent in the phenomena, but do contain something the intellect must conceive of by itself. But we do have a conception of how such a connection may exist between the images in our mind, in general judgments. [These general judgments may take the form of saying that] in one kind of judgment images appear as subjects in relation to predicates, in another kind as cause in relation to effect, and in a third as parts that together constitute a whole. Furthermore, we know *a priori* that without looking upon the image of an object as something definite with regard to one or another of these aspects, we could have no knowledge that could be valid of such an object. If we occupied ourselves with the object in itself there would be no single criterion by which I could know whether it was determined in respect of one or another of the above-mentioned aspects. . . . But then our question is not how things in themselves, but how knowledge based on experience of things in regard to the aforementioned judgments is arrived at, that is, how things as objects of experience can and should be subsumed under the above intellectual concepts. Hence it is clear that I fully understand not only the possibility but also the necessity of subsuming all phenomena under these concepts, that is, of using them as principles of the possibility of experience.

§ 29

In making an attempt to [analyze] Hume's problematical concept (his *crux metaphysicorum*), namely, the concept of Cause,

I am first given generally, *a priori*, and by means of logic, the form of a conditional judgment [which consists in] using one thing known (*Erkenntnis*) as cause and another as effect. But it is possible to meet with a regularity of relation in perception which amounts to saying that one phenomenon always follows another (though the reverse does not happen). If so, it would be a case in which to make use of the hypothetical [form of] judgment and, for instance, to say that if the sun shines long enough upon a body, the body will become warm. Certainly there is no necessary connection here; in other words no concept of cause is involved. But I continue: If the above proposition, which is a mere subjective linking of perceptions, is to become a proposition based on experience, it must be regarded as necessary and generally valid. Such a proposition would run: Sun is the cause of heat through its light. The above empirical regularity is now looked upon as a law, and indeed, not only as valid for phenomena, but valid for them in relation to any possible experience which requires generally, and therefore necessarily, valid rules. Therefore I understand perfectly the concept of cause as a concept belonging necessarily to the mere form of experience, and I understand its possibility as a synthetic linking of perceptions in a consciousness in general. But I do not understand at all how a thing in itself is a possible cause, because the concept of cause does not at all mean a condition attached to things, but only attached to experience. Experience can only be an objectively valid knowledge of phenomena and of their sequence in time, in so far as the antecedent can be united to the consequent according to the rule of hypothetical judgments.

§ 30

Therefore pure intellectual concepts have no meaning whatever when they refer to things in themselves (*noumena*) instead of the objects of experience. They serve, as it were, to "spell out" phenomena so that these may be "read" as experience. The principles that originate from relating these concepts to the realm of the senses are useful to the intellect merely in [interpreting] experience. It can never be known *a priori* whether such combinations are possible nor whether their reference to objects can be verified by an example or even made intelligible, because all examples are borrowed from some possible experience. Consequently the objects of those concepts may not be met with anywhere except in a possible experience.

This complete solution of Hume's problem, although it turns out to be contrary to the presumption of its originator, preserves for the pure intellectual concepts their *a priori* origin, and preserves for the general laws of nature, their validity as intellectual laws. But it does so in such a manner that the use of these concepts is limited to experience because their possibility is grounded solely in the relation of the mind to experience. This is true not because they are derived from experience, but because experience is derived from them. This completely reversed mode of linking [mind and experience] never occurred to Hume.

From this conclusion flows the following result of all previous researches: "All synthetic *a priori* principles are nothing more than principles of possible experience." The synthetic *a priori* principles can never refer to anything more than mere phenomena and can only represent that which makes experience in general possible, or which, inasmuch as experience is derived from these principles, must always be capable of being represented in some possible experience.

§ 31

Thus we at last have something definite upon which to depend in all metaphysical undertakings, which have hitherto boldly enough, but always blindly, tackled everything without discrimination. Dogmatic thinkers have never allowed themselves to imagine that the goal of their efforts was so near by. Nor did those men who were conceited about their supposed common sense or their sane reason realize this. These latter started with concepts and principles of mere reason which, it is true, are legitimate and natural, but are intended merely for use in experience in order to secure insight, for which these men neither knew nor could know any definite boundaries because they had neither reflected nor could reflect on the nature or even the possibility of any such pure intellectual concepts.

Many a naturalist of pure reason (by which I mean the man who considers himself capable of deciding questions of metaphysics without any systematic knowledge) may pretend that long before from the prophetic spirit of his common sense, he not only suspected but knew and comprehended that which has been propounded here with so much preparation, or, if he will have it so, with so much prolix and pedantic pomp: "That with all our reason, we can never get beyond the field of experience." But when he is eventually questioned about his rational principles, he must confess that among them there are many principles that are not drawn from experience and that are therefore valid independently of experience and *a priori*. How then and on what grounds will he restrain himself and the dogmatist who use these concepts and principles outside all possible experience, simply because they are recognized as independent of it? And this adept of sane reason, in spite of all his pretended and cheaply acquired wisdom, is not even proof against wandering unobserved beyond the objects of experience into the field of chimeras. Indeed, in an ordinary way, he is deeply enough involved in such chimeras, although by using popular language, and by putting everything forward as probability, reasonable supposition or analogy, he gives some color to his groundless presumptions.

§ 32

From the earliest days of philosophy students of pure reason have postulated, in addition to the beings known to sense (phenomena) constituting the world of sense, special intellectual beings (noumena) which are supposed to constitute an intellectual world. Since previous students held appearance and illusion *[Erscheinung und Schein]* to be identical, [an error] which may be excused in an undeveloped epoch, they conceded true existence only to the intellectual beings.

Indeed when we rightly regard the objects of sense as mere phenomena we thereby admit that each such object is based upon a thing-in-itself of which we are not aware as it is constituted in itself, but only as known through its appearances, that is, by the manner in which our senses are affected by this unknown something. Therefore the intellect, by assuming phenomena, admits the existence of things-in-themselves. We may even say that the imagining of such beings underlying the phenomena, such mere intellectual beings, is not only permissible, but unavoidable.

Our critical deduction does not exclude by any means such things (noumena), it rather limits the principles of aesthetic so that these principles shall not be extended to everything [as that would mean that] everything would be transformed into mere phenomena. Instead, these principles should only hold with objects of possible experience. Intellectual beings are hereby admitted but only after emphasizing this rule which admits of no exception: that we know nothing definite whatever about these pure intellectual beings, nor can we know anything about them. Our pure intellectual concepts, no less than our pure images, refer to nothing but objects of a possible experience, to mere beings of sense. As soon as we leave these beings of sense, the intellectual concepts retain no meaning whatever.

§ 33

There is indeed something seductive about our pure intellectual concepts which tempt us to a transcendent use; for so I call the use that transcends all possible experience. Not only are our concepts of substance, force, action, reality, etc., entirely independent of experience, but these concepts do not contain any phenomena of sense. They really seem to refer to things-in-themselves (noumena). What confirms this supposition is that they possess a necessary certainty in themselves that experience can never approach. The concept of cause implies a rule according to which one state follows from another in a necessary manner. Experience only teaches us that often, or at most usually, one state of things follows upon another. Therefore experience can produce neither strict universality nor necessity. . . .

§ 34

[In the light of the foregoing], two important and even altogether indispensable, albeit exceedingly dry, investigations are necessary. They have been undertaken in the *Critique of Pure Reason* (*Works,* pp. 141 ff. and pp. 276 ff.). In the first of these investigations it was shown that the senses do not, *in concreto,* furnish pure intellectual concepts, but only the pattern for their use, and that the object that conforms to this pattern is only encountered in experience which [as we have seen] is the product that the intellect fashions from materials of sense. In the second investigation it was shown that [our pure intellectual concepts] cannot be used for thinking about anything outside the field of experience because these concepts merely prescribe the logical form of judgment in respect to images or things-looked-at. But, since no image is given beyond the field of the senses, these pure concepts are entirely void of meaning inasmuch as they cannot be presented *in concreto* in any way. Consequently all these *noumena* together with their sum-total, an intelligible world,[1] are nothing but notions of a task, whose object is conceivable in itself, but whose execution is utterly impossible because of the nature of our intellect. Our intellect is not a faculty for looking at things, but is merely a faculty for joining given images into experience. Therefore experience must comprise all objects for

---

[1] [The footnote justifies the term "intelligible" as contrasted with "intellectual" world.—Ed.]

our concepts; while, outside experience, all concepts will be without meaning as then they cannot be related to any images.

§ 36

How is Nature itself Possible?

This question is the highest point that transcendental philosophy can ever reach and so it must proceed to this point which is its boundary and completion. It properly comprises two questions.

First: How is nature possible at all in its material sense in accordance with what is seen and observed? How are space, time, and what fills them both, namely the object of sensation, possible at all? The answer is that they are possible by means of the quality of our senses; in keeping with this quality our senses are affected in a particular manner by objects that are unknown in themselves and are entirely distinct from these phenomena. This answer has been given in the *Prolegomena* in the solution of the first general question and in the *Critique of Pure Reason* in the section on transcendental aesthetics.

Second: How is nature possible at all in its *formal* sense, as the sum-total of the rules to which all phenomena must be subject if they are to be considered as connected in experience? The answer has to be that nature is only possible in this sense by means of the quality of our mind. In keeping with this quality, all images resulting from sense impressions are necessarily referred to a consciousness. By means of this referring of images to a consciousness, the peculiar method of our thinking according to rules becomes possible, and in turn through this method experience is possible. This answer has been given in the *Critique of Pure Reason* in the section on transcendental logic and in these Prolegomena in the course of the solution of the second general question.

But the question of how this peculiar quality of our senses is possible or how the quality of the intellect and the quality of the necessary perception, upon which intellect and all thinking is based, are possible cannot be analyzed or answered further because we always require these qualities for all our answers and our thinking about objects.

There are many basic laws of nature which we can only know by means of experience, but we can never come to know through experience the fact that phenomena are linked according to laws in general because [the concept of] experience itself presupposes such laws, upon which its possibility is based *a priori*.

Therefore, the possibility of any experience at all is at the same time the universal law of nature, and the principles of that experience are at the same time the laws of nature. For, we only know nature as the sum-total of phenomena, i.e., as the sumtotal of images or representations in our mind. Therefore we can derive the law of their connection only from the principles of the connection of images in ourselves, i.e., from the conditions of a necessary association in a consciousness which provides the possibility of experience.

Even the main proposition that general laws of nature can be known *a priori*, which has been expounded throughout the whole of this section, leads of itself to the further proposition that the highest law-making of nature must apply to ourselves, namely, to our mind, and that we must not seek nature's general laws by means of experience; but that, conversely, we must seek nature's conformity to law only in the conditions of the possibility of experience given by our senses and our mind. For how otherwise could it be possible to know these laws *a priori* since they are not rules of analytic knowledge, but are true synthetic extensions of such knowledge? Such a necessary agreement of the principles of possible experience with the laws of the possibility of nature can only result from one of two causes: That either the laws are borrowed from nature by means of experience, or conversely that nature [as a conceptual manifold] is derived from the laws of the possibility of experience generally and is entirely identical with the mere general conformity to law of such experience. The first hypothesis contradicts itself, for the universal laws of nature can and must be known *a priori*, i.e., known independently of all experience, and be posited as the basis of the empirical use of the intellect; hence only the second [hypothesis] remains to us.

But we must distinguish the empirical laws of nature, which always presuppose particular perceptions, from the pure or universal laws of nature, which, without being based upon any particular perceptions, merely contain the conditions of the necessary association of such perceptions in experience; in respect of the last, nature and possible experience are the same thing. Since in this, nature's conformity to law rests on the necessary linking of phenomena in experience, without which we could not know any object of the world of the senses, in other words, such conformity rests on the original laws of the intellect, it sounds strange at first, but it is none the less true when I say in respect of these laws of the intellect: *The intellect does not derive its laws (a priori) from nature but prescribes them to nature.*

§ 38

If we consider the properties of the circle by which this figure combines in itself under a universal rule so many arbitrary determinations of space, one cannot help but attribute a specific character (*eine Natur*) to this geometrical thing. For instance, two lines that intersect one another and the circle, however they may be drawn, are yet always so regular that the rectangle constructed with the segments of one line is equal to that constructed with the segments of the other. Now I ask, "Does this law originate in the circle or in the intellect?" In other words, does this figure, independently of the intellect, contain the ground of the law itself, or does the intellect introduce this law, that chords cut one another in geometrical proportion, since the intellect itself has constructed the figure according to its own concepts, namely the equality of radii? When we follow the proofs of this law we soon perceive that it can only be derived from the condition upon which the intellect has based the construction of this figure, namely, the equality of radii. If, in order to pursue still further the unity of the manifold properties of geometrical figures under common laws, we extend the concept and consider the circle as a conic section subordinated to the same fundamental conditions of construction as other conic sections, we find that all chords that intersect within the ellipse (parabola and hyperbola) always intersect so that the rectangles under their segments, though indeed not equal, yet stand in the same ratio to one another. If we proceed still further to the fundamental laws of physical astronomy we find a physical law of reciprocal attraction at work over all material nature, whose rule it is that such attraction decreases inversely as the square of the distance from each attracting point, that is as the spherical surfaces increase over which this power radiates. This law seems to be necessarily inherent in the nature of things themselves and is therefore usually propounded as capable of being known *a priori*. Simple as the sources of this law may be, since they rest merely on the relations of spherical surfaces of different radii, its consequences are so valuable as regards the variety of their regularity and agreement that not only are all possible orbits of the celestial bodies [described] in conic sections, but such a relation of these orbits results, that no other law of attraction than that of the inverse square of the distance could be conceived as suitable for a cosmic system.

Therefore nature is resting here on laws that the intellect comes to know *a priori* and to know mainly from general principles for determining spatial relations. Now I ask: Are these natural laws inherent in space and does the intellect learn them by merely seeking to discover the full meaning contained therein, or are they inherent in the intellect and in the manner in which the intellect determines space according to the conditions of uniform synthesis toward which all the concepts of the intellect tend? Space is so uniform a thing and so indeterminate as regards all particular properties that certainly no one will seek any wealth of natural laws in it. But that which shapes space into circular form, the figure of the cone or of the sphere, is the intellect in so far as it contains the grounds of the unity of the construction of these figures. Therefore the mere general form of imagining called space is presumably the substratum of all particular objects of determinate images and this substratum certainly furnishes the condition of the possibility and variety of these images.

[Following this, Kant repeats what he said at the end of § 36. Then, in § 39 he briefly sketches his approach to "categories," rejecting the scheme of Aristotle.—Ed.]

THE THIRD PART OF THE MAIN TRANSCENDENTAL PROBLEM

How is Metaphysics possible at all?

§ 40

For their own security and certainty pure mathematics and pure natural science do not require a deduction such as we have just concluded with respect to them both; for pure mathematics rests upon its own evidence while pure natural science, though arising from the pure sources of the intellect, is dependent upon complete verification by experience, a witness that pure natural science is unable to repudiate and to do altogether without, since, with all its certainty, it can never, when philosophically considered, rival mathematics. Both these sciences did not require the foregoing investigation for their own sake, but for the sake of another science: metaphysics.

Metaphysics has to do not only with concepts of nature which invariably have an application in experience, but also with pure rational concepts which can never be related to any possible experience. Therefore metaphysics has to do with concepts whose objective reality (that they are not mere chimeras) and with assertions whose truth or falsity cannot be confirmed or discovered by any experience. This part of metaphysics is precisely what constitutes its essential purpose, all else being merely a means thereto, and hence this science requires *for its own sake* such a deduction [as Kant has just given for mathematics and pure natural science]. The problem now before us concerns the core and specific nature of metaphysics: The occupation of reason with itself alone and the supposed acquaintance with objects arising from reason as it broods over its own concepts without having need of, nor indeed being able to achieve such knowledge through the meditation of experience. [1]

Reason can never fulfill its rôle without solving this problem. The empirical use to which reason limits pure intellect does not consummate reason's purpose to the utmost extent. Each single experience is but a part of the whole sphere of the intellect's domain. But the *absolute totality of all possible experience is not itself* an experience but is a necessary problem for reason. In order to present this problem reason needs concepts quite different from the pure intellectual concepts [the categories]. The use of these intellectual concepts is only *immanent,* that is, related to experience in so far as it can be given. The rational [spiritual] concepts of reason aim toward complete knowledge, i.e., toward the collective unity of all possible experience and thereby transcending any given experience. Thus these concepts become transcendent.

As the intellect needs the categories for [the acquisition of] experience, so reason contains in itself the basis of ideas, by which I mean necessary concepts whose object *cannot* be given in any experience. These ideas are inherent in the nature of reason as much as the categories are inherent in the nature of

---

[1] If we may say that a science at least exists in all men's thought when it has been established that the problems leading to it are put to everybody by the nature of human reason and consequently that many, though faulty, attempts at solving these problems are constantly and inevitably being made, then we must say that metaphysics exists subjectively (and indeed necessarily). Hence we rightly ask: How is it (objectively) possible?

the intellect. If these ideas involve an appearance that may mislead easily, this appearance is unavoidable, although we may very well guard ourselves against being misled by it.

Since all appearance consists in the subjective grounds of judgment being taken for objective, a self-knowledge of pure reason, in its transcendent use, will be the only protection against the aberrations into which reason falls when it misinterprets its function and relates to an *object,* or thing-in-itself that which only concerns its own *subject* and this subject's guidance in the immanent use of reason.

[In §41 Kant states once again that the distinction between ideas as concepts of pure reason and categories as concepts of the pure intellect is extremely important and that this distinction itself renders the *Critique of Pure Reason* a major contribution to metaphysics. In § 42 Kant reasserts the important differences between ideas and categories as regards experience.—Ed.]

§ 43

It has always been my greatest aim in the *Critique of Pure Reason* not only to distinguish carefully between the ways of [acquiring] knowledge, but also to derive from their common source all the concepts pertaining to these several ways so that by being informed whence they are derived, I should not only be able to determine their [right] use with certainty, but that I should have the never-suspected and priceless advantage of knowing the number, classification and specification of these concepts *a priori,* that is, according to principle. Without this [survey] everything in metaphysics is mere rhetoric and one would never know if what one has is sufficient or if and where something may be wanting in it. We can certainly only have this advantage in pure philosophy, but it constitutes the essence of this philosophy.

Since I had found the origin of the categories in the four

logical functions of all judgments of the intellect, it was only natural to seek the origin of the ideas in the three functions of the syllogisms of reason. For, when such concepts of pure reason (transcendental ideas) are once given, they cannot be found, unless they are supposed to be innate, elsewhere than in an act of reason. As far as mere form is concerned, such an act of reason constitutes the logical element of the syllogisms of reason, while it constitutes the transcendental concepts of pure reason, in so far as such an act presents the judgments of the intellect as determined *a priori* with respect to one or another form.

The formal differences in the syllogisms of reason render necessary their division into categorical, hypothetical and disjunctive syllogisms. The concepts of reason based on them contain: first, the idea of the complete subject (*Substantiale*), second, the idea of the complete series of conditions, and third, the determination of all concepts in [by?] the idea of a complete complex (*Inbegriff*) of the possible.[1] The first idea is psychological, the second cosmological, and the third theological. Since all three give rise to dialectics, although each does so in its own way, the classification of the entire Dialectics of pure reason is based upon these [three ideas]: it is divided into the paralogism, the antinomy, and finally the ideal of such a dialectics. By this division we are fully assured that all requirements of pure reason are completely presented here and that no further requirements can be missing because the capacity of reason is completely surveyed by these three syllogisms.

---

[1] In disjunctive judgments we consider all possibility to be classified in relation to a particular concept. The ontological principle of the complete determination of a thing generally is that of all the possible contradictory predicates one must be attributed to this [given] thing. At the same time this is the principle of all disjunctive judgments and hence this ontological principle is based on the aggregate of all possibilities. This serves as a slight explanation of the above proposition: That the act of reason, in disjunctive syllogisms of reason, is the same, as far as form is concerned, as the act by which reason fashions the idea of an aggregate of all reality; for this idea contains in itself the positive [predicate] of all mutually contradictory predicates.

§ 44

In these general reflections it is noteworthy that rational ideas, unlike categories, are of no service to the intellect for interpreting experience, and can be wholly dispensed with in this connection. In fact, rational ideas are likely to be impediments to the maxims of a rational knowledge of nature, although they are needed for another purpose which has yet to be determined. The question of whether the soul is, or is not, a simple substance need not concern us in so far as the explanation of the soul's phenomena is concerned. We cannot make the concept of a simple being comprehensible by any possible experience related to the senses, i.e., *in concreto.* Hence this concept is quite empty as far as gaining any insight into the cause of phenomena is concerned. It cannot serve as a principle for explaining anything presented by either internal or external experience. The cosmological ideas of the beginning of the world or of the eternity of the world (*a parte ante*) can help us just as little to explain an occurrence in the world itself. Finally, in accordance with a just maxim of the philosophy of nature, we must refrain from all explanations of the order of nature that are derived from the will of a Supreme Being, because that would no longer be a philosophy of nature, but a confession that we are at the end of such a philosophy. Hence, these ideas are destined for quite a different use than the categories. By means of these ideas and the principles based upon them experience itself first becomes possible. But our laborious analysis of the intellect would be quite superfluous if our aim were nothing more than knowledge of nature such as can be provided through experience. Reason accomplishes its work certainly and well both in mathematics and natural science without any of this subtle deduction. Thus our critique of the pure intellect combines with the ideas of pure reason in a direction aiming beyond the empirical use of the intellect. Yet, as we have said above, such empirical use is quite impossible and without object or meaning. Nevertheless there must be an agreement between what belongs to the nature of reason and what belongs to the nature of the intellect and reason must contribute to the perfection of the intellect and cannot possibly confuse it.

The solution of the problem is as follows: Pure reason does not have particular objects in view which lie outside the field of experience, but has in view objects denoted by its ideas. Pure reason requires completeness in the use of the intellect in dealing with experience. This completeness can only be a completeness of principles, not one of images and objects. But in order to be able to present such principles as definite, reason conceives of them as the knowledge of an object. Such knowledge is completely determined in regard to these rules [principles]. But, this object is only an idea designed to bring the knowledge of the intellect as near as possible to the completeness indicated by that idea.

§ 57

The Determination of the Bounds of Pure Reason

After all the very clear proofs we have given above, it would be absurd for us to expect to know more of any object than what belongs to the possible experience of such an object. It would be equally absurd to lay claim to the least knowledge of any conceivable thing of which we can assume that it is not an object of possible experience; we cannot determine what its quality may be or what it is in itself. For how could we effect such a determination? Neither time, space, nor all the intellectual concepts [categories], and certainly not the concepts derived from empirical observation or *perception* in the world of sense have or could have any other use than merely to make experience possible. If we omit this condition from pure intellectual concepts, then these concepts determine no object whatever and have no meaning anywhere.

But it would be even more absurd not to admit [that there might be] things in themselves, or to suggest that our kind of experience is the only possible method of knowing objects, in other words, to pretend that our way of looking at things in space and time is the only possible way, and that our discursive intellect is the prototype of every possible intellect. [This would amount to] insisting that principles of the possibility of experience be considered general conditions of things-in-themselves.

Then our principles, which merely limit the use of reason to possible experience, might accordingly become *transcendent* themselves [which would mean that] the limits of reason would be held to be the limits of things themselves. The *Dialogues* of Hume may serve as an example of this error which results if no careful critique of the limits of our reason watches its empirical use and sets a limit to its pretensions. Scepticism originally arose from metaphysics and its uncontrolled dialectics. At first scepticism, in order to aid the empirical use of the mind, claimed that all that went beyond this empirical use was nugatory and deceptive. But as it gradually became evident that the very same principles that we use in experience were *a priori* and that these principles, imperceptibly and apparently with justification, carried the mind way beyond experience, a doubt began to be thrown on the principles of experience themselves. This doubt means no great danger, for common sense will always assert its rights. But then extraordinary confusion arose in all knowledge, for it could not be determined how far reason was to be trusted and why only so far and no farther. This confusion can only be remedied, and any future relapse prevented, by a formal determination of the limits derived from principles for using reason.

It is true that we cannot form any definite conception of things in themselves, yet we are not entirely free from avoiding an inquiry about them. Considering the nature of our soul, what man can stand attaining a clear consciousness of himself as a subject, and attaining the conviction that the soul's phenomena cannot be explained *materialistically*, without asking what the soul really is? If no concept based on experience suffices for [answering] this question, who can avoid at least assuming a rational concept, namely, that of a simple immaterial being, even though its objective reality cannot be demonstrated in any way? Who can be satisfied with mere knowledge [when it comes to] such cosmological questions as the size and duration of the world, of freedom, or of natural necessity? For, no matter how we start, every answer given according to the principles of experience will generate a new question requiring an answer just as urgently, thereby clearly demonstrating the inadequacy of all physical modes of explanation for satisfying reason. Finally, who does not see how impossible it is to stop with these empirical principles when confronted by the thoroughgoing contingency and dependence of all that he can assume and conceive according to principles based on experience? Who then does not feel himself, though prohibited from losing himself in transcendent ideas, constrained (*notgedrungen*) to go beyond all the concepts verifiable by experience to seek rest and contentment in the concept of a Being whose possibility cannot be perceived by itself but whose possibility cannot be refuted either? This idea is a mere rational being, but without its possibility reason would have to remain unsatisfied forever.

Boundaries, where extended beings are involved, always presuppose a space which is encountered outside a certain place and encloses it. Limits do not require this, since they are mere negations affecting a quantity so far as this quantity is not absolutely complete.* However, our reason sees, so to speak, around itself a space in which things-in-themselves might be known, but it can never have definite concepts of them, since it is limited to phenomena.

As long as knowledge corresponds to reason, no definite boundaries can be conceived for such knowledge. Human reason recognizes limits but no boundaries in mathematics and

---

* [The sharp dichotomy that Kant suggests here between *Grenzen* and *Schranken* does not exist in either German or English. The word *limit* denotes both, but so does *boundary*.—Ed.]

natural science. Reason recognizes that something exists outside itself to which it can never attain, but it does not recognize that it can ever be perfected itself in its inner progress. The extension of our insight into mathematics and the possibility of new discoveries reaches to infinity. The same can be said of the discovery of new qualities in nature, of new forces and laws through continued experience and the linking of such experience by reason. At the same time we cannot fail to acknowledge limits, for mathematics refers only to *phenomena* and that which cannot be an object of observation through the senses, such as the concepts of metaphysics and morals, lies wholly outside the sphere of mathematics. [It lies in a region] to which mathematics can never lead, but then mathematics does not require these concepts. Therefore there is no approach and no continuous progress toward this kind of knowledge. Natural science will never discover the inner [nature] of things; that which is not phenomenon but could serve as the final explanation of phenomena. But natural science does not require this [final solution] for its physical explanations; even if such solutions were offered from other sources, for example the influence of immaterial beings, natural science should reject such solutions and on no account bring them into its own analysis. Natural science should invariably base its analysis on that which is a part of experience, being an object of sense; [for such objects] can be related to our actual perceptions by laws based on experience.

But metaphysics carries us through the dialectical efforts of pure reason to limits [boundaries] which are not initiated arbitrarily or rashly, but which the nature of reason itself impels us [to discover]. Since we cannot deal with transcendental ideas and since transcendental ideas will never allow themselves to be realized, they serve to show us not only the actual boundaries of the use of pure reason, but also the way to determine the boundaries. Indeed, this is the end and use of the natural disposition of our reason, which has given birth to metaphysics as its pet child, whose begetting is not to be ascribed to chance like that of everything else in the world, but ascribed to an original germ, wisely organized for great ends. For, perhaps more than any other science, metaphysics, in its basic outline, is implanted in us by nature itself. Metaphysics can by no means be regarded as the product of an arbitrary choice or as an accidental extension [occurring] in the progress of experience.

Although all reason's concepts and laws of the intellect are adequate for empirical use, i.e., in the world of sense, reason does not find any satisfaction for itself in such, for it is deprived of all hope of completely solving some questions which recur *ad infinitum*. Such problems for reason are the transcendental ideas that aim at this completion [perfection—*Vollendung*]. Reason sees clearly that the world of sense cannot contain such perfection and so it can be contained just as little by those concepts which serve simply for understanding the world of sense, space and time, and by all the concepts we have mentioned under the heading of pure intellectual concepts. The world of sense is nothing but a chain of phenomena connected according to general laws and therefore, being not properly the thing in itself, has no existence by itself. Therefore this world necessarily refers to what provides the basis of this phenomenal world, to beings that cannot be known as things in themselves and cannot be known merely as phenomena. Only in the knowledge of these beings can reason hope to see some time its desire satisfied for completing the progress from the conditioned to its conditions.

We have indicated above (§§ 33, 34) the limits of reason in respect to all knowledge of mere thought beings [rational beings]. We can now determine the boundaries of pure reason, since transcendental ideas have necessitated the progress to these rational beings and they have thus led us, as it were, to the point where filled space is in contact with empty space of which (the *noumena*) we can know nothing. The limits described in the cited paragraphs are not yet sufficient, since we have found that something lies beyond them, even though we can never know what this may be in itself. For now the question is: How does our reason behave in this linking of what we know with what we do not know and never can know? Here is a real link of the known with a wholly unknown which will always remain unknown. Even if the unknown should not become better known in the least [degree]—which indeed is not to be expected—the concept of this link can be determined and made distinctive.

Therefore, it seems, we are to conceive of an immaterial being, of an intellectual world, and of a highest of all beings, all of them *noumena,* because only in these [concepts], as things in themselves, does reason meet with completeness [perfection] and satisfaction. This is because these concepts really refer to something distinct and therefore wholly different from themselves. . . .

Since we can never definitely come to know these intellectual beings [Ed. should read: rational beings] regarding what they may be in themselves and yet we must assume such beings in relation to the world of sense and since we must link these beings to the world of sense through reason, we should at least be able to conceive of this link by means of such concepts as express their relation to the world of sense. We will take an example from the concept of a Supreme Being.

The *deistic* concept [of God] is a very pure, rational concept, but it only represents a thing containing all reality without being able to determine a single [partial reality]. In order to do so, an illustration would have to be borrowed from the world of sense and in that case we would be dealing in every instance with an object of sense and not with something completely different, which cannot be an object of sense. For example, I might attribute intellect to the deistic concept [of God]; yet I have no concept whatever of any intellect other than one like my own, one to which images must be given through the senses, and one which occupies itself with subsuming these images under rules [springing from] the unity of the consciousness. But in that case the elements of my concept would necessarily be those inherent in a phenomenon. Yet it was the inadequacy of the phenomena which forced me [in the first place] to pass beyond the phenomena to the conception of a being in no way dependent on phenomena, or bound up with them as conditions of its definition. On the other hand, if I sever intellect from the senses in order to arrive at a pure intellect nothing remains but the mere form of thought without any images. By such mere form of thought I can know nothing determinate, hence no object. For this purpose I would have to conceive another mind that could look at such objects [things-in-themselves]. I have not the least notion of such a mind because the human mind is discursive and can only know through general concepts. The same happens if I attribute a will to the Supreme Being, for I have this concept only in so far as I derive it from my inner experience. This experience depends upon the satisfaction of [my desires and the] things which we need, and hence upon my senses. Such a dependence completely contradicts the pure concept of a Supreme Being.

The objections of Hume to Deism are weak, hitting upon no more than the proofs and never on the [central] proposition of the deistic assertion. But Hume's objections are very strong as regards Theism, [in which the conception of God] is supposed to be created by a more detailed determination of our concept of the Supreme Being [which] is merely transcendent. Depending on how the concept is constructed, Hume's objections are irrefutable. Hume always maintains that we are really thinking of nothing definite [when we employ] the mere concept of an original being to whom we can attribute none but the ontological predicates of eternity, omnipresence, and omnipotence, and that qualities constituting a concrete concept must be added. It is not enough, says Hume, to state that the original being is cause, but [we must also state] what its causality is like and whether [it operates] perhaps through intellect and will. At this point, Hume's attacks on Theism itself start in earnest, while before he had only assailed the grounds of proof for Deism, which does not constitute any special danger. His dangerous arguments refer entirely to the anthropomorphism which he holds to be inseparable from Theism and to make Theism self-contradictory. For, if this anthropomorphism is left out, [Theism itself] would fall and nothing would remain but a Deism with which one could not accomplish anything that would be useful because it could not serve as a foundation for religion and morals. If it were certain that anthropomorphism were inescapable, the proofs of the existence of a Supreme Being might be what they will, and might all be conceded, the concept of this Being could never be determined by us without involving us in contradictions.

But suppose we combine the apparently contradictory command to proceed to concepts outside the field of the immanent (empirical) use [of the intellect] with the command to avoid all transcendent judgments of pure reason. We then become aware that both commands may prevail together, but just on the *boundary* of all admissible use of reason. This boundary belongs as much to the field of experience as to that of the beings [created by] thought. At the same time we are taught how those strange ideas merely serve to determine the boundaries of human reason. On the one hand, we must not seek to extend beyond all bounds knowledge based on experience, for then nothing but a mere [phenomenal] world remains for us to know. On the other hand, we must not seek to transcend the boundaries of experience and to judge things outside experience as things-in-themselves.

We are keeping to this boundary when we limit our judgment to the relation the world may have to a Being whose concept lies outside all that knowledge of which we are capable within this world. In this case we are not attributing to the Supreme Being itself any of the qualities by which we conceive the objects of experience and we are thus avoiding *dogmatic* anthropomorphism. But we do attribute these qualities to the relations of the Supreme Being to the world. We are thereby allowing ourselves a *symbolical* anthropomorphism which, as a matter of fact, only concerns the language and not the object.

When I say that we are impelled to regard the world *as if* it were the work of a supreme will and intellect, I am not really saying more than the following: As a watch, a ship, or a regiment is related to the craftsman, the shipbuilder or the general, so this world of sense, or all that constitutes the basis of this aggregate of phenomena, is related to the unknown, which I conceive, not according to what it is in itself, but according to what it is for me in regard to the world of which I am a part.

§ 58

An insight such as this is gained by *analogy,* not in the usual meaning of an imperfect resemblance of two things, but of a perfect resemblance of two relations between totally dissimiliar things.[1] By means of this analogy there remains a conception of the Supreme Being which is adequately defined *for our purposes,* although we have left out everything that could determine this conception generally and *in itself.* For, we define this conception in respect of the world and therefore of ourselves and no more is necessary for us.

---

[1] Of this nature is an analogy between the legal relations of human actions and the mechanical relations of moving forces: I can do nothing to another without giving him the right, under the same conditions, to do the same to me; similarly, no body can act upon another body with its moving force without thereby causing that other body to react upon itself to the same extent. Here, right and moving force are quite dissimilar things, but there is complete resemblance in their relation. Hence, by means of an analogy such as this, I can give a relational concept of things absolutely unknown to me. For instance, as the promotion of the happiness of children is related to the love of parents, so the welfare of the human race is related to the unknown [quality] in God which we term love, not as though this unknown quality had the least resemblance to any human affection, but because we can conceive its relation to the world as similar to the relation that things of the world have to each other. But here the relational concept is a mere category; it is the concept of cause which has nothing to do with sense perception.

[Hereafter in this section Kant restates, with slightly different focus, the argument of the previous section.—Ed.]

§ 60

Thus we have fully set forth metaphysics as it is actually given in the natural propensity of human reason and in what constitutes the essential purpose of developing metaphysics. We have done this according to the subjective potentiality of man for metaphysics. We have found in the course of this inquiry that the *merely natural* use of such a propensity of our reason involves reason in extravagant dialectical syllogisms, some of which are illusion, some even [mutually] conflicting, unless discipline bridles our reason and keeps it within limits. This is only possible by means of scientific criticism. Furthermore, [we have found] this speculative metaphysics to be dispensable and even prejudicial to the promotion of the knowledge of nature. Nevertheless, it remains a task worthy of further inquiry to discover the *natural* ends aimed at by this propensity in our reason for [developing] transcendent concepts. For, everything in nature must have been originally designed for some useful purpose.

Such an inquiry is indeed difficult. Moreover I confess that all I say here respecting the primary ends of nature is only conjecture. But I may be permitted to do so in this case as the question does not concern the objective validity of metaphysical judgments, but refers merely to the natural propensity to make such judgments. This inquiry is thus outside the system of metaphysics and belongs to anthropology.

Suppose one compares all transcendental ideas whose aggregate constitutes the peculiar task of natural, pure reason, compelling it to leave mere observation of nature and to pass beyond all possible experience, and in these efforts to produce the thing called metaphysics, whether it be knowledge or mere argumentation. I believe that I can discern that this natural propensity is meant to free our concepts from the restraints of ex·

perience and the limits of mere observation of nature enough so that it may at least see a field opened before it which merely contains objects for the pure intellect that cannot be arrived at by any of the senses. The purpose is not to occupy ourselves speculatively with these objects, because in this we can find no firm ground on which to stand. But we are to occupy ourselves with these objects because principles of action cannot claim general currency if they do not find scope for their necessary expectations and cannot spread and gain the general acceptance that reason requires as indispensable for moral purposes.

Thus the *psychological* idea may offer small insight into the pure nature of the human soul since this nature is beyond all concepts based on experience. But at least this idea reveals to me sufficiently the inadequacy of the concepts of experience and thereby preserves me from materialism. [This is important, because] materialism as a psychological concept is of no use in explaining nature, while it also narrowly restricts reason in its practical aspect [capacity for moral action]. In the same way *cosmological* ideas serve to keep us from a naturalism that proclaims nature to be self-sufficing by (showing) the obvious inadequacy of all possible knowledge of nature in satisfying reason in its justifiable inquiries. Finally, since all natural necessity in the world of sense is invariably conditioned [by antecedent causes] inasmuch as natural necessity always presupposes dependence of things on one another; unconditioned [absolute] necessity must be sought in the unity of a cause differentiated from the world of sense. Yet if the causality of this cause [of causes] were mere nature, it could never make the existence of the contingent comprehensible as its sequence. Therefore reason frees itself from fatalism by means of the *theological idea*, no matter whether such fatalism means a blind natural necessity devoid of a first principle in the context of nature, or whether it means the causality of this principle itself. Instead, reason leads to the conception of causation through freedom, in other words, to a supreme intelligence. Thus the transcendental ideas, if they do not instruct us positively, at least serve to repudiate the audacious assertions of *materialism, naturalism and fatalism* that narrowly restrict the field of reason. At the same time, these ideas procure a place for moral ideas outside the sphere of [mere]speculations. This achievement, it seems to me, will explain in some measure the natural propensity [of man to develop these ideas].

Whatever practical utility a merely speculative science may have lies outside the boundaries of this science and hence can be viewed merely as a scholium, and like all scholia, as not forming a part of the science itself. At the same time, the practical utility of a speculative science at least lies within the boundaries of [general] philosophy, especially in that [part] drawing from the sources of pure reason. Thus the speculative use of reason in metaphysics must necessarily be in concord with its practical use in morals. Hence, when the inescapable dialectics of pure reason in metaphysics are considered as a natural propensity, they deserve to be explained not merely as an illusion requiring to be resolved, but as a natural arrangement [designed] for a highly beneficial end [*überverdienstlich*]. However, as this task is more than meritorious, in justice it cannot be assigned to metaphysics proper.

The solution of these problems, which are discussed in the *Critique of Pure Reason,* might be regarded as a second scholium which is more closely related to the content of metaphysics. For certain principles of reason are expounded there that determine *a priori* the order of nature, or rather the intellect, which is discovering nature's laws through experience. These principles seem to be constitutive and legislative in respect to experience since they arise from mere reason which, like the intellect, cannot be regarded as a principle of possible experience. [It is a question] whether the agreement between intellect and reason rests upon the fact that the intellect can only achieve the thorough uniformity of its use in dealing with the entire possible experience (in a system) by referring to reason, and that therefore experience is directly subject to the laws of reason. . . . This question may be further considered by those who desire to explore the nature of reason apart from its use in metaphysics and how to systematize it in the general principles of a history of nature. This question I have indeed presented as important in the book [*Critique of Pure Reason*] itself, but I have not attempted to solve it.

Thus I conclude the analytical solution of the problem I had proposed myself—How is metaphysics possible at all? I have proceeded from where the use of metaphysics is at least really given in its consequences, to the reasons for the possibility of metaphysics.

SOLUTION OF THE GENERAL PROBLEM OF THE PROLEGOMENA

How is Metaphysics Possible as a Science?

Metaphysics exists as a natural disposition of reason, but it is also dialectical and deceptive when taken by itself as proved in the analytical solution of the third main problem. Hence, attempting to take principles from it and using them to follow natural, but nevertheless misleading, illusions, can never produce science but only an empty dialectical art in which one school may indeed outdo another but none can ever attain a justifiable and lasting success.

In order that metaphysics, as a true knowledge or science, may claim not merely to persuade deceptively but to produce insight and conviction, a critique of reason must exhibit the whole stock of concepts *a priori,* in a complete system arranged according to their different sources: senses, intellect, and reason. Such a critique must also present a complete table of these concepts together with an analysis of them and all that can be deduced from it. But more especially it must present the possibility of synthetic knowledge *a priori* by means of the deduction of these concepts, the principles of their use, and finally the boundaries of such synthetic knowledge, and all of this in a complete system. Thus criticism contains, and it alone contains, the whole plan well tested and approved; indeed, it contains all the means whereby metaphysics may be perfected as a science; by other ways and means this is impossible. The question is now not how this business is possible but only how we are to go about it, how good heads are to be turned from their previous mistaken and fruitless path to a non-deceptive treatment and how such a group may be best directed toward the common end.

This much is certain; that he who has once tried criticism will be revolted forever by all the dogmatic glibness that he was compelled to put up with before because his reason needed something [in the way of general explanation] and could not find anything better with which to entertain itself. Criticism stands to ordinary, academic metaphysics in exactly the same relation as *chemistry* stands to *alchemy,* or as *astronomy* to fortune-telling *astrology.* I guarantee that no one who has comprehended and thought through the conclusions of criticism, even in these *Prolegomena* will ever return to the old sophistical pseudo-science. Instead, he will look forward with a kind of pleasure to a metaphysics which is now within his power and requires no more preparatory discoveries and which alone can procure permanent satisfaction for reason. For this is an advantage upon which metaphysics, alone among all possible sciences, can count with confidence; that metaphysics can be brought to completion and into a firm state where it cannot change any further and where it is not capable of any enlargement through new discoveries. Since the sources of the knowledge of reason are not in objects nor in the imagining of objects (by which it cannot be taught anything additional), these sources are in reason itself. Therefore when reason has presented the basic laws of its capacity completely and determinately (safe) from any interpretation, there remains no knowledge *a priori* for pure reason to seek or even reasonably to inquire after. The certain prospect of so definite and perfect a knowledge has a special attraction, even if all its advantage, of which I shall speak here-after, be set aside.

All false art, all vain wisdom lasts its time, but it destroys itself in the end and its highest cultivation marks at the same time the period of its decline. That this time has now come for metaphysics is proved by the state to which metaphysics has declined among all cultivated nations, notwithstanding the zeal with which every other kind of science is being worked on. The old curriculum of university studies still preserves its shadow, a single academy of sciences bestirs itself now and then by offering prizes to induce another attempt to be made therein. But metaphysics is no longer counted among the fundamental sciences, and anyone may judge for himself how an intellectually gifted man, to whom the term great metaphysician was applied, would take this well-meant compliment.

Although the period of the decline of all dogmatic metaphysics has undoubtedly come, as yet we are far from being able to say that the time of its re-birth by means of a thorough and complete Critique of Reason has already appeared. All transitional phases from one tendency to its opposite pass through the state of indifference and this moment is the most dangerous for an author, but, it seems to me, the most favorable moment for the science. For, when party spirit is extinguished through the complete dissolution of former groups, men's minds are in the best mood for listening eventually to proposals for agreeing on another plan.

When I say that I hope that these *Prolegomena* will perhaps revive inquiry into the field of criticism, and that they will offer to the general spirit of philosophy, which seems to be wanting in nourishment on its speculative side, a new and very promising field for its entertainment, I can foresee already that everyone, who has trodden unwillingly and with vexation the thorny path I have led him in the Critique, will ask me on what I base this hope. I answer: *on the irresistible law of necessity.*

It can be just as little expected that the spirit of man will ever wholly give up metaphysical investigations as that we should stop breathing in order not to be always breathing bad air. Metaphysics will always exist in the world, and what is more, will always [exist] for everyone, but more especially for thoughtful men, who, lacking a public standard, will each fashion it in his own way. What has been termed metaphysics up till now can satisfy no acute mind, but it is impossible to renounce it entirely. Hence, a critique of pure reason itself must be *attempted* at last, and if one exists it must be examined and subjected to general inquiry because there are no other means of relieving this pressing need which is something more than mere thirst for knowledge.

After finishing the perusal of a work on metaphysics, especially if it had entertained as well as instructed me by the definition of its conceptions, its variety and its orderly arrangement in conjunction with its easy style, I cannot, since I have known criticism, forbear asking: Has this author brought metaphysics one step farther? I beg forgiveness of the learned men whose works have been useful to me in other respects and have contributed to the cultivation of my intellectual powers, if I confess that neither in their works, nor in my own lesser efforts in whose favor amour-propre inclines me, have I been able to find that the science has been advanced in the least, and this for the very natural reason that the science did not exist then, nor could it have been brought together piecemeal, for its core had first to be fully formed in the *Critique*. However, in order to avoid all misconception it must be remembered from what has gone before that while the intellect has benefited greatly by analytical treatment of our concepts, the science of metaphysics has not been advanced in the least because these analyses of concepts are only materials out of which the science has to be constructed. We may dissect and define the concept of substance and accident or property as well as possible, for this is useful enough as preparation for its future use. But if I cannot know that in everything that exists substance continues and only the accidents change, science would not be furthered in the least by all this dissection. Now metaphysics has not been able to prove either this proposition *a priori* and validly nor that of sufficient cause, much less any more complex propositions such as those belonging to the doctrine of the soul or to cosmology, and certainly never any synthetic proposition *a priori*. Thus nothing has been accomplished by all this analysis, nothing has been created and nothing furthered and the science, after so much turmoil and noise, remains where it was in Aristotle's time. If only the clue to synthetic knowledge *a priori* had been found first, then [philosophical] efforts would indisputably have been much more effective than they have in fact been formerly.

Should anyone feel offended by what is said here then he can very easily nullify the accusation if he will only abduce a single synthetic proposition belonging to metaphysics which admits of being demonstrated dogmatically *a priori*. For only when he has achieved this shall I concede that he has really advanced the science [of metaphysics], even though the particular proposition may be sufficiently confirmed by common experience. No demand could be more fair and moderate nor, in the unquestionably certain event that the demand is not fulfilled, could any statement be juster than that metaphysics as a science has not hitherto existeɗ at all.

In case the challenge should be accepted, I must forbid two things: First, any playing with *probability* and conjecture, which is as inappropriate to metaphysics as to geometry, and second, any solution by means of the magic rod of so-called *sound common sense* which does not work [alike] for everyone but shifts according to personal characteristics.

As regards the first, nothing could be more absurd in a system of metaphysics, a philosophy of pure reason, than wanting to base judgments on probability and conjecture. All that is to be known *a priori* is claimed as apodictically certain and must be proved as such. We might just as well undertake to found geometry or arithmetic on conjectures. As for calculating probability in the latter, such calculation contains not probable but perfectly certain propositions on the degree of probability in certain cases under given similar conditions which, in the sum of all possible cases, must infallibly occur in accordance with the rule, although the occurrence is not sufficiently determined in respect of any single event. Only in empirical natural science can conjectures be permitted by means of induction and analogy and only in such a manner that at least the possibility of what I assume must be quite certain.

With the *appeal to sound common sense* we are, if possible, still worse off when we are dealing with concepts and principles, not so far as they are allegedly valid for experience, but when these principles are supposedly valid outside the conditions of experience. For what is *sound sense?* It is *common sense* when it judges correctly. And what is common sense? It is the faculty for gathering knowledge and employing rules *in concrete situations* as distinguished from the *speculative sense* or *intellect* which is a faculty for gathering knowledge of rules *in abstract terms*. Thus, common sense will hardly comprehend or understand as a general proposition the rule: that all that happens is determined by means of its cause. Hence common sense demands an example from experience. But when common sense learns that the general [law of causation] means nothing more than what was always apparent when a window pane was broken or a household utensil lost, common sense understands the principle and admits it. Thus sense has no use beyond seeing its rules confirmed in experience, even though these rules are really inherent in it *a priori*. The comprehension of these rules, which is independent of experience, belongs to the speculative understanding and is wholly beyond the horizon of common understanding. Metaphysics is exclusively occupied with this latter kind of knowledge and it is certainly a poor sign of sound sense to appeal to a witness who has no right of judgment here.

V

IDEA FOR A UNIVERSAL HISTORY
WITH COSMOPOLITAN INTENT

[1784]

No MATTER WHAT CONCEPTION ONE MAY FORM OF THE freedom of the will in metaphysics, the phenomenal appearances of the will, i.e., human actions, are determined by general laws of nature like any other event of nature. History is concerned with telling about these events. History allows one to hope that when history considers *in the large* the play of the freedom of human will, it will be possible to discover the regular progressions thereof. Thus (it is to be hoped) that what appears to be complicated and accidental in individuals, may yet be understood as a steady, progressive, though slow, evolution of the original endowments of the entire species. Thus marriages, the consequent births and the deaths, since the free will seems to have such a great influence on them, do not seem to be subject to any law according to which one could calculate their number beforehand. Yet the annual (statistical) tables about them in the major countries show that they occur according to stable natural laws. It is like the erratic weather the occurrence of which cannot be determined in particular instances, although it never fails in maintaining the growth of plants, the flow of streams, and other of nature's arrangements at a uniform, uninterrupted pace. Individual human beings, each pursuing his own ends according to his inclination and often one against another (and even one entire people against another) rarely unintentionally promote, as if it were their guide, an end of nature which is unknown to them. They thus work to promote that which they would care little for if they knew about it.

Since men in their endeavors do not act like animals merely according to instinct, nor like rational citizens according to an agreed plan, no planned history seems to be possible (as in the case of bees and beavers). It is hard to suppress a certain disgust when contemplating men's action upon the world stage. For one finds, in spite of apparent wisdom in detail that everything, taken as a whole, is interwoven with stupidity, childish vanity, often with childish viciousness and destructiveness. In the end, one does not know what kind of conception one should have of our species which is so conceited about its superior qualities. Since the philosopher must assume that men have a flexible *purpose of their own,* it is left to him to attempt to discover an end of nature in this senseless march of human events. A history of creatures who proceed without a plan would be possible in keeping with such an end; the history would proceed according to such an end of nature.

We shall see whether we can succeed in discovering a guide to such a history. We shall leave it to nature to produce a man who would be capable of writing history in accordance with such an end. Thus nature produced a *Kepler* who figured out an unexpected way of subsuming the eccentric orbits of the planets to definite laws, and a *Newton* who explained these laws by a general cause of nature.

First Principle

All natural faculties of a creature are destined to unfold completely and according to their end. External observation and analysis confirms this proposition concerning all authority. An organ which is not to be used, a regulation which does not accomplish its purpose, these are self-contradictions in the teleological theory of nature. If we abandon this principle, we no longer have a nature working according to laws, but an aimlessly playing nature. Then the hapless accident takes the place of reason as guide.

Second Principle

In man (as the only rational creature on earth) those natural faculties which aim at the use of reason shall be fully developed in the species, not in the individual. Reason in a creature is the capacity to enlarge the rules and purposes of the use of his resources far beyond natural instinct. It does not recognize any boundary to its projects. It does not develop instinctively but requires trials, experience and information in order to progress gradually from one level of understanding to the next. Therefore every man would have to live excessively long in order to learn how to make full use of all his faculties. Or, if nature has set man a short term of life (as is, in fact, the case), then (perhaps) nature requires a endless procession of begettings of which one transmits its enlightenment to another, in order finally to push the genus of human kind to that level of development which is appropriate to the purpose of nature. This time must, at least theoretically, be the target of the endeavors of man, because otherwise the natural faculties would have to be considered largely pointless and in vain. This would vitiate all practical principles, as it would suggest that nature, the wisdom of which serves as a principle in judging all other natural arrangements, would have to be suspected of childish play when it comes to man.

Third Principle

Nature has intended that man develop everything which transcends the mechanical ordering of his animal existence, entirely by himself and that he does not partake of any other happiness or perfection except that which he has secured himself by his own reason and free of instinct. Nature does not do things superfluously and is not extravagant in the employment of its means to its end. Since nature gave man reason and the freedom of will which rests upon reason, that serves to show clearly nature's purpose in regard to man's equipment. . . . The discovery of his food, of his clothing, of his external security and defense (for which nature gave man neither the horns of the bull, nor the claws of the lion, nor the teeth of the dog, but only hands), all pleasures that can make life agreeable, even his insight and intelligence, indeed, the kindness of his will should be achieved by man's own work. Nature seems to have delighted in the greatest parsimony; she seems to have barely provided man's animal equipment and limited it to the most urgent needs of a beginning existence, as if nature intended that man should owe all to himself, as though he should eventually struggle up from the greatest backwardness to the greatest skills, to inner perfection of mind, and (as far as it is possible on earth) to blessed happiness. Man alone should have the credit (for having accomplished this), as if nature were more concerned with man's rational *self-esteem* than with his well-being. In the course of human affairs a vast amount of hardship awaits man. It seems as though nature had not cared that man live well, but that by progressing thus far man would prove himself through his conduct worthy of life and well-being. However, it remains perplexing that earlier generations seem to do their laborious work for the sake of later generations, in order to provide a foundation from which the latter can advance the building which nature has intended. Only later generations will have the good fortune to live in the building. But however mysterious this [conclusion] may be, it is nevertheless necessary, if one assumes that an animal species is to have reason, and is to arrive at a complete development of its faculties as a class of reasonable beings who die while their species is immortal.

Fourth Principle

The means which nature employs to accomplish the development of all faculties is the antagonism of men in society, since this antagonism becomes, in the end, the cause of a lawful order of this society. I mean by antagonism the asocial sociability of man, i.e., the propensity of men to enter into a society, which propensity is, however, linked to a constant mutual resistance which threatens to dissolve this society. This propensity apparently is innate in man. Man has an inclination to *associate* himself, because in such a state he feels himself more like a man capable of developing his natural faculties. Man has also a marked propensity to *isolate* himself, because he finds in himself the asocial quality to want to arrange everything according to his own ideas. He therefore expects resistance everywhere, just as he knows of himself that he is inclined to resist others. This resistance awakens all the latent forces in man which drive him to overcome his propensity to be lazy, and so, impelled by vainglory, ambition and avarice, he seeks to achieve a standing among his fellows, whom he does not suffer gladly, but whom he cannot *leave.* Thus the first steps from barbarism to culture are achieved; for culture actually consists in the social value of man. All man's talents are gradually unfolded, taste is developed. Through continuous enlightenment the basis is laid for a frame of mind which, in the course of time, transforms the raw natural faculty of moral discrimination into definite practical principles. Thus a *pathologically* enforced co-ordination of society finally transforms it into a *moral* whole. Without these essentially unlovely qualities of asociability, from which springs the resistance which everyone must encounter in his egoistic pretensions, all talents would have remained hidden germs. If

man lived an Arcadian shepherd's existence of harmony, modesty and mutuality, man, good-natured like the sheep he is herd-
ing, would not invest his existence with greater value than that
his animals have. Man would not fill the vacuum of creation as
regards his end, rational nature. Thanks are due to nature for
his quarrelsomeness, his enviously competitive vanity, and for his
insatiable desire to possess or to rule, for without them all the
excellent natural faculties of mankind would forever remain
undeveloped. Man wants concord but nature knows better
what is good for his kind; nature wants discord. Man wants to
live comfortably and pleasurably but nature intends that he
should raise himself out of lethargy and inactive contentment
into work and trouble and then he should find means of extricating himself adroitly from these latter. The natural impulses, the sources of asociability and continuous resistance from
which so many evils spring, but which at the same time drive
man to a new exertion of his powers and thus to a development
of his natural faculties, suggest the arrangement of a wise creator and not the hand of an evil spirit who might have ruined
this excellent enterprise or spoiled it out of envy.

Fifth Principle

*The latest problem for mankind, the solution of which nature
forces him to seek, is the achievement of a civil society which
administers law* (Recht) *generally.* Nature can achieve its other
intentions regarding mankind only through the solution and
fulfilment of this task, for a completely *just civic constitution*
is the highest task nature has set mankind. This is because only
under such a constitution can there be achieved the supreme
objective of nature, namely, the development of all the faculties
of man by his own effort. It is also nature's intent that man
should secure all these ends by himself only in a society which
not only possesses the greatest freedom and hence a very general
antagonism of its members but also possesses the most precise
determination and enforcement of the limit of this freedom so

that it can coexist with the freedom of other societies: this will serve the highest purpose of nature.

In other words, a society in which *freedom under external laws* is found combined in the highest degree with irresistible force, that is to say, a perfectly *just civic constitution*, must be the supreme task nature has set for mankind. Only through the solution and fulfilment of this task can nature hope to achieve its other objectives concerning man. Want forces man, who so greatly inclines toward unrestricted freedom, to enter into this state of constraint. It takes the greatest want of all to bring men to the point where they cannot live alongside each other in wild freedom but within such an enclosure as the civic association provides. These very same inclinations afterwards have a very good effect. It is like the trees in a forest which, since each seeks to take air and sun away from the other, compel each other to seek both and thus they achieve a beautiful straight growth. Whereas those that develop their branches as they please, in freedom and apart from each other, grow crooked and twisted. All culture and art which adorn mankind, the most beautiful social order, are the fruits of asociability which is self-compelled to discipline itself and thus through a derived art to fulfill completely the germs of its nature.

Sixth Principle

This problem is the most difficult and at the same time the one which mankind solves last. The difficulty which even the mere idea of this task clearly reveals is the following: Man is an animal who, if he lives among others of his kind, *needs a master*, for man certainly misuses his freedom in regard to others of his kind and, even though as a rational being he desires a law which would provide limits for the freedom of all, his egoistic animal inclination misguides him into excluding himself where he can. Man therefore *needs* a master who can break man's will and compel him to obey a general will under which every man could be free. But where is he to get this master? Nowhere else but from mankind. But then this master is in turn an animal who needs a master. Therefore one cannot see how man, try as he will, could secure a master [charged with maintaining] public justice who would be himself just. This is true whether one seeks to discover such a master in a single person or in a group of elected persons. For each of these will always abuse his freedom if he has no one over him who wields power according to the laws. Yet the highest master is supposed to be *just in himself* and yet a *man*. The task involved is therefore most difficult; indeed, a complete solution is impossible. One cannot fashion something absolutely straight from wood which is as crooked as that of which man is made. Nature has imposed upon us the task of approximating this idea.[1] That his task should be the latest that man achieves follows from yet another consideration: the *right conceptions* regarding the nature of a possible constitution. Great *experience* in many activities and a *good will* which is prepared to accept such a constitution are all required. Obviously it will be very difficult, and if it happens it will be very late and after many unsuccessful attempts that three such things are found together.

Seventh Principle

The problem of the establishment of a perfect civic constitution depends upon the problem of a lawful external relationship of the states and cannot be solved without the latter. What use is it to work out a lawful civic constitution among individual men, that is, to order a commonwealth? For the very same asociability which compelled man to do this is again the cause of the fact that each commonwealth in its external relations, that is to

[1] The rule of man is therefore very artificial. We do not know how things are arranged with the inhabitants of other planets and their nature but if we execute this mandate of nature well we may properly flatter ourselves that we occupy a not inconsiderable position among our neighbors in the cosmos. Perhaps with these neighbors an individual can achieve his destiny in his own life. With us mortals it is different: only the species can hope to do so.

say, as a state in relation to other states, is in a condition of unrestricted freedom. Consequently, one commonwealth must expect from the others the very same evils which oppress individual human beings and which compelled them to enter into a lawful civic state. Nature has again used quarrelsomeness, in this case that of the great societies and states, as a means for discovering a condition of quiet and security through the very antagonism inevitable among them. That is to say, wars, the excessive and never-ending preparation for wars, and the want which every state even in the midst of peace must feel—all these are means by which nature instigates attempts, which at first are inadequate, but which, after many devastations, reversals and a very general exhaustion of the states' resources, may accomplish what reason could have suggested to them without so much sad experience, namely; to leave the lawless state of savages and to enter into a union of nations wherein each, even the smallest state, could expect to derive its security and rights —not from its own power or its own legal judgment—but only from this great union of nations (*Foedus Amphictyonum*) and from united power and decisions according to the united will of them all. However fanciful this idea may seem and as such may have been ridiculed when held by the Abbé St. Pierre and Rousseau (perhaps because they believed the idea to be too near its realization), it is, nevertheless, the inevitable escape from the destitution into which human beings plunge each other. It is this which must compel states to the resolution to seek quiet and security through a lawful constitution (however hard it may be for them) and to do that which the wild man is so very reluctantly forced to do, namely, to give up his brutal freedom.

All wars are therefore so many attempts (not in the intention of men, but in the intention of nature) to bring about new relations among the states and to form new bodies by the break-up of the old states to the point where they cannot again maintain themselves alongside each other and must therefore suffer revolutions until finally, partly through the best possible arrangement of the civic constitution internally, and partly through the common agreement and legislation externally, there is created a state which, like a civic commonwealth, can maintain itself automatically.

(The question) whether one should expect that, from an epicurean influence of effective causes, the states, like small fragments of matter, by their accidental collision, make all kinds of formations which are destroyed again by a new impact until eventually and *accidentally* there occurs a formation which can maintain itself in its form (by a lucky accident which will hardly ever occur!); or whether one should rather assume that nature follows a regular sequence to lead our species from the lowest level of animality gradually to the highest level of humanity by man's own, though involuntary, effort and that thus nature is unfolding in this seemingly wild disorder man's original faculties quite according to rule; or whether one prefers to assume that all these effects and counter-effects will in the long run result in nothing, or at least nothing sensible, and that things will remain as they always have been and therefore one cannot predict that the discord which is natural to the species is in the end preparing for us a hell of evils, evil in an ever so civilized state because perhaps nature will destroy, by barbaric devastation, this state and all advances of culture (a fate which one may well suffer with the government of blind accident which is indeed identical with lawless freedom if no wisely conceived direction of nature is imputed thereto)—these three alternatives, in the last analysis, amount to the question: Whether it be reasonable to assume that nature is appropriate in its parts but (as a whole) inappropriate to its end? [2]

Therefore, the feckless condition of the savages did . . . what is also being effected by the barbarian freedom of the

---

[2] The German antithesis here is *Zweckmäsigkeit* and *Zwecklosigkeit.* These terms are very inadequately rendered by appropriate and inappropriate but no other handy pair is available to render the idea that something is appropriate to its end or not. The full German phrase is *ob es wohl vernünftig sei.*

states which have been instituted; by the employment of all the resources of the commonwealth for armaments against one another, by the devastation which war is causing, but even more by the necessity of being constantly prepared for war. The full development of man's natural faculties is being inhibited by the evils which spring from these conditions which compel our species to discover a counter-balance to the intrinsically healthy resistance of many states against each other resulting from their freedom and to introduce a united power which will give support to this balance. In other words these conditions compel our species to introduce a cosmo-political state of public security which is not without all *danger,* [for we must see to it] that neither the vitality of mankind goes to sleep nor these states destroy each other as they might without a principle of balance of *equality* in their mutual *effects* and *counter-effects.* Before this last step, namely, the joining of the states, is taken, in other words, the half-way mark of mankind's development is reached; human nature is enduring the worst hardships under the guise of external welfare and *Rousseau* was not so very wrong when he preferred the condition of savages; [for it is to be preferred], provided one omits this last stage which our species will have to reach. We are highly civilized by art and science, we are civilized in all kinds of social graces and decency to the point where it becomes exasperating, but much (must be discarded) before we can consider ourselves truly ethicized. For the idea of morality is part of culture by the use that has been made of this idea which amounts only to something similar to ethics in the form of a love of honor and external decency (which) constitutes civilization. As long as states will use all their resources for their vain and violent designs for expansion and thus will continually hinder the slow efforts toward the inner shaping of the minds of their citizens, and even withdraw from their citizens all encouragement in this respect, we cannot hope for much because a great exertion by each commonwealth on behalf of the education of their citizens is required for this goal.

Every pretended good that is not grafted upon a morally good frame of mind is nothing more than a pretense and glittering misery. Mankind will probably remain in this condition until, as I have said, it has struggled out of the chaotic condition of the relations among its states.

Eighth Principle

The history of mankind could be viewed on the whole as the realization of a hidden plan of nature in order to bring about an internally—and for this purpose also externally—perfect constitution; since this is the only state in which nature can develop all faculties of mankind. This principle is a conculsion drawn from the previous principle. We can see that philosophy may also have its expectation of a millennium, but this millennium would be one for the realization of which philosophical ideas themselves may be helpful although only from afar. Therefore this expectation is hardly utopian. What matters is whether experience can discover some such progress of nature's intention. I would say *some small part*; for this revolution seems to require so much time that from the small distance which man has so far traversed one can judge only uncertainly the shape of the revolution's course and the relation of the parts to the whole. The situation is similar to that in astronomy where it is likewise difficult to determine from all the observations of the heavens up till now the course which our sun, with all its swarm of satellites, occupies in the system of fixed stars. But when one takes into account the general premise that the world is constituted as a system and considers what little has been observed one can say that the indications are sufficiently reliable to enable us to conclude that such a revolution is real. Our human nature has this aspect that it cannot be indifferent to even the most remote epoch at which our species may arrive if only that epoch may be expected with certainty. Furthermore, it is less feasible in our particular case since it seems that we could hasten by our own rational efforts the time when this state might occur which would be so enjoyable for our descendants. For that reason even feeble traces of an approach to this state become very important. The states are (now) on such artificial terms toward each other that not one of them can relax its efforts at internal development without losing, in comparison to the others, in power and influence. Thus if not progress then at least the maintenance of this end of nature (namely, culture) is safeguarded by the ambitions of those states to some extent. Furthermore, civic freedom cannot now be interfered with without the state feeling the disadvantage of such interference in all trades, primarily foreign commerce, and as a result (there is) a decline of the power of the state in its foreign relations. Therefore this freedom is gradually being extended. If one obstructs the citizen in seeking his welfare in any way he chooses, as long as (his way) can coexist with the freedom of others, one also hampers the vitality of all business and the strength of the whole (state). For this reason restrictions of personal activities are being increasingly lifted and general freedom granted and thus enlightenment is gradually developing with occasional nonsense and freakishness. Enlightenment is a great good which must ever draw mankind away from the egoistic expansive tendencies of its rulers once they understand their own advantage. This enlightenment and along with it a certain participation of the heart (are things) which the enlightened man cannot fail to feel for the good which he fully understands must by and by reach the thrones and have influence upon the principles of government. For example, although our governors have no money to spare for public education nor for anything else that concerns the best interests of the world because all the money has in advance been budgeted for the coming war, they will nevertheless find it to their own advantage at least not to hinder the weak and slow independent efforts of their people in this regard. Eventually, even war will become a very dubious enterprise, not only because its result on both sides is so uncertain and artificial, but because in its aftermath the state consequently finds itself saddled with a growing debt the repayment of which becomes undeterminable. At the same time the effect of each impact of a government upon other governments in our continent, where the states have become so very much linked through commerce, will become so noticeable that the other states, compelled by their own danger, even when lacking a legal basis, will offer themselves as arbiters and thus start a future great government of which there is no previous example in history. Even though this body-politic at present is discernible only in its broadest outline, a feeling (for it) is rising in all member states since each is interested in the maintenance of the whole. . . .

Ninth Principle

A philosophical attempt to write a general world history according to a plan of nature which aims at a perfect civic association of mankind must be considered possible and even helpful to this intention of nature. It is a strange and apparently paradoxical project to write a history according to an idea as to how the world should develop if its development is to have an appropriate rational end. It would seem that such a purpose could only produce a *novel,* but this idea might yet be usable if one could assume that nature and even the play of human freedom does not proceed without plan and intended end. Even though we are too shortsighted to perceive the secret mechanism of nature's plan an otherwise planless *conglomeration* of human activities could be used as a guide when presented as a *system.* If one starts with *Greek* history as the (one) through which all older and contemporary history has been preserved or at least certified,[3] one may trace the influence (of Greek

---

[3] Only a *learned public* which has continued from the beginning uninterruptedly to our time can certify to ancient history. Beyond that all is *terra incognita* and the history of nations which lived beyond that frame can only be started with the time when they entered it. For the *Jewish* people that happened in the time of the Ptolemies through the Greek translation of the Bible without which one would give little credence

history) upon the formation and malformation of the body politic of the Roman people who devoured the Greek state. Again, (if one traces) down to our time the influence of *Rome* upon the *Barbarian* who destroyed the empire; if one then periodically adds the history of the state of other peoples as knowledge of them has come to us through these enlightened nations; then one will discover a regular procession of improvements in constitutional government in our part of the world which will probably give laws to all other (states) eventually. By concentrating primarily on the civic constitution and its laws and on the relations among states, because both served to raise nations, their arts and sciences, one may discover a guide to explain the chaotic play of human affairs. . . . Such a *justification* of nature, or perhaps one should say of providence, is a not unimportant reason for selecting a particular outlook for observing the world. For what good is it to praise the majesty and wisdom of creation in the realm of nature, which is without reason, and to recommend contemplating them if that part of the great arena of supreme wisdom which above all contains that purpose, namely, the history of mankind, remains as a constant objection because its spectacle compels us to turn away our eyes in disgust and as we despair of ever encountering therein a completed rational end causes us to expect such perfection only in another world? It would be a misinterpretation of my intention to maintain that I wished to displace the work on true empirical history by this idea of a universal history which contains a principle *a priori*. This idea is only a notion of what a philosophical mind, who would have to be very knowledgeable in history, could attempt from another standpoint. Furthermore, the complexity, in many ways praiseworthy, with which the history of an age is now composed, naturally causes everyone to worry as to how our later descendants are going to

---

to their *isolated* reports. But one can trace backward from this event once it is adequately ascertained and thus with all peoples. The first page of *Thucydides*, says Hume, is the real beginning of history.

cope with the burden of history which, after some centuries, we are going to leave them. Without doubt they will care for the history of the most ancient period, for which the documents would have long perished, only from the standpoint (which) interests them, namely, what nations and governments have contributed toward world government or how they have damaged it. We may be concerned with this and may also consider (that) the ambition of rulers and their servants (should) be directed toward the only means which could secure a glorious reputation for them in later ages. These considerations may also offer a small reason for attempting such a philosophical history.

VI

WHAT IS ENLIGHTENMENT?

[1784]

ENLIGHTENMENT IS MAN'S LEAVING HIS SELF-CAUSED IM-maturity. Immaturity is the incapacity to use one's intelligence without the guidance of another. Such immaturity is self-caused if it is not caused by lack of intelligence, but by lack of determination and courage to use one's intelligence without being guided by another. *Sapere Aude!* Have the courage to use your own intelligence! is therefore the motto of the enlightenment.

Through laziness and cowardice a large part of mankind, even after nature has freed them from alien guidance, gladly remain immature. It is because of laziness and cowardice that it is so easy for others to usurp the role of guardians. It is so comfortable to be a minor! If I have a book which provides meaning for me, a pastor who has conscience for me, a doctor who will judge my diet for me and so on, then I do not need to exert myself. I do not have any need to think; if I can pay, others will take over the tedious job for me. The guardians who have kindly undertaken the supervision will see to it that by far the largest part of mankind, including the entire "beautiful sex," should consider the step into maturity, not only as difficult but as very dangerous.

After having made their domestic animals dumb and having carefully prevented these quiet creatures from daring to take any step beyond the lead-strings to which they have fastened them, these guardians then show them the danger which threatens them, should they attempt to walk alone. Now this danger is not really so very great; for they would presumably learn to walk after some stumbling. However, an example of this kind intimidates and frightens people out of all further attempts.

It is difficult for the isolated individual to work himself out of the immaturity which has become almost natural for him. He has even become fond of it and for the time being is incapable of employing his own intelligence, because he has never been allowed to make the attempt. Statutes and formulas, these mechanical tools of a serviceable use, or rather misuse, of his natural faculties, are the ankle-chains of a continuous immaturity. Whoever threw it off would make an uncertain jump over the smallest trench because he is not accustomed to such free movement. Therefore there are only a few who have pursued a firm path and have succeeded in escaping from immaturity by their own cultivation of the mind.

But it is more nearly possible for a public to enlighten itself: this is even inescapable if only the public is given its freedom. For there will always be some people who think for themselves, even among the self-appointed guardians of the great mass who, after having thrown off the yoke of immaturity themselves, will spread about them the spirit of a reasonable estimate of their own value and of the need for every man to think for himself. It is strange that the very public, which had previously been put under this yoke by the guardians, forces the guardians thereafter to keep it there if it is stirred up by a few of its guardians who are themselves incapable of all enlightenment. It is thus very harmful to plant prejudices, because they come back to plague those very people who themselves (or whose predecessors) have been the originators of these prejudices. Therefore a public can only arrive at enlightenment slowly. Through revolution, the abandonment of personal despotism may be engendered and the end of profit-seeking and domineering oppression may occur, but never a true reform of the state of mind. Instead, new prejudices, just like the old ones, will serve as the guiding reins of the great, unthinking mass.

All that is required for this enlightenment is *freedom;* and particularly the least harmful of all that may be called freedom, namely, the freedom for man to make *public use* of his reason in all matters. But I hear people clamor on all sides: Don't argue! The officer says: Don't argue, drill! The tax collector: Don't argue, pay! The pastor: Don't argue, believe! (Only a single lord in the world says: *Argue,* as much as you want to and about what you please, *but obey!*) Here we have restrictions on freedom everywhere. Which restriction is hampering enlightenment, and which does not, or even promotes it? I answer: The *public use* of a man's reason must be free at all times, and this alone can bring enlightenment among men: while the private use of a man's reason may often be restricted rather narrowly without thereby unduly hampering the progress of enlightenment.

I mean by the public use of one's reason, the use which a scholar makes of it before the entire reading public. Private use I call the use which he may make of this reason in a civic post or office. For some affairs which are in the interest of the commonwealth a certain mechanism is necessary through which some members of the commonwealth must remain purely passive in order that an artificial agreement with the government for the public good be maintained or so that at least the destruction of the good be prevented. In such a situation it is not permitted to argue; one must obey. But in so far as this unit of the machine considers himself as a member of the entire commonwealth, in fact even of world society; in other words, he considers himself in the quality of a scholar who is addressing the true public through his writing, he may indeed argue without the affairs suffering for which he is employed partly as a passive member. Thus it would be very harmful if an officer who, given an order by his superior, should start, while in the service, to argue concerning the utility or appropriateness of that command. He must obey, but he cannot equitably be prevented from making observations as a scholar concerning the mistakes in the military service nor from submitting these to the public for its judgment. The citizen cannot refuse to pay the taxes imposed upon him. Indeed, a rash criticism of such taxes, if they are the ones to be paid by him, may be punished as a scandal which might cause general resistance. But the same man does not act contrary to the duty of a citizen if, as a scholar, he utters publicly his thoughts against the undesirability or even the injustice of such taxes. Likewise a clergyman is obliged to teach his pupils and his congregation according to the doctrine of the church which he serves, for he has been accepted on that condition. But as a scholar, he has full freedom, in fact, even the obligation, to communicate to the public all his diligently examined and well-intentioned thoughts concerning erroneous points in that doctrine and concerning proposals regarding the better institution of religious and ecclesiastical matters. There is nothing in this for which the conscience could be blamed. For what he teaches according to his office as one authorized by the church, he presents as something in regard to which he has no latitude to teach according to his own preference. . . . He will say: Our church teaches this or that, these are the proofs which are employed for it. In this way he derives all possible practical benefit for his congregation from rules which he would not himself subscribe to with full conviction. But he may nevertheless undertake the presentation of these rules because it is not entirely inconceivable that truth may be contained in them. In any case, there is nothing directly contrary to inner religion to be found in such doctrines. For, should he believe that the latter was not the case he could not administer his office in good conscience; he would have to resign it. Therefore the use which an employed teacher makes of his reason before his congregation is merely a private use since such a gathering is always only domestic, no matter how large. As a priest (a member of an organization) he is not free and ought not to be, since he is executing someone else's mandate. On the other hand, the scholar speaking through his writings to the true public which is the world, like the clergyman making public use of his reason, enjoys an unlimited freedom to employ his own reason and to speak in his own person. For to suggest that the guardians of the people in spiritual matters should always be immature minors is a non-sense which would mean perpetuating forever existing non-sense.

But should a society of clergymen, for instance an ecclesiastical assembly, be entitled to commit itself by oath to a certain unalterable doctrine in order to perpetuate an endless guardianship over each of its members and through them over the people? I answer that this is quite inconceivable. Such a contract which would be concluded in order to keep humanity forever from all further enlightenment is absolutely impossible, even should it be confirmed by the highest authority through parliaments and the most solemn peace treaties. An age cannot conclude a pact and take an oath upon it to commit the succeeding age to a situation in which it would be impossible for the latter to enlarge even its most important knowledge, to eliminate error and altogether to progress in enlightenment. Such a thing would be a crime against human nature, the original destiny of which consists in such progress. Succeeding generations are entirely justified in discarding such decisions as unauthorized and criminal. The touchstone of all this to be agreed upon as a law for people is to be found in the question whether a people could impose such a law upon itself. Now it might be possible to introduce a certain order for a definite short period as if in anticipation of a better order. This would be true if one permitted at the same time each citizen and especially the clergyman to make his criticisms in his quality as a scholar. . . . In the meantime, the provisional order might continue until the insight into the particular matter in hand has publicly progressed to the point where through a combination of voices (although not, perhaps, of all) a proposal may be brought to the crown. Thus those congregations would be protected which had agreed to (a changed religious institution) according to their own ideas and better understanding, without hindering those who desired to allow the old institutions to continue. . . .

A man may postpone for himself, but only for a short time, enlightening himself regarding what he ought to know. But to resign from such enlightenment altogether either for his own person or even more for his descendants means to violate and to trample underfoot the sacred rights of mankind. Whatever a people may not decide for themselves, a monarch may even less decide for the people, for his legislative reputation rests upon his uniting the entire people's will in his own. If the monarch will only see to it that every true or imagined reform (of religion) fits in with the civil order, he had best let his subjects do what they consider necessary for the sake of their salvation; that is not his affair. His only concern is to prevent one subject from hindering another by force, to work according to each subject's best ability to determine and to promote his salvation. In fact, it detracts from his majesty if he interferes in such matters and subjects to governmental supervision the writings by which his subjects seek to clarify their ideas (concerning religion). This is true whether he does it from his own highest insight, for in this case he exposes himself to the reproach: *Caesar non est supra grammaticos;* it is even more true when he debases his highest power to support the spiritual despotism of some tyrants in his state against the rest of his subjects.

The question may now be put: Do we live at present in an enlightened age? The answer is: No, but in an age of enlightenment. Much still prevents men from being placed in a position or even being placed into position to use their own minds securely and well in matters of religion. But we do have very definite indications that this field of endeavor is being opened up for men to work freely and reduce gradually the hindrances preventing a general enlightenment and an escape from self-caused immaturity. In this sense, this age is the age of enlightenment and the age of Frederick (the Great).

A prince should not consider it beneath him to declare that he believes it to be his duty not to prescribe anything to his subjects in matters of religion but to leave to them complete freedom in such things. In other words, a prince who refuses the conceited title of being "tolerant," is himself enlightened. He deserves to be praised by his grateful contemporaries and descendants as the man who first freed humankind of immaturity, at least as far as the government is concerned and who permitted everyone to use his own reason in all matters of conscience. Under his rule, venerable clergymen could, regardless of their official duty, set forth their opinions and views even though they differ from the accepted doctrine here and there; they could do so in the quality of scholars, freely and publicly. The same holds even more true of every other person who is not thus restricted by official duty. This spirit of freedom is spreading even outside (the country of Frederick the Great) to places where it has to struggle with the external hindrances imposed by a government which misunderstands its own position. For an example is illuminating them which shows that such freedom (public discussion) need not cause the slightest worry regarding public security and the unity of the commonwealth. Men raise themselves by and by out of backwardness if one does not purposely invent artifices to keep them down.

I have emphasized the main point of enlightenment, that is of man's release from his self-caused immaturity, primarily *in matters of religion.* I have done this because our rulers have no interest in playing the guardian of their subjects in matters of arts and sciences. Furthermore immaturity in matters of religion is not only most noxious but also most dishonorable. But the point of view of a head of state who favors freedom in the arts and sciences goes even farther; for he understands that there is no danger in legislation permitting his subjects to make *public* use of their own reason and to submit *publicly* their thoughts regarding a better framing of such laws together with a frank criticism of existing *legislation.* We have a shining example of this; no prince excels him whom we admire. Only he who is himself enlightened does not fear spectres when he at the same time has a well-disciplined army at his disposal as a guarantee of public peace. Only he can say what (the ruler of a) free state dare not say: *Argue as much as you want and about whatever you want but obey!* Thus we see here as elsewhere an unexpected turn in human affairs just as we observe that almost everything therein is paradoxical. A great degree of civic freedom seems to be advantageous for the freedom of the *spirit* of the people and yet it establishes impassable limits. A lesser degree of such civic freedom provides additional space in which the spirit of a people can develop to its full capacity. Therefore nature has cherished, within its hard shell, the germ of the inclination and need for free *thought.* This free thought gradually acts upon the mind of the people and they gradually become more capable of acting in freedom. Eventually, the government is also influenced by this free thought and thereby it treats man, who is now more than a machine, according to his dignity.

Koenigsberg, September 30, 1784

VII

METAPHYSICAL FOUNDATIONS OF MORALS

[1785]

FIRST SECTION

Transition from the Common Rational Knowledge of Morality to the Philosophical

NOTHING CAN POSSIBLY BE CONCEIVED IN THE WORLD, OR even out of it, which can be called good without qualification, except a GOOD WILL. Intelligence, wit, judgment, and the other *talents* of the mind, however they may be named, or courage, resolution, perseverance, as qualities of temperament, are undoubtedly good and desirable in many respects. But these gifts of nature may also become extremely bad and mischievous if the will which is to make use of these gifts, and which therefore constitutes what is called *character,* is not good. It is the same with the *gifts of fortune.* Power, riches, honor, even health, and the general well-being and contentment with one's condition which is called *happiness,* all inspire pride and often presumption if there is not a good will to correct the influence of these on the mind, and with this to rectify also the whole principle of acting and adapt it to its end. The sight of a being, not adorned with a single feature of a pure and good will, enjoying unbroken prosperity can never give pleasure to an impartial rational spectator. Thus a good will appears to constitute the indispensable condition for being even worthy of happiness.

Indeed, quite a few qualities are of service to this good will itself and may facilitate its action, yet have no intrinsic, unconditional value, but are always presupposing a good will; this qualifies the esteem that we justly have for these qualities and does not permit us to regard them as absolutely good. Moderation in the affections and passions, self-control and calm deliberation are not only good in many respects, but even seem to constitute part of the intrinsic worth of a person; but they are far from deserving to be called good without qualification, although they have been so unconditionally praised by the ancients. For without the principles of a good will, these qualities may become extremely bad. The coolness of a villain not only makes him far more dangerous, but also immediately makes him more abominable in our eyes than he would have been without it.

A good will is good not because of what it performs or effects, nor by its aptness for attaining some proposed end, but simply by virtue of the volition; that is, it is good in itself and when considered by itself is to be esteemed much higher than all that it can bring about in pursuing any inclination, nay even in pursuing the sum total of all inclinations. It might happen that, owing to special misfortune, or to the niggardly provision of a step-motherly nature, this will should wholly lack power to accomplish its purpose. If with its greatest efforts this will should yet achieve nothing and there should remain only good will (to be sure, not a mere wish but the summoning of all means in our power), then, like a jewel, good will would still shine by its own light as a thing having its whole value in itself. Its usefulness or fruitlessness can neither add to nor detract anything from this value. It would be, as it were, only the setting to enable us to handle it the more conveniently in common commerce and to attract to it the attention of those who are not yet experts, but not to recommend it to true experts or to determine its value.

However, there is something so strange in this idea of the

absolute value of the mere will in which no account is taken of its utility, that notwithstanding the thorough assent of even common reason, a suspicion lingers that this idea may perhaps really be the product of mere high-flown fancy, and that we may have misunderstood the purpose of nature in assigning reason as the governor of the will. Therefore, we will examine this idea from this point of view:

We assume, as a fundamental principle, that no organ [designed] for any purpose will be found in the physical constitution of an organized being, except one which is also the fittest and best adapted for that purpose. Now if the proper object of nature for a being with reason and a will was its *preservation,* its *welfare,* in a word its happiness, then nature would have hit upon a very bad arrangement when it selected the reason of the creature to carry out this function. For all the actions which the creature has to perform with a view to this purpose, and the whole rule of its conduct would be far more surely prescribed by [its own] instinct, and that end [happiness] would have been attained by instinct far more certainly than it ever can be by reason. Should reason have been attributed to this favored creature over and above [such instinct], reason would only have served this creature for contemplating the happy constitution of its nature, for admiring it, and congratulating itself thereon, and for feeling thankful for it to the beneficent cause. But [certainly nature would not have arranged it so that] such a creature should subject its desires to that weak and deceptive guidance, and meddle with nature's intent. In a word, nature would have taken care that reason should not turn into *practical* exercise, nor have the presumption, with its feeble insight, to figure out for itself a plan of happiness and the means for attaining it. In fact, we find that the more a cultivated reason applies itself with deliberate purpose to enjoying life and happiness, so much more does the man lack true satisfaction. From this circumstance there arises in many men, if they are candid enough to confess it, a certain degree of *misology;* that is, hatred of reason, especially in the case of those who are most experienced in the use of reason. For, after calculating all the advantages they derive, not only from the invention of all the arts of common luxury, but even from the sciences (which then seem to them only a luxury of the intellect after all) they find that they have actually only brought more trouble upon themselves, rather than gained in happiness. They end by envying, rather than despising, the common run of men who keep closer to the guidance of mere instinct and who do not allow their reason to have much influence on their conduct. We must admit this much; that the judgment of those, who would diminish very much the lofty eulogies on the advantages which reason gives us in regard to the happiness and satisfaction of life, or would even deny these advantages altogether, is by no means morose or ungrateful for the goodness with which the world is governed. At the root of these judgments lies the idea that the existence of world order has a different and far nobler end for which, rather than for happiness, reason is properly intended. Therefore this end must be regarded as the supreme condition to which the private ends of man must yield for the most part.

Thus reason is not competent enough to guide the will with certainty in regard to its objects and the satisfaction of all our wants which it even multiplies to some extent; this purpose is one to which an implanted instinct would have led with much greater certainty. Nevertheless, reason is imparted to us as a practical faculty; that is, as one which is to have influence on the *will*. Therefore, if we admit that nature generally in the distribution of natural propensities has adapted the means to the end, nature's true intention must be to produce a *will*, which is not merely good as a *means* to something else but *good in itself*. Reason is absolutely necessary for this sort of will. Then this will, though indeed not the sole and complete good, must be the supreme good and the condition of every other good, even of the desire for happiness. Under these circumstances, there is nothing inconsistent with the wisdom of nature in the fact that the cultivation of the reason which is requisite for the first and unconditional purpose, does in many ways interfere, at least in this life, with the attainment of the second purpose: happiness, which is always relative. Nay, it may even reduce happiness to nothing without nature failing thereby in her purpose. For reason recognizes the establishment of a good will as its highest practical destination, and is capable of only satisfying its own proper kind in attaining this purpose: the attainment of an end determined only by reason, even when such an attainment may involve many a disappointment over otherwise desirable purposes.

Therefore we must develop the notion of a will which deserves to be highly esteemed for itself and is good without a specific objective, a notion which is implied by sound natural common sense. This notion needs to be clarified rather than expounded. In evaluating our actions this notion always takes first place and constitutes the condition of all the rest. In order to do this we will take the notion of duty which includes that of a good will, although implying certain subjective restrictions and hindrances. However, these hindrances, far from concealing it or rendering it unrecognizable, rather emphasize a good will by contrast and make it shine forth so much the brighter.

I omit here all actions which are already recognized as inconsistent with duty, although they may be useful for this or that purpose. The question whether these actions are done *from duty* cannot arise at all since they conflict with it. I also leave aside those actions which really conform to duty but to which men have *no* direct *inclination,* performing them because they are impelled to do so by some other inclination. For in this case we can readily distinguish whether the action which agrees with duty is done *out of duty* or from a selfish point of view. It is much harder to make this distinction when the action accords with duty and when besides the subject has a *direct* inclination toward it. For example, it is indeed a matter of duty that a dealer should not overcharge an inexperienced purchaser, and wherever there is much commerce the prudent tradesman does not overcharge, but keeps a fixed price for everyone, so that a child buys of him as well as any other. Men are thus *honestly* served; but this is not enough to make us believe that the tradesman has so acted from duty and from principles of honesty; his own advantage required it. It is out of the question in this case to suppose that he might have besides a direct inclination in favor of the buyers, so that out of love, as it were, he should give no advantage to one over another. Hence the action was done neither out of duty nor because of inclination but merely with a selfish view. On the other hand, it is a duty to maintain one's life; in addition everyone also has a direct inclination to do so. But on this account the often anxious care which most men take of their lives has no intrinsic worth and their maxim has no moral import. No doubt they preserve their life *as duty requires,* but not *because duty requires.* The case is different, when adversity and hopeless sorrow have completely taken away the relish for life; if the unfortunate one, strong in mind, indignant at his fate rather than despondent or dejected, longs for death and yet preserves his life without loving it. [If he does this] not from inclination or fear but from duty, then his maxim has a moral worth.

To be beneficent when we can is a duty; besides this, there are many minds so sympathetically constituted that without any other motive of vanity or self-interest, they find a pleasure in spreading joy [about them] and can take delight in the satisfaction of others so far as it is their own work. But I maintain that in such a case, however proper, however amiable an action of this kind may be, it nevertheless has no true moral worth, but is on a level with other inclinations; e.g. the inclination to honor which, if it is happily directed to that which is actually of public utility and accordant with duty and consequently honorable, deserves praise and encouragement but not respect. For the maxim lacks the moral ingredient that such actions be done *out of duty,* not from inclination. Put the case [another way and suppose] that the mind of that philanthropist were clouded by sorrow of his own, extinguishing all sympathy with the lot of others, and that while he still has the power to benefit others in distress he is not touched by their trouble because he is absorbed with his own; suppose that he now tears himself out of this deadening insensibility, and performs the action without any inclination for it, but simply from duty; only then has his action genuine moral worth. Furthermore, if nature has put little sympathy into the heart of this or that man, if a supposedly upright man is by temperament cold and indifferent to the sufferings of others, perhaps because in respect of his own sufferings he is provided with the special gift of patience and fortitude so that he supposes or even requires that others should have the same; such a man would certainly not be the meanest product of nature. But if nature had not specially shaped him to be a philanthropist, would he not find cause in himself for attributing to himself a value far higher than the value of a good-natured temperament could be? Unquestionably. It is just in this that there is brought out the moral worth of the character which is incomparably the highest of all; namely, that he is beneficent, not from inclination, but from duty.

To secure one's own happiness is a duty, at least indirectly; for discontent with one's condition under pressure of many anxieties and amidst unsatisfied wants might easily become a great *temptation to transgression from duty*. But here again, without reference to duty, all men already have the strongest and most intense inclination to happiness, because it is just in this idea that all inclinations are combined in one total. But the precept for happiness is often of such a sort that it greatly interferes with some inclinations. Yet a man cannot form any definite and certain conception of the sum of satisfying all of these inclinations, which is called happiness. It is not then to be wondered at that a single inclination, definite both as to what it promises and as to the time within which it can be gratified, is often able to overcome such a fluctuating idea [as the precept for happiness.]

For instance, a gouty patient can choose to enjoy what he likes and to suffer what he may, since according to his calculation, at least on this occasion he has not sacrificed the enjoyment of the present moment for a possibly mistaken expectation of happiness supposedly found in health. But, if the general desire for happiness does not influence his will, and even supposing that in his particular case health was not a necessary element in his calculation, there yet remains a law even in this case, as in all other cases; that is, he should promote his happiness not from inclination but from duty. Only in following duty would his conduct acquire true moral worth.

Undoubtedly, it is in this manner that we are to understand those passages of the Scripture in which we are commanded to love our neighbor, even our enemy. For love, as an affection, cannot be commanded, but beneficence for duty's sake can be, even though we are not impelled to such kindness by any inclination, and may even be repelled by a natural and unconquerable aversion. This is *practical* love and not *psychological*. It is a love originating in the will and not in the inclination of sentiment, in principles of action, not of sentimental sympathy.

The second proposition is: That an action done from duty derives its moral worth, *not from the purpose* which is to be attained by it, but from the maxim by which it is determined. Therefore the action does not depend on the realization of its objective, but merely on the *principle* of volition by which the action has taken place, without regard to any object of desire. It is clear from what precedes that the purposes which we may have in view for our actions, or their effects as regarded as ends and impulsions of the will, cannot give to actions any unconditional or moral worth. Then in what can their worth consist if it does not consist in the will as it is related to its expected effect? It cannot consist in anything but the *principle of the will*, with no regard to the ends which can be attained by the action. For the will stands between its *a priori* principle which is formal, and its *a posteriori* impulse which is material, as between two roads. As it must be determined by something, it follows that the will must be determined by the formal principle of volition, as when an action is done from duty, in which case every material impulse has been withdrawn from it.

The third proposition, which is a consequence of the preceding two, I would express thus: *Duty is the necessity of an action, resulting from respect for the law.* I may have an *inclination* for an object as the effect of my proposed action, but I cannot have *respect* for an object just for this reason: that it is merely an effect and not an action of will. Similarly, I cannot have respect for an inclination, whether my own or another's; I can at most, if it is my own, approve it; if it is another's I can sometimes even cherish it; that is, look on it as favorable to my own interest. Only the law itself which is connected with my will by no means as an effect but as a principle which does not serve my inclination but outweighs it, or at least in case of choice excludes my inclination from its calculation; only such a law can be an object of respect and hence a command. Now an action done from duty must wholly exclude the influence of inclination, and with it every object of the will, so that nothing remains which can determine the will objectively except the *law*, and [determine the will] subjectively except *pure respect* for this practical law, and hence [pure respect] for the maxim[1] to follow this law even to the thwarting of all my inclinations.

Thus the moral worth of an action does not consist of the effect expected from it, nor from any principle of action which needs to borrow its motive from this expected effect. For, all these effects, agreeableness of one's condition and even the promotion of the happiness of others, all this could have also been brought about by other causes so that for this there would have been no need of the will of a rational being. However, in this

---

[1] A maxim is the subjective principle of volition. The objective principle, that is, what would also serve all rational beings subjectively as a practical principle if reason had full power over desire; this objective principle is the practical *law*.

will alone can the supreme and unconditional good be found. Therefore the pre-eminent good which we call moral can consist in nothing other than *the concept of law* in itself, *which is certainly only possible in a rational being,* in so far as this conception, and not the expected effect, determines the will. This is a good which is already present in the person acting according to it, and we do not have to wait for good to appear in the result. [2]

But what sort of law can it be the conception of which must determine the will, even without our paying any attention to the effect expected from it, in order that this will may be called good absolutely and without qualification? As I have stripped the will of every impulse which could arise for it from obedience to any law, there remains nothing but the general conformity of the will's actions to law in general. Only this conformity

---

[2] Here it might be objected that I take refuge in an obscure feeling behind the word *respect* instead of giving a distinct solution of the question by a concept of reason. But, although respect is a feeling, it is not a feeling *received* through outside influence, but is self-generated by a rational concept, and therefore is specifically distinct from all feelings of the former kind, which may be related either to inclination or fear. What I recognize immediately as a law, I recognize with respect. This merely signifies the consciousness that my will is *subordinate* to a law, without the intervention of other influences on my sense. The immediate determination of the will by the law and the consciousness of this may be called *respect,* so that this may then be regarded as an effect of the law on the subject and not as the *cause* of it. In a word, respect is the conceiving of a value which reduces my self-love. Accordingly, respect is considered neither an object of inclination nor of fear, though it has something analogous to both. The *object* of respect is the *law* only, a law that we impose on *ourselves* and yet recognize as necessary in itself. We are subjected to it as a law without consulting self-love; but as imposed by us on ourselves, it is a result of our will. In the former aspect it has analogy to fear, in the latter to inclination. Respect for a person is properly only respect for the law (of honesty, etc.) of which he gives us an example. Since we also look on the improvement of our talents as a duty we consider that we see in a person of talents the *example of a law,* as it were, to become like him in this by effort and this constitutes our respect. All so-called moral *interest* consists simply in *respect* for the law.

to law is to serve the will as a principle; that is, I am never to act in any way other than *so I could want my maxim also to become a general law*. It is the simple conformity to law in general, without assuming any particular law applicable to certain actions, that serves the will as its principle, and must so serve it, if duty is not to be a vain delusion and a chimerical notion. The common reason of men in their practical judgments agrees perfectly with this and always has in view the principle suggested here. For example, let the question be: When in distress may I make a promise with the intention of not keeping it? I readily distinguish here between the two meanings which the question may have: Whether it is prudent, or whether it is in accordance with duty, to make a false promise. The former undoubtedly may often be the case. I [may] see clearly that it is not enough to extricate myself from a present difficulty by means of this subterfuge, but that it must be carefully considered whether there may not result from such a lie a much greater inconvenience than that from which I am now freeing myself. But, since in spite of all my supposed *cunning* the consequences cannot be foreseen easily; the loss of credit may be much more injurious to me than any mischief which I seek to avoid at present. That being the case, one might consider whether it would not be more *prudent* to act according to a general maxim, and make it a habit to give no promise except with the intention of keeping it. But, it is soon clear that such a maxim is still only based on the fear of consequences. It is a wholly different thing to be truthful from a sense of duty, than to be so from apprehension of injurious consequences. In the first case, the very conceiving of the action already implies a law for me; in the second case, I must first look about elsewhere to see what results may be associated with it which would affect me. For it is beyond all doubt wicked to deviate from the principle of duty; but to be unfaithful to my maxim of prudence may often be very advantageous to me, although it is certainly wiser to abide by it. However, the shortest way, and an unerring one, to discover the answer to this question of whether a lying promise is consistent with duty, is to ask myself, "Would I be content if this maxim of extricating myself from difficulty by a false promise held good as a general law for others as well as for myself?" Would I care to say to myself, "Everyone may make a deceitful promise when he finds himself in a difficulty from which he cannot extricate himself otherwise"? Then I would presently become aware that while I can decide in favor of the lie, I can by no means decide that lying should be a general law. For under such a law there would be no promises at all, since I would state my intentions in vain in regard to my future actions to those who would not believe my allegation, or, if they did so too hastily, they would pay me back in my own coin. Hence, as soon as such a maxim was made a universal law, it would necessarily destroy itself.

Therefore I do not need any sharp acumen to discern what I have to do in order that my will may be morally good. [As I am] inexperienced in the course of the world and incapable of being prepared for all its contingencies, I can only ask myself: "Can you will that your maxim should also be a general law?" If not, then my maxim must be rejected, not because of any disadvantage in it for myself or even for others, but because my maxim cannot fit as a principle into a possible universal legislation, and reason demands immediate respect from me for such legislation. Indeed, I do not *discern* as yet on what this respect is based; into this question the philosopher may inquire. But at least I understand this much: that this respect is an evaluation of the worth that far outweighs all that is recommended by inclination. The necessity of acting from *pure* respect for the practical law [of right action;] is what constitutes duty, to which every other motive must yield, because it is the condition of a will being good *in itself,* and the value of such a will exceeds everything.

Thus we have arrived at the principle of moral knowledge of common human reason. Although common men no doubt do not conceive this principle in such an abstract and universal form, yet they really always have it before their eyes and use it as the standard for their decision. It would be easy to show here how, with this compass in hand, men are well able to distinguish, in every case that occurs, what is good, bad, conformable to duty or inconsistent with it. Without teaching them anything at all new, we are only, like Socrates, directing their attention to the principle they employ themselves and [showing] that we therefore do not need science and philosophy to know what we should do to be honest and good and even wise and virtuous. Indeed, we might well have understood before that the knowledge of what every man ought to do, and hence also [what he ought] to know is within the reach of every man, even the commonest. We cannot help admiring what a great advantage practical judgment has over theoretical judgment in men's common sense. If, in theoretical judgments, common reason ventures to depart from the laws of experience and from the perceptions of the senses, it plunges into many inconceivabilities and self-contradictions, [or] at any rate into a chaos of uncertainty, obscurity and instability. But in the practical sphere [of just action] it is right that, when one excludes all sense impulses from [determining] practical laws, the power of judgment of common sense begins to show itself to special advantage. It then even becomes a subtle matter as to whether common sense provides tricky excuses for conscience in relation to other claims regarding what is to be called right, or whether, for its own guidance, common sense seeks to determine honestly the value of [particular] actions. In the latter case, common sense has as good a hope of hitting the mark as any philosopher can promise himself. A common man is almost more sure of doing so, because the philosopher cannot have any other [better] principle and may easily perplex his judgment by a multitude of considerations foreign to the matter in hand, and so he may turn from the right way. Therefore would it not be wiser in moral matters to acquiesce in the judgment of common reason, or at most to call in philosophy only for rendering the system of morals more complete and intelligible and its rules more convenient for use, especially for disputation, but not to deflect common sense from its happy simplicity, or to lead it through philosophy into a new path of inquiry and instruction?

Innocence is indeed a glorious thing, only it is a pity that it cannot maintain itself well and is easily seduced. On this account even wisdom, which otherwise consists more in conduct than in knowledge, yet has need of science, not in order to learn from it, but to secure for its own precepts acceptance and permanence. In opposition to all the commands of duty that reason respresents to man as so greatly deserving respect, man feels within himself a powerful counterpoise in his wants and inclinations, the entire satisfaction of which he sums up under the name of happiness. Reason issues its commands unyield-ingly, without promising anything to the inclinations and with disregard and contempt, as it were, for these demands which are so impetuous and at the same time so plausible and which will not allow themselves to be suppressed by any command. Hence there arises a natural *dialectic*; that is, a disposition to argue against these strict laws of duty and to question their validity, or at least to question their purity and strictness. [There is also a disposition] to make them more accordant, if possible, with our wishes and inclinations; that is to say, to corrupt them at their very source and to destroy their value entirely, an act that even common practical reason cannot ultimately approve.

Thus the *common reason of man* is compelled to leave its proper sphere and to take a step into the field of a *practical philosophy*, but not for satisfying any desire to speculate, which never occurs to it as long as it is content to be mere sound rea-son. But the purpose is to secure on practical grounds infor-mation and clear instruction respecting the source of the princi-ple [of common sense] and the correct definition of this principle as contrasted with the maxims which are based on wants and inclinations, so that common sense may escape from the perplexity of opposing claims, and not run the risk of losing all genuine moral principles through the equivocation into which it easily falls. Thus when practical, common reason cultivates itself, there arises insensibly in it a dialectic forcing it to seek aid in philosophy, just like what happens to practical reason in its theoretic use. Therefore in this case as well as in the other, [common sense] will find no rest but in a thorough critical examination of our reason.

SECOND SECTION

Transition from Popular Moral Philosophy to the Metaphysics of Morals

If hitherto we have drawn our concept of duty from the common use of our practical reason, it is by no means to be inferred that we have treated it as an empirical concept. On the contrary, if we attend to the experience of men's conduct, we meet frequent and, as we admit ourselves, just complaints that there is not to be found a single certain example of the disposition to act from pure duty. Although many things are done *in conformity* to what duty prescribes, it is nevertheless always doubtful whether they are done strictly *out of duty* [which would have to be the case if they are] to have a moral value. Hence, in all ages there have been philosophers who have denied altogether that this disposition actually exists in human actions at all, and who have ascribed everything to a more or less refined self-love. Not that they have on that account questioned the soundness of the conception of morality; on the contrary they have spoken with sincere regret of the frailty and corruption of human nature, which though noble enough to take as its law an idea so worthy of respect, is yet too weak to follow it, and employs reason, which ought to give it the law, only for the purpose of accommodating the inclinations, whether single or, at best, in the greatest possible harmony with one another. In fact it is absolutely impossible to ascertain by experience with complete certainty a single case in which the maxim of an action, however right in itself, rested simply on moral grounds and on the conception of duty. Sometimes it happens that with the sharpest self-examination we can find nothing, besides the moral principle of duty, powerful enough to move us to this or that action and to such a great sacrifice; yet we cannot infer from this with certainty that it was not some really secret impulse of self-love, under the false appearance of that idea [of the moral principle of duty] that was the actual determining cause of the will. We then like to flatter ourselves by falsely taking credit for a more noble motive. In fact we can never, even by the strictest self-examination, penetrate completely [to the causes] behind the secret springs of action, since when we ask about moral worth, we are not concerned with actions but with their inward principles which we do not see.

Moreover, we cannot better serve the wishes of those people, who ridicule all morality as a mere chimera of human imagination overstepping itself through vanity, than by conceding to them that concepts of duty must be drawn only from experience, just as people are ready to think out of indolence that this is also the case with all other notions; doing this would prepare a certain triumph for them. Out of love for humanity, I am willing to admit that most of our actions accord with duty, but on examining them more closely we encounter everywhere the cherished self which is always dominant. It is this self that men have consideration for and not the strict command of duty which would often require self-denial. Without being an enemy to virtue, a cool observer who does not mistake an ardent wish for good for goodness itself, may sometimes doubt whether true virtue is actually found anywhere in the world, and do this especially as his years increase and his judgment is in part made wiser by experience and in part more acute by observation. This being so, nothing can save us from altogether abandoning our ideas of duty, nothing can maintain in our soul a well-grounded respect for the law; nothing but the clear conviction that, although there have never been actions really springing from such pure sources, yet . . . reason, by itself and independent of all experience, ordains what ought to be done. Accordingly actions, of which hitherto the world has perhaps never had an example and of which the feasibility might even be very much doubted by anyone basing everything on experience, are nevertheless inflexibly commanded by reason; e.g., even though a sincere friend might never have existed up till now, [just the same] pure sincerity in friendship is required of every man not a whit less, because above and beyond all experience this duty is obligatory in the idea of a reason that determines the will by *a priori* principles.

Unless we deny that the notion of morality has any truth or reference to any possible object, we must admit that its law must be valid not only for men, but for all *rational creatures generally,* not only under certain contingent conditions or with exceptions, but with *absolute necessity.* [When we admit this] then it is clear that no experience could enable us even to infer the possibility of such apodictic laws. What right have we to demand unbounded respect, as for a universal precept of every rational creature, for something that only holds true under the contingent conditions of humanity? Or, how could laws determining *our* will be regarded as laws determining the will of rational beings generally, if these laws were only empirical and did not originate wholly *a priori* from pure and practical reason?

Nor could anything be more ill-advised for morality than our wishing to derive it from examples. Every example set before me must first be tested by principles of morality [to determine] whether it is worthy of serving as an original example; that is, as a model or pattern. An example can by no means furnish authoritatively the concept of morality. Even the Holy One of the Gospels must first be compared with our ideal of moral perfection before we can recognize Him as such; and so He says of himself, "Why call ye Me (whom ye see) good? None is good (the model of good) but God only (whom ye do not see)!" But whence do we acquire the concept of God as the supreme good? Simply from the *idea* of moral perfection which reason sketches *a priori* and connects inseparably with the concept of a free will. Imitation has no place at all in morality, and examples serve only for encouragement; that is, they make feasible beyond any doubt what the law commands and they make visible what the practical rule expresses more generally, but they can never authorize us to set aside the true original existing in reason and to guide ourselves by examples. Therefore, if there is no genuine supreme principle of morality, but only that which rests on pure reason independent of all experience, I think it is unnecessary even to put the question as to whether it is good to exhibit these concepts in their generality (*in abstracto*) as they are established *a priori* along with the principles belonging to them, if our knowledge is to be distinguished from the *vulgar* and called philosophical. Indeed, in our times this question might perhaps be necessary; for if we collected votes on whether pure rational knowledge, apart from everything empirical, that is to say, a metaphysic of morals, is to be preferred to a popular practical philosophy; it is easy to guess which side would carry more weight.

This descent to popular notions is certainly very commendable if the ascent to the principles of pure reason has taken place first and has been accomplished satisfactorily. This implies that first we should establish ethics on metaphysics and, when it is firmly founded, procure a hearing for ethics by giving it a popular character. But it is quite absurd to try to be popular in the first inquiry on which the soundness of the principles depends. Not only can this procedure never lay claim to having the very rare merit of a true *philosophical popularity* for there is no sense in being intelligible if one renounces all thoroughness of insight, but this procedure also produces a disgusting medley of compiled observations and half-reasoned principles. Shallow pates enjoy this because it can be used for everyday chat, but those with deeper understanding find only confusion in this method and, being unsatisfied and unable to assist themselves, turn away their eyes, while philosophers, seeing quite clearly through this confusion, are little heeded when they call men away for a time from this pretended popularity, so they may be rightfully popular after attaining a definite insight.

We only need to look at the attempts of moralists in [using] that favorite fashion and we shall find [a variety of things:] at one point the special destination of human nature including the idea of a rational nature generally, at another point perfection, at another happiness, here moral sense, there fear of God, a little of this and a little of that, all in a marvelous mixture. It does not occur to them to ask whether the principles of morality are to be sought at all in the knowledge of human nature which we can have only from experience. If this is not so, if these principles are completely *a priori* and are to be encountered free from everything empirical only in pure rational concepts and nowhere else, not even in the smallest degree, shall we then adopt the method of making this a separate inquiry as a pure practical philosophy? Or [shall we construct], if one may use a name so decried, a metaphysic of morals[3] and complete it by itself and ask the public wishing for popular treatment to await the outcome of this undertaking?

Such a metaphysic of morals, completely isolated and unmixed with any anthropology, theology, physics, or hyperphysics, and still less with occult qualities which we might call superphysical, is not only an indispensable condition for all sound theoretical knowledge of duties, but at the same time it is a

---

[3] Just as pure mathematics is differentiated from applied and pure logic from applied, so, if we choose, we may also differentiate pure philosophy of morals (metaphysics) from applied (viz., applied to human nature). Also, by this designation we are at once reminded that moral principles are not based on properties of human nature, but must exist *a priori* of themselves; practical rules for every rational nature must be capable of being deduced from such principles and accordingly deduced for the rational nature of man.

desideratum highly important to the actual fulfilment of the precepts of duties. For the pure concept of duty unmixed with any foreign element of experienced attractions, in a word, the pure concept of moral law in general, exercises an influence on the human heart through reason alone. . . . This influence is so much more powerful than all other impulses [4] which may be derived from the field of experience, that in the consciousness of its dignity it despises such impulses and by degrees can become their master. An eclectic ethics compounded partly of motives drawn from feelings and inclinations and partly from concepts of reason, will necessarily make the mind waver between motives which cannot be brought under any one principle, and will therefore lead to good only by mere accident, and may often lead to evil.

It is clear from what has been said that all moral concepts have their seat and origin completely *a priori* in the reason, and have it in the commonest reason just as truly as in what is speculative in the highest degree. Moral concepts cannot be obtained by abstraction from any empirical and hence merely contingent knowledge. It is exactly this purity in origin that makes them worthy of serving our supreme practical principle [for right action] and, as we add anything empirical, we detract in proportion from their genuine influence and from the absolute value of actions. It is not only very necessary from a

---

[4] I have a letter from the late excellent Sulzer, in which he asks me what might be the reason for moral instruction accomplishing so little although it contains much that is convincing to reason. My answer was postponed in order that I might make it complete. But it is simply this: teachers themselves do not have their own notions clear, and when they endeavor to make up for this by suggesting all kinds of motives for moral goodness and in trying to make their medicine strong they spoil it. For, the most ordinary observations show that this is an act of honesty done with steadfast mind and without regard for any advantage in this world or another, and when [persisted in] even under the greatest temptations of need or allurement it will . . . elevate the soul and inspire one with the wish to be able to act in a like manner. Even fairly young children feel this impression and one should never represent duties to them in any other light.

purely speculative point of view, but it is also of the greatest practical importance to derive these notions and laws from pure reason, to present them pure and unmixed, and even to determine the compass of this practical or pure rational knowledge; that is, to determine the entire faculty of pure practical reason. In doing so we must not make the principles of pure practical reason dependent on the particular nature of human reason, though in speculative philosophy this may be permitted and even necessary at times. Since moral laws ought to hold true for every rational creature we must derive them from the general concept of a rational being. Although morality has need of anthropology for its application to man, yet in this way, as in the first step, we must treat morality independently as pure philosophy; that is, as metaphysics, complete in itself. . . . We must fully realize that unless we are in possession of this pure philosophy not only would it be vain to determine the moral element of duty in right actions for purposes of speculative criticism, but it would be impossible to base morals on their genuine principles. This is true even for common practical purposes, but more especially for moral instruction which is to produce pure moral dispositions and to engraft them on men's minds for promoting the greatest possible good in the world.

Our purpose in this study must be not only to advance by natural steps from common moral judgment, which is very worthy of respect, to the philosophical, as has been done already, but also to progress from a popular philosophy which only gets as far as it can by groping with the help of examples, to metaphysics, which does not allow itself to be held back by anything empirical and which goes as far as ideal concepts in measuring the whole extent of this kind of rational knowledge wherever examples fail us. [In order to accomplish this purpose] we must clearly describe and trace the practical faculty of reason, advancing from general rules to the point where the notion of duty springs from it.

Everything in nature works according to laws. Rational beings alone have the faculty for acting according *to the concept* of laws; that is, according to principles. [In other words, rational beings alone] have a will. Since deriving actions from principles requires *reason,* the will is nothing more than practical reason. If reason infallibly determines the will, then the actions of such a being that are recognized as objectively necessary are also subjectively necessary. The will is a faculty for choosing *only that* which reason, independently of inclination, recognizes as practically necessary; that is, as good. But if reason does not sufficiently determine the will by itself, if the latter is also subject to the subjective conditioning of particular impulses which do not always coincide with the objective conditions; in a word, if the will *in itself* does not completely accord with reason, as is actually the case with men, then the actions which are objectively recognized as necessary are subjectively contingent. Determining such a will according to objective laws is compulsory (*Nötigung*). This means that the relation of objective laws to a will not thoroughly good is conceived as the determination of the will of a rational being by principles of reason which the will, because of its nature, does not necessarily follow.

The concept of an objective principle, in so far as it is compulsory for a will, is called a command of reason and the formulation of such a command is called an IMPERATIVE.

All imperatives are expressed by the word *ought* (or *shall*) and are indicating thereby the relation of an objective law of reason to a will, which, because of its subjective constitution, is not necessarily determined by this [compulsion]. Such imperatives may state that something would be good to do or to forbear from doing, but they are addressing themselves to a will which does not always do a thing merely because that thing is represented as good to do. The practically *good* determines the will by means of the concepts of reason, and consequently from objective, not subjective causes; that is, [it determines them] on principles which are valid for every rational being as such.

The practically good is distinguishable from the *pleasant* which influences the will only by means of sensations from subjective causes and which is valid only for the particular sense of this or that man and is not a principle of reason holding true for everyone. [5]

Therefore a perfectly good will would be equally subject to objective laws of good [action], but could not be conceived thereby as *compelled* to act lawfully by itself. Because of its subjective constitution it can only be determined by the concept of the good. Consequently no imperatives hold true for the Divine will, or in general for a *holy* will. *Ought* is out of place here because the act of willing is already necessarily in unison with the law. Therefore imperatives are only formulations for expressing the relation of the objective laws of all volition to the subjective imperfections of the will of this or that rational being; that is, the human will.

All *imperatives* command either *hypothetically* or *categorically*. . . . Since every practical law represents a possible action as good, and on this account as necessary for a subject who can determine practically by reason, all imperatives are formulations determining an action which is necessary according to the principle of a will in some respects good. If the action is good

---

[5] The dependence of the desires on sensations is called inclination, and accordingly always indicates a *want*. The dependence of a contingently determinable will on principles of reason is called an *interest*. Therefore, this dependence is only found in the case of a dependent will, which of itself does not always conform to reason. We cannot conceive of the Divine will having any interest. But the human will can *take an interest* without necessarily acting *from interest*. The former signifies practical interest in the action, the latter *psychological* interest in the object of the action. The first merely indicates dependence of the will on principles of reason in themselves and the second merely indicates dependence on principles of reason for the sake of inclination, reason supplying only the practical rules of how the demands of inclination may be satisfied. In the first case the action interests me in the object of the action, inasmuch as it is pleasant for me. We have seen, in the first section, that in an action done from duty we must not look to the interest in the object but only to the interest in the action itself, and in its rational principle: the law.

only as a means *to something else,* then the imperative is *hypothetical.* If the action is conceived as good *in itself* and consequently as necessarily being the principle of a will which of itself conforms to reason then it is *categorical.*

Thus the imperative declares what, of my possible actions, would be good. It presents the practical rule in relation to a will which does not perform an action forthwith simply because it is good. For, either the subject does not always know that such action is good or, even should the subject know this, its maxims might be opposed to the objective principles of practical reason.

Consequently the hypothetical imperative only states that an action is good for some purpose, *potential* or *actual.* In the first case the principle is *problematical,* in the second it is *assertorial* [positively asserting a claim and may be called a] practical principle. The categorical imperative which declares an action to be objectively necessary in itself without reference to any purpose, i.e., without any other end, is valid as an *apodictic* (practical) principle.

Whatever is possible through the ability of some rational being may also be considered as a possible purpose of some will. Therefore the principles of action concerning the means needed to attain some possible purpose are really infinitely numerous. All sciences have a practical aspect consisting of problems expressing that some end is possible for us, and of imperatives directing how it may be attained. Therefore, these may, in general, be called imperatives of *skill.* There is no question as to whether the end is rational and good, but only as to what one must do in order to attain it. The precepts for the physician to make his patient thoroughly healthy, and for a poisoner to ensure certain death, are equivalent in that each serves to effect its purpose perfectly. Since in early youth it cannot be known what purposes are likely to occur to us in the course of life, parents seek to have their children taught a *great many things* and provide for their *skill* in using means for all sorts of purposes. They cannot be sure whether any particular purpose may perhaps hereafter be an objective for their pupil; it is possible that he might aim at any of them. This anxiety is so great that parents commonly neglect to form and correct their judgment on the value of the things which may be chosen as ends.

However there is *one* end which may actually be assumed to be an end for all rational beings, there is one purpose which they not only *may* have, but which we may assume with certainty that they all actually *do have* by natural necessity; that is *happiness*. The hypothetical imperative expressing the practical necessity of an action as a means for the advancement of happiness is assertorial. We are not presenting it as necessary for an uncertain and merely possible purpose, but for a purpose which we may presuppose with certainty and *a priori* for every man, because it belongs to his being. Now a man's skill in choosing the means to his own greatest well-being may be called *prudence* in the most specific sense. [6] Thus the imperative which refers to the choice of means to one's own happiness, that is, the precept of prudence, is still hypothetical. The action is not commanded absolutely but only as a means to another purpose. Whereas, the categorical imperative directly commands a certain conduct without being conditioned by any other attainable purpose. . . . This imperative may be called the imperative of morality (*Sittlichkeit*).

There is also a marked distinction among the acts of willing according to these three kinds of principles resulting from the *dissimilarity* in the obligation of the will. In order to differentiate them more clearly, I think they would be most suitably classified as either *rules* of skill, *counsels* of prudence, or *com-*

---

[6] The word prudence is taken in two senses: In one it may mean knowledge of the world, in the other, private prudence. The first is a man's ability to influence others so as to use them for his own purposes. The second is the insight to combine all these purposes for his own lasting benefit. This latter is properly that to which the value of even the former is reduced, and when a man is prudent in the former sense, but not in the latter, we might better say of him that he is clever and cunning, but on the whole, imprudent.

mands or laws of morality. For it is only *law* that involves the concept of an *unconditional necessity* which is objective and hence universally valid. Commands are laws that must be obeyed; that is, must be adhered to even when inclination is opposed. Indeed, counsels involve [a certain kind of] necessity, but only one which can hold true under a contingent subjective condition. They depend on whether this or that man counts this or that [object] as essential to his happiness. By contrast, the categorical imperative is not limited by any condition. . . . We might also call the first kind of imperatives *technical* as belonging to art, the second *pragmatic* [7] as belonging to welfare, and the third *moral* as belonging to free conduct generally, that is, to morals.

The question now arises: How are all these imperatives possible? This question is to ascertain, not how the action commanded by the imperative can be carried out, but merely how the compulsion of will expressed by the imperative can be conceived. I should think that no special explanation is needed to show how an imperative related to skill is possible. Whoever wills the end, also wills, so far as reason decisively influences his conduct, the means in his power which are indispensable for achieving this end. This proposition is analytical in regard to the volition. For, in willing an object as an effect, there is already implied therein that I myself am acting as a cause, that is, I make use of the means. From the concept of the willed end, the imperative derives the concept of the actions necessary for achieving this end. No doubt synthetic propositions will have to be employed in defining the means to a proposed end, but they do not concern the principle, the act of the will but

---

[7] It seems to me that the proper meaning of the word *pragmatic* may be most accurately defined in this way: *Sanctions* are called pragmatic when they flow properly not from the law of the states as necessary enactments, but from *precaution* for the general welfare. A history is composed pragmatically when it teaches *prudence;* i.e., instructs the world how it can better provide for its interests, or at least as well as did the men of former times.

only the object and its realization. To give an example: in order to bisect a line I must draw two intersecting arcs from its end points. Admittedly, this is taught by mathematics in synthetic propositions. But if I know that the intended operation can only be performed by this process, then it is an analytical proposition to say that in fully willing the operation, I also will the action required for it. For [assuming that I want a certain thing] it is just the same to conceive that thing as an effect which I can only produce in a certain way as to conceive of myself as acting in this way.

If it were equally easy to give a definite concept of happiness [as of simpler ends], the imperatives of prudence would correspond exactly with those of skill, and would likewise be analytical. It could then be said that whoever wills the end also wills the indispensable means thereto which are in his power. But unfortunately the notion of happiness is so indefinite that although every man wishes to attain it, he never can say definitely and consistently what it is that he really wishes and wills. The reason is that the elements belonging to the notion of happiness are altogether empirical; that is, they must be borrowed from experience. Nevertheless, the idea of happiness implies something absolute and whole; a maximum of well-being in my present and all future circumstances. Now, it is impossible for even the most clear-sighted and most powerful being, as long as it is supposedly finite, to frame for itself a definite concept of what it really wills [when it wants to be happy]. If he wills riches, how much anxiety, envy, and snares might not be drawn upon his shoulders thereby? If he wills knowledge and discernment, perhaps such knowledge might only prove to be so much sharper sight showing him much more fearfully the unavoidable evils now concealed from him, or suggesting more wants for his desires which already give him concern enough. If he should will a long life, who can guarantee him that it will not be a long misery? If he should at least have health, how often has infirmity of the body restrained a man from excesses into which perfect health would have allowed him to fall? And so on. In short, a human being is unable with certainty to determine by any principle what would make him truly happy, because to do so he would have to be omniscient. Therefore, we cannot act on any definite principles to secure happiness, but only on counsels derived from experience; e.g., the frugality, courtesy, reserve, etc., which experience teaches us will promote well-being, for the most part. Hence it follows that the imperatives of prudence do not command at all, strictly speaking; that is, they cannot present actions objectively as practically *necessary* so that they are to be regarded as *counsels* (*consilia*) of reason rather than precepts (*praecepta*). The problem of determining certainly and generally which action would most promote the happiness of a rational being is completely insoluble. Consequently, no imperative respecting happiness is possible, for such a command should, in a strict sense, command men to do what makes them happy. Happiness is an ideal, not of reason, but of imagination resting solely on empirical grounds. It is vain to expect that these grounds should define an action for attaining the totality of a series of consequences that are really endless. However, this imperative of prudence could be an analytical proposition if we assume that the means to happiness could, with certainty, be assigned. For, this imperative is distinguished from the imperative of skill only by this; in the latter the end is merely possible [and available to be chosen]; in the former the end is given. However, both only prescribe the means to an end which we assume to have been willed. It follows that the imperative which calls for the willing of the means by him who wills the end is analytical in both cases. Thus there is no difficulty in regard to the possibility of this kind of imperative either.

On the other hand, the question of how the imperative of *morality* is possible is undoubtedly the only question demanding a solution as this imperative is not at all hypothetical, and the objective necessity it presents cannot rest on any hypothesis, as is the case with hypothetical imperatives. Only we must never leave out of consideration the fact that we *cannot* determine *by any example,* i.e., empirically, whether there is any such imperative at all. Rather is it to be feared that all those apparently categorical imperatives may actually be hypothetical. For instance, when you have a precept such as: thou shalt not promise deceitfully, and it is assumed that the [normative] necessity of this is not a mere counsel to avoid some other evil, [in which case] it might mean: you shall not make a lying promise lest it become known and your credit would be destroyed. On the contrary, an action of this kind should be regarded as evil in itself so that the imperative of the prohibition is categorical. Yet we cannot show with certainty in any instance that the will is determined merely by the law without any other source of action, although this may appear to be so. It is always possible that fear of disgrace, also perhaps obscure dread of other dangers, may have a secret influence on the will. Who can prove by experience the non-existence of a cause when all that experience tells us is that we do not perceive it? In such a case the so-called moral imperative, which appears to be categorical and unconditional, would really only be a pragmatic precept, drawing our attention to our own interests, and merely teaching us to take these interests into consideration.

Therefore we shall have to investigate *a priori* the possibility of a *categorical* imperative, since, in this case, we do not have the advantage that the imperative's reality is given in experience, so that the elucidation of its possibility would be needed only for explaining it, not for establishing it. It can be discerned that the categorical imperative has the purport of a practical law. All the rest may certainly be called *principles* of the will but not laws, since whatever is merely necessary for attaining some casual purpose may be considered contingent in itself, and at any time we can be free from the precept if we give up the purpose. However the unconditional command leaves the will no liberty to choose the opposite, and consequently only the will carries with it that necessity we require in a law.

Secondly, in the case of this categorical imperative or law of morality the difficulty [of discerning its possibility] is very profound. It is *a priori*, a synthetic, practical proposition[8] and as there is so much difficulty in discerning the possibility of speculative propositions of this kind, it may readily be supposed that the difficulty will be no less with the practical.

In [approaching] this problem we will first inquire whether the mere concept of a categorical imperative may not perhaps supply us with its formula also, which contains the proposition that alone can be a categorical imperative. Even if we know the tenor of such an absolute command, yet how it is possible will require further special and laborious study which we will postpone to the last section.

When I conceive of a hypothetical imperative at all, I do not know previously what it will contain until I am given the condition. But when I conceive of a categorical imperative I know at once what it contains. In addition to the law, the imperative contains only the necessity that the maxim[9] conform to this law. As the maxim contains no condition restricting the maxim, nothing remains but the general statement of the law to which the maxim of the action should conform, and it is only this conformity that the imperative properly represents as necessary.

---

[8] I connect the act with the will without presupposing a condition resulting from any inclination but *a priori*, and therefore necessarily (though only objectively; that is, assuming the idea of a reason possessing full power over all subjective motives). Therefore this is a practical proposition which does not analytically deduce the willing for an action from another already presupposed proposition (for we have not such a perfect will), but connects it immediately with the concept of the will of a rational being, as something not contained in it.

[9] A maxim is a subjective principle of action and must be distinguished from an *objective principle*; namely, practical law. The former contains the practical rule set by reason according to the conditions of the subject (often its ignorance or its inclinations); hence it is the principle on which the subject *acts*; but the law is the objective principle valid for every rational being and is the principle on which the being *ought to act*; that is, an imperative.

Therefore there is only one categorical imperative, namely this: *Act only on a maxim by which you can will that it, at the same time, should become a general law.*

Now, if all imperatives of duty can be deduced from this one imperative as easily as from their principle, then we shall be able at least to show what we understand by it and what this concept means, although it would remain undecided whether what is called duty is not just a vain notion.

Since the universality of the law constitutes what is properly called *nature* in the most general sense [as to form]; that is, the existence of things as far as determined by general laws, the general imperative duty may be expressed thus: *Act as if the maxim of your action were to become by your will a general law of nature.*

We will now enumerate a few duties, adopting the usual division of duties to ourselves and to others, and of perfect and imperfect duties. [10]

1. A man, while reduced to despair by a series of misfortunes and feeling wearied of life, is still so far in possession of his reason that he can ask himself whether it would not be contrary to his duty to himself to take his own life. Now he inquires whether the maxim of his action could become a general law of nature. His maxim is: Out of self-love I consider it a principle to shorten my life when continuing it is likely to bring more misfortune than satisfaction. The question then simply is whether this principle of self-love could become a general law of nature. Now we see at once that a system of nature, whose law would be to destroy life by the very feeling designed to compel the maintenance of life, would contradict itself, and therefore could not exist as a system of nature; hence that maxim cannot possibly be a general law of nature and conse-

[10] It must be noted here that I reserve the classification of duties for a future metaphysic of morals; so here I only give a few arbitrary duties as examples.

quently it would be wholly inconsistent with the supreme principle of all duty.

2. Another man finds himself forced by dire need to borrow money. He knows that he will not be able to repay it, but he also sees that nothing will be lent him unless he promises firmly to repay it within a definite time. He would like to make this promise but he still has enough conscience to ask himself: Is it not unlawful and contrary to my duty to get out of a difficulty in this way? However, suppose that he does decide to do so, the maxim of his action would then be expressed thus: When I consider myself in want of money, I shall borrow money and promise to repay it although I know that I never can. Now this principle of self-love or of one's own advantage may perhaps be agreeable to my whole future well-being; but the question is now: Is it right? Here I change the suggestion of self-love into a general law and state the question thus: How would it be if my maxim were a general law? I then realize at once that it could never hold as a general law of nature but would necessarily contradict itself. For if it were a general law that anyone considering himself to be in difficulties would be able to promise whatever he pleases intending not to keep his promise, the promise itself and its object would become impossible since no one would believe that anything was promised him, but would ridicule all such statements as vain pretenses.

3. A third man finds in himself a talent which with the help of some education might make him a useful man in many respects. But he finds himself in comfortable circumstances, and prefers to indulge in pleasure rather than to take pains in developing and improving his fortunate natural capacities. He asks, however, whether his maxim of neglecting his natural gifts, besides agreeing with his inclination toward indulgence, agrees also with what is called duty. He sees then that nature could indeed subsist according to such a general law, though men (like the South Sea Islanders) let their talents rust and devote their

lives merely to idleness, amusement, and the propagation of their species, in a word, to enjoyment. But he cannot possibly *will* that this should be a general law of nature or be implanted in us as such by an instinct of nature. For, as a rational being, he necessarily wills that his faculties be developed, since they have been given to serve him for all sorts of possible purposes.

4. A fourth, prosperous man, while seeing others whom he could help having to struggle with great hardship thinks: What concern is it of mine? Let everyone be as happy as heaven pleases or as he can make himself. I will take nothing from him nor even envy him, but I do not wish either to contribute anything to his welfare or assist him in his distress. There is no doubt that if such a way of thinking were a general law, society might get along very well and doubtless even better than if everyone were to talk of sympathy and good will or even endeavor occasionally to put it into practice, but then [were to] cheat when one could and so betray the rights of man or otherwise violate them. But although it is possible that a general law of nature might exist in terms of that maxim, it is impossible to *will* that such a principle should have the general validity of a law of nature. For a will which resolved this would contradict itself, inasmuch as many a time one would need the love and sympathy of others and by such a law of nature, sprung from one's own will, one would deprive himself of all hope of the aid he desires.

These are a few of the many actual duties, or at least what we regard as such, which derive clearly from the one principle that we have established. We must be *able to will* that a maxim of our action should be a general law. This is the canon of any moral assessment at all of such action. Some actions are such that their maxims cannot even be *conceived* as a general law of nature without contradiction, let alone that one could *will* that these maxims *should* become such laws. Other actions reveal no such intrinsic impossibility, but still it is impossible to *will* that their maxim should be elevated to the universality of a law of nature, since such a will would contradict itself. It can be easily seen that the former would conflict with strict or more specific, inexorable duty, the latter merely with a broader (meritorious) duty. Therefore, all duties, in regard to their compulsory nature (not the object of their action), depend on the same principle as the above illustrations conclusively show.

If we now watch ourselves for any transgression of duty, we shall find that we actually do not will that our maxim should be a general law in such cases. On the contrary, we will that the opposite should remain a general law. We merely take the liberty of making an *exception* in our own favor or (just for this time) in favor of our inclination. Consequently, if we considered all cases from the point of view of reason, we should find a contradiction in our own will; namely, that a certain principle is objectively necessary as a general law and yet is subjectively not general but has exceptions. In regarding our action on the one hand from the point of view of a will wholly conformed to reason, and on the other hand looking at the same action from the point of view of a will affected by inclination, there is really no contradiction but an antagonism on the part of inclination to the precept of reason which turns the universality of the principle into a mere generality, so that the principle of practical reason can meet the maxim half way.

Now although our own impartial judgment cannot justify this, it can prove that we do really acknowledge the validity of the categorical imperative and (with due respect) take just a few liberties with it, which we consider unimportant and at the same time forced upon us.

Thus we have at least established this much; that if duty is a concept which is to have any import and real controlling authority over our actions, it can only be expressed in a categorical and never in hypothetical imperatives. It is also of great importance that the content of the categorical imperative be presented clearly and definitely for every purpose; the categorical imperative must contain the principle of all duty if there is such a thing at all. However, we cannot yet prove *a priori* that such an imperative actually exists; that there is a practical law which commands absolutely by itself and without any other impulse and that compliance with this law is duty.

To be able to do that, it is extremely important to heed the warning that we cannot possibly think of deducing the reality of this principle from *particular attributes of human nature*. Duty is to be the practical, unconditional necessity for action; it must hold therefore for all rational beings (to whom an imperative can refer at all), and *for this reason only* it must also be a law for all human wills. On the other hand, whatever is deduced from the particular natural make-up of human beings, from certain feelings and propensities[11] and, if possible, even from any particular tendency of human reason proper which does not need to show in the will of every rational being. [Whatever is so deduced] may indeed furnish a maxim, but not a law. It may offer us a subjective principle on which we may act and may have propensities and inclinations, but [it does not give us] an objective principle by which we should be *constrained* to act, even though all our propensities, inclinations, and natural dispositions were opposed to it. In fact, the maxim evinces the sublime quality and intrinsic dignity of the command that the more clearly duty holds true, the less its subjective impulses favor it and the more they oppose such duty without being able in the slightest to weaken the binding character of the law, or to diminish its validity. . . .

Therefore, every empirical element is not only quite incapable of aiding the principle of morality, but is even highly prejudicial to the purity of morals. For the proper and inestimable value of a genuine good will consists just in the principle of

---

11 [Kant distinguishes *Hang* (propensity) from *Neigung* (inclination) as follows: *Hang* is a predisposition to the desire of some enjoyment; in other words, it is the subjective possibility of excitement of a certain desire preceding the concept of its object. When the enjoyment has been experienced it produces a *Neigung* (inclination) for it, which accordingly is defined "habitual, sensible desire." See below Pp 368 ff.—Ed.]

action being free from all contingent causes which experience alone can furnish. We cannot repeat our warning too often against this lax and even low habit of thought which searches empirical motives and laws for principles. Human reason when weary likes to rest on this cushion and in a dream of sweet illusions it substitutes for morality a bastard made up of limbs of quite different origin which appears as anything one chooses to see in it, save as virtue to one who has once beheld her in her true form.[12]

The question then is this: Is it a necessary law *for all rational beings* that they should always judge their actions by maxims which they can will themselves to serve as general laws? If this is so, then this must be related (altogether *a priori*) to the very concept of the will of a rational being. But in order to discover this relationship we must, however reluctantly, take a step into metaphysics, although into a domain of it distinct from speculative philosophy; namely, into the metaphysic of morals. In practical philosophy, where one is not concerned with the reasons of what *happens* but with the laws of what *ought to happen* though it never may, that is, with objective practical laws, we need not inquire into the reasons why anything pleases or displeases, how the pleasure of mere sensation differs from taste, and whether the latter differs from a general rational enjoyment. [There we need not ask] for the grounds of pleasure or pain, how desires and inclinations arise from it, and how through the influence of reason from these in turn arise maxims. All this belongs to an empirical psychology which would constitute the second part of the natural sciences viewed as the *philosophy of nature* so far as it is based on *empirical laws*.

However, here we are concerned with objective practical laws and consequently with the relation of the will to itself so

---

[12] To behold virtue in her proper form is but to contemplate morality divested of all admixture of sensible things and of every spurious ornament of reward or self-love. To what extent she then eclipses everything else that charms the inclinations one may readily perceive with the least exertion of his reason, if it be not wholly spoiled for abstraction.

far as it is determined by reason alone, in which case whatever refers to the empirical is necessarily excluded. For, if *reason of itself* determines conduct (which possibility we are about to investigate), it must necessarily do so *a priori*.

The will is conceived as a faculty impelling a man to action *in accordance with the concept of certain laws*. Such a faculty can be found only in rational beings. Now, that which serves the will as the objective ground for its self-determination is the *end*, and if the end is given by reason alone, it must be so given for all rational beings. On the other hand, that which merely contains the ground of a possibility of action is called the *means*. The subjective ground of desire is the *main-spring*, the objective ground of volition is the *motive*; hence the distinction [arises] between subjective ends resting on main-springs, and objective ends depending on motives that hold for every rational being. Practical principles are *formal* when they abstract from all subjective ends, they are *material* when they assume these and, therefore, particular main-springs of action. The ends which a rational being chooses to set himself as *effects* of his action (material ends) are altogether merely relative as only their relation to the specific capacity for desire of the subject gives them their value. Such value therefore cannot furnish general principles, i.e., practical laws valid and necessary for all rational beings and for every volition. Hence all these relative ends can only give rise to hypothetical imperatives. However, supposing that there were something *whose existence* was *in itself* of absolute value, something which, as an *end in itself*, could be a ground for definite laws, then this end and it alone, would be the ground for a possible categorical imperative, i.e., a practical law. Now I say that man, and generally every rational being, *exists* as an end in himself, *not merely as a means* for the arbitrary use of this or that will; he must always be regarded as an end in all his actions whether aimed at himself or at other rational beings. All objects of the inclinations have only a conditional value since, but for the inclinations and their respective wants, their object would be without value. But the inclinations themselves, being sources of want, are so far from having an absolute value that instead of relishing them it must rather be the general wish of every rational being to be wholly free from them. Hence the value of any object which *can be acquired* by our action is always conditional. Beings whose existence depends not on our will but on nature have, nevertheless, if they are irrational beings, only a relative value as means and are therefore called *things*; rational beings, on the other hand, are called *persons*. Their very nature constitutes them as ends in themselves; that is, as something which must not be used merely as means. To that extent, a person is limiting freedom of action and is an object of respect. Therefore persons are not merely subjective ends whose existence is an end for us as the result of our action, but they are objective ends; that is, things whose existence in itself is an end. No other end can be substituted (as a justification) for such an end, making it *merely* serve as a means, because otherwise nothing whatever could be found that would possess *absolute value*. If all value were conditional and therefore contingent, reason would have no supreme practical principle whatever.

Now, if a supreme practical principle ought to exist, or a categorical imperative with respect to the human will, it must be one which turns the concept of what is necessarily an end for everybody because it is *an end in itself* into an *objective* principle of the will which can serve as a general practical law. The basis of this principle is that *rational nature exists as an end in itself*. Man necessarily conceives his own existence as being this rational nature, to the extent that it is a *subjective* principle of human actions. But every other rational being regards its existence similarly for the same rational reason that holds true for me,[13] so at the same time it is an objective principle from which, as a supreme practical ground, all laws of the will must

---

[13] This proposition is stated here as a postulate. Its grounds are to be found in the concluding section.

needs be deductible. Accordingly, the practical imperative will be as follows: *Act so as to treat man, in your own person as well as in that of anyone else, always as an end, never merely as a means.* We shall now inquire whether this principle can be realized.

To use the previous examples:

First: In regard to the concept of necessary duty to oneself, whoever contemplates suicide will ask himself whether his action is consistent with the idea of man as *an end in itself.* If he destroys himself to escape onerous conditions, he uses a person merely a a *means* to maintain a tolerable condition until life ends. But man is not a thing, that is to say, something which can be used *merely* as means, but in all his actions must always be considered as an end in itself. Therefore I cannot dispose in any way of man in my own person so as to mutilate, damage or kill him. (It is a matter of morals proper to define this principle more precisely to avoid all misunderstanding. Therefore I bypass such questions as that of the amputation of the limbs in order to preserve one's life, and of exposing one's life to danger with a view to preserving it, etc.)

Second: As regards necessary or obligatory duties toward others, whoever is thinking of making a lying promise to others will see at once that he would be using another man *merely as a means,* without the latter being the end in itself at the same time. The person whom I propose to use by such a promise for my own purposes cannot possibly assent to my way of acting toward him. . . . This conflict with the principle of duty toward others becomes more obvious if we consider examples of attacks on the liberty and property of others. Here it is clear that whoever transgresses the rights of men intends to use the person of others merely as means without considering that as rational beings they shall always be regarded as ends also; that is, as beings who could possibly be the end of the very same action. [14]

---

[14] This does not mean that the trite saying, *Quod tibi non vis fieri* etc.,

Third: As regards contingent (meritorious) duties to oneself, it is not enough that the action does not violate humanity in our own person as an end in itself; [such action] must also *be congruous to it.* Now, there are in mankind capacities for greater perfection which belong to the end of nature regarding humanity. . . . To neglect these capacities might at best be consistent with the *survival* of humanity as an end in itself, but [it is not consistent] with the *promotion* of nature's end regarding humanity.

Fourth: As regards meritorious duties toward others, the natural end which all men have is their own happiness. Now, humanity might indeed subsist if no one contributed anything to the happiness of others as long as he did not deliberately diminish it; but this would be only negatively congruous to *humanity as an end in itself* if everyone does not also endeavor to promote the ends of others as far as he is able. For the ends of any subject which is an end in himself must be my ends too as far as possible, if that idea is to be *fully* effective in me.

This principle of man, and any rational creature, being *an end in itself,* which is the main limiting condition of every man's freedom of action, is not taken from experience for two reasons. First, its universal character, applying as it does to all rational beings whatever, is a fact which no experience can determine; second, because this principle does not present humanity as a subjective end of men; that is, as an object which actually we set ourselves as an end, but it [presents humanity as] an objective end which, whatever [subjective] ends we may have, is to constitute as a law the supreme limiting condition of all subjective ends. It must, therefore, derive from pure reason.

---

could serve here as the rule or principle. This saying is only a deduction from the above rule, though with several limitations: It cannot be a general law, for it does not contain the principle of duties to oneself, nor the duties of charity to others (for many a person would gladly consent that others need do no good deeds for him, provided only that he might be excused from doing good deeds for them), nor finally, that of obligatory duties to one another; by this reasoning the criminal might argue against judges, and so on.

In fact, according to the first principle, *the rule* and its universal character which enables [such legislation] to be some kind of law, for example, a law of nature, the *subjective* ground is the *end*. Since, according to the second principle the subject of all ends is some rational being, each being an end in itself, the third practical principle of the will follows as the ultimate prerequisite for the congruity [of will] with general practical reason; viz, the idea that *the will of every rational being is a will giving general laws*.

By virtue of this principle all maxims are rejected which cannot co-exist with the will as the general legislator. Thus the will is not being subjected simply to law, but is so subjected that it must be regarded *as giving itself the law*, and for this very reason is subject to the law of which it may consider itself the author. . . . Although a will *which is subject to laws* may be attached to such a law through interest, yet a will which is itself a supreme law-giver cannot possibly depend on any interest, since such a dependent will would still need another law which would restrict the interest of its self-love by the condition that it should be valid as general law.

Thus the principle that every human will *gives general laws through all its maxims*[15] if otherwise correct, could very well be *suited as* the categorical imperative because it is *not grounded in any interest* but rather in the idea of universal law-giving. Therefore, it alone among all possible imperatives can be *unconditional*. Or better still, to reverse the propositon: If there is a categorical imperative, i.e., a law for every [act of] willing by a rational being, it can only command that everything be done on account of maxims of a will which could at the same time consider itself the object of its general laws, because only then both the practical principle and the imperative which it

---

[15] I may be excused from offering examples to elucidate this principle, as those which have explained the categorical imperative and its formula would all serve the same purpose here.

obeys are unconditional, the latter not being based on any interest.

Looking back now on all previous efforts to discover the principle of morality, we need not wonder why they all failed. Man was seen to be bound to laws by duty, but no one realized that he is subject *only to his own general laws* and that he is only bound to act in conformity with his own will, a will designed by nature to make general laws. For, when man was conceived as being only subject to some kind of law, such a law had to be supplemented by some interest, by way either of attraction or of constraint, since it did not originate as a law from *his own* will. [In the absence of such autonomy of the will] the will was obliged by *something else* to act in some manner or other. Through this reasoning, as such entirely necessary, all labor spent in finding a supreme principle of *duty* was irrevocably lost. Its final conclusion was never that of duty, but only that of a necessity of acting from a certain interest, be it a personal or impersonal interest. The imperative had to turn out to be a conditional one and could not by any means serve as a moral command. I will therefore call this principle [of will based on no interest] the principle of *autonomy* of the will as contrasted with every other which I regard as *heteronomy*.[16]

The idea of a rational being which must consider itself as giving general laws through all the maxims of its will in order to evaluate itself and its actions under it, this idea leads to another related and very fruitful idea, namely, that of a *realm of ends.*

By a realm I understand the linking of different rational beings by a system of common laws. Since laws determine the ends and their general validity, we are able to conceive all ends as constituting a systematic whole of both rational beings as ends in themselves, and of the special ends of each being, if we disregard the personal differentiation of rational beings as well as

---

[16] [For an elaboration see the *Critique of Practical Reason,* P. 225 ff. below.—Ed.]

the content of their private ends. In other words, we can conceive a realm of ends which is possible in accordance with
principles stated previously. The reason is that all rational beings
are governed by the *law* that each must treat itself and all other
such beings, *never merely as means,* but also always *as ends in
themselves.* This results in a systematic linking of rational beings
through common objective laws, i.e., a realm which may be
called a realm of ends. In such a realm (admittedly only an
ideal) these laws are directed toward the relations of these beings to one another as ends and means.

A rational being belongs as a *member* to the realm of ends to
the extent to which he is himself subject to these general laws,
although giving them himself. He belongs to it *as ruler*
(*Oberhaupt*) when, while giving laws, he is not subject to the
will of any other.

A rational being must always regard himself as law-making in
a realm of ends made possible by freedom of the will, be it as
member or as ruler. He cannot, however, hold the latter position merely by the maxims of his will but only if he is completely independent, has no wants and possesses unrestricted
power adequate for his will. . . . Reason then relates every
maxim of the will, as general law-giving to every other will and
also to every action toward oneself, not on account of any other
practical motive or any future advantage, but because of the
idea of the *dignity* of a rational being which obeys no law but
that which he himself gives.

In the realm of ends everything has either a price or *dignity.* Whatever has a price can be replaced by something else
which is *equivalent;* whatever is above all price, and therefore
has no equivalent, has dignity.

Whatever is related to the general inclinations and needs of
mankind has a *market price;* whatever answers, without presupposing a need, to a certain taste, that is, to pleasure in the
mere purposeless play of our emotions (*Gemütskröfte*) has a

fancy price. But that which constitutes the condition under which alone anything can be an end in itself has not merely a relative value or price, but has an intrinsic value; it has *dignity.*

Morality is the sole condition under which a rational being can be an end in himself, since only then can he possibly be a law-making member of the realm of ends. Thus, only good morals (*Sittlichkeit*) and mankind, so far as it is capable of it, have dignity. Skill and diligence in work have a market price; wit, lively imagination and whims have a fancy price; but faithfulness to promise, good will as a matter of principle, not as a matter of instinct, have an intrinsic value. Neither nature nor art has anything which, if dignity were lacking, they could put in its place. For, such intrinsic value consists neither in its effects, nor in the utility and advantage which it makes possible, but in convictions; that is, in the maxims of will which are ready to manifest themselves in actions, even when such action does not have the desired effect. These actions need no urging by any subjective taste or sentiment to be regarded with immediate favor and pleasure. They need no immediate propensity or feeling; they represent the will that performs them as an object of an immediate respect. Nothing but reason is required to oblige them. Reason need not *flatter* the will into doing them, which in the case of duties would be a contradiction anyhow. This respect therefore shows that the value of such an outlook is dignity and places it infinitely above all price. Such dignity cannot for a moment be evaluated in terms of price or compared with it without, as it were, violating its sanctity.

What entitles virtue or moral disposition to make such high claims? It is nothing less than the share in the making of general laws which affords the rational being, qualifying him thereby to be a member of a possible realm of ends, for which he was already destined by his own nature. . . . The laws setting all value must for that very reason possess dignity; that is, an unconditional incomparable value. The word *respect* alone offers a fitting expression of the esteem in which a rational being must hold it. *Autonomy* lies at the root of the dignity of human and of every other rational nature.

The aforementioned three modes of presenting the principle of morality are at bottom only so many formulae of the very same law, of which one comprises the other two. There is, however, a difference between them, but it is rather subjective than objective and practical. What is involved is bringing an idea of reason closer to what can be looked at and visualized (*Anschauung*) and thereby closer to feeling. All maxims, in fact, have three aspects.

First, there is *form*, consisting in being generalizations (*Allgemeinheit*). The formula of the moral imperative is stated thus: the maxims must be chosen as if they were as valid as general laws of nature.

Second, there is content or substance (*Materie*), in other words, an end. The formula states that the rational being, as an end by its own nature and therefore as an end in itself, must be for every maxim the condition limiting all merely relative and arbitrary ends.

Third, there is a *complete definition* of all maxims by this formula [of the categorical imperative], to wit: All maxims by virtue of their own lawmaking ought to harmonize so as to constitute together a possible realm of ends as a realm of nature. [17] This progression takes place through the categories of *unity* in the form of will (its generality), of *plurality* of the content or substance (the objects or ends), and of *totality* of their system. In forming a moral *judgment* about actions it is always better to proceed on the strict method and to start with

---

[17]Teleology considers nature as a realm of ends; morals regards a possible realm of ends as a realm of nature. In the first case, the realm of ends is a theoretical idea explaining what actually is. In the latter it is a practical idea bringing about that which is not yet, but which can be realized in conforming to this idea in our conduct.

the general formula of the categorical imperative: *Act according to a maxim which can become a general law.* If, however, we wish to introduce the moral law, it is very useful to evaluate the same action by the three specified concepts and thereby let it approach, as far as possible, something that is clearly envisaged (*Anschauung*).

We can conclude with what we started from, namely, with the concept of an absolutely good will. *That will is thoroughly good* which cannot be evil, or, whose maxim, if made a general law, could never contradict itself. This principle is also its supreme law: Act always on such a maxim as you can will to be a general law. This is the only condition under which a will can never contradict itself; and such an imperative is categorical. Since the validity of the will as a general law for possible actions is analogous to the general linking of the existence of things by general laws which is the formal aspect of nature in general, the categorical imperative can also be expressed as follows: *Act on maxims which can have themselves for their own object as general laws of nature.* Such then is the formula of a thoroughly good will.

Rational nature is distinguished from the rest of nature by setting itself an end. This end would be the content of every good will. But since the idea of an absolutely good will is not limited by any condition of attaining this or that end we must completely disregard every end *to be effected* which would make every will only relatively good. The end here must be understood to be not an end to be effected but an *independently existing* end, consequently only a negative one, i.e., one against which we must never act and therefore every act of willing must never be regarded merely as means, but as an end as well. This end can be nothing but the subject of all possible ends, since it is also the subject of a possible absolutely good will; because such a will cannot be related to any other object without contradiction. The principle: So act toward every rational being (yourself and others), that he may for you always be an end in himself, is therefore essentially identical with this other: Act upon a maxim which is generally valid for every rational being. . . .

In this way an intelligible world (*mundus intelligibilis*) is possible as a realm of ends, by virtue of the lawmaking of all persons as members. . . . Such a realm of ends would be actually realized if maxims conforming to the canon of the categorical imperative for all rational beings *were universally followed*. But a rational being, though punctiliously following this maxim himself, cannot count upon all others being equally faithful to it, nor [can he be certain] that the realm of nature and its purposive design so accord with him as a proper member as to form a realm made possible by himself; that is, favoring his expectation of happiness. Still the law remains in full force: Act according to the maxims of a member of a merely possible realm of ends in making general law since this law commands categorically. Therein lies the paradox; that merely the dignity of man as a rational creature, in other words, respect for a mere idea, should serve as an inflexible precept without any other end or advantage. The sublime character [of this dignity] consists precisely in this independence of maxims from all such springs of action. This makes every rational subject worthy to be a law-making member of the realm of ends. Otherwise he would have to be imagined as subject only to the natural law of his wants. Although we would suppose the realm of nature and the realm of ends to be united under one ruler, so that the realm of ends thereby would no longer be a mere idea but acquire true reality, [such reality] would no doubt gain an additional strong incentive, but never any increase of its intrinsic value. For, this sole unlimited law-giver must nonetheless always be conceived as evaluating the value of rational beings only by their disinterested behavior, as prescribed by the idea of the dignity of man alone. The essence of things is not altered by their external conditions and man must be judged by whatever constitutes his absolute value, irrespective of these [conditions], whoever be the judge, even it be the Supreme Being. Morality then is the relation of actions to the autonomy of the will, that is, to the possible general laws made by its maxims. An action that is consistent with the autonomy of the will is *permissible,* one that is not congruous with it is *forbidden.* A will whose maxims necessarily are congruous with the laws of autonomy is a *sacred,* wholly good will. The dependence of a not absolutely good will on the principle of autonomy (moral compulsion) is [called] obligation. It cannot be applied to a holy being. The objective necessity of an action resulting from obligation is called *duty.*

It is easy to see, from what has been just said, why we ascribe a certain quality and sublime dignity to the person who fulfils all his duties, although we think of the concept of duty as implying subjection to the law. There is no sublime quality in him as far as he is *subject* to the moral law, but there is as far as he is at the same time a maker of that very law and on that account subject to it. Furthermore, we have shown above that neither fear nor inclination but simply respect for the law is the incentive which can give actions a moral value. Our own will, as far as it acts under the condition that its maxims may constitute possible general laws—and such a will is possible as an idea— is the real object of respect. The dignity of mankind consists just in this capacity of making general laws, always provided that it is itself subject to these laws.

The Autonomy of the Will as the Supreme Principle of Morality

Autonomy of the will is that property by which will is a law unto itself, independent of any property of the objects of volition. The principle of autonomy therefore is: always so to choose that in the same act of willing the maxims of this choice are formulated as a general law. We cannot prove by a mere analysis of its concepts that this practical rule is an imperative, i.e., that the will of every rational being is necessarily bound by

it as a condition, since [such rule] is a synthetical proposition.
We would have to go beyond the knowledge of objects to a
critique of the subject; that is to pure practical reason. For this
synthetic proposition which commands apodictically must be
understood and known wholly *a priori*. This matter, however,
does not belong to the present section. But it can readily be
shown by mere analysis of the concepts of morality that the
principle of autonomy is the sole principle of morals. We shall
then find that its principle must be a categorical imperative
and the latter commands neither more nor less than this very
autonomy.

Heteronomy of the Will as the Source of all False Principles of Morality

If the will is concerned with *anything else* but the suitability of
its maxims as general laws of its own making, that is, if it goes
beyond itself and seeks a law by which it is to be determined in
the qualities of any of its objects, *heteronomy* always is the result. The will in that case does not give itself the law, but the
object is given it through its relation to the will. This relation
only admits of hypothetical imperatives, whether the imperative
rests on inclination or on concepts of reason: *I must do something because I want something else.* On the other hand, the
moral and therefore categorical imperative says: I ought to do
thus and so although I want nothing more. For instance, the
hypothetical imperative says: I must lie if I want to retain my
reputation; the latter says: I ought not to lie whether it brings
me the least discredit or not. The latter therefore must disregard the objects to the extent that it has no *influence* on the
will, so that practical reason (the will) may not merely administer an alien interest, but simply prove its own commanding authority as the supreme law-giver. Thus, e.g., I ought to endeavor to promote the happiness of others, not as if I had an
interest in it by immediate inclination or by any pleasure indirectly gained through reason, but simply because a maxim

which excludes [the happiness of others] cannot be comprised in one and the same volition as a general law.

Classification of all Possible Principles of Morality which can be Founded on the Basic Concept of Heteronomy

Human reason has here, as elsewhere in its pure pre-critical use, first tried all kinds of wrong ways before it succeeded in finding the one true way [through criticism]. As we have seen, all principles to be considered from this point of view are either *empirical* or *rational*. As the determining cause of our will, the empirical principles derived from the principle of *happiness* are based on physical or moral sentiments, rational principles derived from the principle of perfection are based as a possible effect either on the rational concept of perfection or on the concept of an autonomous perfection; that is, the will of God.

[Ed: After repeating what he has said concerning the unsuitability of happiness as a foundation for morals, Kant continues:]

Among the *rational* principles of morality, the ontological concept of *perfection,* in spite of its defects, is better than the theological concept which deduces morality from a Divine, absolutely perfect, will. The ontological concept is no doubt empty and indefinite and consequently useless for finding the highest degree [of perfection] in the boundless field of possible reality. Moreover, in attempting to distinguish specifically the reality of which we are now speaking from every other reality, it inevitably tends to go around in circles and cannot avoid presupposing tacitly the morality which this reality is to explain. Nevertheless it is better than the theological concept, not only because we cannot visualize (*anschauen*) the divine perfection and can only deduce it from our own concepts of which the most important is morality itself (and even then our explanation would involve a gross, roundabout, reasoning), but also because the remaining concept of a [divine] will, derived from the attributes of desire for glory and domination and combined with the terrible ideas of power and vengeance, would constitute the basis of a system of morals diametrically opposed to morality.

However, if I had to choose between the concept of moral sense and that of perfection in general (both of which at least do not weaken morality though they are not at all qualified to serve as its foundation) I would decide for the concept of perfection because it, at least, removes the question from the senses and brings it before the court of pure reason. Although even here the concept of perfection decides nothing, at all events it preserves, unadulterated, the indefinite idea of a will good in itself for more precise definition. . . .

Wherever an [external] object of the will has to be supposed and the rule is prescribed for determining it, that rule is simple heteronomy. The imperative is conditional; namely, *if*, or *because*, one desires this object, one should act in this or that way; hence it can never command morally, that is, categorically. Whether the object determines the will through inclination, as in the principle of private happiness, or through reason directed at objects of our possible volition, as in the principle of perfection, in either case the will never determines itself *immediately* through the conceived action, but only through the influence which the foreseen effect of the action has on the will: *I ought to do something because* I am willing something else. Here yet another law must be assumed in me as its subject by means of which I necessarily will this other thing, which law in turn requires an imperative restricting this maxim. The impulse which the concept of an object within the reach of our faculties can give the will of the subject depends on its natural properties, no matter whether the senses (inclination and taste), or intellect and reason are satisfied through use. . . . Consequently, nature would, properly speaking, give the law, and, as such, not only must the law be known and proved by experience and therefore would be contingent and useless as an apodictic practical rule as the moral rule must be, but the law always implies a heteronomy of the will. The will does not give itself the law, the law is given by an extraneous impulse to which the natural constitution of the subject is receptive.

[Ed: After once again stating his views on the autonomy of the good will, Kant continues:]

The problem of how such a synthetic, practical, a priori *proposition is possible and necessary* cannot be solved within the limits of the metaphysics of morals. We have not asserted its truth here, much less professed to have a proof of it. We have simply shown, by the development of the universally accepted concept of morality that autonomy of the will is inevitably connected with this concept or, rather, is its basis. Whoever considers morality real, and not a chimerical idea without truth, must likewise admit its principle as discussed here. This section then, like the first, was merely analytic. To prove that morality is no mere creation of the brain, which it cannot be if the categorical imperative and with it the autonomy of the will are a true idea and are absolutely necessary as an *a priori* principle, requires a synthetic use of pure practical reason. However, we cannot venture into this without first undertaking a critique of this faculty of reason. In the concluding section we shall give the principal features of this critique as far as is necessary for our purpose.

THIRD SECTION

Transition from the Metaphysics of Morals to the Critique of Pure Practical Reason

The Concept of Freedom Is the Key Explanation of the Autonomy of the Will

The *will* is a kind of causality of living beings in so far as they are rational, and *freedom* should be that quality of this causality through which it can be an efficient cause independent of extraneous *determining* causes; just as *physical necessity* is the peculiar quality of the causality of all non-rational beings as impelled into activity by extraneous causes.

The above definition of freedom is *negative* and therefore unsuitable for understanding its essence; but it leads to a *positive* concept which is all the more ample and fruitful. Since the concept of causality implies that of law, according to which something called a cause produces something else called an effect, freedom, though not a quality of the will in so far as it depends on natural laws, is not for that reason without law, but must rather be a causality acting in accordance with immutable laws of a peculiar kind; otherwise free will would be an absurdity. Natural necessity is a heteronomy of efficient causes because every effect if possible only according to the law [of natural causality:] some [antecedent cause] determines the efficient cause to act causally. What else can freedom of the will be but autonomy; that is, the property of the will to be a law unto itself? But the proposition: the will is a law unto itself in every action, only expresses the principle of acting on no other maxim than that which can also aim to be a general law. This is precisely the formula of the categorical imperative and of the principle of ethics, so that a free will and a will subject to moral laws are one and the same.

If freedom of the will is assumed, morality and its principle can be deduced from it by mere analysis of the concept. However, the latter is still a synthetic proposition: that an absolutely good will is one whose maxim can always be stated in terms of a general law, still is a synthetic proposition. This quality of the maxims can never be discovered by analyzing the concept of an absolutely good will. Such synthetic propositions are only possible by uniting both insights (*Erkenntnisse*) with a third in which they both can be found. The *positive* concept of freedom leads to this third [element] which cannot be the nature of the sensible world with its physical causes. This third [element], to which freedom leads us and of which we have an idea *a priori*, cannot be shown here as yet. Nor can we yet explain the deduction of the concept of freedom from pure practical reason, nor the possibility of a categorical imperative. Some further preparation is required.

Freedom Must Be Assumed to Be a Quality of the Will of All Rational Beings

It is not enough to attribute freedom, for whatever reason, to our own will if we have not sufficient grounds for attributing the same to all rational beings. For, as morality serves us as a law only because we are *rational beings,* it must also hold true for all rational beings. As morality must be deduced simply from the quality of freedom, it must be shown that freedom is also a quality of all rational beings. It is not enough then to expound it as derived from certain supposed experiences of human nature (which indeed is quite impossible and can only be shown *a priori*), but we must prove that morality is part of the activity of any and all rational beings endowed with a will. Now I say that every being who cannot act except *under the idea of freedom* is, in practical respects, really free for just that reason. That is to say; all laws inseparably connected with freedom are as valid for this being as though his will had been shown to be free in itself and accepted by theoretical philosophy.[18] I assert that we must necessarily attribute to every rational being having a will the idea of freedom under which alone it acts. In such a being we conceive reason which is practical; that is, which acts causally in reference to its objects. We cannot possibly conceive reason consciously permitting any other quarter to direct its judgments, since then the subject would attribute the control of its judgment not to reason, but to an impulse. Reason must re-

---

[18] I adopt this method of assuming that freedom, merely *as an idea* upon which alone rational beings base their actions, is sufficient for our purpose, in order to avoid the necessity of proving freedom in its theoretical aspect also. Even though the latter is not ascertained, a being that cannot act except under the idea of freedom is bound by the same laws as a being who is actually free. Thus we can escape here from the burden which weighs upon the theory.

gard itself as the author of its principles independent of extraneous influences; consequently, it, as practical reason or as the
will of a rational being, must regard itself as free. That is to say;
the will [of such a being] cannot be a will of its own except
under the idea of freedom. Therefore this idea must, practically
speaking, be attributed to all rational beings.

Of the Interest Attaching to the Ideas of Morality

At last we have reduced the definite concept of morality to the
idea of freedom. However, we could not prove this idea to be
actually a quality of ourselves and of human nature; we saw
merely that we must presuppose it if we want to think of a being as rational and conscious of its causality in its actions, i.e.,
as endowed with a will. So we find that on the very same
grounds we must attribute to every being endowed with reason
and will this quality of obliging itself to act under the idea of
its freedom.

Presupposing these ideas means becoming aware of a law that
the subjective principles of action, i.e., maxims, must always be
taken as being objective, i.e., universal principles, and so serve as
universal laws of our own making. But why should I, simply as a
rational being, subject myself to this principle and thus also
[subject to this principle] all other beings endowed with reason? I will allow that no interest *urges* me to do this, for interest
would not yield a categorical imperative. But I must *take* an interest in it and discern how this comes to pass, as this "I ought"
is properly an "I will" which holds for every rational being, provided only that reason determine his actions without hindrance.
But for beings that are affected also, as we are, by impulses of a
different kind, i.e., our senses, and do not always act according
to reason alike, necessity is only an "ought" and the subjective
necessity differs from the objective one.

Therefore it seems as if moral law, that is, the principle of the
autonomy of the will, were actually only presupposed in the
idea of freedom and as if its reality and objective necessity could

not be proved independently. Even then we would have gained considerably in at least determining the true principle more exactly than had previously been done. But in regard to the validity of the principle and the practical necessity of subjecting oneself to it, we would not have advanced a step. If we were asked why the universal validity of our maxim as a law must be the condition restricting our actions and on what we base the value which we assign to this way of acting, a value so great that there can be no higher interest, [and if we were asked further] why by this alone a man believes to feel his own value compared with which a pleasant or unpleasant condition must be regarded as nothing, to these questions we could give no satisfactory answer.

Sometimes, indeed, we find that we can take an interest in a personal quality not involving any interest or external condition, provided this quality enables us to participate in the condition, in case reason were to bring it about. It can interest us merely in deserving happiness even without sharing the motive [for this happiness]. However this judgment is actually only the effect of the moral law whose importance we have already assumed if we detach ourselves from every empirical interest through the idea of freedom. But we do not realize in this way that we ought to detach ourselves from these interests; that is, consider ourselves as free in action and yet as subject to certain laws, so as to find a value simply in our own person which can compensate us for the loss of everything that gives our condition a value. Nor do we see how all this is possible; in other words, *why moral law is obligatory*.

It must be freely admitted that there appears a sort of circular reasoning here that seems impossible to escape. We assume ourselves to be free in the order of efficient causes so that we may conceive ourselves to be subject to moral laws in the order of ends. Then we consider ourselves as subject to these laws because we have conferred upon ourselves freedom of will. Freedom and law-making of will are both autonomous and are therefore correlative concepts. For this very reason one concept cannot be used to explain the other or set forth its basis, [but can be used] at best to reduce, for the sake of logic, apparently different notions of the same object to one single concept (as we reduce different fractions of equal content to their lowest denominator).

One resource remains: to inquire whether we do not occupy different positions when we think of ourselves as causes efficient *a priori* through freedom and when we consider ourselves as effects of our actions which we see before our eyes.

The remark, which needs no subtle reflection and which can presumably be made by the most average mind (though after his fashion by an obscure discernment of judgment which he calls sentiment) is that all images (*Vorstellungen*) which we get without willing them, such as those of the senses, do not enable us to know objects except as they affect us. Whatever they are in themselves remains unknown. Consequently, regardless of the closest attention and clarity of which the mind is capable, "images" of this kind allow us only to acquire knowledge of *phenomena*, never of *things in themselves*. Once this distinction has been made, (even in just observing a difference between the images or ideas we receive passively from without, and those which we actively produce ourselves), it follows that we must admit and assume behind the phenomena something else that are not phenomena; namely, the things-in-themselves, although we must resign ourselves never to being able to approach them and never to knowing what they are in themselves, but only as they affect us. This must furnish a distinction, no matter how crude, between the world of sense and the world of reason. The former can be distinguished according to the difference of sense impressions in various observers, while the second always remains the same as the basis of the distinction. Man cannot even pretend to know what he is himself from the self-knowledge he has through internal sensation. Since he does not create himself, as it were, and comes by the concept [of man] not *a priori* but empirically, it is natural that he can obtain knowledge of himself only by his inner sense, and consequently only through the phenomena of his nature and the way in which his consciousness is affected. Nevertheless, beyond the structure of his own subject, as made up of mere phenomena, he must suppose something else as the basis of these phenomena; namely, his ego, whatever its nature may be. In regard to mere perception and receptivity of the senses, man must reckon himself as belonging to the *world of sense,* but in regard to what may be pure action in him (reaching consciousness directly and not by affecting the senses), he must reckon himself as belonging to the *world of the mind,* of which, however, he has no further knowledge. . . .

Man actually finds in himself a faculty which distinguishes him from all other things, even from himself as affected by objects, and that is *reason.* Reason, being pure and spontaneous, is superior even to the mind. Though the latter is spontaneous too and does not, like the sense, merely contain images that arise when we are affected by things (and are therefore passive), reason's activity cannot produce any other concepts than those designed *to bring the impressions or images based on sense rules,* to unite them in one consciousness. Without this activity of the senses, the [mind] could not think at all, whereas reason in the form of ideas displays such pure spontaneity that it far transcends anything that the senses can offer it and so proves its most important function in distinguishing the world of sense from that of the intellect, thereby setting the limits of the intellect itself.

A rational being must regard himself *as an intelligence* (not from the viewpoint of his lower faculties) belonging, not to the world of sense, but to that of the intellect. Hence man can regard himself from two points of view and similarly can come to know laws for the exercise of his faculties and consequently laws for all his actions. *First,* so far as he belongs to the world of sense, man is himself subject to laws of nature (heteronomy);

second, so far as he belongs to the intelligible world, [man is] under laws independent of nature which are founded not on experience but on reason alone. . . .

The suspicion which we considered above is now removed. This was the suspicion that our reasoning, from freedom to autonomy and from this to moral law, was mysteriously circular and that we thought the idea of freedom was basic only because of the moral law so that we might then infer the latter from freedom and that then we could offer no explanation at all for this law, but could only [present] it by *begging a principle* which well-disposed minds would gladly concede to us, but which we could never put forward as a provable proposition. Now we see that when we conceive ourselves as free we transfer ourselves into the world of the intellect and recognize the autonomy of the will with its consequence, morality; whereas if we conceive ourselves as obliged we are considering ourselves as belonging at the same time to the world of sense and to the intellectual world (*Verstandeswelt*).

How Is a Categorical Imperative Possible?

Every rational being considers himself as belonging, as an intelligence, to the world of intellect and he calls his causality a will simply as an efficient cause belonging to that world. On the other hand, he is also conscious of being a part of the world of sense in which his actions are displayed as mere phenomena of that causality. However, we cannot discern how they are possible from this causality which we do not know. Instead, these actions must be viewed as determined by other phenomena; namely, desires and inclinations belonging to the sensible world. If I were only a member of the world of the intellect, all my actions would conform perfectly to the principle of the autonomy of pure will; if I were only a part of the world of sense they would be assumed to conform wholly to the natural law of desires and inclinations, i.e., to the heteronomy of nature. (The former would rest on the supreme principle of morality, the latter on that of happiness.) Since *the world of the intellect contains the basis of the world of sense, and consequently of its laws,* and so gives law directly to my will (as belonging entirely to the world of the intellect), I, as an intelligence, must recognize myself as subject to the law of the world of the intellect. [What this means is that I am subject] to reason which contains this law in the idea of freedom, and therefore as subject to the autonomy of the will, though otherwise [I am] a being belonging to the world of sense. Consequently, I must regard the laws of the world of the intellect as imperatives and the corresponding actions as duties.

Therefore categorical imperatives are possible because the idea of freedom makes me a member of an intelligible world whereby, were I nothing else, all my actions *would* always conform to the autonomy of the will. But, since I also see myself as a member of the world of sense, they *ought* so to conform, which *categorical* "ought" is a synthetic *a priori* proposition in so far as there is added to my will, as affected by sensible desires, the idea of the same will belonging to the world of the intellect, pure and practical in itself. . . .

The practical use of common human reason confirms this reflection. There is no one, not even the most consummate villain only provided that he is accustomed to the use of reason, who, when shown examples of honesty of purpose, of steadfastness in obeying good maxims, of sympathy and charity in the face of great sacrifices of advantages and comfort, would not wish that he might also possess these qualities. Only his inclinations and impulses prevent it and he wishes to be free from such troublesome inclinations. Therefore he proves that, with a will free from the impulses of the sense, he can imagine an order of things wholly different from that of his sensible desires. He believes himself to be this better person when he shifts to the viewpoint of a member of the world of the intellect into which he is prompted by the idea of freedom. . . . The moral "ought" is then the necessary "will" of a member of an intelligible world and he conceives it as an "ought" only to the same extent that he considers himself a member of the world of sense.

Of the Extreme Limit of all Practical Philosophy

All men attribute freedom of will to themselves. This explains all judgments of actions that *ought to have been done* but *were not*. Nevertheless this freedom is not a concept based on experience, nor can it be such since it persists even when experience shows the contrary of what are conceived to be its necessary consequences once freedom is presupposed. On the other hand, it is equally necessary that every event should be firmly determined according to laws of nature. This necessity of nature is likewise not an empirical concept in that it involves the notion of necessity; that is, of *a priori* knowledge. But this concept of nature is confirmed by experience and must be presupposed if experience itself is to be possible; that is, if it is to be a coherent knowledge in terms of general laws of sensory objects. Therefore freedom is only an *idea* of reason and its objective reality as such is doubtful, while nature is a *concept* of the *intellect* which proves, and must necessarily prove, its reality in examples of experience.

Although this results in a dialectic of reason since the freedom attributed to the will appears to contradict the necessity of nature, and reason at this parting of the ways for *speculative purposes* finds the road of physical necessity much better trodden and more appropriate than that of freedom, yet for *practical purposes* the narrow path of freedom is the only one by which it is possible to make use of reason in our conduct. Hence it is impossible for the subtlest philosophy as well as for the commonest human reason to argue away freedom. Philosophy must assume that no real contradiction will be found between the freedom and physical necessity of the same human actions, for it cannot give up the concept of nature any more than that of freedom.

It is impossible to escape this contradiction if the subject, thinking itself free, thought of itself *in the same sense* or *in the very same relation* when it calls itself free as when it assumes itself subject to the law of nature with respect to the same action. It is an inescapable problem of speculative philosophy to show at least that this seeming contradiction rests on our thinking of man in a different sense and relation when we call him free, from that when we regard him as part and parcel of nature, and as subject to its laws. It must therefore show not only that both *can* co-exist very well, but that both must be thought of *as necessarily united* in the same subject, since otherwise no explanation could be given for burdening reason with an idea which entangles us in a perplexity sorely embarrassing reason in its theoretic use, though it may be reconciled *without contradiction* with another idea that is sufficiently established. However, this task belongs to speculative philosophy by which it may clear the way for practical philosophy. The philosopher has no option; he must remove the apparent contradiction since if he left it untouched the theory about it would be *bonum vacans* and the fatalist would have a right to acquire it and expel all morality from its supposed domain as occupying it without title.

The title to freedom of will, even that of common reason, is founded on the consciousness and the admitted assumption that reason is independent of mere subjectively determined causes which, as a whole, belong only to sensation, and which consequently come under the general designation of the senses. . . . Man soon realizes that both can hold true, nay even must hold true at the same time. There is not the least contradiction in saying that a *thing-in-appearance* or phenomenon (belonging to the world of sense) is subject to certain laws, of which the very same thing *as a thing* or being *in itself* is independent. [The fact] that he must conceive and think of himself in this two-fold way rests, in regard to the first [way], on his consciousness of being an object affected through the senses, and in regard to the second [way], on his consciousness of being an intelligence; that is, [of being] independent from sense impressions in using his reason and so belonging to the world of the intellect. This explains man claiming the possession of a will which allows nothing to be charged against it merely belonging to his desires and inclinations and, on the other hand, a will which conceives actions as being possible and even necessary that can happen only through disregard of all desires and sensible inclinations. The causality of such actions lies in man as an intelligence, and in the laws of effects and actions according to the principles of an intelligible world, of which he may know nothing other than that there pure reason alone makes the law, independent of the senses. Moreover, since he is his proper self as an intelligence only in that world (as man is only the phenomenon of himself), those laws concern him directly and categorically, so that the incitements of inclinations and appetites (the whole nature of the world of sense) cannot impair the laws of his volition as an intelligence. Furthermore, he does not even hold himself responsible for the former or ascribe them to his proper self, i.e., his will; he only ascribes to his will any indulgence toward them if he allowed them to influence his maxims to the prejudice of the rational laws of the will.

When practical reason *thinks* itself into a world of the intellect it does not thereby transgress its own limits, as it would if it tried to enter it by *looking* at or *sensing* it. This is only a negative thought in respect to the world of sense, which does not give reason any laws to determine the will, and is positive only in the single respect that this freedom as a negative condition is combined with a (positive) faculty and even with a causality of reason, which we call a will, a will of acting so that the principle of the actions conforms to the essential character of a rational motive; i.e., to the condition that the maxim have universal validity as a law. But if practical reason were to borrow an *object* of *will,* that is, a motive from the world of the intellect, it would overstep its bounds and would venture to be acquainted with something of which it knows nothing. The concept of a world of the intellect is only a *position* outside the phenomena which reason finds itself compelled to take in order to *conceive itself as practical,* which would not be possible if the influences of the senses had a determining power over man, but which is necessary unless he is denied the consciousness of himself as an intelligence; that is, as a rational cause acting freely and through reason. This thought certainly involves the idea of an order and a system of laws different from that of the mechanism of nature which governs the sensible world, and it requires the concept of an intelligible world; that is to say, of a whole system of rational beings as things in themselves. But this thought does not in the least entitle us to consider it in terms other than those of its *formal* condition; that is, the autonomy of this intelligible world which alone can co-exist with its freedom. On the other hand, all laws that refer to an object give heteronomy, which is only found in laws of nature and can only apply to the sensible world.

But reason would be overstepping all its bounds if it undertook to *explain how* pure reason could be practical; this would be exactly the same task as explaining *how freedom is possible.*

We can explain nothing but that which we can reduce to laws, whose object can be given in some possible experience. But freedom is a mere idea, whose objective reality can never be shown through laws of nature nor, consequently, through possible experience; therefore it can never be comprehended or even visualized, because we cannot support it by any sort of example or analogy. It is valid only as a necessary hypothesis of reason in a being that believes itself conscious of a will. Where impulse ceases according to laws of nature, there ceases all *explanation* also, leaving nothing but defense, i.e., the removal of the objections of those who pretend to have seen deeper into the nature of things, and who thereupon boldly declare freedom impossible. We can only show them that the contradiction that they believe to have discovered arises only from man having to be considered as a phenomenon in order to apply the law of nature to human actions. When we demand of them that they should also think of him as an intelligence, as a thing-in-itself, they still persist in considering him as [only] phenomenon. [If that were so], to cut off the causality of the same subject, that is, his will, from all the natural laws of the sensible world would unquestionably be a contradiction. But this contradiction disappears if one bethinks oneself and admits as reasonable that beneath the phenomenon must lie at their root [so to speak] the hidden things-in-themselves, and that we cannot expect the laws of these to be identical to those that govern their appearances.

The subjective impossibility of explaining the freedom of the will as identical with the impossibility of discovering and explaining an interest [19] which man could take in the moral law. Nevertheless he does actually take an interest in it, the basis of which in ourselves we call the moral sentiment, which some have falsely pronounced the standard of our moral judgment, whereas it must rather be viewed as the *subjective* effect that the law exercises on the will, for which reason alone furnishes the objective principle.

In order that a rational being, also affected through the senses, should will what reason alone directs such beings to will, reason must have a power *to infuse a sensation of pleasure* or satisfaction in the fulfilment of duty; that is, it should have a causality by which it determines the sensibility according to its own principles. But it is quite impossible to realize, i.e., to make

---

[19] Interest is that which makes reason practical; that is, a cause determining the will. Hence we say of rational beings only that they take an interest in something; irrational beings only feel sensual appetites. Reason takes a direct interest in action only if the universal validity of its maxims is sufficient to determine the will. Such an interest alone is pure. But if it can determine the will only by means of another object of desire or on the assumption of a particular sentiment in the subject, reason takes only an indirect interest in the action. As reason without experience cannot discover either objects of the will or a special sentiment actuating it, this latter interest would only be empirical, and not a pure rational interest. The scholarly interest of reason, for extending its insight, is never direct, but it presupposes purposes for which reason is employed.

it intelligible *a priori,* how a mere thought, itself containing nothing sensible, can produce a sensation of pleasure or pain; for this is a particular kind of causality of which, as of any causality, we can determine *a priori* nothing whatever; we can consult only experience about it. But as experience cannot supply us with any relation of cause and effect as between two objects of experience, whereas in this case the cause is supposed to be pure reason acting through mere ideas which offer no object to experience, although the effect produced lies within experience, it is quite impossible that we human beings explain how and why the *universality of the maxim as a law,* that is, morality, can interest [man]. This much is certain, that it has validity for us not just *because it interests* us, for that would be heteronomy and dependence of practical reason on the senses or a sentiment as its principle, in which case it could never give moral laws. The universal maxim interests us because it is valid for us as human beings as it has its source in our will as intelligences; in other words, in our proper self. *Whereas whatever belongs to mere appearance, reason necessarily subordinates to the nature of the thing in itself.*

The question of how a categorical imperative is possible can be answered to the extent that we can state the only hypothesis on which it is possible, namely, the idea of freedom, and we can also perceive the necessity of this hypothesis which is sufficient for the practical exercise of reason; that is, for convincing us of the *validity of this imperative* and hence of the moral law, but how this hypothesis itself is possible can never be discerned by any human reason. However, on the hypothesis that the will of an intelligence is free, its autonomy is a necessary consequence as the essential formal condition of its determination. Moreover, this freedom of will is not only quite possible as a hypothesis without involving any contradiction to the principle of physical necessity in the nexus of phenomena of the sensible world, as speculative philosophy can show, but a rational being who is conscious of causality through reason, that is to say, of a will distinct from desires, must of *necessity* make it, as an idea, the condition of practically all his voluntary actions. But how pure reason can be practical of itself without the aid of any impulse to action, no matter where such impulse is derived, i.e., how the mere principle of the *universal validity of its maxims as laws* (which would certainly be the form of a pure practical reason) can supply an impulse of itself without any object of the will in which one could antecedently take any original interest; and how it can produce an interest which would be called purely moral; or, in other words, *how pure reason can be practical,* [all this] is beyond the power of human reason to explain and all the labor and pains of seeking an explanation for this are in vain.

The same applies to the attempt to find out how freedom itself is possible as the causality of a will. Here I quit the ground of philosophical explanation and I have no other to go upon. I might revel in the world of intelligences which still remains [open] to me, but though I have an *idea* of it which is well founded, yet I have not the least *knowledge* of it, nor can I ever attain it with all the efforts of my natural faculty of reason. Freedom signifies only a something that remains when I have eliminated everything belonging to the world of sense from the actuating principles of my will, serving merely to restrict the principle of such motives as are taken from the field of sensibility by fixing its limits and showing that it does not contain everything, but that there is more beyond it; but of this "more" I know nothing. After the abstraction of all matter, i.e., knowledge of objects, there remains of pure reason which conceives this ideal nothing but the form, namely, the practical law of the universality of the maxims, and congruous with it the concept of reason in reference to a pure world of the intellect as a possible efficient cause, i.e., a cause determining the will. There must be here a total absence of impulses, unless this idea of an intelligible world is itself the impulse, or the primary interest of reason; but to make this intelligible is precisely the problem that we cannot solve.

This is the extreme limit of all moral inquiry. Yet it is of great importance to determine this limit on this account: that reason may not on the one hand search about in the world of sense to the prejudice of morals for the supreme motive and an interest comprehensible but empirical; and on the other hand so that reason may not impotently raise its wings in the empty space of transcendent concepts which we call the intelligible world without being able to move and so lose itself amidst chimeras. For the rest, the idea remains of a pure world of the intellect as a whole [comprising] all intelligences, to which we ourselves belong [insofar as we are] rational beings, although otherwise we are members of the sensible world. It is a useful and legitimate idea for the purposes of rational belief, even though all knowledge stops at its threshold. It produces in us a lively interest in the moral law by means of the magnificent ideal of a universal realm of *ends in themselves* (of rational beings) to which we can belong as members only when we carefully conduct ourselves according to the maxims of freedom as if they were laws of nature.

Conclusion

The speculative use of reason *with respect to nature* leads to the absolute necessity of some supreme cause for *the world.* The practical use of reason *with a view to freedom* also leads to absolute necessity, but only *for the laws of the actions* of a rational being as such. It is an essential *principle* of reason, however used, to push its knowledge to a consciousness of its *necessity* (without which it would not be rational knowledge). It is, however, an equally essential *restriction* of the same reason that it can neither discern the *necessity* of what is, or of what happens, or of what ought to happen, unless a condition is supposed on which it is, or happens, or ought to happen. By constant inquiry into this condition, the satisfaction of reason is only further and further postponed. Hence reason searches unceasingly for the unconditionally necessary and finds itself forced to assume it without any means of making it comprehensible to itself; reason is fortunate if it can discover a concept which suits this assumption. Therefore our deduction of the supreme principle of morality cannot be blamed but human reason in general should be reproached for not enabling us to conceive the absolute necessity of an unconditional practical law, such as the categorical imperative must be. Reason cannot be blamed for refusing to explain this necessity by a condition; that is to say, by means of some interest assumed as a basis, since the law would then cease to be a supreme law of reason. Thus we do not comprehend the practical, unconditional necessity of the moral imperative, but we comprehend its *incomprehensibility* which is all that, in fairness, can be demanded of a philosophy which aims to carry its principles to the very limit of human reason.

VIII

CRITIQUE OF PURE PRACTICAL REASON

[1788]

INTRODUCTION

THE THEORETICAL USE OF REASON WAS ONLY CONCERNED WITH objects of the cognitive faculty and a critical examination of reason with reference to this use properly applied only to the *pure* faculty of cognition. For this raised the suspicion, which was afterwards confirmed, that the theoretical use of reason might easily pass beyond its limits and be lost among unattainable objects or even contradictory concepts. It is quite different with the practical use of reason. In this enterprise reason is concerned with the grounds for determining the will, which is a faculty, either for producing objects corresponding to concepts, or for determining itself to the effecting of such objects, whether the physical power is sufficient or not; that is, it is a faculty for determining its own causality. For here reason can get to the point of determining the will and reason always has objective reality in so far as only the volition is in question. This is the first question then: Is pure reason sufficient by itself for determining the will, or is it only capable of determining it in dependence on empirical conditions? At this point a special concept of causality enters in, having been justified in the *Critique of Pure Reason,* which is not capable of being presented empirically, the concept of *freedom.* If we can now discover means of proving that this property actually does belong to the human will, and therefore to the will of all rational beings, then it will be shown not only that pure reason can be practical but that it alone, and not reason limited empirically, is indubitably practical. Consequently we shall have to make a critical examination, not of *pure practical* reason, but of *practical* reason generally. For once pure reason has been shown to exist, it needs no critical examination. For reason contains the standard for critically examining every use of itself. Therefore the critique of practical reason as such is bound to prevent the empirically conditioned reason from presuming to be the only ground for determining the will. Once it is proved that there is pure [practical]reason, the employment of this reason by itself is immanent. On the other hand, the empirically conditioned use of reason, for which superiority is claimed, is transcendent and expresses itself in demands and precepts which go quite beyond its sphere. This is just the opposite of what might be said of pure reason in its speculative employment.

However, as it is still the knowledge of pure reason which is the foundation of reason's practical employment there, the general outline of the classification of a critique of practical reason must be arranged in accordance with that of the speculative. Then we must have the *Elements* and the *Methodology* of reason. In the former we must have an *Analytic* as the rule of truth, and a *Dialectic* as the exposition and resolution of illusion in judgments of practical reason. The order in the subdivision of the Analytic will be the reverse of that in the critique of pure speculative reason. For in the present case, we shall commence with *principles* and proceed to concepts, and only then, if possible, come to the senses. Whereas, in the case of speculative reason we began with the senses and had to end with the principles. The reason lies again in this: We now have to do with a will and have to consider reason in relation, not to objects, but to this will and its causality. Therefore we must begin with the principles of a causality not empirically conditioned, following which the attempt can be made to establish our notions of the grounds for determining such a will, of their application to objects and, finally, to the subject and its sense faculty. We have to begin with the law of causality based on freedom, that is, with a pure practical principle, and this determines the objects to which alone it can be applied.

FIRST BOOK

THE ANALYTIC OF PURE PRACTICAL REASON

Chapter I

Of the Principles of Pure Practical Reason

§ 1

Definition

Practical *Principles* are propositions which contain a general determination of the will when several practical rules come under such a determination. They are subjective or *Maxims* when the condition [determination] is regarded by the subject as valid only for his own will. They are objective or practical *laws* when the condition is recognized as objective, that is, as valid for the will of every rational being.

Remark

If we suppose that *pure* reason contains in itself a practical motive, that is, one adequate for determining the will, then there are practical laws; otherwise all practical principles will be mere maxims. In the case that the will of a rational being is psychologically affected, there may occur a conflict between the maxim and the practical laws recognized by this will. For example, a man may make it his maxim to let no offense pass unrevenged and yet he may see that this is not a practical law but only his own maxim; that on the contrary, if it is regarded as being a maxim [constituting] a rule for the will of every rational being, [their conduct] cannot be harmonized. In natural philosophy the principles of what happens, e.g., the principle of equivalence of action and reaction in the communication of motion, are laws of nature at the same time. For, here the use of reason is theoretical and determined by the nature of the object. In practical philosophy, which is concerned only with the reasons determining the will, the principles that a man makes for himself are not laws by which he is inexorably bound. In practical matters reason is concerned with a subject and its faculty of desire, the special character of which may occasion variations in the rule.

The practical rule is always a product of reason because it prescribes action as a means to an intended effect. But in the case of a being whose will is not determined by reason, this rule is an *imperative*. That is, it is a rule characterized by "shall" expressing the objective obligation of the action and signifying that if reason completely determined the will, the action would inevitably take place according to this rule. Imperatives are objectively valid and are quite distinct from maxims which are subjective principles. Imperatives either determine the conditions of the causality of the rational being as an efficient cause, that is, merely in reference to the effect and the means of attaining it, or imperatives determine only the will, as to whether it is adequate to the effect or not. The former would be hypothetical imperatives containing mere precepts of skill and the latter, on the other hand, would be categorical and alone would be practical laws. Maxims are *principles* but they are not *imperatives*. However, when imperatives themselves are conditional, that is, do not determine the will simply as will, but determine it only in respect to a desired effect, in other words, when imperatives are hypothetical, they are practical pre-

cepts but not *laws.* Laws must be sufficient to determine the will as will even before it is asked whether there is power sufficient for a desired effect or the means necessary to produce it. Hence laws are categorical. Otherwise, they are not laws at all because the necessity is lacking which, if the law is to be practical, must be independent of psychological conditions that are only connected with the will by contingency. For example, telling a man that he must be industrious and thrifty in youth so that he will not be indigent in old age is a correct and important practical precept of the will. But in this case it is easy to see that the will is directed to something *else* that it supposedly desires. As to this desire, we must leave it up to the actor himself, whether he looks forward to other resources than those he will acquire himself, or whether he does not expect to become old, or whether he thinks that in the case of future need he will be able to get along with little. Reason, from which alone can spring a rule involving necessity [binding obligation], does indeed give necessity to this precept, for otherwise it would not be an imperative. But this is a necessity dependent on subjective conditions and cannot be supposed in the same degree as all subjects can be. In order to give laws, reason should necessarily only have to presuppose *itself* because rules are objectively and universally valid only when they are without any of the contingent subjective conditions by which one rational being is differentiated from another. Telling a man that he should never make a deceitful promise is a rule that only concerns his will, whether or not the purposes he may have can be attained thereby. It is only the act of willing that is to be determined *a priori* by that rule. Therefore, if it is found that this rule is practically right, then it is a law because it is a categorical imperative. Thus practical laws refer only to the will without considering what is attained by its becoming a cause, and, in order to have the practical laws pure, we may disregard this aspect as belonging to the world of sense.

§ 2

Theorem I

All practical principles presupposing an *object* (material or content) of the faculty of desire as the basis of the will's determination are empirical and can furnish no practical laws.

By the term, material or content of the faculty of desire, I mean an object whose actual existence is desired. Now if this object *precedes* the practical rule and is the condition for our making it a principle, then (*in the first place*) I say that this principle is wholly empirical in that case. For what determines the choice is the idea of an object and the particular relation of this idea to the subject by which the subject's faculty of desire is determined to [seek] its realization. Such a relation to the subject is called the *pleasure* [resulting from] the existence of an object. This pleasure must be presupposed as a condition of the possibility of determining the will. But it is impossible to know *a priori* whether any idea of an object will be connected with *pleasure* or *pain*, or will be indifferent. Therefore, in such cases the principle determining the choice must be empirical and therefore the practical material which presupposed the principle as a condition must also be empirical.

In the second place, since susceptibility to pleasure or pain can only be known empirically and not in the same degree for all rational beings, a principle based on this subjective condition may indeed serve as a *maxim* for the subject who possesses this susceptibility, but may not serve as a law for him. This is because such a principle is lacking in objective necessity which must be recognized *a priori.* Therefore it follows that such a principle can never furnish a practical law.

§ 3

Theorem II

All practical principles relating to content as such, are of one and the same kind and they come under the general principle of self-love or personal happiness.

Pleasure arising from the idea of the existence of a thing, in so far as it is to determine the desire of this thing, is founded on the susceptibility of the subject, since pleasure *depends* on the presence of an object. Hence pleasure belongs to sense (sensation) and not to intellect. Intellect conceives the relation of an idea *to an object* according to concepts, not of an idea to a subject according to feelings. Therefore it is practical only in so far as the faculty of desire is determined by the sensation of agreeableness that the subject expects [to experience] from the actual existence of the object. The consciousness that a rational being has of the pleasure of life that continually accompanies his whole existence is happiness, and making this happiness the supreme ground for determining the will constitutes the principle of self-love. All material principles, that place the determining ground of the will in pleasure or pain received from the existence of any object, are all of the same kind, inasmuch as they all belong to the principle of self-love or individual happiness.

Corollary

All practical rules relating to content place the determining principle of the will in the *lower desires* and if there were no *purely formal* laws of the will adequate for determining it, then we could not admit *any higher desire* at all.

Remark I

It is surprising that otherwise acute men can consider it possible to distinguish between *higher* and *lower desires* according to whether the *ideas* that are connected with the feeling of pleasure have their origin in the *senses* or in the *intellect*. For, when we inquire what are the determining grounds of desire and place them in some expected pleasantness, it is of no consequence whence the *idea* of this pleasing object is derived, but only how much it *pleases*. No matter whether or not an idea has its seat and source in the intellect, if only it can determine the choice by presupposing a feeling of pleasure in the subject,

it follows that its ability for determining the choice depends altogether on the nature of the inner sense and if this can be
agreeably affected by it. However dissimilar the ideas of objects
may be, even though they may be ideas of the intellect or reason in contrast to ideas of sense, yet the feeling of pleasure is of
one and the same kind, not only since it can only be known
empirically, but also since it affects one and the same vital force
manifesting itself in the faculty of desire. In this respect the
feeling of pleasure can differ from every other ground for
determination only in degree. Otherwise how could we compare the *magnitude* of two bases of determination, whose ideas
depend upon different faculties, so as to prefer that which
affects the faculty of desire in the highest degree. The same
man may return unread an instructive book that he cannot obtain again in order not to miss a hunt; he may depart in the
midst of a fine speech in order not to be late for dinner; he may
leave a rational conversation such as he usually values highly to
take his place at the gaming-table; he may even repulse a poor
man whom he at other times takes pleasure in helping because
he has only just enough money in his pocket to pay for his ad-
mission to the theater. If the determination of his will rests on
the feeling of whether something that he expects from a certain
cause is agreeable or not, it is all the same to him by what sort
of ideas he will be affected. The only thing that concerns him
in making his choice is: how great, how long-continued, how
easily obtained, and how often repeated this agreeableness is.
Just as it is all the same to the man wanting money to spend
whether the gold was dug out of the mountain or washed out
of the sand provided it is accepted at the same value, so the
man caring only for the enjoyment of life does not ask whether
the ideas are of the intellect or the senses but only *how much*
and *how great* pleasure they will give for the longest time. It
is only those who would gladly deny to pure reason the power
of determining the will without presupposing any feeling who
could deviate so far from their own definition as to describe as

quite heterogeneous what they had themselves previously brought under one and the same principle. Thus, for example, it is observed that we can find pleasure in the mere *exercise of power,* in the consciousness of our strength of mind in overcoming obstacles which are opposed to our designs, in the culture of our mental talents, etc. We justly call these the more refined pleasures and enjoyments because they are more in our power than others. They do not exhaust, but rather increase our capacity for further enjoyment and while they delight, at the same time they cultivate. But to say on this account that they determine the will in a different way and not through sense, is just the same as when ignorant persons who like to dabble in metaphysics imagine matter so subtle, so super-subtle that they almost become giddy with it and then they think that in this way they have conceived of matter as a *spiritual* and yet extended being. If we follow *Epicurus* and assume that virtue only determines the will by means of the pleasure it promises, we cannot blame him afterwards for considering this pleasure to be of the same kind as those of the coarsest senses. We have no reason whatever to complain about his maintaining that the ideas by which this feeling is excited in us belong merely to the bodily senses. As far as can be conjectured, Epicurus sought the source of many of the ideas in the use of the higher cognitive faculty. But this did not and could not prevent him from maintaining that the pleasure itself which those intellectual ideas give us, and by which alone they can determine the will, is just the same kind [as that of the bodily senses]. *Consistency* is the supreme obligation of a philosopher and yet the most rarely found. The ancient Greek schools give us more examples of it than we find in our *eclectic* age in which some shallow and dishonest *system of compromises* of contradictory principles is devised because such a system commends itself more to a public content to know something of everything and nothing thoroughly. . . .

The principle of one's own happiness, no matter how much intellect and reason may be used in [fashioning] it, cannot contain any determining principles for the will other than those belonging to the lower desires. Either there is no higher faculty of desire at all or *pure* reason alone must be practical. What this means is that reason must be able to determine the will by the mere form of the practical rules without supposing any feeling and consequently without any idea of the pleasant or unpleasant. . . . Only when reason determines the will by itself, and not as the servant of the desires, is that which is determined by feelings really subordinated to a higher desire.

Remark II

To be happy is necessarily the wish of every finite rational being and it is therefore inevitably a determining principle of his faculty of desire. For, we are not originally content with our whole existence—a bliss which would imply a consciousness of our own independent self-sufficiency. This problem is imposed on us by our own finite nature. We have wants and these wants concern the matter of our desires. This matter is something that is relative to a subjective feeling of pleasure or pain which determines what we need in order to be satisfied with our condition. But precisely because this substantive principle of determination can only be empirically known by the subject, it is impossible to regard this task as [resolvable by] a law. For, a law is objective and must contain the *very same principle of determination* of the will in all cases and for all rational beings.

§ 4

Theorem III

A rational being cannot regard his maxims as practical, general laws unless he conceives of them as principles determining the will not by their content or material but only by their form.

[What is meant by the "material" (content) of a practical principle has been explained above, § 2.—Ed.]

Remark

The commonest understanding can distinguish without instruction what form of maxim is adapted for general legislation.
For example, suppose that I have made it my maxim to increase
my fortune by every safe means. Now I have a deposit in my
hands the owner of which has died and left no writing about it.
This is just the sort of case to test whether my maxim can
also hold good as a general, practical law. I ask whether I
can at the same time give a law that everyone may deny a deposit of which no one can produce a proof. I at once become
aware that such a principle, when viewed as a law, would eliminate itself because it would result in no deposits being made. A
practical law that I recognize as such must be qualified for
general legislation; this is an identical proposition and is therefore self-evident.

It is surprising that intelligent men could have thought of
calling the desire for happiness a general, *practical law* on the
ground that the desire and therefore the *maxim* by which
everyone makes this desire determine his will is universal.
While, to be sure, a universal law of nature makes everything
harmonious, on the contrary if in this case we attribute to the
maxim the universality of a law, there will result the extreme
opposite of harmony, the greatest opposition, and the complete
destruction of the maxim itself and of its purpose. For, in regard
to happiness, the will of all has not one and the same object,
but everyone has his own object, his private welfare, which may
fortuitously accord with the purposes of others who are equally
selfish. But this fortuitous accord is far from sufficing for a law
because the recurrent exceptions that it is permitted to make are
endless and cannot be definitely encompassed in one universal
rule. The resulting harmony would be like that which a certain
satirical poem depicts as existing between a married couple bent
on breaking up: "Oh, marvellous harmony of these two, what

he wants strongly, she wants too." It also resembles the pledge of Francis I to the Emperor Charles V: "What my brother Charles wants, that I want also." (Namely, Milan).

§ 5

Problem I

Suppose the mere legislative form of maxims is alone the sufficient determining principle of a will, find the nature of that will which can be determined by it alone.

Since the mere form of the law can only be conceived by reason and consequently is not an object of the senses and does not belong to the class of phenomena, it follows that the idea of the law which determines the will is distinct from all the principles that determine events in nature according to the law of causality because in the case of the latter the determining facts must themselves be phenomena. If no determining principle can serve as a law for the will other than the universal legislative form, such a will must be conceived as wholly independent of the natural law of phenomena in their mutual relation, the law of causality. Such independence is called *freedom* in the strictest, that is in the transcendental, sense. Consequently a will that receives its law from nothing but the mere legislative form of the maxim is a free will.

§ 6

Problem II

Suppose a will is free, find the law which alone is suited for determining it necessarily.

Since the material of a practical law can never be given in any but an empirical way, and since the free will is independent of empirical conditions yet is determinable, it follows that a free will must find its principle of determination in the law, but independent of the material of the law. But nothing, besides the material of the law, is contained in it except the legislative form. Therefore it is the legislative form contained in the maxim which alone can constitute a ground for determining the will.

Remark

Thus, freedom and an unconditional practical law imply each other reciprocally. Now, I am not asking here whether they are actually distinct, or whether an unconditional law is perhaps merely the self-consciousness of a pure practical reason and that such consciousness is identical with the positive concept of freedom. I am only asking where our *knowledge* of the unconditionally practical begins. The knowledge cannot start with freedom for we cannot be conscious of freedom immediately as the first concept of freedom is negative. Nor can we infer such knowledge from experience, for experience gives us only the knowledge of the law of phenomena and hence of the mechanism of nature which is the direct opposite of freedom. Therefore it is moral law that *first* presents itself to us because we become directly conscious of it as soon as we trace for ourselves the maxims of the will. Moral law then leads directly to the concept of freedom inasmuch as reason presents the law as a principle of determination which cannot be outweighed by any sensible conditions and in fact is wholly independent of them. But how is the consciousness of that moral law possible? We can become conscious of pure practical laws just as we are conscious of pure theoretical laws by paying close attention to the necessity with which reason prescribes them, and by attending to the elimination of all empirical conditions as reason directs. The concept of a pure will arises out of such pure practical laws just as that of a pure understanding arises out of pure theoretical laws.

The following consideration may make it evident that this is the correct way of subsuming these [basic] concepts and that morality first reveals the notion of freedom to us and that therefore it is *practical reason* which poses the most insoluble problem to speculative reason with this concept of freedom, thereby placing speculative reason in the greatest perplexity. [As we have seen] no phenomena can be explained by the concept of freedom and so the mechanism of nature must constitute the only clue. Moreover, when pure reason tries to ascend in the series of causes to the un-caused, it becomes involved in an antinomy which is entangled in incomprehensibilities on all sides. Yet mechanism is useful at least in explaining phenomena and therefore no one would have been so rash as to introduce freedom into [natural] science had not moral law and with it practical reason come in and forced the notion of freedom upon us. Experience also confirms this, our pattern of concepts. Suppose someone asserts that when the desired object and the opportunity for satisfying his lascivious appetite are present, it is quite irresistible not to do so. [Ask him] whether, should a gallows be erected before the house wherein he finds this opportunity so that he should be hanged immediately after the gratification of his lust, he could not control his passion then. We need not be long in doubt as to what he would reply. On the other hand, ask him whether, if his ruler should order him on pain of the same immediate execution to bear false witness against an honorable man whom the prince might wish to destroy under some plausible pretext, he would consider it possible in that case to overcome his love of life however great it might be. He would perhaps not venture to say whether he would do so or not, but he would have to admit without qualification that it is possible to do so. Therefore he judges that he can do a certain thing because he is conscious that he ought [to do it]. Thus he recognizes that he is free, a fact which he never would have known but for the moral law.

§ 7

The Fundamental Law of Pure, Practical Reason

Act so that the maxim of your will can be valid at the same time as a principle of universal legislation.

Comment

Pure geometry has postulates which are practical propositions, but which contain nothing more than the assumption that we *can* do something if it is required that we *should* do it; these are the only geometrical propositions that concern existence. They are practical rules under a problematical condition of the will. But the rule [contained in the above law] says that we must absolutely proceed in a certain, definite manner. Therefore this practical rule is unconditional and is conceived *a priori* as a categorical, practical proposition by which the will is objectively determined, absolutely and immediately. . . . For pure reason, which is practical in itself and by itself, is directly legislative in this case. The will is thought of as independent of empirical conditions and therefore it is thought of as pure will determined by the *mere form of the law;* this principle of determination is regarded as the supreme condition of all maxims. The thing is very strange and has no parallel in all the rest of our practical knowledge. For the *a priori* thought of a possible universal legislation which is merely problematical is unconditionally commanded as a law, that is, without borrowing anything from experience or from any external will. This law is not a precept to do something for attaining some desired effect, but it is a rule that determines the will *a priori* only so far as regards the form of its maxims. At least it is not impossible to conceive a law which, while it only applies to the *subjective* form of principles, serves as a principle of determination by means of the *objective* form of law in general. We may call the consciousness of this basic law a fact of reason because we cannot arrive at it by ratiocination from antecedent data of reason, such as the consciousness of freedom for this is not given antecedently. This consciousness presents itself to us as a proposition of *a priori* synthesis which is not based on anything seen, either pure or empirical imagination. The proposition would, indeed, be analytical if the freedom of the will were presupposed, but to presuppose freedom as a positive *concept* would require an intellectual image (*Anschauung*) which cannot be assumed here. However, in order not to fall into any misconception it must be observed that when we regard this law as *given,* it is not an empirical fact but is the sole fact [or datum] of pure reason which thereby announces itself as originally legislative (*sic volo, sic jubeo*).

Corollary

Pure reason is practical by itself alone and gives to man a universal law which we call the *moral law* (*Sittengesetz*).

Remark

The fact [or datum] just mentioned is undeniable. It is only necessary to analyze the judgment that men pass on the lawfulness of their actions, in order to find that, whatever inclination may say to the contrary, reason, incorruptible and self-restrained, always confronts the maxim of the will in any action with the pure will, that is, with itself, considering itself as *a priori* practical. On account of the universality which makes this principle of morality the formal supreme determining principle of the will without regard to any subjective differences, this principle is declared by reason to be a law for all rational beings in so far as they have a will, that is, a power to determine their causality by the concept [of right conduct] of rules. Therefore this principle is declared to be a law so far as such rational beings are capable of acting according to principles and consequently also according to practical *a priori* principles. . . . As stated, this principle is not limited to men only, but applies to all finite beings that possess reason and will; indeed, it even includes the Infinite Being as the supreme intelligence. However in the case of finite beings the law has the form of an imperative because in them, as rational beings, we can suppose a *pure* will. But because they are creatures affected with wants and sensual motives we cannot suppose a sacred will, that is, one which would be incapable of [entertaining] any maxim conflicting with moral law. [To repeat:] in the case of finite beings the moral law is an *imperative*, commanding categorically because the law is unconditioned. The relation of such a will to the [formal] law is one of *dependence* under the name of *obligation*, which implies a *compulsion* to act according to reason and its objective law. Such action is called *duty*, because a discretion subject to psychological affections, though not determined by them and therefore still free, implies a wish that arises from *subjective* causes. Consequently, such a wish often opposes the pure objective determining principle. Such a will is therefore in need [of the moral restraint] of the resistance offered by practical reason; this may be called an inner but intellectual compulsion. In the supreme intelligence the will is rightly conceived as incapable of any maxim which could not be objectively a law at the same time. The notion of holiness belonging to the will places it above not all practical laws but all practically restrictive laws and consequently above obligation and duty. However, this holiness of will is [related to action and hence] practical as an idea which must necessarily serve as a prototype which finite rational beings can only approximate, and which the moral law, itself called sacred on this account, constantly and rightly holds before their eyes. The utmost that finite practical reason can achieve is to be certain of this infinite progress of one's maxims, and of their unchangeable disposition to advance. This highest achievement is virtue and virtue, as a naturally acquired faculty, can never be perfect because in such a case assurance never becomes apodictic certainty, and as mere persuasion it is very dangerous.

§ 8

Theorem IV

The *autonomy* of the will is the sole principle of all moral laws and of all duties which conform to them. On the other hand, *heteronomy* of the will not only cannot be the basis of any

obligation but it is opposed to the principle of such **obligation**
and to the moral quality of the will.* The sole principle **of**
morality consists in moral law being independent of all substantive considerations such as a desired object; it thus consists in the
accompanying determination of the will by the mere general
legislating form of which its maxim must be capable. Now this
independence is *freedom* in the negative sense, and this *self-
legislation* of the pure, and therefore practical, reason is freedom in the positive sense. Thus the moral law expresses nothing
more than the *autonomy* of the pure practical reason, that is, of
freedom. This freedom is itself the formal condition of all
maxims and only when subject to this condition can they agree
with the supreme practical law. Therefore, if the material of
an act of willing, which can be nothing else than the object of
a desire connected with law, enters into the practical law *as the
condition of its possibility*, heteronomy of choice results; that is,
dependence on some [natural] physical law [which causes us to]
follow some impulse or inclination. In that case the will does not
give the law to itself, but gives only a precept on how rationally
to follow psychological laws. In such a case the maxim that
cannot take the universally legislative form, not only produces
no obligation, but is itself contrary to the principle of pure,
practical reason and therefore also to [a basis in pure] convictions [*Gesinnung*] even though the resulting action may be
lawful.

Comment I

A practical precept containing material and therefore empirical
conditions must never be reckoned as a practical law. For the
law of the pure will which is free puts the will into a sphere
quite different from the empirical. As the necessity involved in
the law is not a physical necessity, it can only consist of the
formal conditions of the possibility of a law in general. . . .

* [For a more detailed discussion of "heteronomy" see above Pp. 181 f.
and below Pp. 225 ff.—Ed.]

Yet the happiness of others may be the object of the will of a rational being. If this were the determining principle of the maxim we would have to presuppose that we get a rational satisfaction not only from the welfare of others but also from a need such as is occasioned in some men by their sympathetic disposition. But I cannot assume the existence of this need in every rational being and not at all in God. The material element of the maxim may [be admitted to be present] but it must not be the condition of it, otherwise the maxim would not be a law. Hence the mere form of law limiting the substantive content of a norm must also be a reason for adding this material to the will, not for presupposing it. For example, let the substantive element be my own happiness. If I attribute this [happiness] to everyone, as I actually do in the case of every finite being, then seeking happiness can only become an *objective* practical law if I include the happiness of others. Therefore, the law that we should promote the happiness of others does not arise from the assumption that this is an object of everyone's choice. It merely arises thus; that the form of universality, which reason requires as the condition of giving the objective validity of a law to a maxim of self-love, is itself the determining ground of the will. Therefore, it was not the object, that is, the happiness of others, which determined the pure will, but it was the mere form of law [which did this]. By this mere form of law I qualified a maxim, originally founded on inclination, in order to give it the universality of a law and thus to adapt it to practical reason. It is this qualification alone, and not the addition of an external impulse, which can produce the concept of *obligation* for extending the maxim of my self-love to the happiness of others.

Comment II

The direct opposite of the principle of morality consists in the principle of one's own happiness being made the determining principle of the will. There must be included in this classification all that places the determining principle, which is to serve as a law, anywhere but in the legislative form of the maxim. However, this conflict is not merely logical, such as that which would arise in empirically conditioned rules if one were to raise them to the rank of necessary principles of cognition. This conflict is practical and it would ruin morality altogether were not the voice of reason in reference to the will so clear, so irrepressible, and so distinctly audible to even the most ordinary man. Indeed, this argument can only be maintained by the perplexing speculations of the schools who are bold enough to shut their ears against that heavenly voice in order to support a theory that causes no headaches.

Suppose that an otherwise well-beloved friend were to attempt to justify himself to you for having borne false witness; first, by appealing to what he regarded as the sacred duty of consulting his own happiness, and second, by enumerating the advantages that he had gained thereby, pointing out the prudence he had shown in securing himself against detection, even by yourself, to whom he now reveals the secret only in order that he may be able to deny it at any time. Suppose also that he were to affirm in all seriousness then that he had fulfilled a true human duty. You would either laugh in his face or shrink from him with disgust. Yet, if a man has regulated his principles of action solely with a view to his own advantage you would have no reason whatever for objecting to this mode of behavior. Or, suppose someone recommends to you a steward, a man to whom you can blindly trust all your affairs. In order to inspire you with confidence, he is extolling him as a prudent man who thoroughly understands his own interest and who is so indefatigably active that he lets slip no opportunity for advancing it. Lastly, should you be afraid of finding a vulgar selfishness in him, the good taste with which he lives is praised, not seeking his pleasure in money-making or in coarse wantonness but in the enlargement of his knowledge, in instructive intercourse with a select circle and even in helping the needy. It is then added that this man is not particular as to the means, which of course derive all their value only from the end, and that he is ready to use other people's money for the purpose as if it were his own, only provided he knows that he can do so safely and without discovery. You would either believe that the recommender was mocking you or that he had lost his mind. So sharply and clearly defined are the boundaries of morality and self-love that even the most ordinary eye cannot fail to distinguish whether a thing belongs to one or the other. The few remarks that follow may appear superfluous when the truth is so plain but at least they may serve to give a little more distinctness to the judgment of common sense.

The maxim of self-love (prudence) only *advises,* the law of morality commands. There is a great difference between what we are advised to do and what we are *obliged* to do.

The most ordinary intelligence can see easily and without hesitation what the principle of the autonomy of choice requires to be done. But what is to be done if heteronomy is assumed is quite difficult [to see] and requires worldly prudence. That is to say, what is duty is by itself plain to everyone. But what will bring durable advantage extending to one's whole existence is always veiled in impenetrable obscurity. Much prudence is required for adapting even tolerably the practical rule, founded on such calculations for advantage, to the purposes of life, through making suitable exceptions. But moral law commands the most precise obedience from everyone. Therefore it should not be very difficult to form a judgment as to what moral law calls for so that even the most ordinary unpractised mind can follow it without any worldly prudence.

He who has *lost* at a game may be annoyed with himself and his lack of prudence but if he is conscious of having *cheated* at a game, even though he has gained thereby, he will despise himself as soon as he compares what he has done with the moral law. This moral law must, therefore, be something other than the principle of one's own happiness. When a man is compelled to say to himself, "I am a *worthless* fellow, though I have filled my purse," he must have a different standard from the one he has when he approves of himself and says, "I am a prudent man for I have enriched my account."

Finally, there is something more in the idea of our practical reason that accompanies the transgression of a moral law; namely, the transgression's deserving punishment. Now, the notion of punishment as such cannot be united with that of securing happiness. Although the person inflicting the punishment may be directing it for the benevolent purpose [of making the punished man happier in the end], yet the punishment must be justified in itself as such, that is, as mere injury. The reason is that if injury were all [that was involved] and the person punished could perceive no kindness hidden behind the severity, he would have to admit that justice was done him and that his reward was quite appropriate for his conduct. In every punishment as such there must be justice and this constitutes the essence of the concept. Indeed, benevolence may be connected with it but the man deserving punishment has not the least reason for counting upon this. Therefore punishment is a physical evil which, though it is not connected with moral evil as a *natural* consequence, ought to be connected with it by the principles of moral legislation. Consequently, if every crime, even crime committed with no regard for the physical consequences to its instigator, is punishable in itself, that is, if it forfeits happiness at least in part, it is obviously absurd to say that crime consists only in a man drawing punishment upon himself and thereby injuring his own private happiness. This would be the proper concept of all crime according to the principle of self-love. Therefore, according to this view the [resulting] punishment would be the reason for calling any action a crime, and justice would consist of omitting all punishment and even preventing natural punishment. There would then no longer be any evil in a certain action because the injury which formerly followed it, and only because of which the action was called evil, would now be prevented. Finally, looking on all rewards and punishments as merely machinery in the hand of a higher power for serving only to set rational creatures to strive after their final end of happiness is a viewpoint so evidently a mechanical interpretation of the will and destructive of all freedom that it need not detain us here.

More refined, though equally false, is the opinion of those who conceive of a certain moral sense and who pretend that this sense and not reason determines moral law, and that because of this moral sense, consciousness of virtue is supposed to be directly connected with contentment and pleasure, and consciousness of vice with mental unrest and pain. They thus reduce all morality to a desire for happiness. Without repeating what has been said above, I will only comment briefly here on the fallacy into which they fall. In order to represent a vicious man as tormented by psychic anxiety as a result of being aware of his transgressions, they must first represent him as fundamentally morally good, at least to some degree. Therefore they must represent him as already virtuous who is pleased with the consciousness of dutiful action. Hence the concept of morality and duty must precede any thought of this satisfaction and cannot be derived from it. A man must first appreciate the importance of what we call duty, the authority of moral law, and the immediate worth that obeying it gives a person in his own eyes, before he can feel any satisfaction from consciousness of his conformity to it, or can feel any of the bitter remorse that accompanies consciousness of transgressing it. It is impossible to feel this contentment or anxiety, or to make such contentment the basis of moral law, before knowing the obligation [of moral law]. A man must be at least half honest to be able even to form an idea of these sentiments. Since human will, because of its liberty, is capable of being determined immediately by moral law, I am not denying that frequent practice in accordance with this principle of determination may finally produce a subjective feeling of self-satisfaction. Indeed, it is the duty to establish and cultivate this sentiment that alone properly deserves to be called moral sentiment. But the notion of duty should not be derived from this sentiment lest we should have a sentiment for the law as such. We should have to make that an object of sensation which can only be conceived by reason. If this is not to be a flat contradiction it must [be conceived in a manner] destroying all notion of duty and replacing it by mere mechanical play of refined propensities, though sometimes contending with the coarser propensities.

If we now compare our supreme *formal* principle of pure practical reason of autonomy of the will with all previous substantive principles of morality, we can exhibit them all in a table exhausting all possible cases. This can be done with all except that one formal principle, which may serve to show visibly that there is no use in looking for any principle other than that proposed now. In fact, all possible principles for determining the will are either merely *subjective* and therefore empirical, or they are *objective* and rational; in either case they may be *external* or *internal*.

Practical material (substantive) grounds for determining the principle of morality are:

SUBJECTIVE GROUNDS		OBJECTIVE GROUNDS	
External	*Internal*	*Internal*	*External*
Education	Physical feelings	Perfection	Will of God
(*Montaigne*)	(*Epicurus*)	(*Wolf* and	(Crusius and
Civil constitu-	Moral senti-	the *Stoics*)	other *theolog-*
tion	ments		*ical* Moralists
(*Mandeville*)	(*Hutcheson*)		

Those grounds on the left hand are all empirical and evidently incapable of furnishing the universal principle of morality. But those on the right hand are based on reason. Perfection, as a quality of things and as the highest perfection *substantively* conceived, that is as God, can only be conceived by means of rational concepts. The concept of *perfection* may be taken in a *theoretical* sense and then it means merely the completeness of each thing in its own way (transcendental completeness) or it means merely the completeness of a thing generally (metaphysical completeness); we are not concerned here with those kinds of perfection. On the other hand, the concept of perfection may be taken in a *practical* sense and then it means the fitness or sufficiency of a thing for all sorts of purposes. This perfection, as a *quality* of man and consequently internal, is nothing but *talent* and what strengthens or completes this talent is skill. When the supreme perfection substantively conceived, that is [conceived] as God (hence external), is considered practically, [i.e. as related to action] this perfection is the sufficiency of this being for all ends in general. Only when ends are already given can the notion of *perfection,* whether internal in ourselves or external in God, be the determining principle of the will in relation to the ends. Since an end is an *object* which must precede the determining of the will by a practical rule and since it must contain the grounds for the possibility of this determining of the will, such an end is always empirical. Therefore such an end may serve as the principle of the *Epicurean* theory of happiness, but not as the pure, rational principle of morality and duty. Thus, because talents and their improvement contribute to the advantages of life, or to the will of God, if agreement with [the will of God] may be considered the object of a will with no ante cedent independent practical principle, the improving of talent can be a motive only by reason of the happiness expected therefrom. Hence it follows: *first,* that all the principles stated in such a theory are material (*substantive*); second, that they include all possible substantive principles; and in conclusion, that, since substantive principles are quite incapable of furnishing the supreme moral law as has been shown, the *formal, practical principle* of pure reason, according to which [principle] the mere form of universal legislation must constitute the supreme and immediate determining principle of the will, is the *only possible* principle adequate for furnishing categorical imperatives; that is, practical laws enjoining actions as duty. Only a principle so defined can serve as the principle of morality, both for criticizing conduct and for application to the human will in determining it.

I

Of the Deduction of the Fundamental Principles of Pure Practical Reason

This analytic shows that pure reason can be practical, that it can itself determine the will independently of anything empirical. It does this through the fact in which the pure reason in us proves itself to be actually practical. This is a fact of autonomy as manifest in the principle of morality by which reason determines the will to act.

At the same time this analytic shows that this fact is inseparably linked with consciousness of freedom of the will, and indeed is identical with it. This freedom [determines] the will of a rational being who is conscious of existing in, and being determined by, an intelligible order of things, though, as he belongs to the world of sense, he recognizes himself as necessarily subject to the laws of causality like other efficient causes. He is conscious, not by virtue of a special view (*Anschauung*) of himself, but by virtue of certain dynamic laws which determine his causality in the sensible world. It has been proved elsewhere that if freedom is attributed to us, we are thereby transported into an intelligible order of things.

If we compare this [reasoning] with the analytical part of the critique of pure speculative reason, we shall discover a curious contrast. Not fundamental principles, but pure, sensible *intuition* or visualization (*Anschauung*) was the first *datum* that made *a priori* knowledge possible, though only of objects of the senses. Synthetic principles cannot be derived from mere concepts without visualizing something. They can only occur with reference to such visualizing and therefore with reference to objects of possible experience. For it is when intellectual concepts are united with this act of looking-at-something (*Anschauung*) that the kind of knowledge we call experience is made possible. Beyond objects of experience, and therefore with regard to things as *noumena*, all positive knowledge was rightly disclaimed for speculative reason. However, speculative reason went so far as to establish with certainty the concept of *noumena*, that is, it established the possibility, even the necessity of thinking of them as noumena. For example, speculative reason showed, in the face of all objections, that the assumption of freedom when considered negatively was quite consistent with the principles and limitations of pure theoretic reason. But theoretic reason not only could not give us no definite enlargement of our knowledge with respect to such objects, but cut off all view of them altogether.

On the other hand, moral law presents us with a fact which is absolutely inexplicable in terms of any data of the sensible world and in terms of the whole compass of our theoretic use of reason. This [primary] fact points to a pure world of the intellect, even *defines it positively* and enables us to know something of it, namely, as a law.

As far as rational beings are concerned this law gives the world of sense, as *sensible nature*, the form of an intelligible world, that is, the form of a *supersensible system* of nature, without interfering with its mechanism. In the most general meaning, a system of nature is the existence of things under laws. The sensible nature of rational beings in general is their existence under empirically conditioned laws, which is *heteronomy* from the point of view of reason. On the other hand the supersensible nature of the same beings is their existence under laws that are independent of all empirical conditions and which therefore belong to the *autonomy* of pure reason. Since the laws are practical through which the existence of things depends on knowledge, supersensible nature, as far as we can form any idea of it, is nothing other than a system of nature under the *autonomy* of pure practical reason. Now the law of this autonomy is moral law, which is therefore the fundamental law of a supersensible nature and of a pure intellectual world whose counterpart must exist in the world of sense, but without interfering with its laws. We may call supersensible nature the primal nature (*natura archetypa*) which we only know through reason, and sensible nature the copied or reproduced nature (*natura ectypa*), because it contains the possible effect of the idea of the former which is the determining principle of the will. For, by its idea, moral law actually transfers us into a system where pure reason, if it were accompanied by adequate physical power, would produce the highest good (*summum bonum*) and where moral law would impart to our wills the form of the sensible world, as a whole of rational beings.[1] Paying the least attention to oneself will prove that this idea really serves as a pattern for determining our will.

Whenever the particular maxim that I am disposed to follow in giving testimony is tested by practical reason, I consider what that maxim should be in order to hold true as a general law of nature. It is manifest that when so considered the maxim would oblige everyone to speak the truth. It is incompatible with the generality of a law of nature that statements should be allowed to have the force of proof and yet be purposely untrue. Similarly the particular maxim that I adopt in disposing freely of my life is at once determined when I ask myself what the maxim would have to be like so that a system [of nature] could maintain itself with this maxim as its law. It is obvious that in such a system [of nature] no one could *arbitrarily* put an end to his own life, for such an arrangement could not be a lasting order of nature. And so in all similar cases. In actual nature, as an object of experience, free will is not of itself determined to [adopt] such maxims as could by themselves be the foundation of a natural system subject to general laws, or which could even

---

[1] [The German text is obscure here. It reads: ". . . *und bestimmt unseren Willen die Form der Sinnenwelt, als einem Ganzen vernünftiger Wesen, zu erteilen.*"—Ed.]

be fitted into a system so constituted. On the contrary, maxims of free will are private inclinations which constitute a natural whole in conformity with psychological (physical) laws, but which cannot form part of a system of nature; that would only be possible through our will acting in accordance with pure practical laws. Yet, through reason, we are conscious of a law to which all our maxims are subject, as though a natural order must be originated by our will. Therefore this law must be the idea of a natural system not given in experience and yet possible through freedom. It is therefore a system which is supersensible and to which, at least in its practical aspect, we attribute objective reality since we look on it as an object of our will as pure rational beings.

There is, then, a distinction between the laws of a nature to which the *will is subject* and the laws of a nature which is *subject to a will* as far as nature's relation to the free actions of the will is concerned. This distinction rests on this, that in the former case the objects must be the causes of the ideas which determine the will, whereas in the latter case, the will is the cause of the object. The causality of the will has its determining principle solely in the pure faculty of reason which may therefore be called a pure practical reason.

Therefore there are two very distinct problems. The first is: How can pure reason *a priori* know objects? The second is: How can pure reason be an immediate determining principle of the will; that is, [how can pure reason be an immediate determining principle] of the causality of the rational being with respect to the reality of objects through the mere thought of the universal validity of its own maxims as laws. . . .[2]

The second question, which belongs to the *Critique of Practical Reason,* requires no explaining how objects of the faculty of desire are possible for that, being a problem of the theoretical knowledge of nature, is left to the *Critique of Speculative Reason.* The second question only asks how reason

[2] [See above, *Prolegomena,* 14, Pp. 67.—Ed.]

can determine the maxims of the will. It is left to the theoretic
principles of reason to decide whether or not the causality of
the will suffices for the realization of the objects. This is an inquiry into whether or not the objects of the act of willing are
possible. . . . Here we are concerned only with the determination of the will and the determining principle of the maxims of
such a will as a free will, and not at all with the result [of the
willing]. Provided that the will conforms to the law of pure reason, then no matter what its *power* in execution may be, it is
no concern of the Critique whether or not any system of nature
really results from legislation for a possible system of nature according to such maxims. The critique of practical reason only inquires whether, and in what way, pure reason can be practical;
that is, can directly determine the will.

In this inquiry, criticism can and must begin with pure
practical laws and their actual existence. But instead of anything seen or observable, the conception of their existence in the
intelligible world, namely the concept of freedom, is taken as
their foundation. For freedom has no other meaning and these
[practical] laws are only possible in relation to freedom of
the will, and, freedom being supposed, these laws are necessary. Conversely, freedom is necessary because these laws are
necessary practical postulates. It cannot be explained further
how this consciousness of the moral law is possible, or what
amounts to the same thing, how freedom is possible; however,
its admissibility is well established in the theoretical critique.

The exposition of the supreme principle of practical reason is
now finished. First it was shown what it contains and that it
subsists by itself quite *a priori* and independent of empirical
principles. Then it was shown in what way it is distinguished
from all other practical principles. We cannot expect to succeed
with deducing [this principle], that is, with justifying its objective and universal validity and with understanding the possibility of such a synthetic proposition *a priori*, as well as we did in
the case of the principles of pure theoretical reason. These

latter referred to objects of possible experience: phenomena, and we proved that these phenomena could only be known as objects of experience by being brought under categories in accordance with these [pure practical] laws, and that consequently all possible experience must conform to these laws. But I could not proceed in this way in deducing moral law. For moral law is not concerned with knowledge of the properties of objects which may be given to reason from some other source; rather, it is concerned with knowledge which can itself become the grounds for the existence of objects, and [with knowledge by means of] which reason has causality in a rational being. Our deduction is concerned, therefore, with pure reason in so far as it can be regarded as a faculty immediately determining the will.

All our human insight fails as soon as we reach basic powers or faculties. Their possibility can in no way be understood, yet, [just for that reason] it should not be arbitrarily invented and assumed. Therefore, in the theoretical use of reason, experience alone can justify their assumption. But regarding the pure practical faculty of reason the expedient of adducing empirical proofs instead of deducing from *a priori* sources of knowledge is denied us. Whatever needs to draw the proof of its existence from experience must depend on principles of experience for the grounds of its possibility. Pure, yet practical, reason cannot be regarded as being so derived by its very concept. Furthermore, moral law is given as a fact by pure reason of which we are conscious *a priori* and which is apodictically certain, even though it is granted that no example of its exact fulfilment can be found in experience. Hence the objective reality of moral law cannot be proved through a deduction by any efforts [on the part of] theoretical reason, whether speculative or supported empirically. Therefore, even if we renounced its apodictic certainty, it could not be proved by experience *a posteriori*. Yet the objective reality of moral law is firmly established by itself.

But, instead of this vainly sought deduction of the moral principle, something entirely different and unexpected appears. For, conversely, this moral principle serves as the principle for deducing an inscrutable faculty which no experience can prove, but of which speculative reason is at least compelled to assume the possibility so as not to contradict itself when finding among its cosmological ideas something of unconditioned causality; I mean the faculty of freedom. Moral law, not requiring a justification itself, not only proves the possibility of freedom, but proves that freedom really belongs to those beings who recognize this law as binding on themselves. Moral law is actually a law of the causality of free agents, and is therefore [a law] of the possibility of a supersensible system of nature, just as the metaphysical law of events in the world of sense is a law of causality of the sensible system of nature. Therefore, moral law determines the law for a causality which speculative philosophy was compelled to leave undetermined and only as a negative concept. Therefore for the first time moral law gives this concept [of freedom] objective reality.

This sort of credential for moral law, that moral law is set forth as a principle for deducing freedom as a causality of pure reason, is a sufficient substitute for all *a priori* justification, since theoretical reason was compelled at least to assume the possibility of freedom in order to satisfy a lack of its own. For moral law sufficiently proves its reality even for the critique of speculative reason by the fact that it adds a positive definition to a causality which was previously conceived as merely negative. The possibility of such a causality was incomprehensible to speculative reason, yet had to be assumed by it. For moral law adds to the negative concept of a reason directly determining the will by imposing on its maxims the condition of a general legislative form. Thus for the first time reason can be given an objective, though as yet only a practical, reality, [whereas before] reason always became extravagant when proceeding speculatively with its ideas. [The possibility of such a causality] thus changes the *transcendent* use of reason into an immanent use in which, by means of ideas, reason is itself an efficient cause in the field of experience.

The determination of the causality of beings in the world of sense as such can never be unconditioned; and yet at the end of the entire sequence of conditions there must be something unconditioned. Therefore, there must be a causality which is determined wholly by itself. Hence, the idea of freedom as a faculty of absolute spontaneity was not found to be a need, but to be an analytical principle of pure reason, *as far as its possibility is concerned*. But, we were able only to *defend our premise* that a freely acting cause might be a being in the world of sense provided it is also considered as a *noumenon*. This was because it is absolutely impossible to find in experience any example that accords with this idea [of freedom] since among the causes of things as phenomena it would be impossible to come across any absolutely unconditioned determination of causality. This defense [of our premise] was made by showing that it was not self-contradictory to regard all the actions [of such an unconditioned cause] as subject to physical conditions so far as they are phenomena, and yet [at the same time] to regard the causality of such a being as physically unconditioned, when it is considered as an intellectual being. Thus the concept of freedom is made the regulative principle of reason. However, I do not learn by this principle what is the object to which that sort of causality is attributed. But I remove this difficulty by leaving to [those who explain] the mechanism of physical necessity the right to ascend from condition to condition *ad infinitum* in explaining the course of events in the world and hence also the actions of rational beings, while on the other hand I keep free for speculative reason the as yet vacant place of the intelligible, to which place speculative reason may now transfer the unconditioned. But I was not able [in the *Critique of Pure Reason*] to give *reality* to this idea; that is, I could not transform it into the knowledge of a being acting [in such a way], nor even [into the knowledge] of its possibility. This vacant place is now filled by pure practical reason which sets forth through freedom a definite law of causality in an intelligible world, [that is] moral law. Speculative reason does not fail thereby as regards the *certainty* of its problematical concept of freedom. For here this concept obtains *objective reality* which, though only practical, is nevertheless undoubted. Even the concept of causality, which in application and meaning properly holds true only for the phenomena it connects in experience (as is shown in the *Critique of Pure Reason*);[3] this concept is not so enlarged that its use is extended beyond its proper boundaries. [This is well], for if reason sought so to extend the concept of causality, reason would have to show how the logical relation of cause and effect can be used synthetically for a different way of envisaging than the sensible; that is, how a *causa noumenon* is possible. [Theoretical] reason can never do this and practical reason is not even concerned with this problem. Practical reason only posits the *determining principle* of the causality of man as a given sensible creature in *pure reason* which is therefore called practical. Hence practical reason employs the notion of cause, not in order to know objects, but to determine causality in respect to objects in general. Practical reason can neglect altogether applying this concept of cause to objects, since this concept is at all times encountered *a priori* quite independently of any envisaging of things. Practical reason employs this concept for a practical purpose, and hence we can transfer the determining principle of the will into the intelligible order of things, admitting at the same time that, [in terms of practical reason], we cannot understand what purpose the concept of cause serves in acquiring knowledge of these things. But reason must come to know in a definite manner causality in respect to actions of the will in the world of sense, otherwise practical reason could not really produce any action. Practical reason need not determine theoretically the concept, which it forms of its own causality as

[3] [See above, *Prolegomena*, § 20 et al.—Ed.]

noumenon, with a view to knowing its supersensible existence so as to give the concept of its own causality significance in this way. For this concept acquires significance anyhow, though only for practical use through moral law. . . .

II

Of the Authority of Pure Reason in Its Practical Use to Extend Its Range . . .

In the [form of a] moral principle we have asserted a law of causality whose determining principle is set above all the conditions of the sensible world. We have conceived of the will as determinable inasmuch as it belongs to an intelligible world. Therefore we have conceived of man, the subject of this will, as not only belonging to a world of pure intellect, though he is unknown in this respect, but we have also defined man, in regard to this causality, by means of a law which cannot be reduced to any physical law of the sensible world. We have thus extended our knowledge beyond the limits of that world, a pretension that the *Critique of Pure Reason* declared to be futile for all speculation.[4] How is the practical use of pure reason to be reconciled here with the theoretical use through determining the limits of its faculty?

But what happens when this category of causality and all the other categories, without which there can be no knowledge of any existing thing, are applied to things which are not *objects of possible experience,* but which lie beyond its bounds? For, I was only able to deduce the objective reality of these concepts in reference to objects of possible experience. But the very fact that I have only saved these concepts in this case, and that I have proved that by virtue of them objects may be conceived of, though not determined, *a priori,* this fact gives these concepts a place in the pure intellect from which they are referred to objects in general, whether [the objects are] sensible or not. What

---

[4] [See *Prolegomena,* above, § § 27–30, for what follows here: Kant's critique of Hume's analysis of cause.—Ed.]

is still lacking is the condition for *applying* these categories, and especially that of causality, to objects. This condition is the [ability to visualize things, or] intuition, and when this condition is lacking, it is impossible to apply [the categories] *with a view to knowing theoretically the object* as a *noumenon*.

The objective reality of the concept [of causality] still remains and can even be used in regard to *noumena,* but used without our being able to circumscribe in the least the concept theoretically so as to produce knowledge. It has been shown that this concept contains nothing impossible, even in reference to a [nonmaterial] object. Even when applied to objects of sense, the concept of cause is certainly located in the pure intellect. When referred to things-in-themselves, which cannot be objects of experience, the concept of cause is not capable of being determined for the purpose of imagining a *definite object* of theoretical knowledge. Yet, for any other purpose, such as a practical purpose, the concept of cause might be determinable so as to have such an application. This could not be the case if, as Hume maintained, this concept of causality contained something absolutely inconceivable.

In order to discover the condition under which the concept of causation may be applied to *noumena,* we need only recall why we are not satisfied with just applying it to objects of experience, but also desire to apply it to things-in-themselves. It will then appear that this application is made necessary, not through a theoretical purpose, but through a practical one. Even if in speculation we should be successful in applying the concept, we should not really gain anything in the knowledge of nature, nor gain anything generally with regard to such objects as are given; we would merely be diverging widely from the sensibly conditioned in which we already have enough to do in carefully following the chain of causes to the supersensible in order to complete our knowledge of principles and to fix the limits of that knowledge. But there always remains an infinite chasm gaping between those limits and what we do know, and we would be harkening to a vain curiosity rather than to a firm desire for knowledge [if we should attempt to bridge that chasm.]

But, besides the relation in which the intellect stands to objects in theoretical knowledge, the intellect also has a relation to the faculty of desire, which is therefore called the will and is called the pure will when pure intellect, reason, is practical through the mere concept of a law. . . . [Here follows a restatement of matters covered earlier.—Ed.]

If, like Hume, I had denied all objective reality to the concept of causality in its practical use, not merely with regard to things-in-themselves or to the supersensible, but also with regard to the objects of the senses, the concept of causality would have lost all meaning. Then, being a theoretically impossible concept, it would have been declared quite useless. Since what is nothing cannot be of any use, it would have been absurd to employ practically a concept that is theoretically null and void. But as it is, the concept of a causality free from empirical conditions is theoretically possible although it is empty, that is, devoid of any appropriate visualization. [The concept of such a causality] refers to an indeterminate object, but compensatory significance is given to it in moral law, and consequently in a practical sense. Even though I have nothing to visualize as the objective theoretical reality of the concept, nevertheless the concept has a real application which is exhibited *in concreto* in convictions or maxims. Therefore the concept has a practical reality which can be specified and this is enough to justify it with reference to *noumena*.

When once initiated, this objective reality of a pure intellectual concept in the sphere of the supersensible also gives objective reality to all other categories, but only in so far as they possess a necessary connection with the determining principle of the will, which is the moral law. This reality is only one of practical application. It does not in the least have the effect of enlarging our theoretical knowledge of these objects, or our understanding of their nature by pure reason. We shall thus find in the sequel that these categories refer only to beings as *intelligences* and to them only in the relation of the reason to the will; consequently they refer only to the practical. Beyond this these categories cannot pretend to any knowledge of these beings or intelligences.

CHAPTER II

On the Concept of an Object of Pure Practical Reason

By a concept of practical reason I mean the imagining of an object as possible and to be effected by [the use of one's] freedom. Therefore being an object of practical knowledge as such signifies only the relation of the will to the action by which the object or its opposite would be realized. To decide whether something is an object of *pure* practical reason or not, means discerning the possibility or impossibility of *willing* the action by which a certain object would be realized if we had the required power about which experience must decide. If the object be taken as the determining factor of our desire, it must first be known whether such an object is *physically* possible as a result of the free use of our powers, before we [can] decide whether or not it is an object of practical reason. On the other hand, if the law can be considered *a priori* as the determining principle of the action and the action as therefore determined by pure practical reason, then the judgment of whether or not a thing is an object of pure practical reason does not at all depend on an assessment of our physical power. The question is only whether, if the object were in our power, we should *will* an action that is directed to the existence of an object. Consequently, the *moral possibility* of the action must first be established. For it is not the object, but the law of the will that is the determining principle of the action. The only objects of practical reason are therefore those of *good* and *evil*. For by good is meant an object necessarily desired according to a principle of reason, by evil an object which is necessarily shunned, also according to a principle of reason.

If the concept of the good is not to be derived from an antecedent practical law, but on the contrary is to serve as its foundation, this concept can only be the concept of something whose existence promises pleasure and thus determines the subject [as a cause] for producing it; that is to say, it thus determines the faculty of desire. Now since it is impossible to discern *a priori* what image will be accompanied by *pleasure* and what by *pain*, it will depend on experience alone to find out what is directly good or evil. The quality of the subject, with reference to which alone this experiment can be made, is the *feeling* of pleasure and pain, a receptivity belonging to the inner sense. Thus what would be directly good is that which immediately produces the sensation of *pleasure*, and what [would be] simply evil that which immediately excites *pain*. However, this [way of expressing it] is opposed to ordinary usage which distinguishes the *pleasant* from the *good*, the *unpleasant* from the *evil*, and requires that good and evil shall always be judged by reason and therefore by concepts which can be communicated to everyone and not by mere sensation which is limited to individual subjects and their susceptibility. For this reason and also because pleasure and pain cannot be linked to any idea of an object *a priori*, the philosopher, who though himself obliged to make a feeling of pleasure the foundation of his moral judgments, would call *good* that which is a *means* to the pleasant and *evil* that which is a cause of unpleasantness and pain; for the judgment on the relation of means to ends certainly belongs to reason. But, though reason alone is capable of discerning the connection of means with their ends, so that the will might even be defined as the faculty of ends since these are always determining principles of the desires, yet the practical maxims which would follow from the aforesaid principle of the good being merely a means would never contain as the object of the will anything good in itself, but only something good *for something else*. Hence the good would always be merely the useful and what it is useful for would always lie outside the will in sensation. If such a pleasant sensation were distinguished from the concept of good, there would be nothing directly good at all and the good would have to be sought in the means to something else; namely, something pleasant.

There is an old formula of the schools: *Nihil appetimus nisi sub ratione boni; Nihil aversamus nisi sub ratione mali.* [We desire nothing except by reason of its being good; we reject nothing except by reason of its being bad.] This principle is often used correctly, but also often in a manner damaging to philosophy, because the expressions *boni* and *mali* are ambiguous owing to the limitation of language. These words have a double sense and therefore inevitably cause difficulties for the practical laws. In employing these words philosophy becomes aware of the different meanings in the same word but can find no special expressions for them and so is driven to subtle distinctions. Subsequently, there is no unanimity about these distinctions because the difference cannot be directly signified by a suitable expression.

Fortunately, the German language has expressions which make this difference quite clear. It possesses two very distinct concepts and especially distinct expressions which the Latins express by a single word, *bonum*. For *bonum* German has "*das Gute*" (good) and "*das Wohl*" (well, weal), for *malum,* "*das Böse*" (evil) and "*das Übel*" (ill, bad) or "*das Weh*" (woe). So we express two quite distinct judgments when we consider the *good* and *evil* of an action or the *weal* and *woe* (ill) it brings. Hence it follows that the above-quoted psychological proposition is, at the very least, quite uncertain if it is translated, "we desire nothing except with a view to our *weal* or *woe*." On the other hand, if we render it, "under the direction of reason we desire nothing except as we esteem it to be good or evil," it is quite indubitably certain and at the same time quite clearly expressed. [5]

Weal and *woe* always imply a reference only to our condition, just as *pleasant* and *unpleasant* do. [They describe our condition] as one of pleasure or pain and if we desire or avoid an object on this account, we can only do so by reference to our senses and to the feeling of pleasure or pain that it produces. But *good* or *evil* always implies a reference to the *will*, as determined by the *law of reason* to make something its object. For the will is never determined directly by the object and the idea of the object, but it is a faculty for taking a rule of reason as the motive of an action by which an object may be realized. Good and evil are therefore properly referred to actions, not to the sensations of the person. If anything is to be absolutely good or evil, i.e., in every respect and without any further conditions, or is to be so esteemed, it cannot be a thing but only the manner of acting; the maxim of the will. Consequently the acting person himself may be described as a good or evil man.

Men may laugh at the Stoic who, in the severest paroxysms of gout, cried out, "Pain, no matter how much you torment me, I will never admit that you are an evil," yet he was right. The pain was certainly a bad thing and his cry betrayed that, but he had no reason whatever to admit that any evil attached to him. The pain did not in the least diminish the value of his person, but only that of his condition. If he had been conscious of a single lie it would have lowered his pride, but pain served only to raise it since he was conscious that he had not deserved

---

[5] [Abbot notes that the English language makes the distinction in question, though not perfectly. "Evil" is not absolutely restricted to moral evil. We also speak of physical evils, but certainly when not so qualified it applies usually (as an adjective, perhaps exclusively), to moral evil. "Bad" is more general, but when used with a word connoting moral qualities, it expresses moral evil; for example, "a bad man", a "bad scholar." These words are etymologically the same as the German *"übel"* and *"böse"* respectively. "Good" is as ambiguous, being opposed to "bad" as well as to "evil," but the corresponding German word is equally ambiguous.—Ed.]

it by any unrighteous action by which he had earned such punishment.

What we call good must be an object of desire in the judgment of every rational man, and what we call evil an object of aversion in the eyes of every such man. Therefore, in addition to sense, this kind of judgment requires reason. So it is with truthfulness as opposed to lying, so with justice as opposed to violence, etc. But we may call a thing a bad (or ill) thing, and yet everyone must acknowledge it to be good at the same time, sometimes directly, sometimes indirectly. The man who submits to a surgical operation no doubt feels it to be a bad (ill) thing, but by his reason he and everyone acknowledges the operation to be a good thing. If a man, who delights in annoying and vexing peaceable people, at least receives a right good beating, this is no doubt a bad (ill) thing, but everyone approves it and regards it as a good thing even though nothing else resulted from it. Even the man who receives the beating must acknowledge by his reason that he has met justice because he sees right conduct related to good fortune. Thus what reason places before him as inescapable is here put into practice.

No doubt our weal and woe are of *very great* importance in the estimation of our practical reason. As far as our nature as sensible beings is concerned, our *happiness* is the only thing of *consequence* provided happiness is estimated in terms which reason especially requires; that is, estimated not in terms of transitory sensation, but in terms of the influence that this happiness has on our whole existence and on our satisfaction with it. Man is a being belonging to the world of sense who has wants and in connection with these his reason has a task which it cannot refuse; namely, to attend to the interest of his senses and to form practical maxims with a view to the happiness in this life and, if possible even that of a future [life]. But he is not so completely an animal that he is indifferent to what reason says on its own account, and that he uses reason merely as an instrument for satisfying his wants as a being of sense. The possession alone of reason would not raise his value above that of brutes if it were only to serve him for the same purpose that instinct serves them. In that case reason would be only a particular method which nature had employed as equipment for the same ends for which it has qualified brutes without qualifying man for any higher purpose. Once this arrangement of nature has been made for him, no doubt he needs reason in order to take account of his weal and woe. But he also possesses reason for a higher purpose; namely, to consider what is good or evil in itself. Only pure reason uninfluenced by a sense interest can judge about this and must thoroughly distinguish this estimate from the former [judgment concerning the necessity to fulfill his wants] and make this judgment the supreme condition thereof.

In estimating what is good or evil in itself, as distinguished from what can only relatively be called so, the following points are to be considered: One may assume a rational principle as the determining principle of the will without regard to possible objects of desire and therefore by the mere legislative form of the maxim. In that case the principle is a practical, *a priori* law and pure reason is supposed to be practical of itself. Then the law determines the will directly and the action, which is in conformance with it, is *good in itself*. A will whose maxim always conforms to this law is *absolutely good in every respect* and is the *supreme condition of all good*. Or, one may assume that the will results from a determining principle of desire which presupposes an object of pleasure or pain; something that *pleases* or *displeases*. In this case the maxim of reason that we should pursue the former and avoid the latter determines our actions as good in relation to our inclination, or indirectly good; that is, in relation to a different end to which they are means. Then these maxims can never be called laws but may be called rational practical precepts. The end itself, the pleasure we seek, in the latter case is not a true *good* but a [kind of] *well-being:* not a concept of reason but an empirical concept of an object of sensation. Only the use of the means thereto, the action, is yet called good because rational deliberation is required for it. Even so, the action is not absolutely good, but is good only in relation to our senses with regard to feelings of pleasure and displeasure. The will whose maxim is affected thereby is not a pure will, for pure will is directed only to that in which pure reason by itself can be practical.

This is the proper place to explain the paradox of method in a critique of practical reason; namely, *that the concept of good and evil must not be defined prior to the moral law of which it seems to be the foundation, but only after the moral law and by means of it.* In fact, even if we did not know that the principle of morality is a pure *a priori* law determining the will, yet in order not to assume principles quite freely, we must, anyway at first, leave undecided [the question of] whether the will has merely empirical principles of determination, or whether it also has pure *a priori* principles. It is contrary to all rules of philosophical method to assume as decided that which is the very point in question. Suppose we wish to begin with the concept of good in order to deduce from it the laws of the will. This concept of an object as good would then designate this object as the sole determining principle of the will. Now since this concept had not any practical *a priori* law for its standard, the criterion of good or evil could not be placed in anything but the agreement of the object with our feeling of pleasure or pain. The use of reason could only consist in first determining this pleasure or pain in connection with all the sensations of my existence, and second in determining the means of securing to myself the object of the pleasure. Now as only experience can decide what conforms to the feeling of pleasure, and practical law is to be based hypothetically on this as a condition, the possibility of *a priori* practical laws would be excluded at once because it was in the first place imagined to be necessary to find an object whose concept as a good should constitute the general, though empirical, principle for determining the will. But first it was necessary to explore whether or not there is an *a priori* principle for determining the will. This could never be found anywhere but in a pure practical law in so far as this law merely prescribes for maxims their form without regard to any object. However, since we assumed an object determined by our concepts of good and evil as the basis of all practical law, and whereas without a previous law that object could only be conceived by empirical concepts, we have already deprived ourselves of the possibility of even conceiving a pure practical law. On the other hand, if we had first analytically investigated [pure practical law] we would have found that the concept of good as an object does not determine and make possible moral law, but on the contrary, that it is moral law that first determines and makes possible the concept of good in so far as that concept deserves the name of the absolute good.

The foregoing remark explains what has occasioned all the mistakes of the philosophers with respect to the supreme principle of morals. They sought to find an object of the will which they could make the substance and principle of a law so that the law would not directly determine the will, but do so by means of that object when referred to feelings of pleasure or pain. Instead, philosophers should have first searched for a law that would determine the will *a priori* and directly and afterwards would determine the object in accordance with such a will. It does not matter whether those philosophers saw such an object of pleasure for supplying the supreme concept of goodness in happiness, or in perfection, or in moral sentiment, or in the will of God; in every case their principle implied heteronomy. Inevitably they must come upon empirical conditions for a moral law since their object, which was to be the immediate principle of the will, could not be called good or bad except in its immediate relation to sentiment which is always empirical. Only a formal law, i.e., one prescribing as the supreme condition of its maxims no more than the form of its universal legislation, can be *a priori* a principle for determining practical reason. The ancients revealed this error by directing all their moral inquiries to determining the notion of the highest good, which afterwards they proposed to make the determining principle of the will through moral law. Only much later when moral law has been established and has been shown to be the direct determining principle of the will, can an object such as the highest good be presented to the will whose form has now been determined *a priori*.

In the dialectic of the pure practical reason we shall undertake to show how this is done. The moderns, with whom the question of the highest good has gone out of fashion or at least seems to have become a secondary matter, hid the same error under vague expressions (as they do in many other cases). Nevertheless, the error is revealed in their systems since it always produces heteronomy of practical reason. Never can a moral law giving universal commands be thus deduced.

The concepts of good and evil as consequences of determining the will a priori also imply a pure practical principle and therefore a causality of pure reason. Hence originally they do not refer to objects as do the pure intellectual concepts or the categories of reason in their theoretic employment unifying and synthesizing special modes of the manifold seen things (*Anschauungen*) in one consciousness. On the contrary, the concepts of good and evil presuppose that objects are given. They are all modes (*modi*) of a single category of causality whose determining principle consists in the rational concept of a law, given by reason to itself as a law of freedom, thereby proving itself practical *a priori*. However, actions *on the one side* come under a law which is not a physical law but a law of freedom, and these actions consequently belong to the conduct of intelligible beings, yet, on the *other side*, as events in the world of sense, such actions belong to phenomena. Therefore, the determination of practical reason in reference only to the latter [kind of action] is possible in accordance with these intellectual categories, but only for the purpose of subjecting the manifold of *desires* to the unity of consciousness of a practical reason which gives its commands *a priori* in the moral law, i.e., to the unity of a pure will.

These categories of freedom, for so we propose to call them in contrast to the theoretic categories of nature, have an obvious advantage over theoretic categories inasmuch as these latter are only forms of thought. Theoretic categories designate objects in an indefinite manner by means of general concepts for every possible thing seen (*Anschauung*). Categories of freedom, on the contrary, refer to the determination of a *free choice* for which we cannot indicate anything seen as exactly corresponding, for such free choice is based upon a pure, practical, *a priori* law, which is not the case with any concepts belonging to the theoretic use of our cognitive faculties. These elementary practical concepts are based upon the *form of a pure will* which is given in reason and therefore in the thinking faculty itself. These concepts are not based upon the form of things seen (*Anschauung*), space and time, which does not lie in reason itself but has to be drawn from another source, namely, the sensibility. Thus, since all precepts of pure practical reason have to do only with the *determination of the will* and not with the natural conditions or one's practical capacity for *executing one's purpose,* the practical *a priori* principles at once become knowledge in relation to the supreme principle of freedom and do not have to wait for something seen (*Anschauung*) in order to acquire significance. This is so for the remarkable reason that these principles themselves apply to that to which they refer, namely, the conviction of the will. Obviously, this is not the case with theoretical concepts. But we must be careful to recognize that these categories only apply to the practical reason. Thus they proceed in order from those categories which are still subject to sensible conditions and morally indeterminate, to those categories which are free from sensible conditions and determined merely by moral law.

TABLE OF THE CATEGORIES OF FREEDOM IN RELATION TO THE CONCEPTS OF GOOD AND EVIL

1

Quantity

Subjective, according to maxims (*opinions* of the individual will).

Objective, according to principles (*precepts*).

A priori objective and subjective principles of freedom (*laws*).

2	3
Quality	*Relation*
Practical rules of commission (action) (*praeceptivae*)	To *personality*
Practical rules of *omission* (*prohibitivae*)	To the *state* of the person
Practical rules of exceptions (*exceptivae*)	*Reciprocal,* of one person to the state of the others

4

Modality

The *Permitted* and the *Forbidden*

Duty and *contrary to duty*

Perfect and *imperfect duty*

It will be observed at once that in this table freedom is considered as a sort of causality in regard to actions possible by it, though not as subject to empirical grounds of determination. These actions are phenomena in the world of sense, and consequently freedom is referred to categories related to what is possible in nature. Yet, each category is taken in so universal a connotation that the determining principle of that causality can be placed outside the world of sense and into freedom as a property of an intelligible being. The categories of modality introduce the transition from practical principles generally to those of morality, but only *problematically*. These can be established *dogmatically* only by the moral law.

I add nothing further here in explanation of the present table as it is intelligible enough by itself. A classification of this kind based on principles is very useful in any science for the sake of both thoroughness and intelligibility. Thus we know from the preceding table what we must commence with in practical inquiries: The maxims which everyone bases on his own inclinations; the precepts which hold true for a species of rational beings in so far as they are alike in certain inclinations; and finally the law which holds for all without regard to their inclinations, etc. In this way we can survey the whole plan of what has to be done, every question of practical philosophy that has to be answered, and also the order that is to be followed.

Of the Typology of Pure Practical Judgment

The concepts of good and evil first determine an object of the will. However they themselves are subject to a practical rule of reason which, if it is pure reason, determines the will *a priori* in relation to its object. Whether an action possible in the world of sense falls under the rule or not is a question to be decided by practical judgment, which applies what is usually stated in general terms (*in abstracto*) to a concrete action (*in concreto*). *In the first place* since a practical rule of pure reason concerns the existence of an object, *in the second place,* as it is a practical rule of pure reason, it implies necessity as regards the existence of the action and hence is a practical law. . . . Therefore it seems absurd to expect to find in the world of sense a case which, while depending only on the law of nature, allows the application of a law of freedom to itself and thereby we can apply to it the supersensible idea of the morally good which is to be exhibited in [the case] *in concreto*. Thus the judgment of pure practical reason is subject to the same difficulties as that of pure theoretical reason. However, the judgment of pure theoretical reason could escape from these difficulties because something to be visualized (*Anschauung*) was required to which pure intellectual concepts could be applied. . . . On the other hand, the morally good is something whose object is supersensible and to which, therefore, nothing corresponds or can be found in any sensible visualization (*Anschauung*). Therefore judgment depending on laws of pure reason seems to be subject to special difficulties in that a law of freedom is to be applied to actions which are events taking place in the world of sense and which, therefore, belong to physical nature.

But in spite of this difficulty a favorable prospect for pure practical judgment appears. When I subsume, under a *pure practical law,* an action possible in the world of sense, I am not concerned with the possibility of the *action* as an event in the world of sense. This problem belongs to the judgments formed by reason in its theoretic use according to the law of [physical, natural] causality which is a pure intellectual concept for which reason has a *schema* in sensible visualization (*Anschauung*). Physical causality, or the condition under which it occurs, belongs to concepts based on nature whose schema is sketched by transcendental imagination. However, here we are dealing, not with the schema of a case according to law, but with the *schema* (if the word is allowable here) of the law itself. Since the fact that the will, not the action in relation to its effect, is determined by the law alone without any other ground of determination, the concept of causality is linked to quite different conditions from those which constitute a link [in the chain of) natural [causation].

There must be a *schema* corresponding to the law of nature to which the objects we observe with our sense are subject; that is, it must have a general method for the imagination by which it can exhibit *a priori* to the senses the pure intellectual concept which the law determines. But the law of freedom, and consequently the concept of the unconditionally good, cannot be based upon any things-seen, nor upon any schema supplied for the purpose of applying the laws *in concreto*. Consequently the moral law depends upon the intellect for its application to objects of nature, certainly not upon the imagination. For the purposes of judgment the intellect can provide a law but not a *schema* of the senses for a rational idea, though it is only a law in regard to its form. However, such a law can be exhibited *in concreto* in objects of the senses and is therefore a law of nature. We can therefore call this law the *type* of the moral law.

The rule of judgment according to laws of pure practical reason is this: If the action you propose were to take place by a law of the system of nature of which you are a part yourself, ask yourself whether you could regard it as a possible result of your own will. Everyone does, in fact, decide by this rule as to whether actions are good or evil. Thus people say: Suppose *everyone* permitted himself to deceive when he thought it to his advantage; or thought himself justified in shortening his life as soon as he was thoroughly weary of it; or looked with perfect indifference on the needs of others; if you belonged to such an order of things would you assent to it of your own free will? Now everyone knows well that if he secretly allows himself to deceive, it does not follow that everyone else does the same, or if, unobserved, he is destitute of compassion, others would not necessarily be the same to him. Hence this comparison of the maxim of his actions with a general law of nature is not the determining principle of his will. Nevertheless a law is a *type* of judgment concerning a maxim based on moral principles. If the maxim of the action is not such that it can stand the test of the form of a general law of nature, then it is morally inadmissible. This is also the judgment of common sense; for its ordinary judgments, even those of experience, are always based on the law of nature. Therefore common sense will always use this kind of judgment. However, in cases where *causality based on freedom* is to be evaluated, [common sense] makes that *law of na-*

ture merely the type [pattern] of a *law of freedom.* For without something which it can use as an example when the occasion arises in experience, common sense cannot apply the law of pure practical reason properly.

Therefore it is allowable to use the *nature of the world of sense* as the *type* [or pattern] of a *supersensible (intelligible) nature,* provided one does not transfer to the latter the things seen (*Anschauungen*) and what depends on them, but merely refers to it the *form of law* in general. The concept of this form of law occurs even in the most elementary use of reason, but cannot be definitely known *a priori* for any other purpose than the pure practical use of reason. For laws as such are identical in form no matter what they derive their determining principles from.

Furthermore, absolutely nothing is known of all the supersensible (intelligible world) except freedom through the moral law, and this only in so far as it is inseparably implied in that law, and moreover since all supersensible objects to which reason might lead us following the guidance of that law, still have no reality for us except for the purpose of that law and for the use of mere practical reason. And since reason is authorized and even compelled to use physical nature (in its pure intellectual form) as the type [or pattern] of judgment, the present remark will serve to guard against including among concepts themselves that which belongs only to the *typology* of concepts. This typology of the power of judgment guards against the *empiricism* of practical reason, which founds the practical concepts of good and evil merely on experienced consequences, called happiness. No doubt happiness and the infinite advantages which would result from a will determined by self-love, if at the same time this will formed itself into a universal law of nature, may certainly serve as a quite suitable type for the morally good, but they are not identical with it. The same typology also guards against the *mysticism* of practical reason, which turns what served only as a *symbol* into a *schema.* Such mysticism proposes to provide as a basis for the moral concepts real, yet not sensible visualizations, like those of an invisible Kingdom of God, and thus wanders off into the visionary realm. Only the *rationalism* of the power of judgment is appropriate to the use of moral concepts. This rationalism takes from nature as known to the senses only what pure reason can also conceive by itself; that is, what conforms to law. This rationalism does not transfer anything into the supersensible but what can actually be presented by actions in the world of sense according to the formal rule of a law of nature. However, the caution against *empiricism* is much more important; for mysticism is quite reconcilable with the purity and sublimity of the moral law, and besides it is not very natural or agreeable to common habits of thought to strain one's imagination to supersensible visions; hence the danger on this side is not so general. Empiricism, on the contrary, tears out by the roots the morality of convictions in which, rather than in deeds, consists the high worth that men can and ought to secure through such morality. Empiricism substitutes for duty something quite different, namely, an empirical interest. . . . Moreover empiricism degrades humanity by raising inclinations no matter how they are fashioned to the dignity of a supreme practical principle. . . .

Conclusion

Two things fill the mind with ever new and increasing awe and admiration the more frequently and continuously reflection is occupied with them; the starred heaven above me and the moral law within me. I ought not to seek either outside my field of vision, as though they were either shrouded in obscurity or were visionary. I see them confronting me and link them immediately with the consciousness of my existence. The first [the wonder of the starred heaven] begins with the place I occupy in the external world of sense, and expands the connection in which I find myself into the incalculable vastness of worlds upon worlds, of systems within systems, over endless ages of their periodic motion, their beginnings and perpetuation. The second [the wonder of the moral law within] starts from my invisible self, from my personality, and depicts me as in a world possessing true infinitude which can be sensed only by the intellect. With this I recognize myself to be in a necessary and general connection, not just accidentally as appears to be the case with the external world. Through this recognition I also see myself linked with all visible worlds. The first view of a numberless quantity of worlds destroys my importance, so to speak, since I am an *animal-like being* who must return its matter from whence it came to the planet (a mere speck in the universe), after having been endowed with vital energy for a short time, one does not know how. The second view raises my value infinitely, as an *intelligence*, through my personality; for in this personality the moral law reveals a life independent of animality and even of the entire world of sense. This is true at least as far as one can infer from the purposeful determination of my existence according to this law. This [determination] is not restricted to the conditions and limits of this life, but radiates into the infinite.

Admiration and respect may stimulate further inquiry, but they cannot provide a substitute for the lack of either. Then what can be done in order to pursue such inquiry in a useful way appropriate to the sublime quality of the topic? Examples may serve as a warning, but they may also inspire imitation. The observation of nature began with the most marvelous spectacle that human senses could present and our intellect could bear to trace to its full extent, but it ended in—astrology. Morals started with the noblest quality of human nature whose development and cultivation suggests infinite advantage, but it ended in—idle speculation or superstition. This is what happens to all clumsy attempts in which the use of reason plays the most important part. Such use does not, like the use of one's feet, happen by itself as a result of frequent employment. This is especially true where such use concerns qualities which cannot be presented immediately in common experience. Then, though late, the maxim came into fashion to consider carefully all steps that reason has to take and not to allow reason to proceed except in the tracks of a method carefully thought-out beforehand. After that the judgment concerning the structure of the world took a very different direction and at the same time arrived at a much happier result. The fall of a stone when analyzed into its elements, the forces which manifested themselves were then treated mathematically and eventually produced the clear insight into the structure of the world [which we have now and] which will remain unchanged in the future and which allows the hope that progressive observation will ever extend it, and never have to fear retrogression.

To follow the same road in dealing with the moral qualities of our nature is suggested by that example which offers hope for a similar good result. We have at hand many examples of reason judging morally. To analyze these judgments [and break them down] into their elementary concepts, to employ, in repeated experiments with ordinary common sense, a method similar to that of *chemistry,* (as *mathematics* is not available for the purpose of *separating* the empirical from the rational which may be found in such judgments), should make known *purely* and with certainty both the empirical and the rational and ought to show what each can accomplish by itself. If true, such a procedure ought to be able to forestall the errors of a *coarse,* unskilled judging, as well as *pretensions of genius* which is even more necessary. For imaginary treasures are promised on these pretensions without any methodical inquiry or knowledge of nature, while real treasures are squandered, as happens with the adepts of the stone of wisdom. In a word, scientific knowledge, critically explored and systematically introduced, is the narrow gateway which leads to *wisdom,* if by such wisdom is understood not merely what one ought to *do,* but what ought to serve as a guide for *teachers,* in order to find well and clearly the paths to wisdom on which every man ought to tread, and to preserve others from dead alleys. This is true knowledge, of which philosophy must remain the guardian at all times. In its sophisticated analysis the general public cannot share, but they do share in the doctrines which clearly convince them after such an analysis.

CRITIQUE OF JUDGMENT

[1793]

Part I

CRITIQUE OF ESTHETIC JUDGMENT

INTRODUCTION

I

Division of Philosophy

PHILOSOPHY CONTAINS THE PRINCIPLES FOR RATIONAL KNOWL-edge that concepts afford us of things but not as Logic does, which contains merely the principles of the form of thought in general, irrespective of objects. Hence the usual course of dividing philosophy into the *theoretical* and the *practical* is perfectly sound. But then the concepts, which assign their object to the principles of this rational knowledge, must be different and specific because otherwise they fail to justify a classification. A classification always presupposes that the principles belonging to the rational knowledge of the several parts of a science are antithetical.

Now there are only two kinds of concepts and these yield a corresponding number of distinct principles for the possibility of their objects. These are the concepts of *nature* and the concepts of *freedom*. By the first, *theoretical* knowledge based on *a priori* principles becomes possible. However, in respect of such knowledge, the concept of freedom involves, by its very concept, no more than a negative principle, that of simple antithesis, while for determining the will it establishes principles which enlarge the scope of its activity and which are called *practical* on that account. Hence philosophy is properly divided into two parts, quite distinct in their principles; a theoretical part, as *Philosophy of Nature* and a practical part, as *Philosophy of Morals,* and this last is what is called practical legislation for the reason based upon the concept of freedom. However, up till now these expressions have been grossly misused in dividing the different principles, and through them, philosophy. For, what is practical according to concepts of nature has been taken as identical with what is practical according to the concept of freedom, with the result that a division has been made under these headings of theoretical and practical by means of which there has actually been no division at all, since both parts might have similar principles.

The will as a faculty of desire is one of the many natural causes in the world; it is the cause that acts according to concepts. Whatever is imagined as possible or necessary through the efficacy of will is called practically possible or necessary. This is done in order to distinguish its possibility or necessity from the physical possibility or necessity of an effect where the cause is not determined by concepts, but rather as with lifeless matter by mechanism, and as with animals by instinct. [In treating the matter thus] the question is left open whether the concept which provides the rule for the causality of the will is a concept of nature, or of freedom.

The latter distinction, however, is essential. If the concept determining the causality is a concept of nature, then the principles are *practical* in a *technical* sense, but if it is a concept of freedom, then they are *practical* in a *moral* sense. Now, in the division of a science of reason, everything turns on the difference between objects requiring different principles for their understanding. Hence technical principles belong to theoretical philosophy, as a science of nature, whereas moral principles alone form the second part, practical philosophy, as a science of morals or ethics.

All technical practical rules, those of art and skill in general or those of prudence as a skill exercising an influence over men and their wills, must, so far as their principles rest upon concepts, be considered only as corollaries of theoretical philosophy. They only concern the possibility of things according to concepts of nature and this includes not only the means discoverable in nature for the purpose, but even the will itself as a faculty of desire and hence as a natural faculty, so far as the will may be determined by natural motives according to these rules. Nevertheless these practical rules are not called laws like physical laws but only precepts. This is due to the fact that the will is not merely placed under the concept of nature, but is also placed under the concept of freedom. When related to freedom the principles of the will are called laws, and these principles, with the addition of what follows from them, alone constitute the second or practical part of philosophy.

The solution of the problems of pure geometry is not allocated to a special part of that science, nor does the art of land surveying merit the name of a practical geometry, in distinction to pure geometry, as a second part of the general science of geometry. With as little or perhaps even less right can the mechanical or chemical art of experimentation or of observation be ranked as a practical part of the science of nature. Finally, neither can domestic, agricultural, nor political economy, the art of social intercourse, the principles of dietetics, nor even general instruction for attaining happiness, nor yet the restraining of the passions or the affections for this purpose be denominated as such. None of these may be counted as parts of practical philosophy; even less can they be constituted as the second part of philosophy in general.[1] For all of them contain nothing more than rules of skill which are only practical in a technical sense, as a skill is directed to producing an effect possible according to natural causes and effects. . . .

---

[1] [Hume, following the hedonistic doctrines of the enlightenment, had attempted to do this.—Ed.]

II (omitted)

[Here Kant sums up what the *Critique of Pure Reason* and the *Prolegomena* (see above Chaps. III, IV) and the *Critique of Practical Reason* and his other moral writings (see above, Chaps. VII, VIII) had developed as the basic dualism of the realm of nature and the realm of freedom.—Ed.]

III

The Critique of Judgment as a Means of Linking the Two Parts of Philosophy Into a Whole

Properly speaking the Critique, which deals with what our cognitive faculties are *a priori* capable of yielding, has no field in regard to objects; for it is not a doctrine, but merely investigates whether and how a doctrine may be possible, considering our [mental] faculties. The field of such a critique extends to all the pretensions of our faculties with a view to confining them within their legitimate bounds. But what cannot be included in the division of philosophy may yet be admitted as a principal part into the general critique of our faculty for pure knowledge if it contains principles which are not in themselves adapted for either theoretical or practical use.

The concepts of nature which contain the grounds for all theoretical knowledge *a priori* rest, as we saw, upon the law-giving authority of the intellect. The concept of freedom, which contains the grounds for all practical precepts *a priori* that are not conditioned by the senses, rests upon the authority of reason. Therefore both faculties have their own proper jurisdiction over their content and since there is no higher (*a priori*) jurisdiction over their content, the division of philosophy into theoretical and practical parts is justified.

But in our group of higher thinking faculties there is yet a link between intellect and reason. This link is the *power of judgment* and by analogy we may reasonably surmise that it also contains, if not a special law-giving authority, at least its own principle for discovering laws, even if this principle is merely subjective *a priori*. This principle, even though it has no field of objects appropriate for its realm, may still have some territory of a certain character, for which this principle alone may be valid.

But judging by analogy there is yet a further ground, in addition to the above considerations, upon which judgment may be linked with another order of our powers of imagination. This reason appears to be of even greater importance than the kinship of judgment with the family of cognitive faculties. For all spiritual faculties or capacities may be reduced to three which cannot be further deduced from a common ground: the *faculty of knowledge, the feeling of pleasure* or *displeasure* and the *faculty of desire*. . . . Between the faculties of knowledge and desire [discussed elsewhere] stands the feeling of pleasure, just as judgment stands between intellect and reason. Hence we may at least provisionally assume that judgment likewise contains an *a priori* principle of its own and, since pleasure or displeasure is necessarily connected with desire, that judgment will effect a transition from the faculty of pure knowledge, i.e., from the realm of concepts of nature, to the faculty of the concept of freedom, just as in its logical employment judgment makes possible the transition from intellect to reason.

Despite the fact that philosophy may be divided only into two principal parts, theoretical and practical, and despite also that all we may have to say of the proper principles of judgment may have to be assigned to its theoretical part, i.e., to rational knowledge according to concepts of nature, nevertheless the critique of pure reason, which must figure this all out to determine what is possible before such a system can be constructed, consists of three parts: the critiques of pure intellect, of pure judgment, and of pure reason [proper], which faculties are called pure because they are law-giving *a priori*.

IV

Judgment as a Faculty by which Laws are Prescribed A Priori

In general, judgment is the faculty for thinking of the particular as contained under the general. If the general, i.e., the rule, principle, or law, is given, then the judgment which subsumes the particular under it *is determining*. This is so even where such a judgment is transcendental and as such indicates *a priori* the conditions according to which alone anything can be subsumed under that general [rule or principle]. If only the particular is given and the universal has to be found for it then the judgment is merely *reflecting*.

The determining judgment, which is subject to general transcendental laws furnished by the intellect, merely subsumes; the law is prescribed for it *a priori* and such a judgment has no need to devise a law for its own guidance for subordinating the particular in nature to the general. There are such manifold forms of nature; there are many modifications of the general transcendental concepts of nature that are left undetermined by the laws furnished by pure intellect *a priori* because these laws only concern the general possibility of nature as an object of the senses. Hence there must also be laws on behalf [of the judgment which subsumes the forms under the general concepts of nature]. These laws, being empirical, may be fortuitous as far as *our* intellectual understanding goes, but if they are still to be called laws as the concept of nature requires, they must be regarded as necessary and flowing from a principle of the unity of the manifold, unknown though it may be to us. Therefore the reflecting judgment, obliged to ascend from the particular in nature to the general, stands in need of a principle. The reflecting judgment cannot borrow this principle from experience because it must establish the unity of all empirical principles under higher though likewise empirical principles, and therefore establish the possibility of the systematic subordination of the lower under the higher. The reflecting judgment can give such a transcendental principle as a law only to itself. As long as it derives this law elsewhere, it will remain a determining judgment. Nor can reflecting judgment prescribe such a principle to nature; for reflecting on the laws of nature adjusts itself [the reflection] to nature, and not nature to the conditions according to which we strive to obtain a concept of it— a concept that is quite fortuitous in respect to nature itself.

The principle [needed by the reflecting judgment] can only be this: since general laws of nature have their foundation in our intellect which prescribes them to nature, though only according to the general concept of it as nature, particular empirical laws must be considered in regard to what is left undetermined in them by these general laws. [They must be considered] as though there were a unity such as they would have if an intellect had supplied them for the benefit of our thinking faculties so as to render possible a system of experience according to particular natural laws. This is not to be taken as implying that such an intellect must be assumed as actually existing, for it is the reflecting judgment only that employs this idea as a principle for the purpose of reflecting and not for ascertaining anything. This faculty [reflecting judgment] thereby gives a law to itself alone and not to nature.

The concept of an object so far as it contains at the same time the grounds for the actual existence of this object is called its *end* [or objective or purpose]. The conformance of an object with that quality, which is only possible according to ends, or objectives or purposes, is called the appropriateness of the form [of the object]. Accordingly the principle of judgment regarding the form of the things of nature under empirical laws generally is the *fitness of nature* in its manifoldness and variety. In other words; by this concept nature is imagined as though an intellect contained the grounds for the unity of its manifold though empirical laws.

Therefore the fitness of nature is a particular *a priori* concept having its origin solely in the reflecting judgment. For we can-not ascribe to the products of nature themselves anything like a reference to their purposes. We can only make use of this con-cept for reflecting upon them in respect to the nexus of phe-nomena in nature which is given according to empirical laws. Furthermore, this concept is quite different from practical fit-ness [appropriateness] in human art or even morals, though it is doubtless based on this analogy.

v

The Principle of the Formal Appropriateness of Nature [for its ends] is a Transcendental Principle of Judgment

A transcendental principle is one through which we represent to ourselves *a priori* the only universal condition under which things can generally become objects of our knowledge. On the other hand, a principle is called metaphysical when it represents *a priori* the only condition under which objects, whose concept must be given empirically, may become further determined *a priori*. Thus the principle of the knowledge of bodies as sub-stances, and as changeable substances, is transcendental when it states that the changing must have a cause; but the principle is metaphysical when it asserts that the changing must have an *external* cause. In the first case bodies need only be thought of in terms of ontological predicates (pure intellectual concepts), i.e., as substance, for the proposition is to be understood *a priori*. In the second case, the empirical concept of a body, as a mov-able thing in space, must be introduced to support the proposi-tion; although once this is done it may be seen quite *a priori* that the latter predicate, movement only by means of an exter-nal cause, applies to a body. In this last way, as I shall show presently, the principle of the appropriateness (fitness) of na-ture in the multiplicity of its empirical laws is a transcendental principle. For the concept of objects coming under this princi-ple is only generally the pure concept of objects of possible empirical knowledge and involves nothing empirical. On the other hand, the principle of practical appropriateness, implied in the idea of the *determination* of a free *will*, would be a metaphysical principle, because the concept of a faculty of desire, as will, has to be given empirically; i.e., is not included among transcendental predicates. Nevertheless both these principles are not empirical, but *a priori* principles; because no further experience is required for synthesizing the predicate with the empirical concept of the subject of the judgments of these principles, but it may be apprehended quite *a priori*.

That the concept of nature as related to ends is a transcendental principle is abundantly evident from the maxims of judgment upon which we rely *a priori* in investigating nature, and which only deal with the possibility of experience, and consequently the possibility of the knowledge of nature—but not just nature generally, but nature as determined by a manifold of particular laws. These maxims crop up frequently enough in the course of this science, though only in a scattered way. They are aphorisms of metaphysical wisdom, making their appearance in a number of rules the necessity of which cannot be demonstrated from concepts: "Nature takes the shortest way (*lex parsimoniae*); yet it makes no leap, either in the sequence of its changes, or in the juxtaposition of specifically different forms (*lex continui in natura*); its vast variety in empirical laws is, for all that, unity under a few principles (*principia praeter necessitatem non sunt multiplicanda*)"; and so forth.

If we propose to assign an origin to these elementary rules, and attempt to do so on psychological lines, we fly right in the teeth of their sense. For they tell us, not what happens, that is, according to what rule our powers of judgment actually discharge their functions, and how we judge, but how we ought to judge; and we cannot find this logical objective necessity where the principles are merely empirical. Hence the appropriateness of nature for our thinking faculties and their employment which manifestly radiates from them is a transcendental principle of judgments, and so needs also transcendental deduction, by means of which the grounds for this way of judging must be traced to the *a priori* sources of knowledge.

Now, looking at the grounds for the possibility of an experience, naturally the first thing that meets us is something necessary; namely, the universal laws apart from which nature in general as an object of sense cannot be conceived. These laws rest on the categories, applied to the formal conditions of all observation possible for us, so far as observation is also given *a priori*. Under these laws judgment is determinant; for it has nothing else to do than to subsume under given laws. For instance, the intellect says: all change has its cause (universal law of nature); transcendental judgment has nothing further to do than to furnish *a priori* the condition of subsumption under the concept of the intellect placed before it: this we get in the succession of the determinations of one and the same thing. Now for nature in general, as an object of possible experience, that law is understood as absolutely necessary. But besides this formal time-condition, the objects of empirical knowledge are determined, or so far as we can judge *a priori* are determinable, in diverse ways, so that specifically differentiated nature, over and above what they have in common as things of nature in general, are further capable of being causes in an infinite variety of ways; and each of these modes must, on the concept of a cause in general, have its rule which is a law and consequently imports necessity: although owing to the constitution and limitations of our faculties for knowledge we may entirely fail to see this necessity. Accordingly, in respect to nature's merely empirical laws, we must conceive in nature the possibility of an endless multiplicty of empirical laws, which are yet accidental so far as our insight goes; that is, they cannot be understood *a priori*. According to these laws we evaluate as accidental the unity of nature and the possibility of the unity of experience as a system of empirical laws. Such a unity must be presupposed and assumed as otherwise no thoroughgoing coherence of empirical knowledge would occur [and thus] experience [would not be] a whole. For the general laws of nature certainly provide for such coherence among things of nature generically but they do not provide it for particular things of nature. Hence, for its own use, judgment is compelled to adopt for an *a priori* principle: what appears accidental to human insight in the particular empirical laws of nature, nevertheless contains unity of law in the synthesis of its manifold aspects in an intrinsically possible experience, unfathomable, though still conceivable, as such unity may be for us. Consequently the unity of law in a synthesis is understood by us according to a necessary intention or need of the mind and, though recognized as accidental, is imagined as a fitness of objects of nature. Therefore judgment merely reflects upon things under possible and still to be discovered empirical laws, and must think about nature in respect of the empirical laws according to a *principle of appropriateness*. This principle then finds expression in the above maxims of judgment. This transcendental concept of appropriateness in nature is neither a concept of nature nor of freedom, since it attributes nothing at all to the object: nature. This concept only represents the unique manner in which we must proceed in reflecting upon the objects of nature if we are to get a thoroughly coherent experience. So this concept is a subjective principle or maxim of judgment. Also for this reason, we rejoice as though good fortune favored us when we meet with such systematic unity under merely empirical laws; although we must necessarily assume the presence of such a unity, apart from any ability on our part to perceive or prove its existence.

In order to convince ourselves of the validity of this deduction of the concept before us, and the necessity for assuming it as a transcendental principle of knowledge, let us just consider the magnitude of the task. We have to form a connected experience from given perceptions of a nature containing a perhaps endless multiplicity of empirical laws, and this problem has its basis *a priori* in our intellect. This intellect is no doubt *a priori* in possession of universal laws of nature, apart from which nature would be incapable of being an object of experience at all. But beyond this there is needed a certain order in the particular rules of nature which are only capable of being brought to the knowledge of the intellect empirically, and which are possible as far as the intellect is concerned. These rules, without which we would have no means for advancing from the universal analogy of a possible general experience to a particular experience, must be regarded by the intellect as laws, i.e., as necessary, for otherwise they would not form an order of nature, even though intellect may be unable to comprehend or ever get an insight into their necessity. Although the intellect can determine nothing *a priori* in respect to these objects in pursuit of such empirical so-called laws, it must base all reflections upon them on an *a priori* principle, to the effect that a comprehensible order of nature is possible according to them. A principle of this kind is expressed in the following propositions: In nature there is a subordination of genera and species that we can understand. Each of these genera is approximated to the others on a common principle, so that a transition may be possible from one to the other, and thereby to a higher genus. While it seems unavoidable at the outset that our intellect assume, for the specific variety of natural operations, a like number of various kinds of causality, yet these may all be reduced to a small number of principles, the quest for which is our business. This adaptation of nature to our thinking faculties is presupposed *a priori* by judgment for reflecting upon this adaptation according to empirical laws. But all the while the intellect recognizes this adaptation objectively as accidental, and only judgment attributes it to nature as transcendental fitness, i.e., appropriate to the subject's faculty for knowing. Were it not for this presupposition, we should have no order of nature in accordance with these [principles of causality] in all their variety, or for an investigation of them.

Despite the uniformity of things of nature according to universal laws, without which we would have no form of general empirical knowledge at all, it is quite conceivable that the specific variety of the empirical laws of nature with their effects might still be so great as to make it impossible for our intellect to discover an intelligible order in nature; to divide its products into genera and species so as to avail ourselves of the principles for explaining and comprehending one in order to explain and interpret another, and to make a consistent context of experience out of the material resulting from such confusion, material that properly speaking is infinitely multiform and ill-adapted to our power of apprehension.

Thus judgment also possesses an *a priori* principle for the possibility of nature, but only in a subjective respect. By means of this it prescribes a law, not to nature, but to itself to guide its reflection upon nature. This law may be called *the law of specification of nature* in respect of its empirical laws. It is not a law recognized *a priori* in nature. But judgment adopts such a law for the purpose of making a natural order understandable to our intellect when classifying nature's general laws and subordinating a variety of particular laws to them. So when it is said that nature specifies its universal laws on a principle appropriate to our thinking faculties, we are not thereby either prescribing a law to nature, or learning one from it by observation, although the principle in question may be confirmed by this means. For it is not a principle of the determinant but merely of the reflecting judgment. All that is intended is that, no matter what the order and disposition of nature is in respect to its universal laws, we must investigate the empirical laws throughout nature based on this principle and the maxims founded thereon, because only so far as that principle applies can we make any headway in using our intellect in experience or in gaining knowledge.

VI

The Association of the Feeling of Pleasure with the Concept of the Appropriateness of Nature

So far as our insight goes, the conceived harmony of nature in the manifold of its particular laws, as well as our need for finding universal principles for it, must be deemed contingent and must also be deemed indispensable for the requirements of our intellect and consequently a fitness by which nature is in accord with our aim, but only in so far as it is directed to knowledge. The universal laws of knowledge, which are equally laws of nature, are, though spontaneous, just as necessary to nature as are the laws of motion applicable to matter. Their origin does not presuppose any regard to our thinking faculties, since only by their means can we first have any concept of the meaning of a knowledge of things of nature and they must apply to nature as an object of our general understanding. But so far as we can see it is conditional upon the fact that the order of nature in its particular laws, with their potential wealth of variety and heterogeneity transcending all our powers of comprehension, should still actually be commensurate with these powers. To find out this order of nature is an undertaking for our intellect, which pursues it with a regard to a necessary end of its own; that of introducing unity of principle into nature. This intention must be attributed to nature by judgment, since no law can be prescribed to it by the intellect.

The attainment of any aim is coupled with a feeling of pleasure. Now wherever such attainment has *a priori* for its condition an imagining, as it has here a principle for the reflecting judgment in general, then the feeling of pleasure is also determined by grounds which are *a priori* valid for all men, by merely referring the object to our faculty of knowledge. As the concept of appropriateness (fitness) pays no attention whatever here to the faculty of desire, it differs entirely from all practical fitness of nature.

As a matter of fact we do not and cannot find in ourselves the slightest feeling of pleasure from perceptions coinciding with the laws in accordance with the universal concepts of nature, i.e., the Categories, since in their case the intellect necessarily follows its own bent without ulterior aim. But while this is so, the discovery that two or more empirical laws of nature are linked under one principle embracing them both is the grounds for a very appreciable pleasure, often even for admiration, and is a kind that does not diminish even though we are already familiar enough with its object. It is true that we no longer notice any decided pleasure in comprehending nature, or in the unity of its classification into genera and species, without which the empirical concepts that afford us our knowledge of nature and its particular laws would not be possible. However, such pleasure certainly was experienced at one time. Only because the most common experience would be impossible without comprehending nature, has such comprehension gradually become fused with mere knowledge of any kind and is no longer particularly noticed. Something is required to make us attentive in our estimate of nature to its appropriateness for our understanding; to make us endeavor to bring, wherever possible, nature's heterogeneous laws under higher, though still always empirical laws in order that, on meeting with success, pleasure may be felt in their accord with our thinking faculty, which accord is regarded by us as purely fortuitous. As against this, imagining nature would be altogether displeasing to us, were we to be forewarned that, on the slightest investigation carried beyond the commonest experience, we should come in contact with such a heterogeneity of nature's laws as would make uniting its particular laws under universal empirical laws impossible for our intellect. For this would conflict with the principle of the subjectively final specification of nature in its genera, and with our own reflecting judgment in respect thereof.

Yet this presupposition of judgment is so indeterminate on the question of the extent of the prevalence of that ideal fitness of nature for our thinking faculties, that if we are told that a more searching or enlarged knowledge of nature derived from observation must eventually bring us into contact with a multiplicity of laws that no human understanding could reduce to a principle, we can reconcile ourselves to the thought. But still we listen more gladly to others who hold out to us the hope that the more intimately we come to know the secrets of nature, or the better we are able to compare nature with other aspects as yet unknown to us, the more simple shall we find nature in its principles. The further our experience advances the more harmonious shall we find nature in the apparent heterogeneity of its empirical laws. For our judgment makes it imperative that we proceed on the principle of the conformity of nature to our faculty for knowing, so far as that principle extends, without deciding—for the rule is not given us by a determinant judgment—whether limits are anywhere set to it or not. For while limits may be definitely determined for the rational use of our thinking faculty, in the empirical field no such determination of limits is possible.

IX

Joining the Laws of the Intellect and Reason by Means of Judgment

The intellect prescribes laws *a priori* for nature as an object of the senses, so that we may have a theoretical knowledge of it in a possible experience. Reason prescribes laws *a priori* for freedom and its peculiar causality as the supersensible in the subject, so that we may have a purely practical knowledge. The realm of the concept of nature under the one law, and that of the concept of freedom under the other, are completely cut off from all mutual influence that each, according to its own principles, might exert upon the other, because of the broad gulf that divides the supersensible from phenomena. The concept of freedom determines nothing in respect of the theoretical knowledge of nature, and the concept of nature likewise determines nothing in respect of the practical laws of freedom. To that extent then it is not possible to throw a bridge from the one realm to the other. Although the determining grounds for causality according to the concept of freedom, and the practical rule that this contains, have no place in nature, and although the sensible cannot determine the supersensible in the subject, yet the converse is possible in respect of the consequences arising from the supersensible and bearing on the sensible, though not in respect of the knowledge of nature. Indeed, this much is implied in the concept of a causality by freedom whose *operation* is to take effect in the world in conformity with the formal laws of freedom. However, the word *cause*, when applied to the supersensible only signifies the *grounds* determining the causality of things of nature as an effect in conformity with their appropriate natural laws, and also in unison with the formal principle of the laws of reason—grounds which, while their possibility is impenetrable, may still be completely cleared of the charge of contradiction they allegedly involve.[2] In accordance with the concept of freedom the effect is the final end which, or the

---

[2] One of the supposed contradictions in this radical distinction between the causality of nature and that of freedom is expressed in the objection that when I speak of *hindrances* opposed by nature to causality according to laws of freedom or moral laws, or of *assistance* lent it by nature, I am all the time admitting an *influence* of the former upon the latter. But the misinterpretation is easily avoided, if only attention is paid to the meaning of the statement. The resistance or furtherance is not between nature and freedom, but between the former as phenomenon and *the effects* of the latter as phenomena in the world of sense. Even the causality of freedom, that is, of pure and practical reason, is the causality of a natural cause subordinated to freedom, a causality of the subject regarded as man, and consequently as a phenomenon, and whose grounds for determination are contained in the intelligible; that is, thought under freedom, in a manner that is not further or otherwise explicable. . . .

manifestation of which in the sensible world, is to exist, and this presupposes the condition of the possibility of that end in nature; that is, in the nature of the subject as a being of the sensible world, or man. It is so presupposed *a priori,* and without regard to the practical, by judgment. This faculty, with the concept of the fitness of nature, provides us with the mediating concept between concepts of nature and the concept of freedom—a concept that makes possible the transition from the pure and theoretical (laws of the intellect) to the pure practical (laws of reason) and from conformity to law in accordance with the former to final ends according to the latter. For through that concept we conceive of the possibility of the final end that can only be actualized in nature and in harmony with nature's laws.

The intellect, by the possibility of its supplying *a priori* laws for nature, furnishes a proof of the fact that nature is understood by us only as a phenomenon, and in so doing points to nature's having a supersensible substratum; but the intellect leaves this substratum quite undetermined. Judgment by the *a priori* principle of its evaluation of nature according to its possible particular laws provides this supersensible substratum within, as well as without, us with *determinability through the intellectual faculty.* But reason gives *determination* to the same substratum *a priori* by its practical law. Thus judgment makes possible the transition from the realm of the concept of nature to that of the concept of freedom.

In respect of the faculties of the soul generally, regarded as higher faculties, i.e., as autonomous faculties, intellect is that containing the *constitutive a priori* principles for the faculty of knowledge; that is, the theoretical knowledge of nature. The *feeling of pleasure and displeasure* is provided for by the judgment in its independence from concepts and from sensations that refer to the determination of the faculty of desire and would thus be capable of being immediately practical. For the *faculty of desire* there is reason, which is practical without mediation of any pleasure of whatsoever origin. Reason as a higher faculty determines for the faculty of desire the final end accompanied by pure intellectual delight in the object. Judgment's concept of the fitness of nature falls under the head of natural concepts, but only as a regulative principle for the thinking faculties, although the aesthetic judgment regarding certain objects of nature or of art occasioning that concept is a constitutive principle in respect of the feeling of pleasure or displeasure. The spontaneity in the play of the thinking faculties whose harmonious accord contains the grounds for this pleasure, makes the concept in question in its consequences a suitable mediating link connecting the realm of the concept of nature with that of the concept of freedom, as this accord at the same time promotes the receptivity of the mind for moral sentiments. The following table may facilitate the review of all the above faculties in their systematic unity.[3]

List of Mental Faculties	*Cognitive Faculties*
Thinking faculties	Intellect
Feelings of pleasure and displeasure	Judgment
Faculty of desire	Reason

A Priori Principles	*Application*
Conformity to law	Nature
Appropriateness [to an end]	Art
Final End [and purpose]	Freedom

---

[3] It has been thought somewhat suspicious that my divisions in pure philosophy should almost always come out threefold. But it is due to the nature of the case. If a division is to be *a priori* it must be either analytic, according to the law of contradiction, and then it is always twofold, or else it is *synthetic*. If it is to be derived in the latter case from *a priori* concepts, and not, as in mathematics, from the *a priori* observation corresponding to the concept, then to meet the requirements of synthetic unity in general; namely, (1) a condition, (2) a conditioned, (3) the concept arising from the union of the conditioned with its conditioned, the classification must necessarily be threefold.

FIRST SECTION

ANALYTIC OF AESTHETIC JUDGMENT

FIRST BOOK

ANALYTIC OF THE BEAUTIFUL

FIRST ASPECT

OF THE JUDGMENT OF TASTE:[4] ASPECT OF QUALITY

§ 1

The judgment of taste is aesthetic

If we wish to discern whether anything is beautiful or not, we do not refer its image to the object by means of the intellect with a view to knowledge, but by means of the imagination acting perhaps in conjunction with the intellect we refer the image to the subject and its feeling of pleasure or displeasure. Therefore the judgment of taste is not an intellectual judgment and so not logical, but is aesthetic—which means that it is one whose determining ground *cannot be other than subjective*. Every reference of images is capable of being objective, even that of sensations (in which case it signifies the real in an empirical image). The one exception to this is the feeling of pleasure or displeasure. This denotes nothing in the object, but is a feeling which the subject has by itself and in the manner in which it is affected by the image.

To apprehend a regular and appropriate building with one's thinking faculties, whether the manner of imaginings is clear or confused, is quite different from being conscious of this image

---

[4] The definition of taste here relied upon is that it is the faculty for estimating the beautiful. But the discovery of what is required for calling an object beautiful must be reserved for the analysis of judgments of taste. In my search for the aspects to which attention is paid by this judgment in its reflection, I have followed the guidance of the logical functions of judging, for a judgment of taste always involves a reference to the intellect. I have brought the aspect of quality first under review, because this is what the aesthetic judgment looks to in the first instance.

with an accompanying sensation of delight. Here the image is referred wholly to the subject, and what is more, to its feeling of life—under the name of the feeling of pleasure or displeasure—and this forms the basis of a quite separate faculty for discriminating and estimating, that contributes nothing to knowledge. All it does is to compare the given image in the subject with the entire faculty for imagining of which the mind is conscious in the feeling of its state. Given images in a judgment may be empirical, and so aesthetic; but the judgment which is pronounced by their means is logical, provided it refers them to the object. Conversely, even if the given images are rational, but referred in a judgment solely to the subject (to its feeling), they are always aesthetic to that extent.

§ 2

The delight which determines the judgment of taste is independent of all interest

The delight which we connect with imagining the real existence of an object is called interest. Such a delight, therefore, always involves a reference to the faculty of desire, either as its determining ground, or else as necessarily implicated with its determining ground. Now, where the question is whether something is beautiful, we do not want to know whether we or anyone else are or even could be concerned in the real existence of the thing, but rather what estimate we form of it on mere contemplation (intuition or reflection). If anyone asks me whether I consider that the palace I see before me is beautiful, I may perhaps reply that I do not care for things that are merely made to be gaped at. Or I may reply in the same strain as that Iroquois *sachem* who said that nothing in Paris pleased him better than the eating-houses. I may even go a step further and inveigh with the vigor of a Rousseau against the vanity of the great who spend the sweat of the people on such superfluous things. Or finally, I may quite easily persuade myself that if I found myself on an uninhabited island without hope of ever again coming among men and could conjure such a palace into existence by a mere wish, I should still not trouble to do so as long as I had a hut there that was comfortable enough for me. All this may be admitted and approved; only it is not the point now at issue. All one wants to know is whether the mere image of the object is to my liking, no matter how indifferent I may be to the real existence of the object of this imagining. It is quite plain that in order to say that the object *is beautiful,* and to show that I have taste, everything turns on the meaning which I can give to this representation, and not on any factor which makes me dependent on the real existence of the object. Everyone must allow that a judgment on the beautiful which is tinged with the slightest interest is very partial and not a pure judgment of taste. One must not be in the least prepossessed in favor of the real existence of the thing, but must preserve complete indifference in this respect, in order to play the part of judge in matters of taste.

This proposition, which is of the utmost importance, cannot be better explained than by contrasting the pure disinterested [5] delight which appears in the judgment of taste with that allied to an interest—especially if we can also assure ourselves that there are not other kinds of interest beyond those presently to be mentioned.

§ 3

Delight IN THE AGREEABLE *is coupled with interest*

That is AGREEABLE *which the senses find pleasing in sensation.* This at once affords a convenient opportunity for condemning and directing particular attention to a prevalent con-

---

[5] A judgment upon an object of our delight may be wholly *disinterested* but withal very *interesting,* i.e., it relies on no interest, but it produces one. Of this kind are all pure moral judgments. But, of themselves, judgments of taste do not even set up any interest whatsoever. Only in society is it *interesting* to have taste—a point which will be explained in the sequel.

fusion of the double meaning of which the word "sensation" is capable. All delight (as is said or thought) is itself sensation (of a pleasure). Consequently everything that pleases, and for the very reason that it pleases, is agreeable—and according to its different degrees, or its relations to other agreeable sensations, is attractive, charming, delicious, enjoyable, etc. But if this is conceded, then impressions of sense which determine inclination, or principles of reason which determine the will, or mere observed forms which determine judgment, are all on a par in everything relevant to their effect upon the feeling of pleasure, for this would be agreeableness in the sensation of one's state; and since, in the last resort, all the elaborate work of our faculties must issue in and unite in the practical as its goal, we could credit our faculties with no other appreciation of things and the worth of things than that consisting in the gratification which they promise. How this is attained is in the end immaterial; and as the choice of the means is here the only thing that can make a difference, men might indeed blame one another for folly or imprudence, but never for baseness or wickedness; for they are all, each according to his point of view, pursuing one goal, which for each is the gratification in question.

When a modification of the feeling of pleasure or displeasure is termed sensation, this expression is given quite a different meaning to that which it bears when I call the image of a thing (through sense as a receptivity pertaining to the faculty of knowledge) sensation. For in the latter case the image is referred to the object, but in the former it is referred solely to the subject and is not available for any knowledge, not even for that by which the subject understands itself.

Now in the above definition the word sensation is used to denote an objective image of sense; and to avoid continually running the risk of misinterpretation, we shall call that which must always remain purely subjective, and which is absolutely incapable of imagining an object, by the familiar name of feeling. The green color of the meadows belongs to *objective* sensation, as the perception of an object of sense; but its agreeableness to *subjective* sensation, by which no object is represented: i.e., to feeling, through which the object is regarded as an object of delight (which involves no knowledge of the object).

Now, that a judgment of an object by which its agreeableness is affirmed expresses an interest in it is evident from the fact that through sensation it provokes a desire for similar objects, consequently the delight presupposes, not the simple judgment about it, but the bearing its real existence has upon my state so far as affected by such an object. Hence we do not merely say of the agreeable that it *pleases,* but that it *gratifies.* I do not accord it a simple approval, but inclination is aroused by it, and where agreeableness is of the liveliest type a judgment on the character of the object is so entirely out of place, that those who are always intent only on enjoyment, for that is the word used to denote intensity of gratification, would fain dispense with all judgment.

§ 4

Delight IN THE GOOD *is coupled with interest*

That is *good* which by means of reason commends itself by its mere concept. We call useful that *good for something* which only pleases as a means; but that which pleases on its own account we call *good in itself.* In both cases the concept of an end is implied, and consequently the relation of reason to at least possible willing, and thus a delight in the *existence* of an object or action, i.e. some interest or other.

To deem something good, I must always know what sort of a thing the object is intended to be, i.e. I must have a concept of it. That is not necessary to enable me to see beauty in a thing. Flowers, free patterns, lines aimlessly intertwining—technically termed foliage—have no significance, depend upon no definite concept, and yet please. Delight in the beautiful must depend upon the reflection on an object precursory to some (not definitely determined) concept. It is thus also differentiated from the agreeable, which rests entirely upon sensation.

In many cases, no doubt, the agreeable and the good seem convertible terms. Thus it is commonly said that all (especially lasting) gratification is of itself good; which is almost equivalent to saying that to be permanently agreeable and to be good are identical. But it is readily apparent that this is merely a vicious confusion of words, for the concepts appropriate to these expressions are far from interchangeable. The agreeable, which as such represents the object solely in relation to sense, must in the first instance be brought under principles of reason through the concept of an end, to be called good, as an object of will. But that the reference to delight is wholly different when what gratifies is at the same time called *good,* is evident from the fact that with the good the question always is whether it is mediately or immediately good, i.e., useful or good in itself; whereas with the agreeable this point can never arise, since the word always means what pleases immediately—and it is just the same with what I call beautiful.

Even in everyday parlance a distinction is drawn between the agreeable and the good. We do not scruple to say of a dish that stimulates the palate with spices and other condiments that it is agreeable—owing all the while that it is not good: because, while it immediately *satisfies* the senses, it is mediately displeasing, i.e., in the eye of reason that looks ahead to the consequences. Even in our estimate of health this same distinction may be traced. To all who possess it, it is immediately agreeable —at least negatively, i.e., as remoteness of all bodily pains. But if we are to say that it is good, we must further apply to reason to direct it to ends, that is, we must regard it as a state that puts us in a congenial mood for all we have to do. Finally, in respect of happiness every one believes that the greatest aggregate of the pleasures of life, taking duration as well as number into account, merits the name of a true, nay even of the highest, good. But reason sets its face against this too. Agreeableness is enjoyment.

But if this is all that we are bent on, it would be foolish to be scrupulous about the means that procure it for us—whether it be obtained passively by the bounty of nature or actively by the work of our own hands. But the notion that there is any intrinsic worth in the real existence of a man who merely lives for *enjoyment,* however busy he may be in this respect, even when in so doing he serves others—all like him intent only on enjoyment—as an excellent means to that one end, and does so, moreover, because through sympathy he shares all their gratifications—this is a view to which reason will never let itself be brought round. Only by what a man does heedless of enjoyment, in complete freedom and independently of what he can produce passively from the hand of nature, does he give absolute worth to his existence, as the real existence of a person. Happiness, with all its plethora of pleasures, is far from being an unconditioned good.[6]

But, despite all this difference between the agreeable and the good, they both agree in being invariably coupled with an interest in their object. This is true, not alone of the agreeable (§ 3) and of the mediately good, i.e., the useful, which pleases as a means to some pleasure, but also is true of that which is good absolutely and from every point of view, namely the moral good which carries with it the highest interest. For the good as the object of will, and taking an interest in it, are identical.

§ 5

Comparison of the three specifically different kinds of delight

Both the Agreeable and the Good involve a reference to the faculty of desire, and are thus attended, the former with a delight psychologically conditioned by stimuli, the latter with a

---

[6] An obligation to enjoy is a patent absurdity. The same must also be said of a supposed obligation to actions that have merely enjoyment for their aim, no matter how spiritually this enjoyment may be refined in thought (or embellished), and even if it be a mystical, so-called heavenly, enjoyment.

pure practical delight. Such delight is determined not merely by imagining the object, but also by the represented bond of connection between the subject and the real existence of the object. It is not only the object, but also its real existence that pleases. On the other hand the judgment of taste is simply *contemplative;* i.e., it is a judgment which is indifferent as to the existence of an object, and only decides how its character is related to the feeling of pleasure and displeasure. But this contemplation itself is not even directed to concepts; for the judgment of taste is not a judgment of either theoretical or practical thought, and hence it is not *grounded* on concepts either, nor *intentionally directed* to them.

The agreeable, the beautiful, and the good thus denote three different relations of the imagination to the feeling of pleasure and displeasure, a feeling by which we distinguish different objects or ways of imagining. Also, the corresponding expressions which indicate our satsifaction in them are different. The *agreeable* is what GRATIFIES a man; the *beautiful* what simply PLEASES him; the *good* what is ESTEEMED (approved); i.e., that on which he sets an objective worth. Agreeableness is a significant factor even with irrational animals; beauty has purport and significance only for human beings, both animal and rational but not merely for them as rational—intelligent beings—but only for them as at once animal and rational; whereas the good is good for every rational being in general; a proposition which can only receive its complete justification and explanation in the sequel. Of all these three kinds of delight, that of taste in the beautiful may be said to be the one and only disinterested and *free* delight; for with it no interest, whether of sense or reason, extorts approval. And so we may say that delight, in the three cases mentioned, is related to *inclination,* to *favor,* or to *respect.* For FAVOR is the only free liking. An object of inclination, and one which a law of reason imposes upon our desire, leaves us no freedom to turn anything into an object of pleasure. All interest presupposes a want, or calls one forth; and being a ground determining approval deprives the judgment on the object of its freedom.

So far as the interest or inclination in the case of the agreeable goes, everyone says: Hunger is the best sauce; and people with a healthy appetite relish everything, so long as it is something they can eat. Such delight, consequently, gives no indication of taste having anything to say as to the choice. Only when men have got all they want can we tell who among the crowd has taste or not. Similarly there may be correct habits (conduct) without virtue, politeness without good-will, propriety without honor, etc. For where the moral law dictates, there is no room left for free objective choice as to what one has to do; and to show taste in the way one carries out these dictates, or in estimating the way others do so, is a totally different matter from displaying the moral frame of one's mind. For the latter involves a command and produces a need of judgment.

Definition of the Beautiful Derived from the First Aspect

Taste is the faculty for estimating an object or a mode of representation by means of a delight or aversion *apart from any interest*. The object of such a delight is called *beautiful*.

SECOND ASPECT

OF THE JUDGMENT OF TASTE: ASPECT OF QUANTITY

§6

The beautiful is that which, apart from concepts, is represented as the Object of a UNIVERSAL *delight*

This definition of the beautiful is deducible from the foregoing definition of it as an object of delight apart from any interest. For where anyone is conscious that he has delight in an object independent of interest, it is inevitable that he should look on the object as one containing a basis of delight for all men. For, since the delight is not based on any inclination of the subject (or on any other deliberate interests), but the subject feels himself completely *free* in respect to the liking which he accords to the object, he can find as reasons for his delight no personal conditions to which his own subjective self might alone be party. Hence he must regard it as resting on what he may also presuppose in every other person; and therefore he must believe that he has reason for demanding a similar delight from everyone. Accordingly he will speak of the beautiful as if beauty were a quality of the object and the judgment logical (acquiring a knowledge of the object by concepts of it); although it is only aesthetic, and contains merely a reference of the image of the object to the subject; because it still bears this resemblance to the logical judgment, that it may be presupposed to be valid for all men. But this universality cannot spring from concepts. For from concepts there is no transition to the feeling of pleasure or displeasure (save in the case of pure practical laws, which, however, carry an interest with them; and such an interest does not attach to the pure judgment of taste). The result is that the judgment of taste, with its attendant consciousness of detachment from all interest, must involve a claim to validity for all men, and must do so apart from universality attached to objects; i.e., there must be coupled with it a claim to subjective universality.

§ 7

Comparison of the beautiful with the agreeable and the good by means of the above characteristic

As regards the *agreeable* every one concedes that his judgment, which he bases on a private feeling, and in which he declares that an object pleases him, is restricted merely to himself personally. Thus he does not take it amiss if, when he says that Canary-wine is agreeable, another corrects the expression and reminds him that he ought to say: It is agreeable *to me*. This applies not only to the taste of the tongue, the palate, and the throat, but to what may with anyone be agreeable to eye or ear. A violet color is to one soft and lovely: to another dull and faded. One man likes the tone of wind instruments, another prefers that of string instruments. To quarrel over such points with the idea of condemning another's judgment as incorrect when it differs from our own, as if the opposition between the two judgments were logical, would be folly. With the agreeable, therefore, the axiom holds good: *Everyone has his own taste* (that of the senses).

The beautiful stands on quite a different footing. It would, on the contrary, be ridiculous if anyone who plumed himself on his taste were to think of justifying himself by saying: This object (the building we see, the dress that person has on, the concert we hear, the poem submitted to our criticism) is beautiful *for me*. For if it merely pleases *him*, he must not call it *beautiful*. Many things may possess charm and agreeableness for him—no one cares about that; but when he puts a thing on a pedestal and calls it beautiful, he demands the same delight from others. He judges not merely for himself, but for all men, and then speaks of beauty as if it were a property of things. Thus he says the *thing* is beautiful; and it is not as if he counted on others agreeing in his judgment of liking owing to his having found them in such agreement on a number of occasions, but he *demands* this agreement of them. He blames them if they judge differently, and denies them taste, which he still requires of them as something they ought to have; and to this extent it is not open to men to say: Everyone has his own taste. This would be equivalent to saying that there is no such thing at all as taste, i.e., no aesthetic judgment capable of making a rightful claim upon the assent of all men.

Yet even in the case of the agreeable we find that the estimates men form do betray a prevalent agreement among them, which leads to our crediting some with taste and denying it to others, and that, too, not as an organic sense but as a critical faculty in respect of the agreeable generally. So of one who knows how to entertain his guests with pleasures of enjoyment through all the senses in such a way that one and all are pleased, we say that he has taste. But the universality here is only understood in a comparative sense; and the rules that apply are, like all empirical rules, *general* only, not *universal*—the latter being what the judgment of taste upon the beautiful deals or claims to deal in. The former is a judgment in respect of sociability so far resting on empirical rules. In respect of the good it is true that judgments also rightly assert a claim to validity for every one; but the good is only imagined as an object of universal delight *by means of a concept,* which is the case neither with the agreeable nor the beautiful.

OF JUDGMENTS OF TASTE: ASPECT OF THE RELATION
OF THE ENDS BROUGHT UNDER REVIEW
IN SUCH JUDGMENTS

§ 10

Finality in general

Let us define the meaning of "an end" in transcendental terms (i.e. without presupposing anything empirical, such as the feeling of pleasure). An end is the object of a concept so far as this concept is regarded as the cause of the object (the real ground of its possibility); and the causality of a *concept* in respect of its *object* is finality (*forma finalis*). Then wherever, not merely the knowledge of an object, but the object itself (its form or real existence) as an effect, is thought to be possible only through a concept of it, there we imagine an end. The image of the effect is here the determining ground of its cause and takes the lead of it. The consciousness of the causality of imagining the state of the subject as one tending *to preserve a continuance* of that state, may be said here to denote in a general way what is called pleasure; whereas displeasure is that imagining which contains the ground for converting the state of the images into their opposite (for hindering or removing them).

The faculty of desire, so far as it is determinable only through concepts, i.e. so as to act in conformity with an imagined end, would be the will. But an object, or state of mind, or even an action may, although its possibility does not necessarily presuppose an imagined end, be called final simply on account of its possibility being only explicable and intelligible for us by virtue of an assumption on our part of a fundamental causality according to ends, i.e., a will that would have so ordained it according to a certain represented rule. Finality, therefore, may exist apart from an end, in so far as we do not locate the causes of this form in a will, but yet are able to render the explanation of its possibility intelligible to ourselves only by deriving it from a will. Now we are not always obliged to look with the eye of reason into what we observe (i.e., to consider it in its possibility). So we may at least observe a finality of form, and trace it in objects—though by reflection only—without resting it on an end (as the material of the *nexus finalis*).

§ 11

The sole foundation of the judgment of taste is the FORM OF APPROPRIATENESS *of an object (or mode of imagining it)*

Whenever an end is regarded as a source of delight it always imports an interest as determining ground of the judgment on the object of pleasure. Hence the judgment of taste cannot rest on any subjective end as its ground. But neither can any image of an objective end, i.e., of the possibility of the object itself on principles of final connection, determine the judgment of taste, and, furthermore, neither can any concept of the good. For the judgment of taste is an aesthetic and not a thinking judgment, and so does not deal with any *concept* of the nature or of the internal or external possibility, by this or that cause, of the object, but simply with the relative bearing of the representative powers so far as they are determined by imagination.

Now this relation is present when an object is characterized as beautiful, coupled with the feeling of pleasure. This pleasure is by the judgment of taste pronounced valid for everyone; hence an agreeableness attending the imagining is just as incapable of containing the determining ground of the judgment as imagining the perfection of the object or the concept of the good. We are thus left with the subjective appropriateness in the imagined object, exclusive of any end (objective or subjective)—consequently the bare form of appropriateness in the image whereby an object is *given* to us, so far as we are conscious of it—as that which is alone capable of constituting the delight which, apart from any concept, we estimate as universally communicable, and so of forming the determining ground of the judgment of taste.

§ 12.

The judgment of taste rests upon a priori *grounds*

To determine *a priori* the connection of the feeling of pleasure or displeasure as an effect, with some representation or other (sensation or concept) as its cause, is utterly impossible; for that would be a causal relation which (with objects of experience) is always one that can only be understood *a posteriori* and with the help of experience. True, in the *Critique of Practical Reason* we did actually derive *a priori* from universal moral concepts the feeling of respect as a particular and peculiar modification of this feeling which does not strictly answer either to the pleasure or displeasure which we receive from empirical objects. But there we were further able to cross the border of experience and call in aid a causality resting on a supersensible attribute of the subject, namely that of freedom. But even there it was not this *feeling* exactly that we deduced from the idea of the moral as cause, but from this was derived simply the determination of the will. But the mental state present in the determination of the will by any means is at once in itself a feeling of pleasure and identical with it, and so does not issue from it as an effect. Such an effect must only be assumed where the concept of the moral as a good precedes the determination of the will by the law; for in that case it would be futile to derive the pleasure combined with the concept from this concept as mere knowledge.

Now the pleasure in aesthetic judgments stands on a similar footing: only that here it is merely contemplative and does not bring about an interest in the object; whereas in the moral judgment it is practical. The consciousness of mere formal purpose in the play of the thinking faculties of the subject with imagining an object, is the pleasure itself, because it involves a determining ground for the subject's activity in respect of the quickening of its thinking powers, and thus an internal causality (which is final) in respect of knowledge generally, but without being limited to definite knowledge, and consequently a mere form of the subjective fitness of an image in an aesthetic judgment. This pleasure is also in no way practical, neither resembling that from the psychological ground of agreeableness nor that from the intellectual ground of the imagined good. But still it involves an inherent causality; namely, that of *preserving a continuance* of the state of the image itself and the active engagement of the thinking powers without ulterior aim. We *dwell* on the contemplation of the beautiful because this contemplation strengthens and reproduces itself. The case is analogous (but analogous only) to the way we linger on the charm [we feel] in imagining an object which keeps arresting the attention, the mind all the while remaining passive.

Second Book

Analytic of the Sublime

§ 23

Transition from the faculty for estimating the beautiful to that for estimating the sublime

The beautiful and the sublime agree in that they are pleasing on their own account. Further they agree in not presupposing either a reaction of the senses or a logical judgment, but reflection instead. Hence it follows that the delight does not depend upon a sensation, as with the agreeable, nor upon a definite concept, as does the delight in the good, although it has, for all that an indeterminate reference to concepts. Rather the delight is connected with the mere presentation or faculty of presentation, and is thus taken to express the accord, in a given thing seen (*Anschauung*), of the faculty of presentation, or the imagination, with the *faculty of conceiving* that belongs to understanding or reason, in the sense of the former assisting the latter. Hence both kinds of judgments are *singular*, and yet such as profess to be universally valid in respect of every subject, despite the fact that their claims are directed merely to the feeling of pleasure and not to any knowledge of the object.

There are, however, also important and striking differences between the two. The beautiful in nature relates to the form of the object, and this consists in limitation, whereas the sublime is to be found in an object even devoid of form, so far as it immediately involves, or else by its presence provokes, an image of *limitlessness*, yet with a super-added thought of its totality. Accordingly the beautiful seems to be regarded as a presentation of an indeterminate intellectual concept, the sublime as a presentation of an indeterminate concept of reason. Hence the delight is in the former case coupled with the image of *Quality*, but in this case with that of *Quantity*. Moreover, the former delight is very different from the latter in kind. For the beautiful is directly attended by a feeling of the furtherance of life, and is thus compatible with charms and a playful imagination. On the other hand, the feeling of the sublime is a pleasure that only arises indirectly, being brought about by the feeling of a momentary check to the vital forces followed at once by a discharge all the more powerful, and so it is an emotion that seems to be no sport, but a dead earnest affair of the imagination. Hence charms are repugnant to it; and, since the mind is not simply attracted by the object but is also alternately repelled thereby, the delight in the sublime does not so much involve positive pleasure as admiration or respect; i.e., merits the name of a negative pleasure.

But the most important and vital distinction between the sublime and the beautiful is certainly this: that if, as is allowable, we here confine our attention in the first instance to the sublime in objects of nature (that of art being always restricted by the conditions of an agreement with nature) we observe that whereas natural beauty (such as is self-subsisting) conveys a finality in its form making the object appear, as it were, preadapted to our power of judgment, so that it thus forms of itself an object of our delight, that which, without our indulging in any refinements of thought but simply in our apprehension of it excites the feeling of the sublime, may appear in point of form to contravene the ends of our power of judgment, to be ill-adapted to our faculty for imagining, and to be, as it were, an outrage on the imagination, yet it is judged all the more sublime on that account.

From this it may be seen at once that we express ourselves on the whole inaccurately if we term any *object of nature* sublime, although we may with perfect propriety call many such objects beautiful. For how can that which is apprehended as inherently contra-final be noted with an expression of approval? All that we can say is that the object lends itself to the presentation of a sublimity discoverable in the mind. For the sublime, in the strict sense of the word, cannot be contained in any sensuous form, but rather concerns rational ideas, which, although no adequate presentation of them is possible, may be excited and called into the mind by that very inadequacy itself which does not admit of presentation through the senses. The broad ocean agitated by storms cannot be called sublime. Its aspect is horrible, and one must have stored one's mind in advance with a rich stock of ideas, if such an intuition is to raise it to the pitch of a feeling which is itself sublime—sublime because the mind has been incited to go beyond the senses, and employ itself upon ideas involving higher ends.

Self-subsisting natural beauty reveals to us a technique of nature which shows it in the light of a system ordered in accordance with laws whose principle is not to be found within the range of our entire faculty of the intellect. This principle is that of a finality relative to the employment of judgment in respect of phenomena which have thus to be assigned, not merely to nature regarded after the analogy of art. Hence it gives a veritable extension, not of course to our knowledge of objects of nature, but to our concept of nature itself—nature as mere mechanism being enlarged to the concept of nature as art—an extension inviting profound inquiries as to the possibility of such a form. But in what we are wont to call sublime in nature there is such an absence of anything leading to particular objective principles and corresponding forms of nature, that it is rather in its chaos, or in its wildest and most irregular disorder and desolation, provided it gives signs of magnitude and power, that nature chiefly excites the ideas of the sublime. Hence we see that the concept of the sublime in nature is far less important and rich in consequences than that of its beauty. It gives on the whole no indication of any final purpose in nature itself, but only in the possible *employment* of our observation of it inducing a feeling in our own selves of appropriateness quite independent of nature. For the beautiful in nature we must seek a ground outside ourselves, but for the sublime merely one inside ourselves: the attitude of mind that introduces sublimity into the image of nature. This is a very needful preliminary remark. It entirely separates the ideas of the sublime from those of the appropriateness of *nature,* and makes the theory of the sublime a mere appendage to the aesthetic estimate of the appropriateness of nature, because it does not give an image of any particular form in nature, but involves no more than the development of a final employment by the imagination of its own image.

Critique of Aesthetic Judgment

SECOND SECTION

§ 55

Dialectic of Aesthetic Judgment

For a power of judgment to be dialectical it must first of all be rationalizing; that is to say, its judgments must lay claim to universality,[7] and do so *a priori*, for it is in the antithesis of such judgments that dialectic consists. Hence there is nothing dialectical in the irreconcilability of aesthetic judgments based on sense (the agreeable and disagreeable). And in so far as each person appeals merely to his own private taste even the conflict of judgments of taste does not form a dialectic of taste—for no one is proposing to make his own judgment into a universal rule. Hence the only concept left to us of a dialectic affecting taste is one of a dialectic of the *Critique* of taste (not of taste itself) in respect to its *principles*: for, on the question of the ground of the possibility of judgments of taste in general, mutually conflicting concepts naturally and unavoidably make their appearance. The transcendental *Critique* of taste will, therefore, only include a part capable of bearing the name of a dialectic of the aesthetic judgment if we find an antinomy of the principles of the faculty which throws doubt upon its conformity to law, and hence also upon its inner possibility.

§ 56

Image of the antinomy of taste

The first commonplace of taste is contained in the proposition under cover of which everyone devoid of taste thinks to shelter

---

[7] Any judgment which claims to be universal may be termed a rationalizing judgment (*iudicium ratiocinans*); for so far as it is universal it may serve as the major premise of a syllogism. On the other hand, only a judgment which is thought as the conclusion of a syllogism, and, therefore, as having an *a priori* foundation, can be called rational (*iudicium ratiocinatum*).

himself from reproach: *everyone has his own taste*. This is only another way of saying that the determining ground of this judgment is merely subjective (gratification or pain), and that the judgment has no right to the necessary agreement of others.

Its second commonplace, to which even those resort who concede the right of the judgment of taste to pronounce with validity for everyone, is: *there is no disputing about taste*. This amounts to saying that even though the determining ground of a judgment of taste be objective, it is not reducible to definite concepts, so that in respect of the judgment itself no *decision* can be reached by proofs, although it is quite open to us to *contend* upon the matter, and to contend with right. For though *contention* and *dispute* have this point in common, that they aim at bringing judgments into accordance out of and by means of their mutual opposition; yet they differ in the latter hoping to effect this from definite concepts, as grounds of proof, and, consequently, adopting *objective concepts* as grounds of the judgment. But where this is considered impracticable, dispute is regarded as alike out of the question.

Between these two commonplaces an intermediate proposition is readily seen to be missing. It is one which has certainly not become proverbial, but yet it is at the back of everyone's mind. It is that *there may be contention about taste* (although not a dispute). This proposition, however, involves the contrary of the first one. For in a matter in which contention is to be allowed, there must be a hope of coming to terms. Hence one must be able to count on grounds of judgment that possess more than private validity and are thus not merely subjective. And yet the above principle, *everyone has his own taste,* is directly opposed to this.

The principle of taste, therefore, exhibits the following antinomy:

1. *Thesis.* The judgment of taste is not based upon concepts; for, if it were, it would be open to dispute (decision by means of proofs).

2. *Antithesis.* The judgment of taste is based on concepts; for otherwise, despite diversity of judgment, there could be no room even for contention in the matter (a claim to the necessary agreement of others with this judgment).

§ 57

Solution of the antinomy of taste

There is no possibility of removing the conflict of the above principles, which underlie every judgment of taste (and which are only the two peculiarities of the judgment of taste previously set out in the Analytic) except by showing that the concept to which the object is made to refer in a judgment of this kind is not taken in the same sense in both maxims of the aesthetic judgment; that this double sense, or point of view, in our estimate, is necessary for our power of transcendental judgment; and that nevertheless the false appearance arising from the confusion of one with the other is a natural illusion, and so unavoidable.

The judgment of taste must have reference to some concept or other, as otherwise it would be absolutely impossible for it to lay claim to necessary validity for everyone. Yet it need not on that account be provable from a concept. For a concept may be either determinable, or else at once intrinsically undetermined and indeterminable. An intellectual concept, which is determinable by means of predicates borrowed from sensible looking-at-things and corresponding to it, is of the first kind. But of the second kind is the transcendental rational concept of the supersensible, which lies at the basis of all that sensible looking-at-things and is hence incapable of being further determined theoretically.

Now the judgment of taste applies to objects of sense, but not so as to determine a *concept* of them for the intellect; for it is not a logical judgment. Rather it is a singular image or observation referable to the feeling of pleasure, and, as such, only a private judgment. And to that extent it would be limited in its validity to the individual judging: the object is *for me* an object of delight, for others it may be otherwise—everyone according to his taste.

For all that, the judgment of taste contains beyond doubt an enlarged reference by imagining the object in such a way as to lay the foundation for an extension of judgments of this kind so as to make them binding for everyone. This must of necessity be founded upon some concept or other, but such a concept as does not admit of being determined by observation, and affords no knowledge of anything. Hence, too, it is a concept *which does not afford any proof* of the judgment of taste. But the mere pure rational concept of the supersensible lying at the basis of the object (and of the judging subject for that matter) as object of sense, and thus as phenomenon, is just such a concept. For unless such a point of view were adopted there would be no means of saving the claim to universal validity of the judgments of taste. And if the concept forming the required basis were an intellectual concept, though a mere confused one, as, let us say, of perfection, answering to which the sensible observation of the beautiful might be adduced, then it would be at least intrinsically possible to found the judgment of taste upon proofs, which contradicts the thesis.

All contradiction disappears, however, if I say: The judgment of taste does depend upon a concept (namely that of a general ground of the subjective appropriateness of nature for the power of judgment), but one from which nothing can be known of the object, and nothing proved, because it is in itself indeterminable and useless for knowledge. Yet by means of this very concept the judgment acquires at the same time validity for everyone (but for each individual, no doubt, as a specific judgment immediately accompanying his observation): because its determining ground lies, perhaps, in the concept of what may be regarded as the supersensible substratum of humanity.

The solution of an antinomy turns solely on the possibility of two apparently conflicting propositions not being in fact contradictory, but rather being capable of consisting together, although the explanation of the possibility of their concept transcends our faculties for knowledge. That this illusion is also natural and for human reason unavoidable, as well as why it is so, and remains so, although upon the solution of the apparent contradiction it no longer misleads us, may be made intelligible from the above considerations.

For the concept which a judgment must have as a basis for its universal validity is taken in the same sense in both the conflicting judgments, yet two opposite predicates are asserted of it. The thesis should therefore read: The judgment of taste is not based on *determinate* concepts; but the antithesis: The judgment of taste does rest upon a concept, although an *indeterminate* one (namely, that of the supersensible substratum of phenomena), and then there would be no conflict between them.

Beyond removing this conflict between the claims and counter-claims of taste we can do nothing. To supply determinate objective principles of taste in accordance with which its judgments might be derived, tested, and proved, is an absolute impossibility, for then it would not be a judgment of taste. The subjective principle—that is to say, the indeterminate idea of the supersensible within us—can only be indicated as the unique key to the riddle of this faculty, itself concealed from us in its sources; and there is no means of making it any more intelligible.

The antinomy here exhibited and resolved rests upon the proper concept of taste as a merely reflective aesthetic judgment, and the two seemingly conflicting principles are reconciled on the ground that *they may both be true*, and this is sufficient. If, on the other hand, owing to the fact that the image lying at the basis of the judgment of taste is singular, the determining ground of taste is taken, as by some it is, to be *agreeableness*, or, as others, looking to its universal validity, would have it, the principle of *perfection*, and if the definition of taste is framed accordingly, the result is an antinomy which is absolutely irresolvable unless we show *the falsity of both propositions* as contraries (not as simple contradictories). This would force the conclusion that the concept upon which each is founded is self-contradictory. Thus it is evident that the removal of the antinomy of the aesthetic judgment pursues a course similar to that followed by the Critique in the solution of the antinomies of pure theoretical reason; and that the antinomies, both here and in the *Critique of Practical Reason,* compel us, whether we like it or not, to look beyond the horizon of the sensible, and to seek in the supersensible the point of union of all our faculties *a priori*: for we are left with no other expedient to bring reason into harmony with itself.

THE CRITIQUE OF JUDGMENT

PART II

Critique of Teleological Judgment

§ 61

Objective appropriateness in nature [for its ends]

We do not need to look beyond the critical explanation of the possibility of knowledge to find ample reason for assuming a subjective appropriateness on the part of nature in its particular laws. This is a purpose relative to comprehensibility—man's power of judgment being such as it is—and to the possibility of uniting particular experiences into a connected system of nature. In this system, then, we may further anticipate the possible existence of some among the many products of nature that, as if put there with quite special regard to our judgment, are of a form particularly adapted to that faculty. Forms of this kind are those which by their combination of unity and heterogeneity serve as it were to strengthen and entertain the mental powers that enter into play in the exercise of the faculty of judgment, and to them the name of *beautiful forms* is accordingly given.

But the universal idea of nature, as the complex of objects of sense, gives us no reason whatever for assuming that things of nature serve one another as means to ends, or that their very possibility is only made fully intelligible by a causality of this sort. For since, in the case of the beautiful forms above mentioned, imagining things is something in ourselves, it can quite readily be thought of even *a priori* as well-adapted and convenient for disposing our thinking faculties to an inward and final harmony. But where the ends are not ends of our own, and do not belong even to nature (which we do not take to be an intelligent being), there is no reason at all for presuming *a priori* that they may or ought nevertheless to constitute a special kind of causality or at least a quite peculiar order of nature. What is more, the actual existence of these ends cannot be proved by experience—save on the assumption of an antecedent process of mental jugglery that only reads the concept of an end into the nature of the things, and that, not deriving this concept from the objects and what it knows of them from experience, makes use of it more for the purpose of rendering nature intelligible to us by an analogy to a subjective ground upon which our imaginings are brought into inner connection, than for that of understanding nature from objective grounds.

Besides, objective appropriateness, as a principle upon which physical objects are possible, is so far from attaching *necessarily* to the concept of nature, that it is the stock example adduced to show the fortuitousness of nature and its form. So where the structure of a bird, for instance, the hollow formation of its bones, the position of its wings for producing motion and of its tail for steering, are cited, we are told that all this is in the highest degree accidental if we simply look to the *nexus effectivus* in nature, and do not call in aid a special kind of causality, namely, that of ends (*nexus finalis*). This means that nature, regarded as mere mechanism, could have fashioned itself in a thousand other different ways without lighting precisely on the unity based on a principle like this, and that, accordingly, it is only outside the conception of nature, and not in it, that we may hope to find some shadow of ground *a priori* for that unity.

We are right, however, in applying the teleological estimate, at least problematically, to the investigation of nature; but only with a view to bringing it under principles of observation and research by *analogy* to the causality that looks to ends, while not pretending to *explain* it by this means. Thus it is an estimate of the reflective, not of the determinant, judgment. Yet the concept of combinations and forms in nature that are determined by ends is at least *one more principle* for reducing its phenomena to rules in cases where the laws of its purely mechanical causality do not carry us sufficiently far. For we are bringing forward a teleological ground where we endow a concept of an object—as if that concept were to be found in nature instead of in ourselves—with causality in respect of the object, or rather where we picture to ourselves the possibility of the object on the analogy of a causality of this kind—a causality such as we experience in ourselves—and so regard nature as possessed of a capacity of its own for acting like a technician; if we did not ascribe such a mode of operation to nature its causality would have to be regarded as blind mechanism. But this is a different thing from crediting nature with causes acting *designedly,* to which it may be regarded as subjected in following its particular laws. The latter would mean that teleology is based, not merely on a *regulative* principle, directed to the simple *estimate* of phenomena, but is actually based on a *constitutive* principle available for *deriving* natural products from their causes: with the result that the concept of an end of nature now exists for the determinant, rather than the reflective judgment. But in that case the concept would not really be specially connected with the power of judgment, as is the concept of beauty as a formal subjective appropriateness. Natural ends would, on the contrary, be a concept of reason, and would introduce a new causality into science—one which we are borrowing all the time solely from ourselves and attributing to other beings, although we do not mean to assume that they and we are similarly constituted.

ANALYTIC OF TELEOLOGICAL JUDGMENT

§ 64

The distinctive character of things considered as physical ends

A thing is possible only as an end where the causality to which it owes its origin must not be sought in the mechanism of nature, but in a cause whose capacity of acting is determined by concepts. What is required in order that we may perceive that a thing is only possible in this way is that its form is not possible on purely natural laws—that is to say, such laws as we may understand by means of unaided intellect applied to objects of sense—but that, on the contrary, even to know it empirically in respect of its cause and effect presupposes concepts of reason. Here we have, as far as any empirical laws of nature go, a *fortuitousness* of form of the thing in relation to reason. Now reason in every case insists on understanding the necessity of the form of a natural product, even where it only desires to perceive the conditions involved in its production. In the given form above mentioned, however, it cannot get this necessity. Hence the fortuitousness is itself a ground for making us look upon the origin of the thing as if, just because of that fortuitousness, it could only be possible through reason. But the causality, so construed, becomes the faculty of acting according to ends— that is to say, a will; and the object, which is represented as only deriving its possibility from such a will, will be represented as possible only as an end.

Suppose a person was in a country that seemed to him uninhabited and was to see a geometrical figure, say a regular hexagon, traced on the sand. As he reflected, and tried to get a concept of the figure, his reason would make him conscious, though perhaps obscurely, that in the production of this concept there was unity of principle. His reason would then forbid him to consider the sand, the neighboring sea, the winds, or even animals with their footprints, as causes familiar to him, or any other irrational cause, as the ground of the possibility of such a form. For the fortuitousness of coincidence with a concept like this, which is only possible in reason, would appear to him so infinitely great that there might just as well be no law of nature at all in the case. Hence it would seem that the cause of the production of such an effect could not be contained in the mere mechanical operation of nature, but that, on the contrary a conception of such an object, as a conception that only reason can give and compare the object with, must likewise be what alone contains that causality. On these grounds it would appear to him that this effect was one that might without reservation be regarded as an end, though not as a natural end. In other words he would regard it as a product of art—*vestigium hominis video.*

But when a thing is recognized to be a product of nature, then something more is required—unless, perhaps, our very estimate involves a contradiction—if, despite its being such a product, we are yet to estimate it as an end, and, consequently, as an *end of nature.* As a provisional statement I would say that a thing exists as an end of nature *if it is* (in a double sense) *both cause and effect of itself.* For this involves a kind of causality that we cannot associate with the mere concept of a nature unless we make that nature rest on an underlying end, but which can then, though incomprehensible, be thought without contradiction. Before analysing the component factors of this idea of an end of nature or natural end, let us first illustrate its meaning by an example.

A tree produces, in the first place, another tree, according to a familiar law of nature. But the tree which it produces is of the same genus. Hence, in its *genus,* it produces itself. In the genus, now as effect, now as cause, continually generated from itself and likewise generating itself, it preserves itself generically.

Secondly, a tree produces itself even as an *individual*. It is true that we only call this kind of effect growth; but growth is here to be understood in a sense that makes it entirely different from any increase according to mechanical laws, and renders it equivalent, though under another name, to generation. The plant first prepares the matter that it assimilates and bestows upon it a specifically distinctive quality which the mechanism of nature outside it cannot supply, and it develops itself by means of a material which, in its composite character, is its own product. For, although in respect of the constituents that it derives from nature outside, it must be regarded as only a product, yet in the separation and recombination of this new material we find an original capacity of selection and construction on the part of natural beings of this kind such as infinitely outdistances all the efforts of art, when the latter attempts to reconstitute those products of the vegetable kingdom out of the elements which it obtains through their analysis, or else out of the material which nature supplies for their nourishment.

Thirdly, a part of a tree also generates itself in such a way that the preservation of one part is reciprocally dependent on the preservation of the other parts. An eye taken from the sprig of one tree and set in the branch of another produces in the alien stock a growth of its own species, and similarly a scion grafted on the body of a different tree. Hence even in the case of the same tree each branch or leaf may be regarded as engrafted or inoculated into it, and, consequently, as a tree with a separate existence of its own, and only attaching itself to another and living parasitically on it. At the same time the leaves are certainly products of the tree, but they also maintain it in turn; for repeated defoliation would kill it, and its growth is dependent upon the action of the leaves on the trunk. The way nature comes, in these forms of life, to her own aid in the case of injury, where the want of one part necessary for the maintenance of the neighboring parts is made good by the rest; the abortions or malformations in growth, where, on account of some chance defect or obstacle, certain parts adopt a completely new formation, so as to preserve the existing growth, and thus produce an anomalous form: are matters which I only desire to mention here in passing, although they are among the most wonderful properties in the forms of organic life.

§ 65

Things considered as physical ends are organisms

Where a thing is a product of nature and yet, so regarded, has to be understood as possible only as a natural end, it must from its character, as set out in the preceding section, stand to itself reciprocally in the relation of cause and effect. This is, however, a somewhat inexact and indeterminate expression that needs derivation from a definite concept.

In so far as the causal connection is thought about merely by means of the intellect, it is a nexus constituting a series of causes and effects that is invariably progressive. The things that as effects presuppose others as their causes cannot themselves in turn be also causes of the latter. This causal connection is termed that of efficient causes (*nexus effectivus*). On the other hand, however, we are also able to think of a causal connection according to a rational concept, that of ends, which, if regarded as a series, would involve regressive as well as progressive dependency. It would be one in which a thing designated at first as an effect deserves none the less, if we take the series regressively, to be called the cause of the thing of which it was said to be the effect. In the domain of practical matters, such as in art, we readily find examples of a nexus of this kind. Thus a house is certainly the cause of the money that is received as rent, but yet, conversely, the imagining of this possible income was the cause of the building of the house. A causal nexus of this kind is termed that of final causes (*nexus finalis*). The former might, perhaps, more appropriately be called the nexus of real and the latter the nexus of ideal causes, because with this use of terms it would be understood at once that there cannot be more than these two kinds of causality.

Now the *first* requisite of a thing, considered as an end of nature, is that its parts, both as to their existence and form, are only possible by their relation to the whole. For the thing is itself an end, and is, therefore, comprehended under a concept or an idea that must determine *a priori* all that is to be contained in it. But so far as the possibility of a thing is only thought of in this way, it is simply a work of art. It is the product, in other words, of an intelligent cause, distinct from the matter, or parts, of the thing, and of one whose causality, in bringing together and combining the parts, is determined by its idea of a whole made possible through that idea, and, consequently, not by external nature.

But if a thing is a product of nature, and as such is necessarily to possess intrinsically and in its inner possibility a relation to ends, in other words, is to be possible only as an end of nature and independently of the causality of the concepts of external rational agents, then this *second* requisite is involved, namely, that the parts of the thing combine of themselves into the unity of a whole, being reciprocally cause and effect of their form. For this is the only way in which it is possible that the idea of the whole may conversely, or reciprocally, determine in its turn the form and combination of all parts, not as cause—for that would make it an art-product—but as the epistemological basis upon which the systematic unity of the form and combination of all the manifold contained in the given matter becomes understandable for the person studying it.

What we require, therefore, in the case of a body which in its intrinsic nature and inner possibility has to be considered as nature's end, is as follows. Its parts must in their collective unity reciprocally produce one another alike as to form and combination, and thus by their own causality produce a whole, the concept of which, conversely—in a being possessing the causality according to concepts that is adequate for such a product—could in turn be the cause of the whole according to a principle, so that, consequently, the nexus of *efficient causes* might as well be interpreted as an *operation brought about by final* [end-related] *causes*.

In such a natural product as this every part is thought as *owing* its presence to the *agency* of all the remaining parts, and also as existing *for the sake of the others* and of the whole, that is as an instrument, or organ. But this is not enough—for it might be an instrument of art, and thus have no more than its general possibility referring to an end. On the contrary the part must be an organ *producing* the other parts—each, consequently reciprocally producing the others. No instrument of art can answer to this description, but only the instrument of that nature from whose resources the materials of every instrument are drawn—even the materials for instruments of art. Only under these conditions and upon these terms can such a product be an *organized* and *self-organized being,* and, as such, be called a *natural end.*

In a watch one part is the instrument by which the movement of the others is effected, but one wheel is not the efficient cause of the production of the other. One part is certainly present for the sake of another, but it does not owe its presence to the agency of that other. For this reason, also, the producing cause of the watch and its form is not contained in the nature of this material, but lies outside the watch in a being that can act according to ideas of a whole which its causality makes possible. Hence one wheel in the watch does not produce the other, and, still less, does one watch produce other watches, by utilizing, or organizing, foreign material; hence it does not of itself replace parts of which it has been deprived, nor, if these are absent in the original construction, does it make good the deficiency by the support of the rest; nor does it, so to speak, repair its own casual disorders. Yet these are all things which we are justified in expecting from organized nature. An organized being is, therefore, not a mere machine. For a machine has solely *motive power,* whereas an organized being possesses inherent *formative* power, and such, moreover, as it can impart to material devoid of it—material which it organizes. This, therefore, is a self-propagating formative power, which cannot be explained by the capacity of movement alone, that is to say, by mechanism.

We do not say half enough of nature and her capacity in organized products when we speak of this capacity as being the *analogue of art.* For what is here present to our minds is an artist—a rational being—working from without. But nature, on the contrary, organizes itself, and does so in each species of its organized products—following a single pattern, certainly, as to general features, but nevertheless admitting deviations calculated to secure self-preservation under particular circumstances. We might perhaps come nearer to the description of this impenetrable property if we were to call it an analogue of life. But then either we should have to endow matter as mere matter with a property (hylozoism) that contradicts its essential nature; or else we should have to associate with it a foreign principle *being in communion* with it (a soul). But, if such a product is to be a natural product, then we have to adopt one or other of two courses in order to bring in a soul. Either we must presuppose organized matter as the instrument of such a soul, which makes organized matter no whit more intelligible, or else we must make the soul the artificer of this structure, in which case we must withdraw the product from (corporeal) nature. Strictly speaking, therefore, the organization of nature has nothing analogous to any causality known to us.[1] Natural beauty

---

[1] We may, on the other hand, make use of an analogy to the above-mentioned immediate physical ends to throw light on a certain union, which, however, is to be found more often in idea than in fact. Thus in the case of a complete transformation, recently undertaken, of a great people into a state, the word *organization* has frequently, and with much propriety, been used for the constitution of the legal authorities and even of the entire body politic. For in a whole of this kind certainly no mem-

may justly be termed the analogue of art, for it is only ascribed to the objects in respect of reflection upon the *external* view of them and, therefore, only on account of their superficial form. But *intrinsic natural perfection*, as possessed by things that are only possible as *ends of nature*, and that are therefore called organisms, is unthinkable and inexplicable on any analogy to any known physical, or natural, agency, not even excepting—since we ourselves are part of nature in the widest sense—the suggestion of any strictly apt analogy to human art.

The concept of a thing as intrinsically a natural end is, therefore, not a constitutive concept either by the intellect or by reason, but yet it may be used by reflective judgment as a regulative conception for guiding our investigation of objects of this kind by a remote analogy with our own causality according to ends generally, and as a basis of reflection upon their supreme source. But in the latter connection it cannot be used to promote our knowledge either of nature or of such original sources of those objects, but must on the contrary be confined to the service of just the same practical faculty of reason in analogy with which we considered the cause of this finality.

Organisms are, therefore, the only beings in nature that, considered in their separate existence and apart from any relation to other things, cannot be thought possible except as ends of nature. It is they, then, that first provide objective reality to the concept of an *end* that is an end *of nature* and not a practical end. Thus they supply natural science with the basis for a teleology, or, in other words, a mode of estimating its objects on a special principle that it would otherwise be absolutely unjustifiable to introduce into that science—seeing that we are quite unable to perceive *a priori* the possibility of such a kind of causality.

---

ber should be a mere means, but should also be an end, and, seeing that he contributes to the possibility of the entire body, should have his position and function in turn defined by the idea of the whole.

§ 66

The principle on which the intrinsic finality [relation to ends] in organisms is estimated

This principle, the statement of which serves to define what is meant by organisms, is as follows: *an organized natural product is one in which every part is reciprocally both end and means.* In such a product nothing is in vain, without an end, or to be ascribed to a blind mechanism of nature.

It is true that the occasion for adopting this principle must be derived from experience—namely, from such experience as is methodically arranged and is called observation. But owing to the universality and necessity which that principle predicates of such finality, it cannot rest merely on empirical grounds, but must have some underlying *a priori* principle. This principle, however, may be one that is merely regulative, and it may be that the ends in question only reside in the idea of the person forming the estimate and not in any efficient cause whatever. Hence the above-named principle may be called a *maxim* for estimating the intrinsic finality of organisms.

It is common knowledge that scientists who dissect plants and animals, seeking to investigate their structure and to see into the reasons why and the end for which they are provided with such and such parts, why the parts have such and such a position and interconnection, and why the internal form is precisely what it is, adopt the above maxim as absolutely necessary. So they say that nothing in such forms of life is in *vain*, and they put the maxim on the same footing of validity as the fundamental principle of all natural science, that *nothing* happens *by chance*. They are, in fact, quite as unable to free themselves from this teleological principle as from that of general physical science. For just as the abandonment of the latter without any experience at all, so the abandonment of the former would leave them with no clue to assist their observation of a type of natural things that have once come to be thought under the concept of natural ends.

Indeed this concept leads reason into an order of things entirely different from that of a mere mechanism of nature, since *mere mechanism* no longer proves adequate in this domain. An idea has to underlie the possibility of the natural product. But this idea is an absolute unity of the representation, whereas the material is a plurality of things that of itself can afford no definite unity of composition. Hence, if that unity of the idea is actually to serve as the *a priori* determining ground of a natural law of the causality of such a form of the composite, the end of nature must be made to extend to *everything* contained in its product. For once we lift such an effect out of the sphere of the blind mechanism of nature and relate it *as a whole* to a supersensible ground of determination, we must then consider it entirely on this principle. We have no reason for assuming the form of such a thing to be still partly dependent on blind mechanism, for with such confusion of heterogeneous principles every reliable rule for estimating things would disappear.

No doubt in an animal body, for example, many parts might be explained as accretions resulting from simple mechanical laws (as skin, bone, hair). Yet the cause that accumulates the appropriate material, modifies and fashions it, and deposits it in its proper place, must always be estimated teleologically. Hence, everything in the body must be regarded as organized, and everything, also, in a certain relation to the thing is itself in turn an organ.

§ 67

The principle on which nature in general is estimated teleologically as a system of ends

We have said above that the *extrinsic* finality of natural things affords no adequate justification for taking them as ends of nature to explain the reason of their existence, or for treating their accidentally final effects as ideally the grounds for their existence on the principle of final causes. Thus we are not entitled to consider *rivers* as natural ends then and there, because they facilitate international intercourse in inland countries, or *mountains*, because they contain the sources of the rivers and hold stores of snow for the maintenance of their flow in dry seasons, or, similarly, the *slope* of the land, that carries down these waters and leaves the country dry. For, although this configuration of the earth's surface is very necessary for the origination and sustenance of the vegetable and animal kingdoms, yet intrinsically it contains nothing the possibility of which should make us feel obliged to invoke a causality according to ends. The same applies to plants utilized or enjoyed by man; or to animals, as the camel, the ox, the horse, dog, etc., which are so variously employed, sometimes as servants of man, sometimes as food for him to live on, and mostly found quite indispensable. The external relationship of things that we have no reason to regard as ends in their own right can only be hypothetically estimated as related to ends.

There is an essential distinction between estimating a thing as a natural end in virtue of its intrinsic form and regarding the real existence of this thing as an end of nature. To maintain the latter view we require, not merely the concept of a possible end, but a knowledge of the final end (*scopus*) of nature. This involves our referring nature to something supersensible, a reference that far transcends any teleological knowledge we have of nature; for, to find the end of the real existence of nature itself, we must look beyond nature. That the origin of a simple blade of grass is only possible on the rule of ends is, to our human critical faculty, sufficiently proved by its internal form. But let us lay aside this consideration and look only to the use to which the thing is put by other natural beings—which means that we abandon the study of the internal organization and look only to external adaptations to ends. We see, then, that the grass is required as a means of existence by cattle, and cattle similarly, by man. But we do not see why after all it should be necessary that men should in fact exist (a question that might not be so easy to answer if the specimens of humanity that we had in mind were, say, the New Hollanders or Fuegians). We do not then arrive in this way at any categorical end. On the contrary all this adaptation is made to rest on a condition that has to be removed to an ever-retreating horizon. This condition is the unconditional condition—the existence of a thing is not a natural end either, since it (or its entire genus) is not to be regarded as a product of nature.

Hence it is only in so far as matter is organized that it necessarily involves conceiving of it as an end of nature, because here it possesses a form that is at once specific and a product of nature. But, brought so far, this concept necessarily leads us to the idea of aggregate nature as a system following the rule of ends, to which idea, again, the whole mechanism of nature has to be subordinated on principles of reason—at least for the purpose of testing phenomenal nature by this idea. The principle of reason is one which it is competent for reason to use as a merely subjective principle, that is as a maxim: everything in the world is good for something or other; nothing in it is in vain; we are entitled, nay incited, by the example that nature affords us in its organic products, to expect nothing from it and its laws but what is related to ends or final when things are viewed as a whole.

It is evident that this is a principle to be applied not by the determinant, but only by the reflective, judgment, that it is regulative and not constitutive, and that all that we obtain from it is a clue to guide us in the study of natural things. These things it leads us to consider in relation to a ground of determination already given, and in the light of a new uniformity, and it helps us to extend physical science according to another principle, namely, that of final causes, yet without interfering with the principle of the mechanism of physical causality. Furthermore, this principle is altogether silent on the point of whether

anything considered according to it is, or is not, an end of nature *by design:* whether, that is, the grass exists for the sake of
the ox or the sheep, and whether these and the other things
of nature exist for the sake of man. We do well to consider even
things that are unpleasant to us, and that in particular connections are contrafinal, from this point of view also. Thus, for
example, one might say that the vermin which plague men in
their clothes, hair, or beds, may, by a wise provision of nature,
be an incitement toward cleanliness, which is of itself an important means for preserving health. Or the mosquitoes and
other stinging insects that make the wilds of America so trying
for the savages may be so many goads to urge these primitive
men to drain the marshes and bring light into the dense forests
that shut out the air, and, by so doing, as well as by the tillage
of the soil, to render their abodes more sanitary. Even what appears to man to be contrary to nature in his internal organization affords, when treated on these lines, an interesting, and
sometimes even instructive, outlook into a teleological order of
things, to which mere unaided study from a physical point of
view apart from such a principle would not lead us. Some persons say that men or animals that have a tapeworm receive it as
a sort of compensation to make good some deficiency in their
vital organs. Now, just in the same way, I would ask if dreams
(from which our sleep is never free, although we rarely remember what we have dreamed) may not be a regulation of nature
adapted to ends. For when all the muscular forces of the body
are relaxed dreams serve the purpose of internally stimulating
the vital organs by means of the imagination and the great
activity which it exerts—an activity that in this state generally
rises to psychophysical agitation. This seems to be why imagination is usually more actively at work in the sleep of those who
have gone to bed at night with a loaded stomach, just when this
stimulation is most needed. Hence, I would suggest that without this internal stimulating force and fatiguing unrest that
makes us complain of our dreams, which in fact, however, are

probably curative, sleep, even in a sound state of health, would amount to a complete extinction of life.

Once the teleological estimate of nature, supported by the natural ends actually presented to us in organic beings, has entitled us to form the idea of a vast system of natural ends we may regard even natural beauty from this point of view, such beauty being an accordance of nature with the free play of our thinking faculties as engaged in grasping and estimating its appearance. For then we may look upon it as an objective finality of nature in its entirety as a system of which man is a member. We may regard it as a favor[8] that nature has extended to us, that besides giving us what is useful it has dispensed beauty and charms in such abundance, and for this we may love it, just as we view it with respect because of its immensity, and feel ourselves ennobled by such contemplation—just as if nature had erected and decorated its splendid state with this precise purpose in mind.

The general purport of the present section is simply this: once we have discovered a capacity in nature for bringing forth products that can only be thought by us according to the concept of final causes, we advance a step farther. Even products which do not (either as to themselves or the relation, however final, in which they stand) make it necessarily incumbent upon us to go beyond the mechanism of blind efficient causes and seek out some other principle on which they are possible, may nevertheless be justly estimated as forming part of a system of ends. For the idea from which we started is one which, when we consider its foundation, already leads beyond the world

---

[8] In the Part on Aesthetics the statement was made: *we regard nature with favor,* because we take a delight in its form that is altogether free (disinterested). For in this judgment of mere taste no account is taken of any end for which these natural beauties exist: whether to excite pleasure in us, or irrespective of us as ends. But in a teleological judgment we pay attention to this relation; and so we can *regard it as a favor of nature,* that it has been disposed to promote our culture by exhibiting so many beautiful forms.

of sense, and then the unity of the supersensible principle must be treated, not as valid merely for certain species of natural beings, but as similarly valid for the whole of nature as a system.

DIALECTIC OF TELEOLOGICAL JUDGMENT

§ 69

Nature of an antinomy of judgment

The *determinant* judgment does not possess as its own separate property any principles upon which *concepts of objects* are founded. It is not autonomous; for it *subsumes* merely under given laws, or concepts, as principles. Just for this reason it is not exposed to any danger from inherent antinomy and does not run the risk of a conflict of its principles. Thus transcendental judgment, which was shown to contain the conditions of subsumption under categories, was not independently *nomothetic*. It only specified the conditions of visualizing by the senses upon which reality, that is, application, can be provided for a given concept as a law of the intellect. In doing this, judgment could never fall into a state of internal disunion, at least in the matter of principles.

But the *reflecting* judgment has to subsume under a law that is not yet given. It has, therefore, in fact only a principle of reflection upon objects for which we are objectively at a complete loss for a law, or concept of the object, sufficient to serve as a principle covering the particular cases as they come before us. Now as there is no permissible employment of the thinking faculties apart from principles, the reflecting judgment must in such cases be a principle to itself. As this principle is not objective and is unable to introduce any basis of knowledge of the object sufficient for the required purpose of subsumption, it must serve as a mere subjective principle for the employment of our thinking faculties in a final manner, namely, for reflecting upon objects of a particular kind. The reflecting judgment provides, therefore, maxims applicable to such cases—maxims that are in fact necessary for obtaining a knowledge of the natural laws to be found in experience, and which are directed to assist us in attaining to concepts, be these even concepts of reason, wherever such concepts are absolutely required for the mere purpose of getting to know nature's empirical laws. Between these necessary maxims of the reflecting judgment a conflict may arise, and consequently an antinomy. This antinomy provides the basis of a dialectic; and if each of the mutually conflicting maxims has its foundation in the nature of our thinking faculties, his dialectic may be called a natural dialectic, which creates an unavoidable illusion which it is the duty of critical philosophy to expose and to resolve lest it should deceive us.

§ 70

Exposition of this Antinomy

In dealing with nature as the complex of objects of external sense, reason is able to rely upon laws, some of which are prescribed by the mind itself *a priori* to nature, while others are capable of indefinite extension by means of the empirical determinations occurring in experience. For the application of the laws prescribed *a priori* by the intellect, that is, of the *universal* laws of material nature in general, judgment does not need any special principle of reflection; for there it is determinant, an objective principle being furnished to it by the intellect. But in respect of the particular laws with which we can become acquainted through experience alone, there is such a wide scope for diversity and heterogeneity that judgment must be a principle to itself, even for the mere purpose of searching for a law and tracing one in the phenomena of nature. For it needs such a principle as a guiding thread, if it is even to hope for a consistent body of empirical knowledge based on a thoroughgoing uniformity of nature—that is a unity of nature in its empirical laws. Now from the fact of this accidental unity of particular laws it may come to pass that judgment acts upon two maxims in its reflection, one of which it receives *a priori* from mere intellect, but the other of which is prompted by particular experiences that bring reason into play to institute an estimate of corporeal nature and its laws according to a particular principle. What happens then is that these two different maxims seem to all appearance unable to be harmonized, and a dialectic arises that throws judgment into great confusion as to the principle of its reflection.

The first maxim of such reflection is the *thesis*: All production of material things and their forms must be estimated as possible on mere mechanical laws.

The second maxim is the *antithesis*: Some products of material nature cannot be estimated as possible on mere mechanical laws (that is, for estimating them quite a different law of causality is required; namely, that of final causes).

If now these regulative principles of investigation were converted into constitutive principles of the possibility of the objects themselves, they would read thus:

Thesis: All production of material things is possible on mere mechanical laws.

Antithesis: Some production of such things is not possible on mere mechanical laws.

In this latter form, as objective principles for the determinant judgment, they would contradict one another, so that one of the pair would necessarily be false. They would then form an antinomy certainly, though not one of judgment, but rather a conflict in the laws of reason. But reason is unable to prove either one or the other of these principles: seeing that we can have no *a priori* determining principle of the possibility of things [based] on mere empirical laws of nature.

On the other hand, looking at the maxims of a reflecting judgment as first set out, we see that they do not in fact contain any contradiction at all. For if I say: I must inquire into the possibility of all events in material nature, and, consequently, also all forms considered as its products, as resulting from mechanical laws, I do not thereby assert that they *are solely possible in this way*, that is, to the exclusion of every other kind of causality. On the contrary this assertion is only intended to indicate that I *ought* at all times to *reflect* upon these things *according to the principle* of the simple mechanism of nature, and, consequently, push my investigation with it as far as I can, because unless I make it the basis of research there can be no knowledge of nature in the true sense of the term at all. Now this does not stand in the way of the second maxim when a proper occasion for its employment presents itself—that is to say, in the case of some natural forms (and, at their instance, in the case of entire nature), we may, in our reflection upon them, follow the trail of a principle which is radically different from explanation by the mechanism of nature, namely, the principle of final causes. For reflection according to the first maxim is not in this way superseded. On the contrary we are directed to pursue it as far as we can. Further it is not asserted that those forms were not possible as the result of the mechanism of nature. It is only maintained that *human reason,* adhering to this maxim and proceeding on these lines, could never discover a particle of foundation for what constitutes the specific character of a natural end, whatever additions it might make in this way to its knowledge of natural laws. This leaves it an open question, whether in the unknown inner basis of nature itself the physicomechanical and the final nexus present in the same things may not cohere in a single principle; it being only our reason that is not in a position to unite them in such a principle, so that our judgment, consequently, remains *reflective,* not determinant, that is, acts on a subjective ground, and not according to an objective principle of the possibility of things in their inherent nature, and, accordingly, *is* compelled to conceive a different principle from that of the mechanism of nature as a ground of the possibility of certain forms in nature.

§71

Introduction to the solution of the above antinomy

We are wholly unable to prove the impossibility of the production of organized natural products in accordance with the simple mechanism of nature. For we cannot see into the first and inner ground of the infinite multiplicity of the particular laws of nature, which, being only known empirically, are for us contingent, and so we are absolutely incapable of reaching the intrinsic and all-sufficient principle of the possibility of a nature —a principle which lies in the supersensible. But may not the productive capacity of nature be just as adequate for what we estimate to be formed or connected according to the idea of ends as it is for what we believe merely calls for mechanical functions on the part of nature? Or may it be that in fact things are genuine natural ends (as we must necessarily estimate them to be), and as such founded upon an original causality of a completely different kind, which cannot be an incident of material nature or of its intelligible substratum, but instead are caused by a constructing mind? What has been said shows that there are questions upon which our reason, very narrowly restricted to the specific *a priori,* can give absolutely no answer. But that, relatively to our thinking faculties, the mere mechanism of nature is also unable to furnish any explanation of the creation of organisms, is a matter just as indubitably certain. *For the reflective judgment,* therefore, this is a perfectly sound principle: that for the clearly manifest nexus of things according to final causes, we must think a causality distinct from mechanism, namely, a world-cause acting according to ends, that is, an intelligent cause—however rash and undemonstrable a principle this might be *for the determinant judgment.* In the first case the principle is a simple maxim of judgment. The concept of causality which it in-volves is a mere idea to which we in no way undertake to con-cede reality, but only make use of it as a guide to reflection that still leaves the door open for any available mechanical explana-tion, and that never strays from the world of sense. In the sec-ond case the principle would be an objective principle. Reason would prescribe it and judgment would have to be subject to it and be determined accordingly. But in that case reflection wanders from the world of sense into transcendent regions, and possibly gets led astray.

All semblance of an antinomy between the maxims of the strictly physical or mechanical mode of explanation and the teleological or constructive, rests, therefore, on our confusing a principle of the reflective with one of the determinant judg-ment. The *autonomy* of the former, which is valid merely subjectively for the use of our reason in respect of particular empirical laws, is mistaken for the *heteronomy* of the second, which has to conform to the laws, either universal or particular, given by the mind.

§ 74

The impossibility of treating the concept of a construc-tion of nature dogmatically springs from the inexplicability of a natural end

Even though a concept is to be placed under an empirical con-dition we deal dogmatically with it, if we regard it as con-tained under another concept of the object—this concept form-ing a principle of reason—and determine it in accordance with the latter. But we deal merely critically with the concept if we only regard it in relation to our thinking faculties, and con-sequently to the subjective conditions of thinking it, without undertaking to decide anything as to its object. Hence the dog-matic treatment of a concept is treatment which is authoritative for the determinant judgment: the critical treatment is such as is authoritative merely for the reflective judgment.

Now the concept of a thing as a natural end is one that subsumes nature under a causality that is only thinkable by the aid of reason, and so subsumes it for the purpose of letting us judge of what is given of the object in experience [on the basis of] this principle. But in order to make use of this concept dogmatically for the determinant judgment we should have first to be assured of its objective reality, as otherwise we could not subsume any natural thing under it. The concept of a thing as a natural end is, however, certainly one that is empirically conditioned, that is, is one only possible under certain conditions given in experience. Yet it is not one to be abstracted from these conditions, but, on the contrary, it is only possible [if based] on a rational principle in the estimating of the object. We have no insight into the objective reality of such a principle, that is to say, we cannot perceive that an object answering to it is possible. We cannot establish it dogmatically; and we do not know whether it is a mere logical fiction and an objectively empty concept (*conceptus ratiocinans*), or whether it is a rational concept, supplying a basis of knowledge and substantiated by reason (*conceptus ratiocinatus*). Hence it cannot be treated dogmatically on behalf of the determinant judgment. In other words, not only is it impossible to decide whether or not things of nature, considered as natural ends, require for their production a causality of a quite peculiar kind, namely, an intentional causality, but the very question is quite out of order. For the concept of a natural end cannot at all be proved by reason to have objective reality, which means that it is not constitutive for the determinant judgment, but merely regulative for the reflective judgment.

That a natural end is not provable is clear from the following considerations. Being a concept of a *natural product* it involves necessity. Yet it also involves in one and the same thing, considered as an end, an accompanying fortuitousness in the form of the object in respect of mere laws of nature. Hence, if it is to escape self-contradiction, besides containing a basis of the possibility of the thing in nature it must further contain a basis of the possibility of this nature itself and of its reference to something that is not an empirically understandable nature, namely to something supersensible, and, therefore, to what is not understandable by us at all. Otherwise in judging of its possibility, we should not have to estimate it in the light of a kind of causality different from that of natural mechanism. Accordingly the concept of a thing as a natural end is transcendent *for the determinant judgment* if its object is viewed by reason—albeit for the reflective judgment it may be immanent in respect of objects of experience. Objective reality, therefore, cannot be procured for it on behalf of the determinant judgment. Hence we can understand how it is that all systems that are devised with a view to the dogmatic treatment of the concept of natural ends or of nature as a whole as owing its consistency and coherence to final causes, fail to settle anything whatever either by their objective affirmations or by their objective denials. For, if things are subsumed under a concept that is merely problematic, the synthetic predicates attached to this concept—as, for example, in the present case, whether the natural end which we suppose for the production of the thing is designed or undesigned—must yield judgments about the object of a like problematic character, be they affirmative or negative, since one does not know whether one is judging about what is something or nothing. The concept of a causality through ends, that is, ends of art, has certainly objective reality, just as that of a causality according to the mechanism of nature has. But the concept of a natural causality following the rule of ends, and still more of such a Being as is utterly incapable of being given to us in experience—a Being regarded as the original creator of nature—while it may no doubt be thought without self-contradiction, is nevertheless useless for the purpose of dogmatic definitive assertions. For, since it is incapable of being extracted from experience, and besides is unnecessary for its possibility, there is nothing that can give any guarantee of its objective reality. But even if this could be assured, how can I count among products of nature things that are definitely posited as products of divine art, when it was the very incapacity of nature to produce such things according to its own laws that necessitated the appeal to a cause distinct from nature?

APPENDIX

THEORY OF THE METHOD OF APPLYING THE
TELEOLOGICAL JUDGMENT

§ 80

The necessary subordination of the principle of mecha-
nism to the teleological principle in the explanation
of a thing regarded as a physical end.

Our *right to aim at* an explanation of all natural products on simple mechanical lines is in itself quite unrestricted. But the constitution of our mind, as engaged upon things in the shape of natural ends, is such that our *power* of meeting *all demands* from the unaided resources of mechanical explanation is not only very limited, but is also circumscribed within clearly marked limits. For by a principle of judgment that adopts the above procedure alone nothing whatever can be accomplished in the way of explaining natural ends. For this reason our estimate of such products must at all times be subordinated to a concurrent teleological principle.

Hence there is reason, and indeed merit, in pursuing the mechanism of nature for the purpose of explaining natural products so far as this can be done with probable success, and in fact never abandoning this attempt on the ground that it is *intrinsically* impossible to encounter the appropriateness of nature along this road, but only on the ground that it is impossible *for us* as men. For in order to get results along this line of investigation we should require a capacity of looking-at-things different from our senses and a determinate knowledge of the intelligible substratum of nature from which we could show the reason of the very mechanism of phenomena and their particular laws. But this wholly surpasses our capacity.

So where it is established beyond question that the concept of a natural end applies to things, as in the case of organized beings, if the naturalist is not to throw his labor away, he must always in forming an estimate of them accept some original organization or other as fundamental. He must consider that this organization avails itself of the very mechanism above mentioned for the purpose of producing other organic forms, or for evolving new structures from those given—such new structures, however, always issuing from and in accordance with the end in question.

It is praiseworthy to employ a comparative anatomy and go through the vast creation of organized beings in order to see if there is not discoverable in it some trace of a system, and indeed of a system following a genetic principle. For otherwise we should be obliged to content ourselves with the mere critical principle—which tells us nothing that gives any insight into the production of such beings—and to abandon in despair all claim to *insight into nature* in this field. When we consider the agreement of so many genera of animals in a certain common schema, which apparently underlies not only the structure of their bones, but also the disposition of their remaining parts, and when we find here the wonderful simplicity of the original plan, which has been able to produce such an immense variety of species by the shortening of one member and the lengthening of another, by the involution of this part and the evolution of that, there gleams upon the mind a ray of hope, however faint, that the principle of the mechanism of nature, apart from which there can be no natural science at all, may yet enable us to arrive at some explanation in the course of organic life. This analogy of forms, which in all their differences seem to be produced in accordance with a common type, strengthens the suspicion that they have an actual kinship due to descent from a common parent. This we might trace in the gradual approximation of one animal species to another, from that in which the principle of ends seems best authenticated, namely, from man, back to the polyp, and from this back even to mosses and lichens, and finally to the lowest perceptible stage of nature. Here we come to crude matter; and from this, and the forces which it exerts in accordance with mechanical laws (laws resembling those by which it acts in the formation of crystals) seems to be developed the whole construction of nature which, in the case of organized beings, is so incomprehensible to us that we feel obliged to imagine a different principle for its explanation.

Here the archeologist of nature is at liberty to go back to the traces that remain of nature's earliest revolutions, and, appealing to all he knows of or can conjecture about its mechanism, to trace the genesis of that great family of living things (for it must be pictured as a family if there is to be any foundation for the consistently coherent affinity mentioned). He can suppose that the womb of mother earth as it first emerged, like a huge animal, from its chaotic state, gave birth to creatures whose form displayed less relation to ends, that these bore others which adapted themselves more perfectly to their native surroundings and their relations to each other, until this womb, becoming rigid and ossified, restricted its birth to definite species incapable of further modification, and the multiplicity of forms was fixed as it stood when the operation of that fruitful formative power had ceased. Yet, for all that, he is obliged eventually to attribute to this universal mother an organization suitably constituted with a view to all these forms of life, for unless he does so, the possibility of the final form of the products of the animal and plant kingdoms is quite unthinkable.[9] But when he

---

[9] An hypothesis of this kind may be called a daring venture on the part of reason; and there are probably few even among the most acute scientists to whose minds it has not sometimes occurred. For it cannot be said to be absurd, like the *generatio aequivoca*, which means the

does attribute all this to nature he has only pushed the explanation a stage farther back. He cannot pretend to have made the genesis of those two kingdoms intelligible independently of the condition of final causes.

Even as regards the alteration which certain individuals of the organized genera contingently undergo, where we find that the character thus altered is transmitted and taken up into the generative power, we can form no other plausible estimate of it than that it is an occasional development of a purposive capacity originally present in the species with a view to the preservation of the race. For in the complete inner appropriateness of an organized being, the generation of its like is intimately associated with the condition that nothing shall be taken up into the generative force which does not also belong, in such a system of ends, to one of its undeveloped native capacities. Once we depart from this principle we cannot know with certainty whether many constituents of the form at present found in a species may not be of equally accidental and purposeless origin, and the principle of teleology, that nothing in an organized being which is preserved in the propagation of the species should be estimated as devoid of a relation to ends, would be made very unreliable and could only hold good for the parent stock, to which our knowledge does not go back.

In reply to those who feel obliged to adopt a teleological

---

generation of an organized being from crude inorganic matter. It never ceases to be *generatio univoca* in the widest acceptation of the word, as it only implies the generation of something organic from something else that is also organic, although, within the class of organic beings, differing specifically from it. It would be as if we supposed that certain water animals transformed themselves by degrees into marsh animals, and from these after some generations into land animals. In the judgment of plain reason there is nothing *a priori* self-contradictory in this. But experience offers no example of it. On the contrary, as far as experience goes, all generation known to us is *generatio homonyma*. It is not merely *univoca* in contradistinction to generation from an unorganized substance, but it brings forth a product which in its very organization is of like kind with that which produced it, and a *generatio heteronyma* is not met with anywhere within the range of our experience.

principle of critical judgment, that is of constructing intellect in the case of all such natural ends, Hume raises the objection that one might ask with equal justice how such an intellect is itself possible. By this he means that one may also ask how it is possible that there should be such a teleological coincidence in one being of the manifold faculties and properties presupposed in the very concept of a mind possessing at once intellectual and executive capacity. But there is nothing in this point. For the whole difficulty that besets the question as to the genesis of a thing that involves ends (purposes) and that is solely comprehensible by their means rests upon the demand for unity in the source of the synthesis of the multiplicity of *externally existing* elements in this product. For, if this source is to be understood as a simple substance regarded as a productive cause, the above question, as a teleological problem, is abundantly answered, whereas if the cause is merely sought in matter, as an aggregate of many externally existing substances, the unity of principle requisite for the intrinsically end-related form of its complex structures is wholly absent. The *autocracy* of matter in productions that by our understanding are only conceivable as ends is a word with no meaning.

This is the reason why those who look for a supreme ground of the possibility of the objectively end-related forms of matter, and yet do not concede an intellect to this ground, choose nevertheless to make the universe either an all-embracing substance (Pantheism), or else—and this is only the preceding in more refined form—a complex of many determinations inhering in a single *simple substance* (Spinozism). Their object is to derive from this substance that *unity* which all relation to ends presupposes. And in fact, thanks to their purely ontological concept of a simple substance, they really do something to satisfy *one* condition of the problem—namely, that of the unity implied in the reference to an end. But they have nothing to say on the subject of the *other* condition, namely, the relation of the substance to its consequence regarded as an *end*, this relation being what gives to their ontological ground the more precise determination which the problem demands. The result is that they in no way answer the *entire* problem. For our intellect the problem is absolutely unanswerable except on the following terms. First, the original source of things must be pictured by us as a simple substance. Then its attribute, as a simple substance, in its relation to the specific character of the natural forms whose source it is, i.e., the character of unity through ends, must be pictured as the attribute of an intelligent substance. Lastly, the relation of this intelligent substance to the natural forms must, owing to the contingency which we find in everything which we imagine to be possible only as an end, be pictured as one of causality.

§ 81

The association of mechanism with the teleological principle which we apply to the explanation of an end of nature considered as a product of nature

We have seen from the preceding section that the mechanism of nature is not sufficient to enable us to conceive the possibility of an organized being, but that in its root origin it must be subordinated to a cause acting by design—or, at least, that the type of our thinking faculty is such that we must conceive it to be so subordinated. But just as little can the mere teleological source of a being of this kind enable us to consider and to estimate it as at once an end and a product of nature. With that teleological source we must further associate the mechanism of nature as a sort of instrumental cause acting by design and contemplating an end to which nature is subordinated even in its mechanical laws. The possibility of such a union of two completely different types of causality, namely, that of nature in its universal conformity to law and that of an idea which restricts nature to a particular form of which nature, as nature, is in no way the source, is something which our reason does not comprehend. For it resides in the supersensible substratum of nature, of which we are unable to make any definite affirmation, further than that it is the self-subsistent being of which we know merely the phenomenon. Yet, for all that, this principle remains in full and undiminished force, and everything which we assume to form part of phenomenal nature and to be its product must be thought as linked with nature by mechanical laws. For, apart from this type of causality, organized beings, although they are ends of nature, would not be natural products.

Now suppose we adopt the teleological principle of the production of organized beings, as indeed we cannot avoid doing, we may then base their internal form as related to ends either on the *occasionalism* or on the *pre-establishment* of the cause. According to occasionalism the Supreme Cause of the world would directly supply on the occasion of each impregnation the organic formation, stamped with the impress of His idea, to the commingling substances united in the generative process. On the premise of pre-establishment the Supreme Cause would only endow the original products of His wisdom with the inherent capacity by means of which an organized being produces another after its own kind, and the species preserves its continuous existence, while the loss of individuals is ever being repaired through the agency of a nature that concurrently labors toward their destruction. If the occasionalism of the production of organized beings is assumed, all co-operation of nature in the process is entirely lost, and no room is left for the exercise of reason in judging of the possibility of products of this kind. So we may take it for granted that no one will embrace this system who cares anything for philosophy.

Again the system of pre-establishment may take either of two forms. Thus it treats every organized being produced from one of its own kind either as its *educt* or as its *product*. The system which regards the generations as educts is termed that of *individual preformation*, or, sometimes, the *theory of evolution*; that which regards them as products is called the system of *epigenesis*. The latter may also be called the system of *generic preformation,* inasmuch as it regards the productive capacity of the parents, in respect of the inner final tendency that would be part of their original stock, and, therefore, the specific form, as still having been *virtualiter* preformed. On this statement the opposite theory of individual preformation might also more appropriately be called the *theory of involution* (or *encasement*).

The advocates of the *theory of evolution* exclude all individuals from the formative force of nature, for the purpose of deriving them directly from the hand of the Creator. Yet they would not venture to describe the occurrence on the lines of the hypothesis of occasionalism, so as to make the impregnation an idle formality, which takes place whenever a supreme intelligent Cause of the world has made up His mind to form a foetus directly with His own hand and relegate to the mother the mere task of developing and nourishing it. They would avow adherence to the theory of preformation; as if it were not a matter of indifference whether a supernatural origin of such forms is allowed to take place at the start or in the course of the world-process. They fail to see that in fact a whole host of supernatural contrivances would be spared by acts of creation as occasion arose, which would be required if an embryo formed at the beginning of the world had to be preserved from the destructive forces of nature, and had to keep safe and sound all through the long ages till the day arrived for its development, and also that an incalculably greater number of such preformed entities would be created than would be destined ever to develop, and that all those would be so many creations thus rendered superfluous and in vain. Yet they would like to leave nature some role in these operations, so as not to lapse into an unmitigated hyperphysics that can dispense with all explanation on naturalistic lines. Of course they would still remain unshaken in their hyperphysics; so much so that they would discover even in abortions—which yet cannot possibly be deemed ends of nature —a marvelous appropriateness, even if directed to no better purpose than that of being a meaningless employment intended to put some chance anatomist at his wit's end, and make him fall on his knees with admiration. However, they would be absolutely unable to make the generation of hybrids fit in with the system of preformation, but would be compelled to allow to the seed of the male creature, to which in other cases they had denied all but the mechanical property of serving as the first means of nourishment for the embryo, a further and additional formative force directed to ends. And yet they would not concede this force to either of the two parents when dealing with the complete product of two creatures of the same genus.

As against this, even supposing we failed to see the enormous advantage on the side of the advocate of *epigenesis* in the matter of empirical evidence in support of his theory, still we should at the outset be strongly prepossessed in favor of his line of explanation. For as regards things the possibility of whose origin can only be represented to the mind according to a causality of ends, epigenesis none the less regards nature as at least itself productive in respect of the continuation of the process, and not as merely unraveling something. Thus with the least possible expenditure of the super-natural it entrusts to nature the explanation of all steps subsequent to the original beginning, which is what baffles all the attempts of physics, no matter what chain of causes it adopts.

No one has rendered more valuable services in connection with this theory of epigenesis than Herr Hofrat Blumenbach. This is as true of what he has done toward establishing the correct principles of its application—partly by setting due bounds to an over-liberal employment of it—as it is of his contributions to its proof. He makes organic substance the starting-point for physical explanations of these formations. For to suppose that crude matter, obeying mechanical laws, was originally its own architect, that life could have sprung up from the nature of what is void of life, and matter have spontaneously adopted the form of a self-maintaining finality, he justly declares to be contrary to reason. But at the same time he leaves to the mechanism of nature, in its subordination to this inscrutable *principle* of a primordial *organization*, an indeterminable yet also unmistakable function. The capacity of matter here required he terms— in contradistinction to the simply mechanical *formative force* universally residing in it—in the case of an organized body a *formative impulse*, standing, so to speak, under the higher guidance and direction of the above principle.

§ 82

The teleological system in the extrinsic relations of organisms

By extrinsic appropriateness I mean the appropriateness that exists where one thing in nature serves another as a means to an end. Now even things which do not possess any intrinsic relevancy, and whose possibility does not imply any, such as earth, air, water, and the like, may nevertheless be extrinsically, that is in relation to other beings, very well adapted to ends. But then those other beings must in all cases be organized, that is be nature's ends, for unless they are ends the former could not be considered means. Thus water, air, and earth cannot be regarded as means to the upgrowth of mountains. For intrinsically there is nothing in mountains that calls for their being a source of somehow possibly serving ends. Hence their cause can never be referred to such a source and represented under the predicate of a means subservient thereto.

Extrinsic appropriateness is an entirely different concept from that of intrinsic appropriateness, the latter being connected with the possibility of an object irrespective of whether its actuality is itself an end or not. In the case of an organism we may further inquire: For what end does it exist? But we can hardly do so in the case of things in which we recognize the simple effect of the mechanism of nature. The reason is that in the case of organisms we have already pictured to ourselves a causality according to ends—a creative intellect—to account for their intrinsic appropriateness, and have referred this active faculty to its determining ground, the design. There is one extrinsic appropriateness which is the single exception—and it is intimately bound up with the intrinsic purpose of an organization. This case does not leave open the question as to the end for which the nature so organized must have existed, and yet it is an extrinsic relation of a means to an end. This is the organization of the two sexes in their mutual relation with a view to the propagation of their species. For here we may always ask, just as in the case of an individual: Why was it necessary for such a pair to exist? The answer is: In this pair we have what first forms an *organizing* whole, though not an organized whole in a single body.

Now when it is asked to what end a thing exists, the answer may take one of two forms. It may be said that its existence and generation have no relation whatever to a cause acting designedly. Its origin is then understood to be always derived from the mechanism of nature. Or it may be said that its existence, being that of a contingent natural entity, has some ground or other involving design. And this is a thought which it is difficult for us to separate from the concept of a thing that is organized. For inasmuch as we are compelled to rest its intrinsic possibility on the causality of final causes and an idea underlying this causality, we cannot but think that the real existence of this product is also an end. For where the imagining of an effect is at the same time the ground determining an intelligent efficient cause to its production, the effect so imagined is termed an *end*. Here, therefore, we may either say that the end of the real existence of a natural being of this kind is inherent in itself, that is, that it is not merely an end, but also a *final end*; or we may say that the final end lies outside it in other natural beings, that is, that its real existence, which is adapted to ends, is not itself a final end, but is necessitated by its being at the same time a means.

But if we go through the whole of nature we do not find in it, as nature, any being capable of laying claim to the distinction of being the final end of creation. In fact it may even be proved *a priori*, that what might do perhaps as an *ultimate end* for nature, endowing it with any conceivable qualities or properties we choose, could nevertheless in its character of a natural thing never be a final end.

Looking to the vegetable kingdom we might at first be induced by the boundless fertility with which it spreads itself abroad upon amost every soil to think that it should be regarded as a mere product of the mechanism which nature displays in its formations in the mineral kingdom. But a more intimate knowledge of its indescribably wise organization precludes us from entertaining this view, and drives us to ask: For what purpose do these forms of life exist? Suppose we reply: For the animal kingdom, which is thus provided with the means of sustenance, so that it has been enabled to spread over the face of the earth in such a manifold variety of genera. The question again arises: For what purpose then do these herbivora exist? The answer would be something like this: For the carnivora, which are only able to live on what itself has animal life. At last we get down to the question: What is the end and purpose of these and all the preceding natural kingdoms? Man, we say, and the multifarious uses to which his intelligence teaches him to put all these forms of life. He is the ultimate end of creation here upon earth, because he is the one and only being upon it that is able to form a concept of ends, and from an aggregate of things purposively fashioned is able to construct by the aid of his reason a system of ends.

We might also follow the Chevalier Linné and take the seemingly opposite course. Thus we might say: The herbivorous animals exist for the purpose of checking the profuse growth of the vegetable kingdom by which many species of that kingdom would be choked; the carnivora for the purpose of setting bounds to the voracity of the herbivora; and finally man exists so that by pursuing the latter and reducing their numbers a certain equilibrium between the productive and destructive forces of nature may be established. So, on this view, however much man might in a certain relation be esteemed as end, in a different relation he would in turn only rank as a means.

If we adopt the principle of an objective relation to ends in the manifold variety of the specific forms of terrestrial life and in their extrinsic relations to one another as beings with a structure adapted to ends, it is only reasonable to go on and imagine that in this extrinsic relation there is also a certain organization and a system of the whole kingdom of nature related to ends as causes. But experience seems here to give the lie to the maxim of reason more especially as regards an ultimate end of nature—an end which nevertheless is necessary to the possibility of such a system, and which we can only place in man. For, so far from making man, regarded as one of the many animal species, an ultimate end, nature has no more exempted him from its destructive than from its productive forces, nor has it made the smallest exception to its subjection of everything to a mechanism of forces devoid of an end.

The first thing that would have to be expressly arranged in a system ordered with a view to a final whole of natural beings upon the earth would be their habitat—the soil or the element upon or in which they are intended to thrive. But a more intimate knowledge of the nature of this basal condition of all organic production shows no trace of any causes but those acting altogether without design, and in fact tending toward destruction rather than calculated to promote genesis of forms, order, and ends. Land and sea not alone contain memorials of mighty primeval disasters that have overtaken both them and all their brood of living forms, but their entire structure—the strata of the land and the coast lines of the sea—has all the appearance of being the outcome of the wild and all-subduing forces of a nature working in a state of chaos. However wisely the configuration, elevation and slope of the land may now seem to be adapted for the reception of water from the air, for the subterranean channels of the springs that well up between the diverse layers of earth (suitable for various products) and fo. the course of the rivers, yet a closer investigation of them shows that they have resulted simply as the effect partly of volcanic eruptions, partly of floods, or even invasions of the ocean. And this is not alone true as regards the genesis of this configuration, but more particularly of its subsequent transformation, attended with the disappearance of its primitive organic productions.[10] If now the abode for all these forms of life—the lap of the land and the bosom of the deep—points to none but a wholly undesigned mechanical generation, how can we, or what right have we to ask for or to maintain a different origin for these latter products? And even if man, as the most minute examination of the remains of those devastations of nature seems, in Camper's judgment, to prove, was not comprehended in such revolutions, yet his dependence upon the remaining forms of terrestrial life is such that, if a mechanism of nature whose power overrides these others is admitted, he must be regarded as included within its scope, although his intelligence, to a large extent at least, has been able to save him from its work of destruction.

But this argument seems to go beyond what it was directed to prove. For it would seem to show not merely that man could not be an ultimate end of nature, or, for the same reason, the aggregate of the organized things of terrestrial nature be a system of ends, but that even the products of nature previously

---

[10] If the name of *natural history,* now that it has once been adopted, is to continue to be used for the description of nature, we may give the name of *archaeology* of *nature,* as contrasted with art, to that which the former literally indicates, namely, an account of the bygone or *ancient* state of the earth—a matter on which, though we dare not hope for any certainty, we have good ground for conjecture. Fossil remains would be objects for the archaeology of nature, just as rudely cut stones, and things of that kind, would be for the archeology of art. For, as work is actually being done in this department, under the name of a theory of the earth, steadily though, as we might expect, slowly, this name would not be given to a purely imaginary study of nature, but to one to which nature itself invites and summons us.

deemed to be ends of nature could have no other origin than the mechanism of nature.

But, then, we must bear in mind the results of the solution above given of the antinomy of the principles of the mechanical and teleological generation of organic natural beings. These principles, as we there saw, are merely principles of reflective judgment in respect of formative nature and its particular laws, the key to whose systematic correlation is not in our possession. They tell us nothing definite as to the origin of the things in their own intrinsic nature. They only assert that by the constitution of our understanding and our reason we are unable to conceive the origin in the case of beings of this kind otherwise than in the light of end-related causes. The utmost persistence, nay even a boldness, is allowed us in our endeavors to explain them on mechanical lines. More than that, we are even summoned by reason to do so, albeit we know we can never complete such an explanation—not because there is an inherent inconsistency between the mechanical generation and an origin according to ends, but for subjective reasons involved in the particular type and limitations of our intellect. Lastly, we saw that the reconciliation of the two modes of picturing the possibility of nature might easily lie in the supersensible principle of nature, both external and internal. For the imagining based on end-related causes is only a subjective condition of the exercise of our reason in cases where reason is not merely seeking the proper estimate to be made of objects arranged as phenomena, but is bent rather on referring these phenomena, principles and all, to their supersensible substratum, for the purpose of recognizing the possibility of certain laws of their unity, which are capable of being figured by the mind only as means toward an end (of which reason also possesses examples of the supersensible type).

§ 83

The ultimate end of nature as a teleological system

We have shown in the preceding section that, looking to principles of reason, there is ample ground—for the reflective, though not of course for the determinant, judgment—to make us consider man as not merely an end of nature, such as all organized beings are, but as the being upon this earth who is the *ultimate end* of nature, and the one in relation to whom all other natural things constitute a system of ends. What now is the end in man, and the end which, as such, is intended to be promoted by means of his connection with nature? If this end is something which must be found in man himself, it must either be of such a kind that man himself may be satisfied as a result of nature and its beneficence, or else it is the aptitude and skill for all manner of ends for which he may employ nature both external and internal. The former end of nature would be the *happiness* of man, the latter his *culture*.

The concept of happiness is not one which man abstracts more or less from his instincts and so derives from his animal nature. It is, on the contrary, a mere *idea* of a state, and one to which he seeks to make his actual state of being adequate under purely empirical conditions—an impossible task. He projects this idea himself, and, thanks to his intellect and its complicated relations with imagination and sense, projects it in such different ways, and even alters his concept so often, that were nature a complete slave to his elective will, it would nevertheless be utterly unable to adopt any definite, universal and fixed law by which to accommodate itself to this fluctuating concept and so bring itself into accord with the end that each individual arbitrarily sets before himself. But even if we sought to reduce this concept to the level of the true wants of nature in which our species is in complete and fundamental accord, or, trying the other alternative, sought to increase to the highest level man's skill in reaching his imagined ends, nevertheless what man means by happiness, and what in fact constitutes his peculiar ultimate physical end, as opposed to the end of freedom, would never be attained by him. For his own nature is not so constituted as to rest or be satisfied in any possession or enjoyment whatever. Also external nature is far from having made a particular favorite of man or from having preferred him to all other animals as the object of its beneficence. For we see that in its destructive operations—plague, famine, flood, cold, attacks from animals great and small, and all such things—it has as little spared him as any other animal. But, besides all this, the discord of inner *natural tendencies* betrays man into further misfortunes of his own invention, and reduces other members of his species, through the oppression of lordly power, the barbarism of wars, and the like, to such misery, while he himself does all he can to work ruin to his race, that, even with the utmost goodwill on the part of external nature, its end, supposing it were directed to the happiness of our species, would never be attained in a system of terrestrial nature, because our own nature is not capable of it. Man, therefore, is ever but a link in the chain of nature's ends. True, he is a principle in respect of many ends to which nature seems to have predetermined him, seeing that he makes himself so; but, nevertheless, he is also a means toward the preservation of the appropriateness in the mechanism of the remaining members. As the single being upon earth that possesses intellect, and, consequently, a capacity for setting before himself ends of his deliberate choice, he is certainly titular lord of nature, and, supposing we regard nature as a teleological system, he is born to be its ultimate end [goal]. But this is always on condition that he has the intelligence and the will to give to nature and to himself such ends as can be self-sufficing independently of nature, and, consequently, [can constitute] a final end. Such an end, however, must not be sought in nature.

But where in man, at any rate, are we to place this *ultimate end* of nature? To discover this we must seek out what nature can supply for the purpose of preparing him for what he him-self must do in order to be a final end, and we must segregate it from all ends whose possibility rest upon conditions that man can only expect at the hand of nature. Earthly happiness is an end of the latter kind. It is understood to mean the complex of all possible human ends attainable through nature whether in man or external to him. In other words it is the material sub-stance of all his earthly ends and what, if he converts it into his sole end, renders him incapable of positing a final end [aim] for his own real existence and of harmonizing them. Therefore of all his ends in nature, we are left only with a formal, subjective condition, namely, that of the aptitude for setting goals before himself at all, and, independent of nature in his power of determining goals, of employing nature as a means in accordance with the maxims of his free goals gener-ally. This alone remains of what nature can effect relative to the final end that lies outside it, and of what may therefore be regarded as its ultimate end. The development in a rational being of an aptitude for any ends whatever of his own choosing, consequently of being able to use his freedom, is *culture*. Hence it is only culture that can be the ultimate end which we have cause to attribute to nature in respect of the human race. His individual happiness on earth, and, we may say, the mere fact that he is the chief instrument for instituting order and harmony in irrational external nature, are ruled out.

But not every form of culture can fill the function of this ulti-mate end [purpose] of nature. *Skill* is a culture that is certainly the principal subjective condition of the aptitude for the further-ing of ends of all kinds, yet it is incompetent for giving assistance to the *will* in its determination and choice of its ends. But this is an essential factor, if an aptitude for ends [goals] is to have its full meaning. This latter condition of aptitude, involv-ing what might be called culture by way of discipline, is nega-tive. It consists in the liberation of the will from the despotism of desires whereby, in our attachment to certain natural things, we are rendered incapable of exercising a choice of our own. This happens when we allow ourselves to be enchained by impulses with which nature only provided us that they might serve as leading strings to prevent our neglecting, or even impairing, the animal element in our nature, while yet we are left free enough to tighten or slacken them, to lengthen or shorten them, as the ends of our reason may dictate.

Skill can hardly be developed in the human race otherwise than by means of inequality among men. For the majority, in a mechanical kind of way that calls for no special art, provide the necessaries of life for the ease and convenience of others who apply themselves to the less necessary branches of culture in science and art. These keep the masses in a state of oppression, with hard work and little enjoyment, though in the course of time much of the culture of the higher classes spreads to them also. But with the advance of this culture—the culminating point of which, where devotion to what is superfluous begins to be prejudicial to what is indispensable, is called luxury—misfortunes increase equally on both sides. With the lower classes they arise by force of domination from without, with the upper from seeds of discontent within. Yet this splendid misery is connected with the development of natural tendencies in the human race, and the end pursued by nature itself, though it be not our end, is thereby attained. The formal condition under which nature can alone attain this, its real end, is the existence of a constitution so regulating the mutual relations of men that the abuse of freedom by individuals striving one against another is opposed by a lawful authority centered in a whole, called a *civil community*. For it is only in such a constitution that the greatest development of natural tendencies can take place. In addition to this we should also need a *cosmopolitan* whole—had men but the ingenuity to discover such a constitution and the wisdom voluntarily to submit themselves to its constraint. It would be a system of all states that are in danger of acting injuriously to one another. In its absence, and with the obstacles that ambition, love of power, and avarice, especially on the part of those who hold the reins of authority, put in the way even of the possibility of such a scheme, *war* is inevitable. Sometimes this results in states splitting up and resolving themselves into lesser states, sometimes one state absorbs other smaller states and endeavors to build up a larger unit. But if on the part of men war is a thoughtless undertaking, being stirred up by unbridled passions, it is nevertheless a deep-seated, maybe far-seeing, attempt on the part of supreme wisdom, . . . to prepare the way for a rule of law governing the freedom of states, and thus bring about their unity in a system established on a moral basis. And, in spite of the terrible calamities which it inflicts on the human race, and the hardships, perhaps even greater, imposed by the constant preparation for it in time of peace, yet—as the prospect of the dawn of an abiding reign of national happiness keeps ever retreating farther into the distance—it is one further spur for developing to the highest pitch all talents that minister to culture.

We turn now to the discipline of inclinations. In respect of these our natural equipment is very purposively adapted to the performance of our essential functions as an animal species, but they are a great impediment to the development of our humanity. Yet here again, in respect of this second requisite for culture, we see nature striving on purposive lines to give us that education which opens the door to higher ends than it can itself afford. The preponderance of evil is indisputable which a taste refined to the extreme of idealization, and which even luxury in the sciences, considered as food for vanity, diffuses among us as the result of the mass of insatiable inclinations which they beget. But, while that is so, we cannot fail to recognize the end of nature—ever more and more to prevail over the rudeness and violence of inclinations that belong more to the animal part of our nature and are most inimical to an education that would fit us for our higher vocation (inclinations toward enjoyment), and to make way for the development of our humanity. Fine art and the sciences, if they do not make man morally better, yet, by conveying a pleasure that admits of universal communication and by introducing polish and refinement into society, make him civilized. Thus they do much to overcome the tyrannical propensities of sense, and so prepare man for a sovereignty in which reason alone shall have sway. Meanwhile the evils visited upon us, now by nature, now by the truculent egoism of man, evoke the energies of the soul, and give it strength and courage to submit to no such force, and at the same time quicken in us a sense that in the depths of our nature there is an aptitude for higher ends.[11]

§ 84

The final end of the existence of a world, that is, of creation itself

A *final end* [ultimate purpose] is an end that does not require any other end as condition of its possibility.

If the simple mechanism of nature is accepted as the explanation of the point of it all, it is not open to us to ask: For what end do the things in the world exist? For in such an imagined system we have only to reckon with the physical possibility of things—and things that it would be mere empty sophistry to imagine as ends. Whether we refer this form of things to chance,

---

[11] The value of life for us, measured simply by *what we enjoy* (by the natural end of the sum of all our inclinations, that is, by happiness), is easy to decide. It is less than nothing. For who would enter life afresh under the same conditions? Who would even do so according to a new, self-devised plan (which should, however, follow the course of nature), if it also were merely directed to enjoyment? We have shown above what value life receives from what it involves when lived according to the end with which nature is occupied in us, and which consists in *what we do,* not merely what we enjoy, we being, however, in that case always but a means to an undetermined final end. There remains then nothing but the worth which we ourselves assign to our life by what we not alone do, but do with a view to an end so independent of nature that the very existence of nature itself can only be an end subject to the condition so imposed.

or whether we refer it to blind necessity, such a question would in either case be meaningless. But if we suppose the final nexus in the world to be real, and assume a special type of causality for it, namely, the activity of a cause *acting designedly*, we cannot then stop short at the question: What is the end for which things in the world, namely, organized beings, possess this or that form, or are placed by nature in this or that relation to other things? On the contrary, once we have conceived an intellect that must be regarded as the cause of the possibility of such forms as they are actually found in things, we must go on and seek in this intellect for an objective ground capable of determining such creative intellectual power for producing an effect of this kind. That ground is then the final end for which such things exist.

I have said above that the final end is not an end which nature would be competent to realize or produce in terms of its idea, because it is one that is unconditioned. For in nature, as a thing of sense, there is nothing whose determining ground, discoverable in nature itself, is not always in turn conditioned. This is not merely true of external or material nature, but also of internal or thinking nature—it being of course understood that I am only considering what in us is strictly nature. But a thing, which by virtue of its objective characterization is to exist necessarily as the final end of an intelligent cause, must be of such a kind that in the order of ends it is dependent upon no further or other condition than simply its idea.

Now we have in the world beings of but one kind whose causality is teleological, or directed to ends, and which at the same time are beings of such a character that the law according to which they have to determine ends for themselves is imagined by them themselves as unconditioned and not dependent on anything in nature, but as necessary in itself. A being of this kind is man, but man regarded as noumenon. He is the only natural creature whose peculiar objective characterization is nevertheless such as to enable us to recognize in him a supersensible faculty—his *freedom*—and to perceive both the law of its causality and the object of freedom which that faculty is able to set before itself as the highest end—the supreme good in the world.

Now it is not open to us in the case of man, considered as a moral agent, or similarly in the case of any rational being in the world, to ask the further question: For what end (*quem in finem*) does he exist? His existence inherently involves the highest end—the end to which, as far as in him lies, he may subject the whole of nature, or contrary to which at least he must not deem himself subjected to any influence on its part. Now assuming that things in the world are beings that are dependent in point of their real existence and as such stand in need of a supreme cause acting according to ends, then man is the final end of creation. For without man the chain of mutually subordinated ends would have no ultimate point of attachment. Only in man, and only in him as the individual being to whom the moral law applies, do we find unconditional legislation in respect of ends. This legislation, therefore, is what alone qualifies him to be a final end to which all of nature is teleologically subordinated.[12]

---

[12] It would be possible for the happiness of the rational beings in the world to be an end of nature, and were it so, it would also be the *ultimate end of nature*. At least it is not obvious *a priori* why nature should not be so ordered, for, so far as we can see, happiness is an effect which it would be quite possible for nature to produce by means of its mechanism. But morality, or a causality according to ends that is subordinate to morality, is an absolutely impossible result of natural causes. For the principle that determines such causality of action is supersensible. In the order of ends, therefore, it is the sole principle possible which is absolutely unconditioned in respect to nature, and it is what alone qualifies the subject of such causality to be the *final end* of creation, and the one to which all of nature is subordinated. *Happiness*, on the other hand, as an appeal to the testimony of experience showed in the preceding section, so far from being a *final end of creation,* is not even an *end of nature* as regards man in preference to other creatures. It may ever be that individual men will make it their ultimate subjective end. But if, seeking for the final end of creation, I ask: For what end was it necessary that men should exist? my question then refers to an objective supreme

§ 91

The type of assurance produced by a practical faith

If we look merely to the manner in which something can be an object of knowledge (res cognoscibilis) for us, that is, having regard to the subjective nature of our powers of imagination, we do not in that case compare our concepts with the objects, but merely with our faculty for knowing and the use that it is able to make of the given image from a theoretical or practical point of view. So the question whether something is an understandable entity or not is a question which touches, not the possibility of the things themselves, but the possibility of our knowledge of them.

Understandable things are of three kinds: *matters of opinion, matters of fact, and matters of faith.*

1. The objects of mere ideas of reason, being wholly incapable of presentation on behalf of theoretical knowledge in any possible experience whatever, are to that extent also things altogether *unknowable,* and, consequently, we cannot even *form an opinion* about them. For to form an opinion *a priori* is absurd on the face of it and the straight road to pure figments of the brain. Either our *a priori* proposition is, therefore, certain or it involves no element of assurance at all. Hence, *matters of opinion* are always objects of an empirical knowledge that is at least intrinsically possible. They are, in other words, objects belonging to the world of sense, but objects of which other than em-

---

end, such as the highest reason would demand for their creation. If we reply to this question: So that beings may exist upon whom that supreme Cause may exercise this beneficence, we then belie the condition to which the reason of man subjects even his own inmost wish for happiness, namely, harmony with his own inner moral laws. This proves that happiness can only be a conditional end and therefore that it is only as a moral being that man can be the final end of creation; while, as regards his state of being, happiness is only incident thereto as a consequence proportionate to the measure of his harmony with that end, as the end of his existence.

pirical knowledge is impossible because the degree of empirical knowledge we possess is as it is. Thus the ether of our modern physicists—an elastic fluid interpenetrating all other substances and completely permeating them—is a mere matter of opinion, yet it is in all respects of such a kind that it could be perceived if our external senses were sharpened to the highest degree, but its presentation can never be the subject of any observation or experiment. To assume rational inhabitants of other planets is a matter of opinion; for if we could get nearer the planets, which is intrinsically possible, experience would decide whether such inhabitants are there or not; but as we shall never get so near to them, the matter remains one of opinion. But to entertain an opinion that there exist in the material universe pure unembodied thinking spirits is mere romancing—supposing, I mean, that we dismiss from our notice, as well we may, certain phenomena that have been passed off for such. Such a notion is not a matter of opinion at all, but an idea pure and simple. It is what remains over when we take away from a thinking being all that is material and yet let it keep its thought. But whether, when we have taken away everything else, the thought—which we only know in man, that is, in connection with a body—would still remain, is a matter we are unable to decide. A thing like this is a *fictitious logical entity* (*ens rationis ratiocinantis*), not a *rational entity* (*ens rationis ratiocinatae*). With the latter it is anyway possible to substantiate the objective reality of its concept, at least in a manner sufficient for the practical use of reason, for this use, which has its peculiar and apodictically certain *a priori* principle, in fact demands and postulates that conception.

The objects that answer to concepts whose objective reality can be proved are *matters of fact* [13] (*res facti*). Such proof may

---

[13] I here extend the concept of a matter of fact beyond the usual meaning of the term, and, I think, rightly. For it is not necessary, and indeed not practicable, to restrict this expression to actual experience where we are speaking of the relation of things to our thinking faculties, as we do not need more than a merely possible experience to enable us to speak of things as objects of a definite kind of knowledge.

be afforded by pure reason or by experience, and in the former case may be from theoretical or practical data of reason, but in all cases it must be effected by means of an observation corresponding to the concepts. Examples of matters of fact are the mathematical properties of geometrical magnitudes, for they admit of *a priori presentation* for the theoretical employment of reason. Further, things or qualities of things that are capable of being verified by experience, be it one's own personal experience or that of others (supported by evidence), are in the same way matters of fact—an idea which does not of itself admit of being visualized as an image, or, consequently, of any theoretical proof of its possibility. The idea in question is that of *freedom*. Its reality is the reality of a particular kind of causality (whose concept would be transcendent if considered theoretically), and as a causality of that kind it admits of verification by means of practical laws of pure reason and in the actual actions that take place in obedience to them, and, consequently, in experience. It is the only one of all the ideas of pure reason whose object is a matter of fact and must be included among them.

Objects that must be thought of *a priori*, either as consequences or as grounds, if pure practical reason is to be used as duty commands, but which are transcendent for the theoretical use of reason, are mere *matters of faith*. Such is the *summum bonum* which has to be realized in the world through freedom— a concept whose objective reality cannot be proved in any experience possible for us, or in any way so as to satisfy the requirements of the theoretical employment of reason. At the same time we are enjoined to use it for the purpose of realizing that end through pure practical reason in the best way possible, and, accordingly, its possibility must be assumed. This effect which is commanded, *together with the only conditions on which its possibility is conceivable by us,* namely, the existence of God and the immortality of the soul, are *matters of faith (res fidei)* and moreover, are of all objects the only ones that can be so called.[14] For although we have to believe **what we** can only learn by *testimony* from the experience of others, **yet** that does not make what is so believed in itself a matter of faith, for with *one* of those witnesses it was personal experience and matter of fact, or is assumed to have been so. In addition it must be possible to arrive at knowledge by this path—the path of historical belief; for the objects of history and geography, as, in general, everything that the nature of our thinking faculties makes at least a possible subject of knowledge are to be classed among matters of fact, not matters of faith. It is only objects of pure reason that can be matters of faith at all, and even they must then not be regarded as objects simply of pure speculative reason; for this does not enable them to be reckoned with any certainty whatever among matters, or objects, of that knowledge which is possible for us. They are ideas, that is, concepts, whose objective reality cannot be guaranteed theoretically. On the other hand, the supreme final purpose to be realized by us, which is all that can make us worthy of being ourselves the final purpose of a creation, is an idea that has objective reality for us in practical matters, and is a matter of faith. For since we cannot provide objective reality for this conception from a theoretical point of view, it is a mere matter of faith on the part of pure reason, as are also God and immortality, they being the sole conditions under which, owing to the frame of our human reason, we are able to conceive the possibility of that effect of the use of our freedom according to law. But assurance in matters of faith is an assurance from a purely practical point of view. It is a moral faith that proves nothing for pure rational

---

[14] Being a matter of faith does not make a thing an *article of faith,* if by articles of faith we mean such matters of faith as one can be bound to *acknowledge,* inwardly or outwardly—a kind therefore that does not enter into natural theology. For, being matters of faith, they cannot, like matters of fact, depend on theoretical proofs, and, therefore, the assurance is a free assurance, and it is only as such that it is compatible with the morality of the subject.

knowledge as theoretical, but only for it as practical and directed to the fulfilment of its obligations. It in no way extends either speculation or the practical rules of prudence actuated by the principle of self-love. If the supreme principle of all moral laws is a postulate, this involves the possibility of its supreme object, and, consequently, the condition under which we are able to conceive such possibility is also being postulated. This does not make knowing the postulate into any knowledge or opinion of the existence in nature of these conditions, as a mode of theoretical knowledge. The postulate is a mere assumption, confined to matters practical and commanded in practical interests, on behalf of the moral use of our reason.

Were we able with any plausibility to make the ends of nature which natural teleology sets before us in such abundance the basis of a *determinate* concept of an intelligent world-cause, the existence of this being would not then be a matter of faith. For as it would not be assumed on behalf of the performance of our duty, but only for the purpose of explaining nature, it would simply be the opinion and hypothesis best suited to our reason. Now the teleology in question does not lead in any way to a determinate concept of God. On the contrary such a concept can only be found in that of a moral author of the world, because this alone assigns the final end to which we can attach ourselves but only so far as we live in accordance with what the moral law prescribes to us as the final end, and, consequently imposes upon us as a duty. Hence, it is only by relation to the object of our duty, as the condition which makes its final end possible, that the concept of God acquires the position of figuring in our assurance as a matter of faith. On the other hand, this very same concept cannot make its object valid as a matter of fact, for although the necessity of duty is quite plain for a practical reason, yet the attainment of its final end, so far as it does not lie entirely in our own hands, is merely assumed in the interests of the practical employment of reason, and, therefore, is not practically necessary in the way duty itself is.[15]

Faith as *habitus*, not as *actus*, is the moral attitude of reason in its assurance of the truth of what is beyond the reach of theoretical knowledge. It is the steadfast principle of the mind, therefore, according to which the truth of what must necessarily be presupposed as the condition of the supreme final purpose being possible is assumed as true in consideration of the fact that we are under an obligation to pursue that end[16]—and assumed not-

[15] The final end which we are enjoined by the moral law to pursue is not the foundation of duty. For duty lies in the moral law which, being a formal practical principle, directs categorically, irrespective of the objects of the faculty of desire—the subject-matter of volition—and, consequently, of any end whatever. This formal character of our actions— their subordination to the principle of universal validity—which alone constitutes their intrinsic moral worth, lies entirely in our own power; and we can quite easily make abstraction from the possibility or the impracticability of the ends that we are obliged to promote in accordance with that law—for they only form the extrinsic worth of our actions. Thus we put them out of consideration, as what does not lie altogether in our own power, in order to concentrate our attention on what rests in our own hands. But the object in view—the furthering of the final end of all rational beings, namely, happiness so far as consistent with duty—is nevertheless imposed upon us by the law of duty. But speculative reason does not in any way perceive the practicability of that object—whether we look at it from the standpoint of our own physical power or from that of the co-operation of nature. On the contrary, so far as we are able to form a rational judgment on the point, speculative reason must, apart from the assumption of the existence of God and immortality, regard it as a baseless and idle, though well-intentioned, expectation, to hope that mere nature, internal or external, will from such causes bring about such a result of our good conduct, and could it have perfect certainty as to the truth of this judgment, it would have to look on the moral law itself as a mere delusion of our reason in respect of practical matters. But speculative reason is fully convinced that the latter can never happen, whereas those ideas whose object lies beyond nature may be thought without contradiction. Hence for the sake of its own practical law and the task which it imposes, and, therefore, in respect of moral concerns, it must recognize those ideas to be real, in order not to fall into self-contradiction.
[16] It is a confidence in the promise of the moral law. But this promise is not regarded as one involved in the moral law itself, but rather as one which we import into it, and so import on morally adequate grounds.

withstanding that we have no insight into its possibility, though likewise none into its impossibility. Faith, in the plain acceptation of the term, is a confidence of attaining a purpose the furthering of which is a duty, but whose achievement is a thing of which we are unable to *perceive* the possibility—or, consequently, the possibility of what we can alone conceive to be its conditions. Thus the faith that has reference to particular objects is entirely a matter of morality, provided such objects are not objects of possible knowledge or opinion, in which latter case, and above all in matters of history, it must be called credulity and not faith. It is a free assurance, not of any matter for which conclusive proofs can be found for the theoretical determinant judgment, nor of what we consider a matter of obligation, but of that which we assume in the interests of a purpose which we set before ourselves in accordance with laws of freedom. But this does not mean that it is adopted like an opinion formed on inadequate grounds. On the contrary it is something that has a foundation in reason (though only in relation to its practical employment), and *a foundation that satisfies the purpose of reason*. For without it, when the moral attitude comes into collision with theoretical reason and fails to satisfy its demand for a proof of the possibility of the object of morality, it loses all its stability, and wavers between practical commands and theoretical doubts. To be *incredulous* is to adhere to the maxim of

For a final end cannot be commanded by any law of reason, unless reason, though it be with uncertain voice, also promises its attainability, and at the same time authorizes assurance as to the sole conditions under which our reason can imagine such attainability. The very word *fides* expresses this; and it must seem suspicious how this expression and this particular idea get a place in moral philosophy, since it was first introduced by Christianity, and its acceptance might perhaps seem only a flattering imitation of the language of the latter. But this is not the only case in which this wonderful religion has in the great simplicity of its statement enriched philosophy with far more definite and purer conceptions of morality than morality itself could have previously supplied. But once these concepts are found, they are *freely* approved by reason, which adopts them as concepts at which it could quite well have arrived itself and which it might and ought to have introduced.

placing no reliance on testimony; but a person is *unbelieving* who denies all validity to the above ideas of reason because their reality has no theoretical foundation. Hence, such a person judges dogmatically. But a dogmatic *unbelief* cannot stand side by side with a moral maxim governing the attitude of the mind—for reason cannot command one to pursue an end that is recognized to be nothing but a fiction of the brain. But the case is different with a *doubting faith*. For such a faith the want of conviction on grounds of speculative reason is only an obstacle—one which a critical insight into the limits of this faculty can deprive of any influence upon conduct and for which it can make amends by a paramount practical assurance.

*   *   *   *   *   *

If we desire to replace certain mistaken efforts in philosophy, and to introduce a different principle, and gain influence for it, it gives great satisfaction to see just how and why such attempts were bound to miscarry.

God, freedom, and the *immortality of the soul* are the problems to whose solution, as their ultimate and unique goal, all the laborious preparations of metaphysics are directed. Now it was believed that the doctrine of freedom was only necessary as a negative condition for practical philosophy, whereas that of God and the nature of the soul, being part of theoretical philosophy had to be proved independently and separately. Then each of those two concepts was subsequently to be united with what is commanded by the moral law (which is only possible on terms of freedom) and a religion was to be arrived at in this way. But we perceive at once that such attempts were bound to miscarry. For from simple ontological conceptions of things in the abstract, or of the existence of a necessary being, we can form absolutely no concept of an original being determined by predicates which admit of being given in experience and which are therefore available for knowledge. But should the concept be founded on experience of the physical appropriateness of nature, it could then in turn supply no proof adequate for morality, or, consequently, the knowledge of a God. Just as little could knowledge of the soul drawn from experience—which we can only obtain in this life—furnish a concept of its spiritual and immortal nature, or, consequently, one that would satisfy morality. *Theology* and *pneumatology*, regarded as problems framed in the interests of sciences pursued by a speculative reason, are in their very implication transcending all our faculties of knowledge, and cannot, therefore, be established by means of any empirical data or predicates. These two concepts, both that of God and that of the soul (in respect to its immortality), can only be defined by means of predicates which, although they themselves derive their possibility entirely from a supersensible source, must, for all that, prove their reality in experience, for this is the only way in which they can make possible a knowledge of a wholly supersensible being. Now the only concept of this kind to be found in human reason is that of the freedom of man subject to moral laws and, in conjunction therewith, to the final end which freedom prescribes by means of these laws. These laws and this final end enable us to ascribe, the former to the author of nature, the latter to man, as the properties which contain the necessary conditions for the possibility of both. Thus it is from this idea that an inference can be drawn to the real existence and the nature of both God and the soul—beings that otherwise would be entirely hidden from us.

Hence, the source of the failure of the attempt to attain to a proof of God and immortality by the merely theoretical route lies in the fact that no knowledge of the supersensible is possible if the path of natural concepts is followed. The reason why the proof succeeds, on the other hand, when the path of morals, that is of the concept of freedom, is followed, is because from the supersensible, which in morals is fundamental (i.e. as freedom), there issues a definite law of causality. By means of this law the supersensible here not only provides material for the knowledge of the supersensible, that is of the moral final end and the conditions of its practicability, but it also substantiates its own reality, as a matter of fact, in actions. For that very reason, however, it is unable to afford any valid argument other than from a practical point of view—which is also the only one needful for religion.

There is something very remarkable in the way this whole matter stands. Of the three ideas of pure reason, God, freedom, and immortality, that of freedom is the one and only concept of the supersensible which (owing to the causality implied in it) proves its objective reality in nature by its possible effect there. By this means it makes possible the connection of the two other ideas with nature, and the connection of all three to form a religion. We are thus ourselves in possession of a principle which is capable of determining the idea of the supersensible within us, and, in that way, also of the supersensible without us, so as to constitute knowledge—a knowledge, however, which is only possible from a practical point of view. This is something of which mere speculative philosophy—which can only give a simply negative concept even of freedom—must despair. Consequently the concept of freedom, as the root-concept of all unconditionally practical laws, can extend reason beyond the bounds to which every natural or theoretical concept must remain hopelessly restricted.

X

RELIGION WITHIN THE LIMITS OF REASON ALONE

[1793]

BOOK ONE

Concerning the Indwelling of the Evil Principle with the Good, or on the Radical Evil in Human Nature

THAT "THE WORLD LIETH IN EVIL" IS A PLAINT AS OLD AS HIS-TORY, old even as the older art, poetry; indeed, as old as that old-est of all fictions, the religion of priestcraft. All agree that the world began in a good estate, whether in a Golden Age, a life in Eden, or a yet more happy community with celestial beings. But they represent that this happiness vanished like a dream and that a fall into evil (moral evil, with which physical evil ever went hand in hand) presently hurried mankind from bad to worse with accelerated descent; [1] so that now (this "now" is also as old as history) we live in the final age, with the Last Day and the destruction of the world at hand. In some parts of India the Judge and Destroyer of the world, Rudra (sometimes called Siwa or Siva), already is worshipped as the reigning God—Vishnu, the Sustainer of the world, having some centuries ago

---

[1]
Aetas parentum peior avis tulit
Nos nequiores, mox daturos
Progeniem vitiosorem.

Horace

grown weary and renounced the supreme authority which he inherited from Brahma, the Creator.

More modern, though far less prevalent, is the contrasted optimistic belief, which indeed has gained a following solely among philosophers and, of late, especially among those interested in education—the belief that the world steadily (though almost imperceptibly) forges in the other direction, to wit, from bad to better; at least that the predisposition to such a movement is discoverable in human nature. If this belief, however, is meant to apply to *moral* goodness and badness (not simply to the process of civilization), it has certainly not been deduced from experience; the history of all times cries too loudly against it. The belief, we may presume, is a well-intentioned assumption of the moralists, from Seneca to Rousseau, designed to encourage the sedulous cultivation of that seed of goodness which perhaps lies in us—if, indeed, we can count on any such natural basis of goodness in man. We may note that since we take for granted that man is by nature sound of body (as at birth he usually is), no reason appears why, by nature, his soul should not be deemed similarly healthy and free from evil. Is not nature herself, then, inclined to lend her aid to developing in us this moral predisposition to goodness? In the words of Seneca: *Sanabilibus aegrotamus malis, nosque in rectum genitos natura, si sanari velimus, adiuvat.*

But since it well may be that both sides have erred in their reading of experience, the question arises whether a middle ground may not at least be possible, namely, that man as a species is neither good nor bad, or at all events that he is as much the one as the other, partly good, partly bad. We call a man evil, however, not because he performs actions that are evil (contrary to law) but because these actions are of such a nature that we may infer from them the presence in him of evil maxims. In and through experience we can observe actions contrary to law, and we can observe (at least in ourselves) that they are performed in the consciousness that they are unlawful; but a man's maxims, even his own, are not thus observable; consequently the judgment that the agent is an evil man cannot be made with certainty if grounded on experience. In order, then, to call a man evil, it would have to be possible *a priori* to infer from several evil acts done with consciousness of their evil, or from one such act, an underlying evil maxim; and further, from this maxim to infer the presence in the agent of an underlying common ground, itself a maxim, of all particularly morally evil maxims.

Lest difficulty at once be encountered in the expression *nature*, which, if it meant (as it usually does) the opposite of *freedom* as a basis of action, would flatly contradict the predicates *morally* good or evil, let it be noted that by "nature of man" we here intend only [to imply] the subjective ground of the exercise (under objective moral laws) of man's freedom in general; this ground—whatever may be its character—is necessarily antecedent of every act apparent to the senses. But this subjective ground, again, must itself always be an expression of freedom (for otherwise the use or abuse of man's power of choice in respect of the moral law could not be imputed to him nor could the good or bad in him be called moral). Hence the source of evil cannot lie in an object *determining* the will through inclination, nor yet in a natural impulse; it can lie only in a rule made by the will for the use of its freedom, that is, in a maxim. But now it must not be considered permissible to inquire into the subjective ground in man of the adoption of this maxim rather than of its opposite. If this ground itself were not ultimately a maxim, but a mere natural impulse, it would be possible to trace the use of our freedom wholly to determination by natural causes; this, however, is contradictory to the very notion of freedom. When we say, then, Man is by nature good, or, Man is by nature evil, this means only that there is in him an ultimate ground (inscrutable to us) [2] of the

---

[2] That the ultimate subjective ground of the adoption of moral maxims is inscrutable is indeed already evident from this, that since this adop-

adoption of good maxims or of evil maxims (i.e. those contrary to law), and this option he has, being a man; and hence he thereby expresses the character of his species.

We shall say, therefore, of the character (good or evil) distinguishing man from other possible rational beings, that it is *innate* in him. Yet in doing so we shall ever take the position that nature is not to bear the blame (if it is evil) or take the credit (if it is good), but that man himself is its author. But since the ultimate ground of the adoption of our maxims, which must itself lie in free choice, cannot be a fact revealed in experience, it follows that the good or evil in man (as the ultimate subjective ground of the adoption of this or that maxim with reference to the moral law) is termed innate only in *this* sense, that it is posited as the ground antecedent to every use of freedom in experience (in earliest youth as far back as birth) and is thus conceived of as present in man at birth—though birth need not be the cause of it.

Observation

The conflict between the two hypotheses presented above is based on a disjunctive proposition: *Man is* (by nature) *either morally good or morally evil*. It might easily occur to anyone, however, to ask whether this disjunction is valid, and whether some might not assert that man is by nature neither of the two, others, that man is at once both, in some respects good, in other respects evil. Experience actually seems to substantiate the middle ground between the two extremes.

It is, however, of great consequence to ethics in general to avoid admitting, so long as it is possible, of anything morally in-

tion is free, its ground (why, for example, I have chosen an evil and not a good maxim) must not be sought in any natural impulse, but always again in a maxim. Now since this maxim also must have its ground, and since apart from maxims no *determining ground* of free choice can or ought to be adduced, we are referred back endlessly in the series of subjective determining grounds, without ever being able to reach the ultimate ground.

termediate, whether in actions (*adiophora*) or in human characters; for with such ambiguity all maxims are in danger of forfeiting their precision and stability. Those who are partial to this strict mode of thinking are usually called *rigorists* (a name which is intended to carry reproach, but which actually praises); their opposites may be called *latitudinarians*. These latter, again, are either latitudinarians of neutrality, whom we may call *indifferentists*, or else latitudinarians of combination, whom we may call *syncretists*.[3]

According to the rigoristic diagnosis, [4] the answer to the ques-

---

[3] If the good = a, then its diametric opposite, the not-good is the result either of a mere absence of a basis of goodness, = o, or of a positive ground of the opposite of good, = − a. In the second case the not-good may also be called positive evil. (As regards pleasure and pain there is a similar middle term, whereby pleasure = a, pain = − a, and the state in which neither is to be found, indifference, = o.) Now if the moral law in us were not a motivating force of the will, the morally good (the agreement of the will with the law) would = a, and the not-good would = o; but the latter, as merely the result of the absence of a moral motivating force, would = a × o. In us, however, the law is a motivating force, = a; hence the absence of agreement of the will with this law (= o) is possible only as a consequence of a real and contrary determination of the will, i.e., of an *opposition* to the law, = − a, i.e., of an evil will. Between a good and an evil disposition (inner principle of maxims), according to which the morality of an action must be judged, there is therefore no middle ground.

A morally indifferent action (*adiaphoron morale*) would be one resulting merely from natural laws, and hence standing in no relation whatsoever to the moral law, which is the law of freedom; for such action is not a morally significant fact at all and regarding it neither *command*, nor *prohibition*, nor *permission* (legal *privilege*) occurs or is necessary.

[4] Professor Schiller, in his masterly treatise (*Thalia*, 1793, Part III) on grace and dignity in morality, objects to this way of representing obligation as carrying with it a monastic cast of mind. Since, however, we are at one upon the most important principles, I cannot admit that there is disagreement here, if only we can make ourselves clear to one another. I freely grant that by very reason of the dignity of the *idea of duty* I am unable to associate *grace* with it. For the idea of duty involves absolute necessity, to which grace stands in direct contradiction. The majesty of the moral law (as of the law on Sinai) instils awe (not dread, which repels, nor yet charm, which invites familiarity); and in this instance,

tion at issue rests upon the observation, of great importance to morality, that freedom of the will is of a wholly unique nature in that an incentive can determine the will to an action *only so far as the individual has incorporated it into his maxim* (has made it the general rule in accordance with which he will conduct himself); only thus can an incentive, whatever it may be, co-exist with the absolute spontaneity of the will (i.e. freedom). But the moral law, in the judgment of reason, is in itself an incentive, and whoever makes it his maxim is *morally* good. If, now, this law does not determine a person's will in the case of an action which has reference to the law, an incentive contrary to it must influence his choice; and since, by hypothesis, this can

---

since the ruler resides within us, this *respect,* as of a subject toward his ruler, awakens a *sense of the sublimity* of our own destiny which enraptures us more than any beauty. *Virtue,* also, i.e., the firmly grounded disposition strictly to fulfil our duty, is also *beneficent* in its results, beyond all that nature and art can accomplish in the world; and the august picture of humanity, as portrayed in this character, does indeed allow the attendance of the *graces.* But when duty alone is the theme, they keep a respectful distance. If we consider, further, the happy results which virtue, should she gain admittance everywhere, would spread throughout the world, [we see] morally directed reason (by means of the imagination) calling the sensibilities into play. Only after vanquishing monsters did Hercules become Musagetes, leader of the Muses—after labors from which those worthy sisters, trembling, drew back. The attendants of Venus Urania become wantons in the train of Venus Dione as soon as they meddle in the business of determining duty and try to provide springs of action therefor.

Now if one asks, What is the *aesthetic character,* the *temperament,* so to speak, *of virtue,* whether courageous and hence *joyous* or fearridden and dejected, an answer is hardly necessary. This latter slavish frame of mind can never occur without a hidden *hatred* of the law. And a heart which is happy in the *performance* of its duty (not merely complacent in the *recognition* thereof) is a mark of genuineness in the virtuous spirit—of genuineness even in *piety,* which does not consist in the self-inflicted torment of a repentant sinner (a very ambiguous state of mind, which ordinarily is nothing but inward regret at having infringed upon the rules of prudence), but rather in the firm resolve to do better in the future. This resolve, then, encouraged by good progress, must needs beget a joyous frame of mind, without which man is never certain of having really *attained a love* for the good, i.e., of having incorporated it into his maxim.

only happen when a man adopts this incentive (and thereby the deviation from the moral law) into his maxim (in which case he is an evil man) it follows that his disposition in respect to the moral law is never indifferent, never neither good nor evil.

Neither can a man be morally good in some ways and at the same time morally evil in others. His being good in one way means that he has incorporated the moral law into his maxim; were he, therefore, at the same time evil in another way, while his maxim would be universal as based on the moral law of obedience to duty, which is essentially single and universal, it would at the same time be only particular; but this is a contradiction. [5]

To have a good or an evil disposition as an inborn natural constitution does not here mean that it has not been acquired by the man who harbors it, that he is not author of it, but rather, that it has not been acquired in time (that he has *always* been good, or evil, *from his youth up*). The disposition, i.e., the ultimate subjective ground of the adoption of maxims, can be one only and applies universally to the whole use of freedom. Yet this disposition itself must have been adopted by free choice, for otherwise it could not be imputed. But the subjective ground or cause of this adoption cannot further be known (though it is inevitable that we should inquire into it), since

---

[5] The ancient moral philosophers, who pretty well exhausted all that can be said upon virtue, have not left untouched the two questions mentioned above. The first they expressed thus: Must virtue be learned? (Is man by nature indifferent as regards virtue and vice?) The second they put thus: Is there more than one virtue (so that man might be virtuous in some respects, in others vicious)? Both questions were answered by them, with rigoristic precision, in the negative and rightly so; for they were considering virtue *as such*, as it is in the idea of reason as that which man ought to be. If, however, we wish to pass moral judgment on this moral being, man *as he appears*, i.e., as experience reveals him to us, we can answer both questions in the affirmative; for in this case we judge him not according to the standard of pure reason (at a divine tribunal) but by an empirical standard (before a human judge). This subject will be treated further in what follows.

otherwise still another maxim would have to be adduced in which this disposition must have been incorporated, a maxim which itself in turn must have its ground. Since, therefore, we are unable to derive this disposition, or rather its ultimate ground, from any original act of the will in time, we call it a property of the will which belongs to it by nature (although actually the disposition is grounded in freedom). Further, the man of whom we say, "He is by nature good or evil," is to be understood not as the single individual (for then one man could be considered as good, by nature, another as evil), but as the entire race; that we are entitled so to do can only be proved when anthropological research shows that the evidence, which justifies us in attributing to a man of these characters as innate, is such that it gives no ground for excepting anyone, and that the attribution therefore holds for the race.

I. Concerning the Original Predisposition to Good in Human Nature

We may conveniently divide this predisposition, with respect to function, into three divisions, to be considered as elements in the fixed character and destiny of man.

(1) The predisposition to *animality* in man, taken as a *living* being.

(2) The predisposition to *humanity* in man, taken as a living and at the same time a *rational* being.

(3) The predisposition to *personality* in man, taken as a rational and at the same time an *accountable* being.[6]

---

[6] We cannot regard this as included in the concept of the preceding, but necessarily must treat it as a special predisposition. For from the fact that a being has reason it by no means follows that this reason, by the merely imagining its maxims as fit to be laid down as general laws, is thereby rendered capable of determining the will unconditionally, so as to be "practical" of itself; at least, not so far as we can see. The most rational mortal being in the world might still stand in need of certain incentives, originating in objects of desire, to determine his choice. He might, indeed, bestow the most rational reflection on all that concerns not only the greatest sum of these incentives in him but also the means

1. The predisposition to *animality* in mankind may be brought under the general title of physical and purely *mechanical* self-love, wherein no reason is demanded. It is threefold: first, for self-preservation; second for the propagation of the species, through the sexual impulse, and for the care of offspring so begotten; and third, for community with other men, i.e., the social impulse. On these three stems can be grafted all kinds of vices (which, however, do not spring from this predisposition itself as a root). They may be termed vices of the coarseness of nature, and in their greatest deviation from natural purposes are called the *beastly* vices of *gluttony* and *drunkenness, lasciviousness,* and wild lawlessness (in relation to other men).

2. The predisposition to humanity can be brought under the general titles of a self-love which is physical and yet *compares* (for which reason is required); that is to say, we judge ourselves happy or unhappy only by making comparison with others. Out of this self-love springs the desire *to acquire value in the opinion of others.* This is originally a desire merely for *equality,* to allow no one superiority above oneself, bound up with a constant care lest others strive to attain such superiority; but from this arises gradually the unjustifiable craving to win such superiority for oneself over others. Upon this twin stem of *jealousy* and *rivalry* may be grafted the very great vices of secret and open animosity against all whom we look upon as not belonging to us—vices, however, which really do not sprout of themselves from nature as their root; rather are they desires, aroused in us by the anxious endeavors of others to attain a hated superiority over us, to attain for ourselves as a measure of

---

of attaining the end thereby determined, without ever suspecting the possibility of such a thing as the absolutely imperative moral law which proclaims that it is itself an incentive, and indeed, the highest. Were it not given us from within, we should never by any ratiocination subtilize it into existence or win over our will to it; yet this law is the only law which informs us of the independence of our will from determination by all other incentives (of our freedom) and at the same time of the accountability of all our actions.

precaution and for the sake of safety such a position over others. For nature, indeed, wanted to use the idea of such rivalry (which in itself does not exclude mutual love) only as a spur to culture. Hence the vices which are grafted upon this desire might be termed vices of *culture*, in their highest degree of malignancy, as, for example, in *envy, ingratitude, spitefulness*, etc. (where they are simply the idea of a maximum of evil going beyond what is human), they can be called the *diabolical vices*.

3. The predisposition to *personality* is the capacity for respect for the moral law *as in itself a sufficient incentive of the will*. This capacity simply to respect the moral law within us would thus be moral sentiment, which in and through itself does not constitute an end of the natural predisposition except so far as it is the motivating force of the will. Since this is possible only when the free will incorporates such moral sentiment into its maxim, the character of the free will is something which can only be acquired; its possibility, however, demands the presence in our nature of a predisposition on which it is absolutely impossible to graft anything evil. We cannot rightly call the idea of the moral law, and the respect which is inseparable from it, *a predisposition to personality*; it is [the essence of] personality itself (the idea of humanity considered quite intellectually). But the subjective ground for the adoption into our maxims of this respect as a motivating force seems to be an adjunct to our personality, and thus to deserve the name of a predisposition to its furtherance.

If we consider the three predispositions named, in terms of the conditions of their possibility, we find that the first requires no reason, the second is based on practical reason, but a reason thereby subservient to other incentives, while the third alone is rooted in reason which is practical in itself, that is, reason which dictates laws unconditionally. All of these predispositions are not only *good* in a negative way in that they do not contradict the moral law; they are also predispositions *toward good* enjoining the observance of the law. They are *original,* for they are bound up with the possibility of human nature. Man can indeed use the first two contrary to their ends, but he can extirpate none of them. By the predispositions of a being we understand not only its constituent elements which are necessary to it, but also the forms of their combination, by which the being is what it is. They are *original* if they are involved necessarily in the possibility of such a being, but *contingent* if it is possible for the being to exist of itself without them. Finally, let it be noted that here we treat only those predispositions which have immediate reference to the faculty of desire and the exercise of the will.

II. Concerning the Propensity to Evil in Human Nature

By *propensity (propensio)* I understand the subjective ground of the possibility of an inclination (habitual craving, *concupiscentia*) so far as mankind in general is liable to it.[7] A propensity is distinguished from a predisposition by the fact that although it can indeed be innate, it *ought* not to be represented merely thus; for it can also be regarded as having been *acquired* (if it is good), or *brought* by man *upon himself* (if it is evil). Here, however, we are speaking only of the propensity to genuine, that is, moral evil; for since such evil is possible only as a determination of the free will, and since the will can be appraised as

---

[7] A *propensity (Hang)* is really only the *predisposition* to crave a delight which, when once experienced, arouses in the subject an *inclination* to it. Thus all savage peoples have a propensity for intoxicants; for though many of them are wholly ignorant of intoxication and in consequence have absolutely no craving for an intoxicant, let them but once sample it and there is aroused in them an almost inextinguishable craving for it.

Between inclination, which presupposes acquaintance with the object of desire, and propensity there still is *instinct,* which is a felt want to do or to enjoy something of which one has as yet no conception such as the constructive impulse in animals, or the sexual impulse. Beyond inclination there is finally a further stage in the faculty of desire; not *emotion,* for this has to do with the feeling of pleasure and pain, but passion which is an inclination that excludes any mastery over oneself.

good or evil only by means of its maxims, this propensity to evil must consist in the subjective ground of the possibility of the deviation of the maxims from the moral law. If, then, this propensity can be considered as belonging to mankind in general and hence as part of the character of the race, it may be called a *natural* propensity in man to evil. We may add further that the will's capacity or incapacity, arising from this natural propensity, to adopt or not to adopt the moral law into its maxim, may be called *a good or an evil heart*.

In this capacity for evil there can be distinguished three distinct degrees. First, there is the weakness of the human heart in the general observance of adopted maxims, or in other words, the *frailty* of human nature; second, the propensity for mixing unmoral with moral motives which causes *impurity*, even when it is done with good intent and under maxims of the good, third, the propensity to adopt evil maxims, that is the *wickedness* of human nature or of the human heart.

First: the frailty (*fragilitas*) of human nature is expressed even in the complaint of an Apostle, "What I would, that I do not!" In other words, I adopt the good (the law) into the maxim of my will, but this good, which objectively, in its ideal conception (*in thesi*), is an irresistible incentive, is subjectively (*in hypothesi*), when the maxim is to be followed, the weaker (in comparison with inclination).

Second: the impurity (*impuritas, improbitas*) of the human heart consists in this, that although the maxim is indeed good in respect of its object (the intended observance of the law) and perhaps even strong enough for practice, it is yet not purely moral; that is, it has not, as it should have, adopted the law *alone* as its *all-sufficient* objective: instead, it frequently (perhaps continually) stands in need of other incentives beyond this, in determining the will to do what duty demands; in other words, actions called for by duty are done not purely for duty's sake.

Third: the wickedness (*vitiositas, pravitas*) or, if you like, the *corruption* (*corruptio*) of the human heart is the propensity of the will to maxims which neglect the incentives springing from the moral law in favor of others which are not moral. It may also be called the *perversity* (*perversitas*) of the human heart, for it reverses the ethical order [of priority] among the incentives of a *free* will; and although conduct which is lawfully good (i.e., legal) may result from it, yet the cast of mind is thereby corrupted at its root so far as the moral disposition is concerned, and the man is hence designated as evil.

It will be remarked that this propensity to evil is here ascribed as regards conduct to men in general, even to the best of them; this must be the case if it is to be proved that the propensity to evil in mankind is universal, or, what here comes to the same thing, that it is woven into human nature.

There is no difference, however, as regards conformity of conduct to the moral law, between a man of good morals (*bene moratus*) and a morally good man (*moraliter bonus*)—at least there ought to be no difference, save that the conduct of the one has not always, perhaps has never, the law as its sole and supreme incentive while the conduct of the other has it *always*. Of the former it can be said: He obeys the law according to the *letter*, that is, his conduct conforms to what the law commands; but of the second: he obeys the law according to the *spirit*, the spirit of the moral law consisting in this, that the law is sufficient in itself as an incentive. *Whatever is not done out of such faith is sin,* as regards cast of mind. For when incentives other than the law itself, such as ambition, self-love in general, yes, even a kindly instinct such as sympathy, are necessary to bend the will to conduct which is *conformable to the law,* it is merely accidental that these causes coincide with the law, for they could equally well impel a man to violate it. The maxim, then, in terms of whose goodness all moral worth of the individual must be appraised, is thus contrary to the law, and the man, despite all his good deeds, is nevertheless evil.

The following explanation is also necessary in order to define the concept of this propensity. Every propensity is either physical, i.e., pertaining to the will of man as a natural being, or moral, i.e., pertaining to his will as a moral being. In the first sense there is no propensity to moral evil, for such a propensity must spring from freedom; and a physical propensity grounded in sense impulses toward any use of freedom whatsoever—whether for good or bad—is a contradiction. Hence a propensity to evil can inhere only in the moral capacity of the will. But nothing is morally evil and capable of being so imputed but that which is our own *act*. On the other hand, by the concept of a propensity we understand a subjective determining ground of the will which *precedes all acts* and which, therefore, is itself not an act. Hence in the concept of a simple propensity to evil there would be a contradiction were it not possible to take the word "act" in two meanings, both of which are reconcilable with the concept of freedom. The term "act" can apply in general to that exercise of freedom whereby the supreme maxim in harmony with the law or contrary to it is adopted by the will, but also to the exercise of freedom whereby the actions themselves, considered substantively, that is with reference to the objects of volition, are performed in accordance with that maxim. The propensity to evil, then, is an act in the first sense (*peccatum originarium*), and at the same time the formal ground of all unlawful conduct in the second sense, which latter, considered substantively, violates the law and is termed vice (*peccatum derivatum*). The first offense remains, even though the second, from incentives which are not comprised by the law itself may be repeatedly avoided. The former is intelligible action, known by means of pure reason alone, apart from every temporal condition; the latter is sensible action, empirical, given in time (*factum phaenomenon*). The former, particularly when compared with the latter, is called a simple propensity and innate, [first] because it cannot be eradicated, since for such eradication the highest maxim would have to be that of the good—whereas in this propensity it already has been postu-

lated as evil, but chiefly because we can no more assign a further cause for the corruption in us by evil of just this highest
maxim, although this is our own action, than we can assign a
cause for any fundamental attribute belonging to our nature.
Now it can be understood, from what has just been said, why it
was that in this section we sought, at the very first, the three
sources of the morally evil solely in what, according to laws of
freedom, touches the ultimate ground of the adoption or the
observance of our maxims, and not in what touches sensibility
when regarded as receptivity.

III. Man Is Evil by Nature

Vitiis nemo sine nascitur. HORACE

In view of what has been said above, the proposition, Man is
evil, can mean only, he is conscious of the moral law but has
nevertheless adopted into his maxim the occasional deviation
therefrom. He is evil *by nature* means but this, that evil can be
predicated of man as a species; not that such a quality can be inferred from the concept of his species, that is, of man in general
—for then it would be necessary. It rather means that from
what we know of man through experience we cannot judge
otherwise of him, or, (to put it another way) that we may presuppose evil to be subjectively necessary to every man, even to
the best. Now this propensity must itself be considered as
morally evil, yet not as a natural predisposition but rather as
something that can be imputed to man. Consequently this
propensity must consist in maxims of the will which are contrary to the (moral) law. Further, for the sake of freedom,
these maxims must in themselves be considered contingent, a
circumstance which, on the other hand, will not tally with
the universality of this evil *unless* the ultimate subjective ground
of all maxims somehow or other is entwined with and, as it
were, rooted in humanity itself. Hence we can call this a natural propensity to evil, and as we must, after all, ever hold man
himself responsible for it, we can further call it a *radical* innate

evil in human nature (yet none the less brought upon us by ourselves).

That such a corrupt propensity must indeed be rooted in man need not be formally proved in view of the multitude of crying examples which experience *of the actions* of men puts before our eyes. If we wish to draw our examples from that state in which various philosophers hoped pre-eminently to discover the natural goodliness of human nature, namely, from the so-called *state of nature*, we need but compare with this hypothesis the scenes of unprovoked cruelty in the murderous scenes enacted in Tofoa, New Zealand, and in the Navigator Islands, and the unending cruelty of which Captain Hearne tells (occurring) in the wide deserts of northwestern America, from which, indeed, not a soul reaps the smallest benefit;[8] and we have vices of barbarity more than sufficient to (cause us to) abandon such an opinion. If, however, we incline to the opinion that human nature can better be known in the civilized state, in which its predispositions can more completely develop, we must listen to a long melancholy litany of indictments against humanity: of secret falsity even in the closest friendship, so that it is reckoned a universal maxim of prudence in intercourse to limit one's trust in the mutual confidences of even the best friends; of a propensity to hate him to whom one is indebted, for which a benefactor must always be prepared; of

---

[8] Thus the war ceaselessly waged between the Arathapescaw Indians and the Dog Rib Indians has no other object than mere slaughter. Bravery in war is, in the opinion of savages, the highest virtue. Even in a civilized state it is an object of admiration and a basis for the special regard commanded by that profession in which bravery is the sole merit; and this is not without rational cause. For that man should be able to possess a thing (i.e., honor) and make it an end to be valued more than life itself, and because of it renounce all self-interest, surely bespeaks a certain nobility in his natural disposition. Yet we recognize in the complacency with which victors boast their mighty deeds such as massacre, butchery without quarter, and the like that it is merely their own superiority and the destruction they can wreak, without any other objective, in which they really take satisfaction.

a hearty well-wishing which yet allows of the remark that "in the misfortunes of our best friends there is something which is not altogether displeasing to us"; and of many other vices concealed under the appearance of virtue, to say nothing of the vices of those who do not conceal them, for we are content to call him good *who is a man bad in a way common to all;* and we shall have enough of the vices of *culture* and civilization which are the most offensive of all to make us rather turn away our eyes from the conduct of men lest we ourselves contract another vice, misanthropy. But if we are not yet content, we need but contemplate a state which is compounded in strange fashion of both the others, that is, the international situation. Here civilized nations stand toward each other in the relation obtaining in the barbarous state of nature, which is a state of continuous readiness for war; civilized nations seem to be firmly determined never to give up this state. We then become aware of the fundamental principles of the great societies called *states*[9]—principles which flatly contradict their public pronouncements but are never laid aside, and which no philosopher has yet been able to bring into agreement with morality. Nor, sad to say, has any philosopher been able to propose better

---

[9] When we survey the history of these, merely as the phenomenon of the inner predispositions of mankind which are for the most part concealed from us, we become aware of a certain machine-like movement of nature toward ends which are nature's own rather than those of the nations. Each separate state, so long as it has a neighboring state which it dares hope to conquer, strives to aggrandize itself through such a conquest, and thus to attain a world-empire, a polity wherein all freedom, and as a consequence virtue, taste, and learning, would necessarily expire. Yet this monster in which laws gradually lose their force, after it has swallowed all its neighbors, finally dissolves of itself, and through rebellion and disunion breaks up into many smaller states. These, instead of striving toward a league of nations, a republic of federated free nations, begin the same game over again, each for itself, so that war, the scourge of humankind, may not be allowed to cease. Although indeed war is not so incurably evil as that tomb, a universal autocracy (or even as a confederacy which exists to hasten the weakening of a despotism in any single state), yet, as one of the ancients put it, war creates more evil than it destroys.

principles which at the same time can be brought into harmony with human nature. The result is that the *philosophical utopianism,* which hopes for a state of perpetual peace based on a league of peoples as a world-republic, and the *theological utopianism,* which waits for the complete moral regeneration of the entire human race, is universally ridiculed as day-dreaming.

Now the ground of this evil (1) cannot be placed, as is so commonly done, in man's *senses* (*Sinnlichkeit*) and the natural inclinations to evil (rather do they afford the occasion for what the moral disposition in its power can manifest, namely, virtue); we cannot, must not even be considered responsible for their existence since they are implanted in us and we are not their authors. We are accountable, however, for the propensity to evil, which, as it affects the morality of the subject, is to be found in him as a free-acting being and for which it must be possible to hold him accountable as the offender—this, too, despite the fact that this propensity is so deeply rooted in the will that we are forced to say that it is to be found in man by nature. Neither can the ground of this evil (2) be placed in a *corruption* of the reason-giving moral laws—as if reason could destroy the authority of the very law which is its own, or deny the obligation arising therefrom; this is absolutely impossible. To conceive of oneself as a freely acting being and yet as exempt from the law which is appropriate to such a being (the moral law) would be tantamount to conceiving a cause operating without any laws whatsoever (for determination according to natural laws is excluded by the fact of freedom); this is a self-contradiction. In seeking, therefore, a ground of the morally-evil in man, (we find that) *the senses* comprise too little, for when the incentives which can spring from freedom are taken away, man is reduced to a mere *animal* being. On the other hand, a reason exempt from the moral law, a *malignant reason* as it were, a thoroughly evil will, comprises too much, for thereby opposition to the law would itself be set up as an incentive since in the absence of all incentives the will cannot be determined, and thus the subject would be made a *satanic* being. Neither of these designations is applicable to man.

But even if the existence of this propensity to evil in human nature can be demonstrated by experiential proofs of the real opposition, in time, of man's will to the law, such proofs do not teach us the essential character of that propensity or the ground of this opposition. Rather, because this character concerns a relation of the will which is free and the concept of which is therefore not empirical to the moral law as an incentive the concept of which, likewise, is purely intellectual, it must become known *a priori* through the concept of evil, so far as evil is possible under the laws of freedom, of obligation and accountability. This concept may be developed in the following manner.

Man, even the most wicked, does not under any maxim whatsoever repudiate the moral law in the manner of a rebel who renounces obedience to it. The law rather forces itself upon him irresistibly by virtue of his moral predisposition. If no other incentive were working in opposition, he would adopt the law into his supreme maxim as the sufficient determining ground of his will, that is, he would be morally good. But by virtue of an equally innocent natural predisposition he depends upon the incentives of his senses and adopts them also in accordance with the subjective principle of self-love into his maxim. If he took the latter into his maxim *as in themselves wholly adequate* to the determination of the will, without troubling himself about the moral law which, after all, he does have in him, he would be morally evil. Now, since he naturally adopts *both* into his maxim, and since furthermore he would find either, if it were alone, adequate in itself for the determining of the will, it follows that if the difference between the maxims amounted merely to the difference between the two incentives, that is the substance of the maxims, in other words, if it were merely a question as to whether the law or the sense impulse were to furnish the incentive, man would be at once good and evil: this, however, as we saw in the Introduction, is a contradiction. Hence the distinction between a good man and one who is evil cannot lie in the difference between the incentives which they adopt into their maxim; that is not in the substance of the maxim, but rather must depend upon the *subordination* or the form of the maxim, in other words, *which of the two incentives he makes the condition of the other*. Consequently even the best man is evil, but only in that he reverses the moral order of the incentives when he adopts them into his maxim. He adopts, indeed, the moral law along with the law of self-love; yet when he becomes aware that they cannot remain on a par with each other but that one must be subordinated to the other as its supreme condition, he makes the incentive of self-love and its inclinations the condition of obedience to the moral law; whereas, on the contrary, the moral law, as the *supreme condition* of the satisfaction of self-love, ought to have been adopted into the universal maxim of the will as the sole incentive.

Yet, even with this reversal of the ethical order of the incentives in and through his maxim, a man's actions still may prove to be as much in conformity to the law as if they sprang from true basic principles. This happens when reason employs the unity of the maxims in general, a unity which is inherent in the moral law, merely to bestow upon the incentives of desire, under the name of *happiness*, a unity of maxims which otherwise they cannot have. For example, truthfulness, if adopted as a basic principle, delivers us from the anxiety of making our lies agree with one another and of not being entangled by their serpent coils. The empirical character is then good, but the intelligible character is still evil.

Now if a propensity to this does lie in human nature, there is in man a natural propensity to evil; and since this very propensity must in the end be sought in a will which is free, and can therefore be imputed, it is morally evil. This evil is *radical*, because it corrupts the ground of all maxims; it is, moreover, as a natural propensity, *eradicable* by human effort, since eradication could occur only through good maxims, and cannot take place when the ultimate subjective ground of all maxims is postulated as corrupt; yet at the same time it must be possible to *overcome* it, since it is found in man, a being whose actions are free.

We are not, then, to call the depravity of human nature *wickedness*, taking the word in its strict sense as a subjective *principle* of the maxims or a disposition to adopt evil *as evil* into our maxims as an incentive, for that is satanic; we should rather term it the *perversity* of the heart, which then because of what follows from it is also called an *evil heart*. Such a heart may co-exist with a will which in general is good: it arises from the frailty of human nature, the lack of sufficient strength to follow out the principles it has chosen for itself, joined with its impurity, the failure to distinguish the incentives (even of well-intentioned actions) from each other by the gauge of morality; and so at last, if the extreme is reached, [it results] from looking only to the squaring of these actions with the [moral] law and not to the derivation of them from the law **as** the sole motivating spring. Now even though there does **not** always follow therefrom an unlawful act and a propensity thereto, namely, *vice,* yet the outlook which considers the absence of such vice as if it were virtue and such mentality to the [moral] law [imposed by] duty itself deserves to be called a radical perversity in the human heart—since in this case no attention whatever is being paid to the incentives involved in the maxim but only to the observance of the letter of the law.

This *innate* guilt (*reatus*), which is so denominated because it may be observed in man as early as the first manifestations of the exercise of freedom, but which, none the less, must have originated in freedom and hence can be imputed—this guilt may be judged in its first two stages (those of frailty and impurity) to be unintentional guilt (*culpa*), but in the third to be deliberate guilt (*dolus*). It displays the character [of this guilt] in a certain *insidiousness* of the human heart (*dolus malus*), which deceives itself in regard to its own good and evil convictions. If only its conduct has no evil consequences which it might well have, with such maxims, the human heart does not trouble itself about its convictions but rather considers itself justified before the law. Thence arises the peace of conscience of so many men, conscientious in their own estimation when, in the course of conduct concerning which they did not take the [moral] law into their counsel, or at least in which the [moral] law was not the supreme consideration, they merely eluded evil consequences by good fortune. They may even picture themselves as meritorious, feeling themselves guilty of no such offenses as they see others burdened with; nor do they ever inquire whether good luck should not have the credit, or whether by reason of the frame of mind which they could discover, if they only would, in their own inmost nature, they would not have practised similar vices, had not inability, temperament, training, and circumstances of time and place which serve to tempt one and for which a man is not responsible, kept them away from those vices. This dishonesty by which we "kid" ourselves and which thwarts the developing of genuine moral convictions, broadens itself into falsehood and deception of others. If this is not to be termed wickedness, it at least deserves the name of worthlessness, and is an element in the radical evil of human nature. Inasmuch as such evil puts out of commission the moral capacity to judge what a man is to be taken for, and renders wholly uncertain both internal and external attribution of responsibility, it constitutes the foul taint in our race. So long as we do not eradicate it, it prevents the seed of goodness from developing as it otherwise would.

A member of the British Parliament once exclaimed in the heat of debate, "Every man has his price, for which he sells himself." If this is true, a question to which each must make his own answer, if there is not virtue for which some temptation cannot be found capable of overthrowing it, and if whether the good or evil spirit wins us over to his party depends merely on which bids the most and pays us most promptly, then certainly it holds true of men universally, as the Apostle said: "They are all under sin—there is none righteous (in the spirit of the law), no, not one."[10]

IV. *Concerning the Origin of Evil in Human Nature*

A first origin is the derivation of an effect from its first cause, that is, from that cause which is not in turn the effect of another cause of the same kind. It can be considered either as an *origin in reason* or as an *origin in time*. In the former sense, regard is had only to the *existence* of the effect; in the latter, to its *occurrence*, and hence it is related as an event to its *first cause in time*. If an effect is referred to a cause to which it is bound under the laws of freedom, as is true in the case of moral evil, then the determination of the will to the production of this effect is conceived of as bound up with its determining ground not in time but merely in rational image (*Vorstellung*); such an effect cannot be derived from any *preceding* state whatsoever. Yet derivation of this sort is always necessary when an evil action, as an *event* in the world, is referred to its natural cause. To seek the temporal origin of free acts as such as though they were operations of nature is thus a contradiction. Hence it

---

[10] The special proof of this sentence of condemnation by morally judging reason is to be found in the preceding section rather than in this one, which contains only the confirmation of it by experience. Experience, however, never can reveal the root of evil in the supreme maxim of the free will relating to the law, a maxim which, as *intelligible act*, precedes all experience. Hence from the singleness of the supreme maxim, together with the singleness of the law to which it relates itself, we can also understand why, for the pure intellectual judgment of mankind, the rule of excluding a mean between good and evil must remain fundamental; yet for the empirical judgment based on *sensible conduct* (the actual performance or failure to act), the rule may be laid down that there *is* a mean between these extremes—on the one hand, a negative mean of indifference prior to all education, on the other hand, a positive, a mixture, partly good and partly evil. However, this latter is merely a judgment upon the morality of mankind as appearance, and must give place to the former in a final judgment.

is also a contradiction to seek the temporal origin of man's moral character, so far as it is considered as contingent, since this character signifies the ground of the *exercise* of freedom; this ground like the determining ground of the free will generally must be sought in purely rational images.

Whatever the origin of moral evil in man may be like, surely of all the explanations of the spread and propagation of this evil through all members and generations of our race, the most inept describes it as descending to us as an *inheritance* from our first parents; for one can say of moral evil precisely what the poet said of good: *genus, et proavos, et quae non fecimus ipsi, vix ea nostra puto.*[11] Yet we should note that, in our search for the origin of this evil, we do not deal first of all with the propensity thereto (as *peccatum in potentia*); rather do we direct our attention to the actual evil of given actions with respect to what [inner defeat] makes them possible—to what must take place within the will if evil is to be performed.

In the search for the rational origin of evil actions, every such

---

[11] The three so-called "higher faculties" (in the universities) would explain this transmission of evil each in terms of its own specialty, as *inherited disease, inherited debt,* or *inherited sin.* (1) The *faculty of medicine* would represent this hereditary evil somewhat as it represents the tapeworm, concerning which several naturalists actually believe that, since no specimens have been met with anywhere but in us, not even (of this particular type) in other animals, it must have existed in our first parents. (2) The *faculty of law* would regard this evil as the legitimate consequence of succeeding to the patrimony bequeathed us by our first parents, [an inheritance] encumbered, however, with heavy forfeitures (for to be born is no other than to inherit the use of the earthly goods so far as they are necessary to our continued existence). Thus we must fulfil payment (atone) and at the end still be dispossessed (by death) of the property. How just is legal justice! (3) The *theological faculty* would regard this evil as the personal participation by our first parents in the *fall* of a condemned rebel, maintaining either that we ourselves then participated (although now unconscious of having done so) or that even now, born under the rule of the rebel (as prince of this world), we prefer his favors to the supreme command of the heavenly Ruler, and do not possess enough faith to free ourselves; wherefore we must also eventually share his doom.

action must be regarded as though the individual had fallen into it directly from a state of innocence. For whatever his previous deportment may have been, whatever natural causes may have been influencing him, and whether these causes were to be found within him or outside him, his action is yet free and determined by none of these causes; hence it can and must always be judged as an *original* use of his will. He should have refrained from that action, whatever his temporal circumstances and entanglements; for through no cause in the world can he cease to be a freely acting being. Rightly is it said that to a man's account are set down the *consequences* arising from his former free acts which were contrary to the law; but this merely amounts to saying that man need not involve himself in the evasion of seeking to establish whether or not these consequences are free, since there exists in the admittedly free action, which was their cause, ground sufficient for holding him responsible. However evil a man has been up to the very moment of an impending free act so that evil has actually become custom or second nature it was not only his duty to have been better [in the past], it is *now* still his duty to better himself. To do so must be within his power, and if he does not do so, he is susceptible of, and subjected to, being held responsible in the very moment of that action, just as much as though, endowed with a predisposition to good which is inseparable from freedom, he had stepped out of a state of innocence into evil. Hence we cannot inquire into the temporal origin of this deed, but solely into its rational origin, if we are thereby to determine and, wherever possible, to elucidate the propensity, if it exists, i.e., the general subjective ground of the adoption of transgression into our maxim.

The foregoing agrees well with that manner of presentation which the Scriptures use, whereby the origin of evil in the human race is depicted as having a [temporal] *beginning*, this beginning being presented in a narrative, wherein what in its essence must be considered as primary (without regard to the element of time) appears as coming first in time. According to this account, evil does not start from a propensity thereto as its underlying basis, for otherwise the beginning of evil would not have its source in freedom; rather does it start from *sin* (by which is meant the transgressing of the moral law as a *divine command*). The state of man prior to all propensity to evil is called the state of *innocence*. The moral law became known to mankind, as it must to any being not pure but tempted by desires, in the form of a *prohibition* (Genesis II, 16–17). Now instead of straightway following this law as an adequate incentive (the only incentive which is unconditionally good and regarding which there is no further doubt), man looked about for other incentives (Genesis III, 6) such as can be good only conditionally (namely, so far as they involve no infringement of the law). He then made it his maxim—if one thinks of his action as consciously springing from freedom—to follow the law of duty, not as duty, but, if need be, with regard to other aims. Thereupon he began to call in question the severity of the commandment which excludes the influence of all other incentives; then by sophistry he reduced [12] obedience to the law to the merely conditional character of a means, subject to the principle of self-love; and finally he adopted into his maxim of conduct the ascendancy of the sense impulse over the incentive which springs from the law—and thus occurred sin (Genesis III, 6). *Mutato nomine de te fabula narratur.* From all this it is clear that we daily act in the same way, and that therefore "in Adam all have sinned" and still sin; except that in us there is

[12] All homage paid to the moral law is an act of hypocrisy, if, in one's maxim, ascendancy is not at the same time granted to the law as an incentive sufficient in itself and higher than all other determining grounds of the will. The propensity to do this is inward deceit, that is, a tendency to deceive oneself in the interpretation of moral law, to its detriment (Genesis III, 5). Accordingly, the Christian portion of the Bible denominates the author of evil who is within us as the liar from the beginning, and thus characterizes man with respect to what seems to be the chief ground of evil in him.

presupposed an innate propensity to transgression, whereas in the first man, from the point of view of time, there is presupposed no such propensity but rather innocence; hence transgression on his part is called a *fall into sin;* but with us sin is represented as resulting from an already innate wickedness in our nature. This propensity, however, signifies no more than this, that if we wish to address ourselves to the explanation of evil in terms of its *beginning in time,* we must search for the causes of each deliberate transgression in a previous period of our lives, far back to that period wherein the use of reason had not yet developed, and thus back to a propensity to evil as a natural ground which is therefore called innate—the source of evil. But to trace the causes of evil in the instance of the first man, who is depicted as already in full command of the use of his reason, is neither necessary nor feasible, since otherwise this, the evil propensity, would have had to be created in him; therefore his sin is set forth as engendered directly from innocence. We must not, however, look for an origin in time of a moral character for which we are to be held responsible; though to do so is inevitable if we wish to *explain* the contingent existence of this character, and perhaps it is for this reason that Scripture, in conformity with this weakness of ours, has thus pictured the temporal origin of evil.

But the rational origin of this perversion of our will whereby it makes lower incentives supreme among its maxims, that is, of the propensity to evil, remains inscrutable to us, because this propensity itself must be set down to our account and because, as a result, that ultimate ground of all maxims would in turn involve the adoption of an evil maxim [as a basis]. Evil could have sprung only from the morally evil, not from mere limitation in our nature; and yet the original predisposition which no one other than man himself could have corrupted, if he is to be held responsible for this corruption, is a predisposition to good; there is then for us no conceivable ground from which the moral evil in us could originally have come. This inconceivability, together with a more accurate specification of the wickedness of our race, the Bible expresses in the historical narrative as follows.[13] It finds a place for evil at the creation of the world, yet not in man, but in a *spirit* of an originally loftier destiny. Thus is the *first* beginning of all evil represented as having fallen into evil only *through seduction,* and hence as being *not basically* corrupt even as regards his original predisposition to good but rather as still capable of an improvement, in contrast to a seducing *spirit,* that is, a being for whom temptation of the flesh cannot be accounted as an alleviation of guilt. For man, therefore, who despite a corrupted heart yet possesses a good will, there remains hope of a return to the good from which he has strayed.

BOOK TWO

Concerning the Conflict of the Good with the Evil Principle for Rule Over Man

To become morally good it is not enough merely to allow the seed of goodness implanted in our species to develop without hindrance; there is also present in us an active and opposing cause of evil to be combatted. Among the ancient moralists it was pre-eminently the Stoics who called attention to this fact by their watchword *virtue,* which in Greek as well as in Latin

---

[13] What is written here must not be read as though intended for Scriptural exegesis, which lies beyond the limits of the domain of bare reason alone. It is possible to explain how an historical account is to be put to moral use without deciding whether this is the intention of the author or merely our interpretation, provided this meaning is true in itself, apart from all historical proof. Moreover this moral use is the only one whereby we can derive something conducive to our betterment from a passage which otherwise would be only an unfruitful addition to our historical knowledge and which, when understood, in no way helps us to be better men. That which can afford such help is discovered without historical guidance, and indeed must be understood without it. Historical knowledge which has no inner bearing valid for all men belongs to the class of *adiaphora,* which each man is free to cherish if he finds it edifying.

signifies courage and valor and thus presupposes the presence of an enemy. In this regard the word *virtue* is a noble one, and that it has often been ostentatiously misused and derided, as has of late the word "Enlightenment," can do it no harm. For simply to make the demand for courage is to go half-way toward infusing it; on the other hand, the lazy and pusillanimous frame of mind in morality and religion which entirely mistrusts itself and hesitates waiting for help from without, is weakening to all a man's powers and makes him unworthy even of this assistance.

Yet those valiant men [the Stoics] mistook their enemy: for he is not to be sought merely in the undisciplined natural inclinations which present themselves so openly to everyone's consciousness; rather is he, as it were, an invisible foe who hides himself behind reason and is therefore all the more dangerous. They called out *wisdom* against *folly*, which allows itself to be deceived by the inclinations through mere carelessness, instead of summoning her against the *wickedness* of the human heart, which secretly undermines the convictions with soul-destroying principles.[14]

---

[14] These Stoic philosophers derived their universal ethical principle from the dignity of human nature, that is, from its freedom regarded as an independence from the power of the inclinations, and they could not have used as their foundation a better or nobler principle. They then derived the moral laws directly from reason, which alone makes moral laws and whose command, through these laws, is absolute. Thus everything was quite correctly defined—objectively, with regard to the rule, and subjectively, with reference to the incentive—provided one ascribes to man an uncorrupted will to incorporate these laws unhesitatingly into his maxims. Now it was just in the latter presupposition that their error lay. For no matter how early we direct our attention to our moral state, we find that this state is no longer a *res integra*, but that we must start by dislodging from its stronghold the evil which has already entered in, and it could never have done so, had we not ourselves adopted it into our maxims; that is, the first really good act that a man can perform is to forsake the evil, which is to be sought not in his inclinations, but in his perverted maxim, and so in freedom itself. Those inclinations merely make difficult the *execution* of the good maxim which opposes them; whereas genuine evil consists in this, that a man does not *will* to withstand those inclinations when they tempt him to

Natural inclinations, *considered in themselves,* are *good,* that is, not a matter of reproach, and it is not only futile to want to extirpate them but to do so would also be harmful and blameworthy. Rather, let them be tamed and instead of clashing with one another they can be brought into harmony in a wholeness which is called happiness. Now the reason which accomplishes this is termed *prudence.* But only what is opposed to the moral law is evil in itself, absolutely reprehensible, and must be completely eradicated; and only a reason which teaches this truth, and more especially one which puts it into actual practice, alone deserves the name of *wisdom.* The vice corresponding to this may indeed be termed *folly,* but again only when reason feels itself strong enough not merely to *hate* vice as something to be feared, and to arm itself against it, but to *scorn* vice with all its temptations.

So when the Stoic regarded man's moral struggle simply as a conflict with his inclinations, so far as these inherently innocent inclinations had to be overcome as hindrances to the fulfilment of his duty, he could locate the cause of transgression only in man's failure to combat these inclinations, for he admitted no special, positive principle such as evil in itself. Yet since this failure is itself contrary to duty and a transgression and no mere lapse of nature, and since the cause thereof cannot without arguing in a circle be sought once more in the inclinations but only in something which determines the will as a free will,

---

transgress—so it is really this disposition that is the true enemy. The inclinations are but the opponents of basic principles in general (be they good or evil); and so far that high-minded principle of morality [of the Stoics] is of value as an initiatory lesson and a general discipline of the inclinations in allowing oneself to be guided by basic principles. But so far as specific principles of moral *goodness* ought to be present but are not present, as maxims, we must assume the presence in the agent of some other opponent with whom virtue must join combat. In the absence of such an opponent all virtues would not, indeed, be *splendid vices,* as the Church Father has it; yet they would certainly be *splendid frailties.* For though it is true that thus the rebellion is often stilled, the rebel himself is not being conquered and exterminated.

that is, in the first and inmost ground of the maxims which accord with the inclinations, we can well understand how philosophers could mistake the real opponent of goodness.[15]

It is not surprising that an Apostle imagines this *invisible* enemy, who is known only through his effect upon us and who destroys basic principles, as being outside us and, indeed, as an evil *spirit:* "We wrestle not against flesh and blood (the natural inclinations) but against principalities and powers—against evil spirits." This is an expression which seems to have been used not to extend our knowledge beyond the world of sense but only to make clear *for practical use* the conception of what is for us unfathomable. Moreover, as far as its practical value is concerned, it is all one whether we place the seducer merely within ourselves or without, for guilt touches us not a whit less in the latter case then in the former, inasmuch as we would not be led astray by him at all were we not already in secret league with him.[16] We shall treat of this whole subject in two sections.

---

[15] It is a very common assumption of moral philosophy that the existence of moral evil in man may easily be explained by the power of the incentives of his senses on the one hand, and the impotence of his rational impulses (his respect for the law) on the other, that is, by *weakness.* But then the moral goodness in him, his moral predisposition, would have to allow of a still easier explanation, for to comprehend the one apart from comprehending the other is quite unthinkable. Now reason's ability to master all opposing motivating forces through the bare idea of a [moral] law is utterly inexplicable; it is also inconceivable, therefore, how the incentives of the senses would be able to gain the ascendancy over a reason which commands with such authority. For if all the world were to proceed in conformity with the precepts of the [moral] law, we should say that everything came to pass according to natural order, and no one would so much as think to inquire after the cause.

[16] It is a peculiarity of Christian ethics to represent moral goodness as differing from moral evil not as heaven from *earth* but as heaven from *hell.* Though this representation is figurative, and, as such, disturbing, it is none the less philosophically correct in meaning. That is, it serves to prevent us from regarding good and evil, the realm of light and the realm of darkness, as bordering on each other and as losing themselves in one another by gradual steps (of greater and lesser brightness); but rather to represent those realms as being separated from one another by

Concerning the Lawful Claim of the Good Principle to Rule Over Man

A. The Personified Idea of the Good Principle

Mankind or rational earthly existence in general *in its complete moral perfection* is that which alone can render a world the object of a divine decree and the end of creation. With such perfection as the prime condition, happiness is the direct consequence, according to the will of the Supreme Being. Man so conceived, alone pleasing to God, "is in Him through eternity," the idea of him proceeds from God's very being; hence he is no created thing but His only-begotten Son, "the *Word* (the *Fiat!*) through which all other things are, and without which nothing is in existence that is made," since for him, that is, for rational existence in the world, so far as he may be regarded in the light of his moral destiny, all things were made. "He is the brightness of His glory." "In him God loved the world," and only in him and through the adoption of his disposition can we hope "to become the sons of God," etc.

Now it is our common duty as men to *elevate* ourselves to this ideal of moral perfection, that is, to this archetype of the moral disposition in all its purity—and for this the idea itself, which reason presents to us for our zealous emulation, can give us power. But just because we are not the authors of this idea, and because it has established itself in man without our comprehending how human nature could have been capable of receiving it, it is more appropriate to say that this archetype has *come down* to us from heaven and has assumed our humanity; for it is less

an immeasurable gulf. The complete dissimilarity of the basic principles, by which one can become a subject of this realm or that, and the danger, too, which attends the notion of a close relationship between the characteristics which fit an individual for one or for the other, justify this manner of representation—which, though containing an element of horror, is none the less very exalting.

possible to conceive how man, by nature *evil,* should of himself lay aside evil and *raise* himself to the ideal of sanctity, than that the latter should *descend* to man and assume a *humanity* which is, in itself, not evil. Such union with us may therefore be regarded as a state of *humiliation* of the Son of God if we represent to ourselves this godly-minded person, regarded as our archetype, as assuming sorrows in fullest measure in order to further the world's good, though he himself is holy and therefore is bound to endure no sufferings whatsoever. Man, on the contrary, who is never free from guilt even though he has developed the very same disposition, can regard as truly merited the sufferings that may overtake him, how they come; consequently he must consider himself unworthy of having his character identified with the idea of God, even though this idea serves him as an archetype.

This ideal of a humanity pleasing to God and hence of such moral perfection as is possible to an earthly being who is subject to wants and inclinations we can imagine only as the idea of a person who would be willing not merely to discharge all human duties himself and to spread about him goodness as widely as possible by precept and example, but even, though tempted by the greatest allurements, to take upon himself every affliction, up to the most ignominious death, for the good of the world and even for his enemies. For man can frame to himself no concept of the degree and strength of a force like that of moral convictions except by picturing it as encompassed by obstacles, and yet, in the face of the fiercest onslaughts, victorious.

Man may then hope to become acceptable to God (and so be saved) through *a practical faith in this Son of God,* so far as He is represented as having taken upon Himself man's nature. In other words, he, and he alone, is entitled to look upon himself as an object not unworthy of divine approval who is conscious of such moral convictions as enable him to have a well-grounded confidence in himself and to *believe* that, under like temptations and afflictions, so far as these are made the touchstone of that idea, he would be loyal unswervingly to the archetype of humanity and, by faithful imitation, remain true to his exemplar.

B. The Objective Reality of This Idea

From the practical point of view this idea is completely existential in its own right, for it resides in our morally legislative reason. We *ought* to conform to it; consequently we must *be able* to do so. Did we have to prove in advance the possibility of man's conforming to this archetype, as is absolutely essential in the case of concepts of nature, if we are to avoid the danger of being deluded by empty notions, we should have to hesitate before allowing even to the moral law the authority of an unconditioned and yet sufficient determining ground of our will. For how it is possible that the mere idea of conformity to law, as such, should be a stronger incentive for the will than all the incentives conceivable whose source is personal gain, can neither be understood by reason nor yet proved by examples from experience. As regards the former, the law commands unqualifiedly; and as regards the latter, even though there had never existed an individual who yielded unqualified obedience to this law, the objective necessity of being such an one would yet be undiminished and self-evident. We need, therefore, no empirical example to make the idea of a person morally well-pleasing to God our pattern; this idea as a pattern is already present in our reason. Moreover, if anyone, in order to acknowledge, for his imitation, a particular individual as such an example which conforms to that idea, and therefore demands more than what he sees, more, that is, than a course of life entirely blameless and as meritorious as one could wish; and if he goes on to require, as credentials requisite to belief, that this individual should have performed miracles or had them performed for him—he who demands this thereby confesses to his own moral *unbelief,* that is, to his lack of faith in virtue. This is a lack which no belief that rests upon miracles and is therefore merely historical can repair. For only a faith in the practical validity of that idea which lies in our reason has moral value. Only this idea, to be sure, can establish the truth of miracles as possible effects of the good principle; but it can never itself derive from them its own verification.

Just for this reason an experience must be possible in which the example of such a [morally perfect] human being is presented (so far, at least, as we can expect or demand from any merely external experience the evidences of an inner moral disposition). According to the [moral] law, each man ought really to furnish an example of this idea in his own person. To this end does the archetype always reside in the reason: and this just because no example in outer experience is adequate to it; for outer experience does not disclose the inner nature of the character but merely allows of an inference about it though not one of strict certainty. For not even does a man's inner experience with regard to himself enable him so to fathom the depths of his own heart as to obtain, through self-observation, quite certain knowledge of the basis of the maxims which he professes, or of their purity and stability.

Now if it were indeed a fact that such a truly godly-minded man at some particular time had descended, as it were, from heaven to earth and had given men in his own person through his teachings, his conduct, and his sufferings as perfect an *example* of a man well-pleasing to God as one can expect to find in external experience (for be it remembered that the *archetype* of such a person is to be sought nowhere but in our own reason), and if he had, through all this, produced immeasurably great good upon earth by effecting a revolution in the human race—even then we should have no cause for supposing him other than a man naturally begotten. Indeed, the naturally begotten man feels himself under obligation to furnish himself just such an example. This is not, to be sure, absolutely to deny that he might be a man supernaturally begotten. But to suppose this can in no way benefit us practically, inasmuch as the archetype which we find embodied in this manifestation must, after all, be sought in ourselves, even though we are but natural men. And the presence of this archetype in the human soul is in itself sufficiently incomprehensible without our adding to its supernatural origin the assumption that it is hypostasized in a particular individual. The elevation of such a holy person above all the frailties of human nature would rather, so far as we can see, hinder the adoption of the idea of such a person for our imitation. For let the nature of this individual pleasing to God be regarded as human in the sense of being encumbered with the very same inclinations [as man], hence with the same temptations to transgress [the moral law]; let him, however, be regarded as superhuman to the degree that his unchanging purity of will, not achieved with effort but innate, makes all transgression on his part utterly impossible: his distance from the natural man would then be so infinitely great that such a divine person could no longer be held up as an *example to* him. Man would say: If I too had a perfectly sanctified will, all temptations to evil would of themselves be thwarted in me; if I too had the most complete inner assurance that, after a short life on earth, I should by virtue of this sanctity become at once a partaker in all the eternal glory of the kingdom of heaven, I too should take upon myself not only willingly but joyfully all sorrows, however bitter they might be, even to the point of a most ignominious death, since I would see before my eyes the glorious and imminent sequel. To be sure, the thought that this divine person was in actual possession of this eminence and this bliss from all eternity and needed not first of all to earn them through such afflictions, and that he willingly renounced them for the sake of those absolutely unworthy, even for the sake of his enemies, to save them from everlasting perdition—this thought must inspire our hearts to admiration, love, and gratitude. Similarly the idea of a demeanor in accordance with so perfect a standard of morality would no doubt be valid for us, as a model for us to copy. Yet he himself could *not* be presented to us an *example* for our imitation, nor, consequently, as a proof of the feasibility and attainability *for us* of so pure and exalted a moral goodness.[17]

---

[17] It is indeed a limitation of human reason, and one which is ever inseparable from it, that we can conceive of no considerable moral worth in the actions of a personal being without representing that person, or his manifestation, in human guise. This is not to assert that such value is in itself and in truth so conditioned, but merely that we must always resort to some analogy to natural existences to render supersensible qualities intelligible to ourselves. Thus a philosophical poet assigns a higher place in the moral gradation of beings to man, so far as he has to fight a propensity to evil within himself, nay, just in consequence of this fact, if only he is able to master the propensity, than to the inhabitants of heaven themselves who, by reason of the holiness of their nature, are placed above the possibility of going astray:

"The world with all its faults
Is better than a realm of will-less angels."   (Haller)

The Scriptures too accommodate themselves to this mode of representing [God] when, in order to make us comprehend the degree of His love for the human race, they ascribe to Him the very highest sacrifice which a loving being can make, a sacrifice performed in order that even those who are unworthy may be made happy ("For God so loved the world . . ."); though we cannot indeed rationally conceive how an all-sufficient Being could sacrifice a part of what belongs to His state of bliss or rob Himself of a possession. Such is the *schema of analogy* [pattern of reason], with which as a means of explanation we cannot dispense. But to transform it into a *schema of objective determination* for the extension of our knowledge is *anthropomorphism,* which has, from the moral point of view (in religion), most injurious consequences.

At this point let me remark incidentally that while, in proceeding from the sensible to the supersensible it is indeed allowable to *schematize,* that is, to render a concept intelligible by the help of an analogy to something sensible, it is on no account permitted to *infer* and thus to *extend* our concept by this analogy, so that what holds of the former must also be attributed to the latter. Such an inference is not possible, for the simple reason that it would run *directly counter* to all analogy to conclude that, because we absolutely need a schema to render a concept intelligible to ourselves, it therefore follows that this schema must necessarily belong to the object itself as its predicate. Thus, I cannot say: I can *make comprehensible* to myself the cause of a plant or of any organic creature, or indeed of the whole purposive world only by attributing intelligence to it, on the analogy of an artificer in his

Now such a godly-minded teacher, even though he was completely human, might nevertheless truthfully speak of himself as though the ideal of goodness were displayed incarnate in his teachings and conduct. In speaking thus he would be alluding only to the convictions which he makes the rule of his actions. Since he cannot make these convictions visible, as an example for others, by and through themselves, he places them before their eyes only through his teachings and actions: "Which of you convinceth me of sin?" For in the absence of proofs to the contrary it is no more than right to ascribe the faultless example which a teacher furnishes of his teaching—when, moreover, this is a matter of duty for all—to the supremely pure moral character of the man himself. When a character such as this, together with all the afflictions assumed for the sake of the world's highest good, is taken as the ideal of mankind, it is, by standards of supreme righteousness, a perfectly valid ideal for all men, at all times and in all places, whenever man moulds his own character to be like it, as he ought to do. To be sure, such an attainment will ever remain a righteousness not our own, inasmuch as it would have to consist of a course of life completely and faultlessly harmonious with that perfect character. Yet an appropriation of this righteousness for the sake of our own must be possible when our own character is made similar to that of the archetype. However, the greatest difficulties will stand in the way of our rendering this act of appropriation comprehensible.

---

relation to his work, say a watch; therefore the cause of the plant and of the world in general must itself *possess* intelligence. That is, I cannot say that this postulated intelligence of the cause conditions not merely my comprehending it but also conditions the possibility of its being a cause. On the contrary, between the relation of a schema to its concept and the relation of this same schema of a concept to the objective fact itself there is no analogy, but rather a chasm, the overleaping of which leads us at once to anthropomorphism. The proof of this I have given elsewhere.

BOOK THREE

The Victory of the Good Over the Evil Principle, and the Founding of a Kingdom of GOD on Earth

The combat which every morally well-disposed man must sustain in this life, under the leadership of the good principle, against the attacks of the evil principle, can procure him, however much he exerts himself, no greater advantage than freedom from the *rule* of evil. To become *free,* "to be freed from bondage under the law of sin, to live for righteousness"—this is the highest prize he can win. He continues to be exposed, none the less, to the assaults of the evil principle; and in order to assert his freedom, which is perpetually being attacked, he must ever remain armed for the fray.

Now man is in this perilous state through his own fault; hence he is *bound* at the very least to strive with all his might to extricate himself from it. But how? That is the question. When he looks around for the causes and circumstances which expose him to this danger and keep him in it, he can easily convince himself that he is subject to these not because of his own gross nature, so far as he is here a separate individual, but because of mankind to whom he is related and bound. It is not at the instigation of the former that what should properly be called the *passions,* which cause such havoc in his original good predisposition, are aroused. His needs are but few and his frame of mind in providing for them is temperate and tranquil. He is poor (or considers himself so) only in his anxiety lest other men consider him poor and despise him on that account. Envy, the lust for power, greed, and the malignant inclinations bound up with these, besiege his nature, contented within itself, *directly he is among men.* And it is not even necessary to assume that these are men sunk in evil and examples to lead him astray; it suffices that they are at hand, that they surround him, and that they are men, for them mutually to corrupt each other's predispositions and make one another evil. If no means could be discovered for the forming of an alliance uniquely designed as a protection against this evil and for the furtherance of goodness in man—of a society, enduring, ever extending itself, aiming solely at the maintenance of morality, and counteracting evil with united forces—this association with others would keep man constantly in danger of falling again under its dominion, however much he may have done as a single individual to throw off the sovereignty of evil. As far as we can see, therefore, the sovereignty of the good principle is attainable, so far as men can work toward it, only through the establishment and spread of a society in accordance with, and [established] for the sake of, the laws of virtue, a society whose task and duty it is rationally to impress these laws in all their scope upon the entire human race. For only thus can we hope for a victory of the good over the evil principle. In addition to prescribing laws to each individual, morally legislative reason when giving moral laws also unfurls a banner of virtue as a rallying point for all who love the good, that they may gather beneath it and thus at the very start gain the upper hand over the evil which is attacking them without interruption.

A union of men under merely moral laws, patterned on the above idea, may be called an *ethical* society, and so far as these laws are public, an ethico-civil, in contrast to a juridico-civil, society; or [it may be called] an *ethical* commonwealth. It can exist within a political commonwealth and may even be made up of all its members; indeed, unless it is based upon such a commonwealth it can never be brought into existence by man. It has, however, a special and unique principle of union, virtue, and hence a form and constitution which fundamentally distinguish it from the political commonwealth. At the same time there is a certain analogy between these two kinds of commonwealths, in view of which the former may also be called an *ethical state, i.e.,* a *realm* of virtue, or of the good principle. The idea of such a state possesses a thoroughly well-grounded objective existence in human reason and in man's duty to join such a state, even though, subjectively, we can never hope that man's good will may lead mankind to decide to work with unanimity toward this goal.

DIVISION ONE

Philosophical Account of the Victory of the Good Principle in the Founding of a Kingdom of God on Earth

I. Concerning the Ethical State of Nature

A *juridico-civil* (political) *state* is the relation of men to each other in which they all alike stand socially under *public juridical laws* (which are, as a class, laws of coercion). An *ethico-civil* state is that in which they are united under noncoercive laws, that is, *laws of virtue* alone.

Now just as the rightful but not therefore always righteous, or *juridical state of* NATURE is opposed to the first, *the ethical state of* NATURE is distinguished from the second. In both, each individual is his own judge, and there exists no powerful *public* authority to determine with legal power, according to laws, what is each man's duty in every situation that arises, and to bring about the universal performance of duty.

In an already existing political commonwealth all the political citizens, as such, are in an *ethical state of nature* and are entitled to remain therein; for it would be a contradiction (in terms) for the political commonwealth to compel its citizens to enter into an ethical commonwealth, since the very concept of the latter involves freedom from coercion. Every political commonwealth may indeed wish to be able to rule, according to laws of virtue, over the spirits [of its citizens]; for then, when its methods of compulsion do not avail, for the human judge cannot penetrate into the depths of other men, their convictions about virtue would bring about what was required. But woe to the legislator who wishes to establish through force a polity directed to ethical ends! For in so doing he would not merely achieve the very opposite of an ethical polity but also under-mine his political state and make it insecure. The citizen of the political commonwealth remains therefore, so far as its legisla-tive function is concerned, completely free to enter with his fellow-citizens into an ethical association or group in addition [to the political] or to remain in this kind of state of nature, as he may wish. Only so far as an ethical commonwealth must rest on *public* laws and possess a constitution based on these laws are those who freely pledge themselves to enter into this ethical state bound, not [indeed] to accept orders from the political power as to how they shall or shall not fashion this ethical constitution internally, but to agree to limitations. Namely, to the condition that this constitution shall contain nothing which contradicts the duty of its members as *citizens of the state*—al-though when the ethical pledge is of the genuine sort the political limitation need cause no anxiety.

Further, because the duties of virtue apply to the entire human race, the concept of an ethical commonwealth is ex-tended ideally to the whole of mankind, and thereby distin-guishes itself from the concept of a political commonwealth. Hence even a large number of men united in that purpose can be called not the ethical commonwealth itself but only a par-ticular society which strives toward harmony with all men, finally even with all rational beings in order to form an absolute ethical whole of which every partial society is only a representa-tion or schema; for each of these societies in turn, in its relation to others of the same kind, can be represented as in the ethical state of nature and subject to all the defects thereof. This is precisely the situation of separate political states which are not united through a public international law.

II. Man ought to leave his Ethical State of Nature in order to become a Member of an Ethical COMMONWEALTH

Just as the juridical state of nature is one of war of every man against every other, so too is the ethical state of nature one in which the good principle, which resides in each man, is continually attacked by the evil which is found in him and also in everyone else. Men as was noted above mutually corrupt one another's moral predispositions. Despite the good will of each individual, because they lack a principle which unites them, men abandon, through their dissensions, the common goal of goodness and, just as though they were *instruments of evil*, expose one another to the risk of falling once again under the rule of the evil principle. Again, just as the state of a lawless external and brutish freedom and independence from coercive laws is a state of injustice and of war, everyone against everyone, which a man ought to leave in order to enter into a politico-civil state: so is the ethical state of nature one of *open* conflict between principles of virtue and a state of inner immorality which the natural man ought to bestir himself to leave as soon as possible.

Now here we have a duty which is *sui generis,* not of men toward men, but of the human race toward itself. For the species of rational beings is objectively, through the idea of reason, destined for a social goal, namely, the promotion of the highest good as a social good. But because the highest moral good cannot be achieved merely by the exertions of the single individual toward his own moral perfection, but requires such individuals to unite into a whole directed toward the same goal, that is into a system of well-disposed men, in which and through whose unity alone the highest moral good can be achieved, the idea of such a whole as a universal republic based on laws of virtue is an idea sharply distinguished from all moral laws which concern what we know to lie in our own power. It involves working toward a union of which we do not know whether, as such, it lies in our power or not. Hence this duty is distinguished from all others both in kind and in principle. We can already foresee that this duty will require the presupposition of another idea, namely, that of a higher moral Being through whose universal dispensation the forces of separate individuals, insufficient in themselves, are united for a common end. First of all, however, we must follow up the clue of that moral need [for social union] and see whither this will lead us.

III. The Concept of an Ethical Commonwealth is the Concept of a PEOPLE OF GOD under Ethical Laws

If an ethical commonwealth is to come into being, all single individuals must be subject to public legislation, and all the laws which bind them must be capable of being regarded as commands of a common lawgiver. Now if the commonwealth to be established is to be *juridical,* the mass of people uniting itself into a whole would itself have to be the lawgiver, of constitutional laws, because legislation proceeds from the principle of *limiting the freedom of each to those conditions under which it can be consistent with the freedom of everyone else according to a common law,* and because, as a result, the general will sets up an external legal control. But if the commonwealth is to be *ethical,* the people as a people cannot itself be regarded as the lawgiver. For in such a commonwealth all the laws are expressly designed to promote the *morality* of actions, which is something *inner* and hence cannot be subject to public human laws, whereas, in contrast, these public laws are directed only toward the *legality* of actions, which meets the eye, and not toward inner morality, which alone is in question here. There must therefore be someone other than the populace capable of being specified as the public lawgiver for an ethical commonwealth. And yet, ethical laws cannot be thought of as emanating *originally* merely from the will of this superior being as statutes, which, had he not first commanded them, would perhaps not be binding, for then they would not be ethical laws and the duty proper to them would not be the free duty of virtue but the coercive duty of law. Hence only he can be thought of as highest lawgiver of an ethical commonwealth with respect to whom all *true duties,* hence also the ethical, only must be represented as *at the same time* his commands. He must therefore also be "one who knows the heart," in order to see into the innermost parts of the convictions of each individual and, as is necessary in every commonwealth, to bring it about that each receives whatever his actions are worth. But this is the concept of God as moral ruler of the world. Hence an ethical commonwealth can be thought of only as a people under divine commands, i.e., as *a people of God,* and indeed *under laws of virtue.*

We might indeed conceive of a people of God under *statutory laws,* under such laws that obedience to them would concern not the morality but merely the legality of acts. This would be a juridical commonwealth, of which, indeed, God would be the lawgiver. Hence the *constitution* of this state would be theocratic. But men as priests receiving His behests from Him directly, would build up an aristocratic *government.* Such a constitution however, whose existence and form rest wholly on an historical basis, cannot settle the problem of the morally-legislative reason giving moral laws. It is this problem the solution of which alone we are to effect. An institution under politico-civil laws whose lawgiver through God is yet external and therefore will come under review in the historical section. Here we have to do only with an institution whose laws are purely inward—a republic under laws of virtue, that is, a people of God "zealous of good works."

IV. The Idea of a People of God can be Realized through Human Organization only in the Form of a Church

The sublime, yet never wholly attainable, idea of an ethical commonwealth dwindles markedly under men's hands. It becomes an institution which, at best capable of representing only the pure form of such a commonwealth, is by the conditions created by man being a creature of senses, greatly circumscribed in its means for establishing such a whole. How indeed can one expect something perfectly straight to be fashioned out of such crooked wood?

To found a moral people of God is therefore a task whose consummation can be looked for not from men but only from

God Himself. Yet man is not entitled on this account to be idle in this business and to let Providence rule, as though each could apply himself exclusively to his own private moral affairs and relinquish to a higher wisdom all the affairs of the human race as regards its moral destiny. Rather must man proceed as though everything depended upon him; only on this condition dare he hope that higher wisdom will grant the completion of his well-intentioned endeavors.

The wish of all well-disposed people is, therefore, "that the kingdom of God come, that His will be done on earth." But what preparations must they now make that it shall come to pass?

An ethical commonwealth under divine moral legislation is a *church* which, so far as it is not an object of possible experience, is called the *church invisible,* a mere idea of the union of all the righteous under direct and moral divine world-government, an idea serving all as the archetype of what is to be established by men. The *visible Church* is the actual union of men into a whole which harmonizes with that ideal. So far as each separate society maintains under public laws an order among its members in the relation of those who obey its laws to those who direct their obedience, the group, united into a whole, the church, is a *congregation* under authorities, who while called teachers or shepherds of souls, merely administer the affairs of the invisible supreme head thereof. In this function they are all called *servants* of the church, just as in the political commonwealth the visible ruler occasionally calls himself the highest servant of the state even though he recognizes no single individual over him and ordinarily not even the people as a whole. The true visible church is that which exhibits the moral kingdom of God on earth so far as it can be brought into existence by men. The requirements upon and, hence the tokens, of the true church are the following:

1. *Universality,* and hence its numerical oneness; for which it must possess this characteristic, that although divided and at variance in unessential opinions it is none the less with respect

RELIGION WITHIN LIMITS OF REASON 411

to its fundamental intention founded upon such basic principles as must necessarily lead to a general unification in a single church, hence no sectarian divisions.

2. Its *nature* or quality is *purity*, that is, a union under no motivating forces other than *moral* ones purified [and freed from] the stupidity of superstition and the madness of fanaticism.

3. Its *relation* under the principle of *freedom;* both the internal relation of its members to one another, and the external relation of the church to political power—both relations as in a *republic.* Hence neither a *hierarchy,* nor an *illuminatism,* which is a kind of *democracy* through special inspiration, where the inspiration of one man can differ from that of another, according to the whim of each.

4. Its *modality,* the *unchangeableness* of its *constitution,* yet with the reservation that incidental regulations concerning merely its *administration* may be changed according to time and circumstance; to this end, however, it must already contain within itself *a priori* settled principles in the idea of its purpose. (Thus [it operates] under primordial laws, once [for all]) laid down, as it were out of a book of laws, for guidance; not under arbitrary symbols which, since they lack authenticity, are fortuitous, exposed to contradiction, and changeable.

An ethical commonwealth, then, in the form of a church, that is as a mere *representative* of a city of God, really has, as regards its basic principles nothing resembling a political constitution. For its constitution is neither *monarchical* under a pope or patriarch, nor *aristocratic* under bishops and prelates, nor *democratic* (as of sectarian *illuminati*). It could best of all be likened to that of a household or family under a common, though invisible, moral Father, whose holy Son, knowing His will and yet standing in blood relation with all members of the household, takes His place in making His will better known to them; these accordingly honor the Father in him and so enter with one another into a voluntary, universal, and enduring union of hearts.

XI

THEORY AND PRACTICE CONCERNING THE COMMON SAYING: THIS MAY BE TRUE IN THEORY BUT DOES NOT APPLY TO PRACTICE

[1793]

Introduction

WE CALL A SYNTHESIS (EVEN A SYNTHESIS OF PRACTICAL RULES) a theory if the rules concerned are principles of a certain generality, and if in that condition we abstract them from many conditions, which necessarily have an influence in the application of such principles. Conversely, not every activity can be called a practice but only a realization of that end which is conceived as a result of following certain general principles of procedure. It is evident that a link and transition is needed between theory and practice no matter how complete a theory may be. An act of judgment must be added to the rational concept which contains a rule and it is by this act of judgment that the practitioner can decide whether something is to be subsumed under the rule or not. Since there cannot again be rules for judgment on how a subsumption is to be achieved, for this would go on into the infinite, there will be theoreticians who, in their whole lives, can never become practical because they lack judgment. For example, there are doctors and lawyers who, although they did well in school, do not know what to do when they are called upon to give counsel.

But even where a natural gift [of judgment] is encountered there may be a lack of premises. That is to say, the theory may be incomplete and must be supplemented, perhaps by additional experiments and experience from which a doctor, an agriculturalist, a cameralist could derive new rules and thus complete this theory. In such cases, theory is of little practical use, not because of theory as such, but because there is not enough theory that an experienced man could have used, and what theory there is, is true theory even though it may not be systematically teachable. . . .

No man has the right to pretend that he is practically expert in a science and yet show contempt for theory without revealing that he is an ignoramus in his field. Apparently such a man believes that he can get further than he can by using theory, by groping about in experience on experiments without developing certain principles which constitute what I call theory and without having thought out an integrated approach to his work which, when it is developed according to method, is called a system.

However, it is more nearly permissible that an ignoramus should declare theory to be unnecessary and dispensable for his imagined peace than that a smart aleck could concede the value of theory for academic purposes, perhaps as an exercise of the mind, but then at the same time assert that things work quite differently in practice; that when one goes from school out into the world one will discover that one has pursued empty ideals and philosophic dreams.

Everyone would ridicule an empirical machinist who denounced general mechanics or an artilleryman who denounced the mathematical doctrine of ballistics, by declaring that the theory might be skillfully conceived but that it did not apply to practice because the execution [of these tasks] produced from very different results what the theory suggested. For, if the theory of friction were added to the knowledge of general mechanics and the theory of the resistance of air were added to the doctrine of ballistics; if, in other words, some more theory were added, these theories would indeed coincide with experience. Still, [it might be urged] that a theory which is concerned with objects of observation is quite different from a theory in which these objects are only present through concepts, as in the case with objects of mathematics and philosophy. The objects of mathematics and philosophy may be *thought of* quite well and without objection by reason but perhaps they can never be *given* but [will remain] only empty ideas. In practice, such ideas could be used either not at all or with disadvantage. If this were true, the common saying would yet be right in such cases. But in a theory which is founded on the *concept of duty,* the concern over the empty ideality of that concept is eliminated, for it would not be a duty to pursue a certain effect of our will if this effect were not possible in experience, even if experience is imagined as complete or approaching completion. In the present discussion we are only dealing with this kind of theory. . . .

This maxim about theory and practice which has become common in our wordy and deedless times causes very great damage if it is applied to moral questions; i.e., moral or legal duty. For the canon of practical reason is involved in this realm. Here the value of [a given] practice depends upon its appropriateness to the theory upon which it is based. All is lost if empirical, and consequently accidental, conditions of the execution of the law are made the conditions of the law itself. Then a practice which is calculated in relation to the probable result of previous experience is accorded the right of determining the theory itself. The following essay is divided according to three standpoints: First, that of the private individual or businessman; second, the statesman; third, the cosmopolitan or world citizen. [1]

---

[1] [Ed: We are offering here only the second of these three.]

II

Of the Relation of Theory to Practice in Constitutional Law

(Contra Hobbes)

Of all the compacts by which a number of people join themselves into a society (*pactum sociale*), the compact for the
establishment of a *civic constitution* (*pactum unionis civilis*) is
of such a particular kind that this compact is intrinsically distinct from all other compacts in the principle of its constitution
(*constitutionis civilis*). . . . The joining of many persons for
some common end which they all share is an element in all
social compacts. But a joining of many is an end in itself which
every one of them *ought to have*. In other words, a joining
which is an absolute and first duty in any external relations
among human beings who cannot avoid having mutual influence, such a union is only to be encountered in a society which
has reached the civic state; that is, the state constituting a
commonwealth (*gemeines Wesen*). The end which is a duty in
itself in such external relations and which is itself the supreme
formal condition of all other external duties, is the *right* of human beings [to live] *under public-coercive laws* by which every
man's [right] is determined and secured against the interference
of every other man.

The concept of an external right is derived from the concept
of freedom in the external relation of human beings to each
other. This concept has nothing at all to do with the purpose
which all human beings naturally have; namely, a desire for
happiness, nor has it anything to do with the means of achieving such happiness. Thus the desire for happiness must not be
included as a ground for determining laws of external right.
Right is the limitation of every man's freedom so that it harmonizes with the freedom of every other man in so far as
harmonization is possible according to a general law. *Public
Law* is the totality of external laws which makes such a gen-

eral consonance possible, since every limitation of freedom by the will of another is called coercion. It follows that the civic constitution is a relationship of *free* men who, despite their freedom for joining with others, are nevertheless placed under coercive laws. This is so because it is so willed by pure *a priori* legislating reason which has no regard for empirical purposes such as are comprised under the general name of happiness. For men have many different ideas about happiness and what can be conceived as constituting it. Therefore, if happiness is adopted as a basic criteria for what ought to be law, men's will cannot be brought under a common principle nor under an external law which harmonizes with every man's freedom.

The civic state, considered merely as a legal state, is based on the following *a priori* principles:

1. The freedom of each member of society as a *man*.

2. The *equality* of each member with every other as a *subject*.

3. The autonomy of each member of a commonwealth as a *citizen*.

These principles are not laws given by a constituted state; they are rather the only principles according to which a state could be constituted, [and be in keeping with] the rational principles of the external law of man. Therefore; (1) I will state the *freedom* of man as man as a principle for the constitution of the commonwealth in the following formula: No one may force anyone to be happy according to his manner of imagining the well-being of other men; instead, everyone may seek his happiness in the way that seems good to him as long as he does not infringe on the freedom of others to pursue a similar purpose, when such freedom may coexist with the freedom of every other man according to a possible and general law.

A government might be constituted on the principle of benevolence, with an attitude toward the people such as a father has toward his children, that is, a paternal government under which the subjects are obliged to behave merely passively like minor children who cannot distinguish between what is truly useful or noxious, the idea being that they are to learn how to be happy according to the judgment of the head of the state, depending entirely upon his kindness. But such a government is the greatest conceivable *despotism,* having a constitution which suspends all the freedom of the subjects who thereby have no rights whatsoever. Not a *paternal* but only a *patriotic* government can be concerned with men who are capable of [enjoying their rights] even in relation to the benevolence of the ruler. For a patriotic attitude influences everyone in the state, including its head, to regard the commonwealth as his maternal womb, or the country as the paternal soil from which he has sprung and which he must leave as a beloved token to his descendants. [To put it another way; a patriotic attitude is one] which makes the citizens consider themselves authorized to protect the rights of the commonwealth by laws, but not authorized to subject the commonwealth to the absolute discretion [of the head] for his purposes. This right of freedom belongs to man as the member of a commonwealth in so far as he is a being who is capable of having rights.

(2) [We may state the principle of] the *equality* [of each member of society] as a subject in the following formula: Every member of the commonwealth has a right of coercion against every other member and the head of the state is exempted from that right only because he is not a member but the creator and maintainer of the commonwealth. The head of the state alone has the authority to coerce without being himself subject to coercion. . . . For if he could also be coerced he would not be the head of the state and the sequence of authority would go upward into the infinite. If there were two persons free from coercion neither would be subject to coercive laws and neither could do to the other anything contrary to right, all of which is impossible. The general equality of men as subjects in a state coexists quite readily with the greatest inequality in degrees of the possessions men have, whether the possessions consist of cor-

poreal or spiritual superiority or in material possession besides. Hence the general equality of men also coexists with great inequality of specific rights of which there may be many. Thus it follows that the welfare of one man may depend to a very great extent on the will of another man, just as the poor are dependent on the rich and the one who is dependent must obey the other as a child obeys his parents or the wife her husband or again, just as one man has command over another, as one man serves and another pays, etc. Nevertheless, all subjects are equal to each other before the law which, as a pronouncement of the general will, can only be one. This law concerns the form and not the matter of the object regarding which I may possess a right. For no man can coerce another [under constitutional government] except through publicly-known law and through its executor, the head of the state, and by this same law every man may resist to the same degree. No one can lose this right to coerce others except through a crime. In other words, no one can make an agreement or other legal transaction to the effect that he has no rights but only duties. By such a contract he would deprive himself of [the right to] make a contract, and thus the contract would nullify itself.

From this concept of the equality of men as subjects in a commonwealth the following formula is derived: Every member of a commonwealth must be able to reach every level of status in the commonwealth which can belong to a subject and which [he can achieve] by his talent, his industry or his good fortune. No subject may stand in his way as a result of hereditary privilege and thus keep him and his descendants down forever.

The birth is no deed of him who is born. Therefore no inequality of legal status and no subjection under coercive laws can come through birth except that which a man has in common with all others as subjects under the sole supreme legislative power. . . . No one can pass on to his descendants the privileged status which he occupies in a commonwealth. To put it another way; a man cannot forcibly prevent his descendants from reaching a superior status by their own merit by qualifying them for such status through their birth. He may bequeath everything else because material things do not concern the personality and can be acquired as property and disposed of again. In a line of succession this may cause a considerable inequality of wealth among members of the commonwealth (such as the inequality between the mercenary and his employer, the estate-owner and the hired man). . . . No man can lose the equality [he has in a commonwealth as a subject] except through his own crime and especially he cannot lose that equality through a contract or as a result of military occupation. For he cannot cease, by any legal act, either his own or another's, to be master of himself. No man may enter into the class of domestic animals, which can be used for all services the master pleases and which are maintained in service without their consent as long as the master wishes, even though he is subject to the restriction not to cripple or kill them (which may, as with the Indians, be sanctioned by religion). Man may be considered happy in any condition if he is conscious that his condition is due to himself, his ability, or his earnest effort or to circumstances for which others cannot be blamed. But [he may not be considered happy] if his condition is due to the irresistible will of another and if he does not rise to the same status as others who, as his co-subjects, have no advantage over him as far as his rights are concerned.[2]

(3) [The principle of] the autonomy (*sibisufficientia*) or self-sufficiency of a member of a commonwealth as a citizen; that is, as a co-legislator may be stated as follows: As regards legislation, all who are free and equal under pre-existing public laws must be considered equal, but not as concerns the right to give these laws. Those who are not capable of exercising that right are

---

[2] [Here follows a footnote in which Kant protests against the use of the appellation *gnädiger Herr*, or benevolent lord.—Ed.]

nevertheless, as members of the commonwealth, obliged to obey these laws and are thereby entitled to the protection of the law, but not as citizens.

All right depends upon laws. A publicly-known law determining what everyone shall be legally permitted or forbidden [to do] is an act of the public will from which all right proceeds and which cannot itself act contrary to right. For this purpose no other will is possible but the will of the entire people because [through this will] all men decide about all men and hence everyone decides about himself. For no one can be considered unjust to himself. This basic law which originates only in the general and united will of the people is called the *original contract.*

He who has the right to vote on basic legislation is called a citizen (*citoyen,* i.e., *Staatsbürger,* not *Stadtbürger,* i.e., *bourgeois*). The requisite quality for this [status], apart from the natural one that the person not be a child nor a woman, is only this: that such a person be *his own master* (*sui iuris*) and hence that he have some property (under which we may include any art, craft or science) that would provide him with sustenance. [To put this another way, he must be] a man who, when he must earn a livelihood from others, acquires property only by selling what is his own and not by conceding to others the right to make use of his strength. Consequently he *serves* no one, in the strict sense of the word, but the commonweal. In this respect artisans and great or small property-owners are all equal and each is entitled to only one vote. Regarding large property owners we leave aside the question of how a man might rightfully come into possession of more land than he can himself work, for acquisition by military conquest is no first acquisition. We also leave aside how it happened that many men who otherwise might have acquired permanent property have thus been reduced merely to serve others in order to live. In any case it would be contrary to the principle of equality if a law established the privileged status for those large estate owners so that their descendants would always remain large estate owners as under feudalism without there being any possibility that the estates would be sold or divided by inheritance and thus made useful for more people. Nor is it proper that only certain arbitrarily selected classes acquire some of these divided properties. Thus the big estate owner destroys the many smaller owners and their voice [in the commonwealth] who might be occupying his place. He does not vote in their stead for he has only *one* vote. . . . Not the amount of property, but merely the number of those owning any property, should serve as a basis for the number of voters.

All who possess the right to vote must agree on this basic law of how to arrive at public justice; [for if they did not] there would be a conflict of law between those who agree to it and those who do not, which would necessitate a still higher legal principle to decide the issue. Since such general agreement cannot be expected of an entire people, only a majority of the votes must be considered to be the best that can be attained. In a large nation even this majority will not be that of the voters, but merely that of delegates representing the people. But then this principle of being satisfied by a majority will have to be presumed as having been accepted by general agreement; that is, through a contract, and hence [this principle will have to be presumed to be] the supreme reason for constituting a civic constitution.

Conclusion

In the foregoing we have an original contract upon which alone can a civic, and therefore completely legal, constitution among men be established. But this contract, which is called *contractus originarius* or *pactum sociale* . . . need not be assumed to be a fact, indeed it is not [even possible as such. To suppose that would be like insisting] that before anyone would be bound to respect such a civic constitution, that it be proved first of all from history that a people, whose rights and obligations we have entered into as their descendants, had *once upon a time* executed such an act and had left a reliable document or instrument, either orally or in writing, concerning this contract. Instead, this contract is a *mere idea* of reason which has undoubted practical reality; namely, to oblige every legislator to give us laws in such a manner that the laws *could* have originated from the united will of the entire people and to regard every subject in so far as he is a citizen as though he had consented to such [an expression of the general] will. This is the testing stone of the rightness of every publicly-known law, for if a law were such that it was impossible for an entire people to give consent to it (as for example a law that a certain class of subjects, by inheritance, should have the privilege of the *status of lords*), then such a law is unjust. On the other hand, if there is a mere *possibility* that a people might consent to a (certain) law, then it is a duty to consider that the law is just, even though at the moment the people might be in such a position or have a point of view that would result in their refusing to give their consent to it if asked. [3]

But this limitation is evidently valid only for the judgment of the legislator, not for that of the subject. Therefore if a people should judge that they will probably lose their happiness from certain actual legislation, then what should they do? Should they not resist? The answer can only be that they can do nothing but obey. We are not interested here in the happiness of the subjects supposedly resulting from the institutions or the

---

[3] For example, if a war tax, proportional for all subjects, were imposed, the subjects cannot, because the tax is onerous, claim that the tax is unjust because the war is unnecessary in their opinion. On that question they are not entitled to judge, as it is always possible that the war was inevitable and hence the tax is indispensable and so must be considered rightful in the judgment of the subjects. But if, in such a war, certain estate owners were bothered with requisitions which others in the same position were spared, then it is easy to see that an entire people could never consent to such a law. The people are therefore entitled at least to make representations against the law because they could not consider so uneven a distribution of burdens.

administration of the commonwealth but are interested only [in the law which is to be secured] for everyone by this institution and administration. This is the supreme principle with which all maxims concerning the commonwealth must begin and which is not restricted by any other. With regard to happiness no generally valid principle can be offered for legislation. For the conditions of the time as well as the very contradictory and constantly changing illusions as to what constitutes happiness—and no one can prescribe for anyone wherein he should seek happiness—render impossible all fixed principles and make the idea of happiness by itself unfit to be a principle of legislation. The proposition: *salus publica suprema civitatis lex est* remains unreduced in value and authority but the public weal which must be considered first is precisely that legal constitution which secures freedom for each man under the law. At the same time each man is free to seek his happiness in any way that seems best to him as long as he does not infringe upon the general lawful freedom and thereby on the rights of his fellow-citizens.

* * * * * *

From this it follows that all resistance against the supreme legislative power, all instigation to rebellion, is the worst and most punishable crime in a commonwealth because this destroys the foundation of a commonwealth. The prohibition (of rebellion) is absolute. Even when the [supreme legislative] power, or its agent, the head of the state, has violated the original contract and he thereby, in the opinion of the subject, loses the right to legislate because the supreme power has authorized the government to be run thoroughly tyrannically, even in this case no assistance is allowed the subject for a countermeasure. The reason is that under an already existing civic constitution the people have no lawful judgment as to how the constitution should be administered. For, if one assumes that the people have such a power of judgment and have exercised it contrary to that of the real head of the state, who is to decide which one is right?

Neither can do so, being judge in his own cause. Therefore there would have to be a head above the head of the state to decide between the people and the head of the state, which is self-contradictory.

Nor can some kind of emergency law, having a presumed right to do what is unlawful in the most extreme crisis, be introduced here and provide the key for closing the gate to restrict the power of the people. The head of the state may believe that he can justify his harsh procedure by the insubordination of his subjects, as readily as the subjects can justify their rebellion from complaints regarding their exceptional suffering. Who then shall decide? Only he who controls the supreme enforcement of the law can do this, and that is precisely the head of the state and hence there cannot be anyone in a commonwealth with the right to deny him this power.

Nevertheless I know respected men who assert this right of the subject to resist his superior under certain circumstances. Among these I will mention here only Achenwall who is very cautious, definite and modest in his doctrines concerning natural law. He says: "If the danger which threatens a commonwealth as a result of the continued endurance of injustice from its head is greater than the danger which may be feared from using arms against him, then may the people resist him and on behalf of this right may they deviate from their part of submission and dethrone him as a tyrant." Then he concludes: "The people thus return into a state of nature." [4]

I can well believe that in any actual case neither Achenwall nor any of the other honest men who, agreeing with him have reasoned concerning this matter, would have ever given counsel or assent to such dangerous undertakings. It cannot be doubted that if the rebellions, by which Switzerland, the United Netherlands and Great Britain have achieved their highly praised

---

[4] [These views attributed here to Achenwall are common among natural-law writers and are familiar in the classical form given them by Locke in his second treatise, Chap. XVIII and XIX.—Ed.]

constitutions, had failed, the readers of the history of those rebellions would regard the execution of their celebrated originators as nothing more than the well-earned punishment of great
criminals. For, concerning the grounds of legality [for such a
venture] our judgment is usually affected by the outcome, although the outcome was uncertain at a time when the grounds
of legality were certain. But it is clear that, even granting that
no injustice is done through such a rebellion to a prince who
violates a real contract with the people such as the *Joyeuse
Entrée,* nevertheless the people have acted highly illegally by
seeking their rights in this manner.

[Ed: After repeating his previous discussion regarding the impossibility of basing law upon the principle of happiness, Kant
continues:] I can see here what damage [is caused in public law
by] the principle of happiness, which is actually incapable of
forming a distinct principle just as [that principle causes difficul-
ties] in ethics even when those who teach this doctrine have the
best intentions. The sovereign makes the people happy according to his own ideas and becomes a despot; the people do not
want to surrender the general human desire for seeking their
own happiness and become rebels. If one had first of all asked
what is right (for these principles which are certain *a priori*
cannot be upset by empiricists), the idea of the social contract
would remain in indisputable authority, not as a fact . . . but
merely as a rational principle for evaluating every public legal
constitution. [If one knew what was right] then one would understand that until there is a general will the people have no
coercive right against their lord because they can only legally
coerce through him. But if there is a general will there still can
be no force exercised against it because then the people themselves are the supreme authority. In short, people are never entitled to use force against the head of the state or to obstruct
him in work or deed.

In practice, we see this theory quite adequately confirmed by
the constitution of Great Britain where the people are as proud

of their constitution as though it were the matrix of the whole world. We find that the constitution is silent regarding any authority of the people [to resist] in case the monarch should violate the contract of 1688. Does this mean that, because there is no law concerning this aspect, there is reserved the secret right of rebellion? For, a constitution which would contain a law authorizing anyone to overthrow the existing constitution upon which all specific laws rest, involves a clear contradiction because then the constitution would have to contain a *publicly constituted* counter-force. [5] This would mean having a second head of the state who would protect the rights of the people against the first head and then in turn a third to decide between the two.

Those leaders of the [British] people, or if you wish, guardians, being worried over such an accusation in case their enterprise should fail, invented a voluntary abandonment of the government by the monarch whom they scared away and they did this instead of claiming the right to depose him whereby they would have brought the constitution into contradiction with itself. Since no one, I trust, will accuse me of flattering the princes too much by asserting their inviolability, I also hope that I will be spared the accusation that I assert too much on the part of the people when I say that they likewise have inalienable rights against the head of the state even though those rights cannot be coercive.

Hobbes is of the opposite opinion. According to him (*de Cive*, Chap. 7, 14) the head of the state is not obliged to anything by contract and he can act contrary to law and right against the citizen in whatever way he might decide regarding him. This proposition would be correct if that which is contrary to law

---

[5] No right in a state can be kept under cover by a secret mental reservation, least of all the right [of revolution] which the people claim as belonging to the constitution, because all laws derived from it must be considered to have sprung from a public will. Therefore the constitution would, if it permitted revolution, have to declare this right publicly as well as the procedure by which to make use of it.

and right were understood to mean a kind of injury providing the injured with a right against him who has acted contrary to law and right. But stated generally as Hobbes does, the proposition is terrifying. The non-resisting subject must be able to assume that his ruler does not want to do him injustice, for every man has his inalienable rights which he cannot give up even should he want to and concerning which he is entitled to form his own judgments. But the injustice, which in his opinion he is suffering occurs according to the above assumption only because of error and ignorance of certain (unforseen) consequences of the law the supreme power has made. Therefore the citizen must have the privilege of making public his opinion on the ordinances of the supreme power when it seems to him that they constitute an injustice against the commonwealth. Indeed, this privilege should be supported by the ruler himself, for to assume that the ruler could not err sometimes or be unaware of things would mean that we imagine him to be gifted with divine intuition and to be superior to mankind. As a result, the freedom of the pen is the sole shield of the rights of the people. Of course, this [freedom] should be kept within the limits of respect and loyalty for the constitution under which one lives, [and it should be used in the spirit of] the liberal frame of mind which that constitution inspires in the subjects. To some extent this sort of limitation is imposed by writers on each other so they do not lose their freedom. Denying the subject this freedom does not only mean, as in Hobbes, depriving him of all claim to justice before a sovereign; it also means depriving the sovereign of all knowledge of those matters which he himself would change if he knew the views of the subject and thus he would be put into self-contradiction. [In this connection it must be remembered that] the will of the sovereign only gives commands to the subject merely as a citizen because he represents the general will of the people. Insinuating to the sovereign that he should be worried about disturbances being created in the state by such thoughts and speeches would arouse an awakening in him and make him distrust his own power and come to hate the people. To sum up: the general principle according to which a people may judge negatively what is not ordered by the supreme legislative power in accordance with the best will of the people is contained in the proposition: *What a people cannot decide concerning themselves, the legislator cannot decide concerning the people.*

[What follows here is very similar to what Kant developed in his short essay, "What is Enlightenment?" See above Pp. 132 ff. —Ed.]

* * * * * *

Nowhere do people engaged in practical pursuits speak with more pretentiousness derogatively of theory and neglecting all pure rational principles, than on the question of what is required for a good constitution. This is because a legal constitution which has existed a long time accustoms people to its rule by and by and makes them inclined to evaluate their happiness as well as their rights in the light of the conditions under which everything has been quietly going forward. Men fail to do the opposite; namely, to evaluate the existing constitution according to concepts [standards] provided by reason in regard to both happiness and right. As a result, men prefer this passive state to the dangerous task of seeking a better one. They are following the maxim which Hippocrates urges doctors to keep in mind: *Judgment is uncertain and experiment dangerous. (Judicium anceps, experimentum pericolosum.)* In spite of their differences, all constitutions which have existed a long time, whatever their faults, produce one and the same result; namely, that people become satisfied with what they have. It follows from this that in considering people's welfare, theory is apparently not valued but all depends upon practices derived from experience.

[Against this I assert that] in reason there exists a concept which may be expressed by the words constitutional law (or constitutional justice—*Staatsrecht*). If this concept has binding force for men who are pitched against each other through the antagonism of their freedom, [perhaps we can further assume that] this concept has objective practical reality without our considering what good or ill may result; for knowledge of these results is based purely on experience. If this be so then constitutional law is based upon principles *a priori,* since what is right cannot be taught by experience. A theory of constitutional law exists with which practice must agree in order to be valid [from a moral standpoint].

Nothing can be brought forward against this proposition except [the fact] that human beings, even though they have a concept of their rights, are incapable and unworthy of being treated according to their rights because of their refractoriness and therefore a supreme power must proceed to keep them in order according to rules of prudence. However, this desperate conclusion (*salto mortale*) implies that, since there no longer is any mention of right but only of force, then people may also try their own power and thus endanger every legal constitution. For, if there is nothing which compels immediate respect through reason, such as basic human rights, then all attempts to influence men's arbitrary will cannot restrain their [arbitrary] freedom. On the other hand, if in addition to benevolence, right (law—*Recht*) speaks loudly, then human nature does not appear so corrupted that it does not hear this voice with respect. . . .

XII

ETERNAL PEACE

[1795]

"TO ETERNAL PEACE."

Whether the above satirical inscription, once put by a certain Dutch innkeeper on his signboard on which a graveyard was painted, holds of men in general, or particularly of the heads of states who are never sated with war, or perhaps only of those philosophers who are dreaming that sweet dream of peace, may remain undecided. However, in presenting his ideas, the author of the present essay makes one condition. The practical statesman should not, in case of a controversy with the political theorist, suspect that any danger to the state lurks behind the opinions which such a theorist ventures honestly and openly to express. Consistency demands this of the practical statesman, for he assumes a haughty air and looks down upon the theorist with great self-satisfaction as a mere theorizer whose impractical ideas can bring no danger to the state, since the state must be founded on principles derived from experience. The worldly-wise statesman may therefore, without giving himself great concern, allow the theorizer to throw his eleven bowling balls all at once. By this "saving clause" the author of this essay knows himself protected in the best manner possible against all malicious interpretation.

FIRST SECTION

Which Contains the Preliminary Articles of an Eternal Peace Between States

1. "No treaty of peace shall be held to be such, which is made with the secret reservation of the material for a future war."

For, in that event, it would be a mere truce, a postponement of hostilities, not *peace*. Peace means the end of all hostilities, and to attach to it the adjective "eternal" is a pleonasm which at once arouses suspicion. The pre-existing reasons for a future war, including those not at the time known even to the contracting parties, are all of them obliterated by a genuine treaty of peace; no search of documents, no matter how acute, shall resurrect them from the archives. It is Jesuitical casuistry to make a mental reservation that there might be old claims to be brought forward in the future, of which neither party at the time cares to make mention, because both are too much exhausted to continue the war, but which they intend to assert at the first favorable opportunity. Such a procedure, when looked at in its true character, must be considered beneath the dignity of rulers; and so must the willingness to attempt such legal claims be held unworthy of a minister of state.

But, if enlightened notions of political wisdom assume the true honor of the state to consist in the continual increase of power by any and every means, such a judgment will, of course, evidently seem academic and pedantic.

2. "No state having an independent existence, whether it be small or great, may be acquired by another state through inheritance, exchange, purchase or gift."

A state is not a possession (*patrimonium*) like the soil on which it has a seat. It is a society of men, which no one but they themselves is called upon to command or to dispose of. Since, like a tree, such a state has its own roots, to incorporate it as a graft into another state is to take away its existence as a moral person and to make of it a thing. This contradicts the idea of the original contract, without which no right over a people can even be conceived. [1] Everybody knows into what danger, even in the most recent times the supposed right of thus acquiring states has brought Europe. Other parts of the world have never known such a practice. But in Europe states can even marry each other. On the one hand, this is a new kind of industry, a way of making oneself predominant through family connections without any special effort; on the other, it is a way of extending territorial possessions. The letting out of troops of one state to another against an enemy not common to the two is in the same class. The subjects are thus used and consumed like things to be handled at will.

3. "Standing armies shall gradually disappear."

Standing armies incessantly threaten other states with war by their readiness to be prepared for war. States are thus stimulated to outdo one another in number of armed men without limit. Through the expense thus occasioned peace finally becomes more burdensome than a brief war. These armies are thus the cause of wars of aggression, undertaken in order that this burden may be thrown off. In addition to this, the hiring of men to kill and be killed, an employment of them as mere machines and tools in the hands of another (the state), cannot be reconciled with the rights of humanity as represented in our own person. The case is entirely different where the citizens of a state voluntarily[2] drill themselves and their fatherland against attacks from without. It would be exactly the same with the accumula-

---

[1] An hereditary monarchy is not a state which can be inherited by another state. Only the right to govern it may be transferred by heredity to another person. Thus the state acquired a ruler, not the ruler a state.
[2] [Presumably, the word *"freiwillig"* here refers to the citizens acting as a whole, and through a majority, not the individuals separately.—Ed.]

tion of a war fund if the difficulty of ascertaining the amount of the fund accumulated did not work a counter effect. Looked upon by other states as a threat of war, a big fund would lead to their anticipating such a war by making an attack themselves, because of the three powers—the power of the army, the power of alliance, and the power of money—the last might well be considered the most reliable instrument of war.

4. "No debts shall be contracted in connection with the foreign affairs of the state."

The obtaining of money, either from without or from within the state, for purposes of internal development—the improvement of highways, the establishment of new settlements, the storing of surplus for years of crop failure, etc.—need create no suspicion. Foreign debts may be contracted for this purpose. But, as an instrument of the struggle between the powers, a credit system of debts endlessly growing though always safe against immediate demand (the demand for payment not being made by all the creditors at the same time)—such a system, the ingenious invention of a trading people in this century, constitutes a dangerous money power. It is a resource for carrying on war which surpasses the resources of all other states taken together. It can only be exhausted through a possible deficit of the taxes, which may be long kept off through the increase in commerce brought about by the stimulating influence of the loans on industry and trade. The facility thus afforded of making war, coupled with the apparently innate inclination thereto of those possessing power, is a great obstacle in the way of eternal peace. Such loans, therefore, must be forbidden by a preliminary article—all the more because the finally unavoidable bankruptcy of such a state must involve many other states without their responsibility in the disaster, thus inflicting upon them a public injury. Consequently, other states are at least justified in entering into an alliance against such a state and its pretensions.

5. "No state shall interfere by force in the constitution and government of another state."

For what could justify it in taking such action? Could perhaps some offense do it which that state gives to the subjects of another? Such a state ought rather to serve as a warning, because of the example of the evils which a people brings upon itself by its lawlessness. In general, the bad example given by one free person to another (as a *scandalum acceptum*) is no violation of the latter's rights. The case would be different if a state because of internal dissension should be split into two parts, each of which, while constituting a separate state, should lay claim to the whole. An outside state, if it should render assistance to one of these, could not be charged with interfering in the constitution of another state, as that state would then be in a condition of anarchy. But as long as this inner strife was not decided, the interference of outside powers would be a trespass on the rights of an independent people struggling only with its own inner weakness. This interference would be an actual offense which would so far tend to render the autonomy of all states insecure.

6. "No state at war with another shall permit such acts of warfare as must make mutual confidence impossible in time of future peace: such as the employment of assassins, of poisoners, the violation of articles of surrender, the instigation of treason in the state against which it is making war, etc."

These are dishonorable stratagems. Some sort of confidence in an enemy's frame of mind must remain even in time of war, for otherwise no peace could be concluded, and the conflict would become a war of extermination. For after all, war is only the regrettable instrument of asserting one's right by force in the primitive state of nature where there exists no court to decide in accordance with law. In this state neither party can be declared an unjust enemy, for this presupposes a court decision.

The outcome of the fight, as in the case of a so-called "judgment of God," decides on whose side the right is. Between states no war of punishment can be conceived, because between them there is no relation of superior and subordinate.

From this it follows that a war of extermination, in which destruction may come to both parties at the same time, and thus to all rights too, would allow eternal peace only upon the graveyard of the whole human race. Such a war, therefore, as well as the use of the means which might be employed in it, is wholly forbidden.

But that the methods of war mentioned above inevitably lead to such a result is clear from the fact that such hellish arts, which are in themselves degrading, when once brought into use do not continue long within the limits of war but are continued in time of peace, and thus the purpose of the peace is completely frustrated. A good example is furnished by the employment of spies, in which only the dishonorableness of others (which unfortunately cannot be exterminated) is taken advantage of.

Although all the laws above laid down would objectively— that is, in the intention of the powers, be negative laws, (*leges prohibitiae*) yet some of them are strict laws, which are valid without consideration of the circumstances. They insist that the abuse complained of be abolished at once. Such are our rules number 1, 5, and 6. The others, namely rules number 2, 3, and 4, though not meant to be permitting exception from the "rule of law," yet allow for a good deal of subjective discretion in respect to the application of the rules. They permit delay in execution without their purpose being lost sight of. The purpose, however, does not admit of delay till doomsday—"to the Greek Calends," as Augustus was wont to say. The restitution, for example, to certain states of the freedom of which they have been deprived, contrary to our second article, must not be indefinitely put off. The delay is not meant to prevent restitution, but to avoid undue haste which might be contrary to the intrinsic purpose. For the prohibition laid down by the article relates only to the mode of acquisition, which is not to be allowed to continue, but it does not relate to the present state of possessions. This present state, though not providing the needed just title, yet was held to be legitimate at the time of the supposed acquisition, according to the then current public opinion.

SECOND SECTION

Which Contains the Definitive Articles for Eternal Peace Among States

The state of peace among men who live alongside each other is no state of nature (*status naturalis*). Rather it is a state of war which constantly threatens even if it is not actually in progress. Therefore the state of peace must be *founded;* for the mere omission of the threat of war is no security of peace, and consequently a neighbor may treat his neighbor as an enemy unless he has guaranteed such security to him, which can only happen within a state of law.[3]

---

[3] It is often assumed that one is not permitted to proceed with hostility against anyone unless he has already actively hurt him, and this is indeed very true if both live in a civic state under law, for by entering into this state one man proffers the necessary security to another through the superior authority which has power over both.—But man (or the nation) in a mere state of nature deprives me of this security and hurts me by this very state, simply by being near me, even though not actively (*facto*). He hurts me by the lawlessness of his state (*statu iniusto*) by which I am constantly threatened, and therefore I can compel him either to enter into a communal state under law with me or to leave my vicinity.—Hence the postulate which underlies all the following articles is this: all men who can mutually affect each other should belong under a joint civic constitution.

There are three kinds of constitution under law as far as concerns the persons who belong under it: (1) the constitution according to the law of national citizenship of all men belonging to a nation (*ius civitatis*); (2) the constitution according to international law regulating the relation of states with each other (*ius gentium*); (3) the constitution according to the law of world citizenship which prevails insofar as men and states standing in a relationship of mutual influence may be viewed as citizens of a universal state of all mankind (*ius cosmopoliticum*).

First Definitive Article of the Eternal Peace

The civil constitution in each state should be republican.

A republican constitution is a constitution which is founded upon three principles. First, the principle of the *freedom* of all members of a society as men. Second, the principle of the *dependence* of all upon a single common legislation as subjects, and third, the principle of the *equality* of all as *citizens*. This is the only constitution which is derived from the idea of an original contract upon which all rightful legislation of a nation must be based.[4]

This classification is not arbitrary but necessary in relation to the idea of eternal peace. For if even one of these were in a relation of physical influence upon the other and yet in a state of nature, the state of war would be connected with it, and to be relieved of this state is our very purpose.

[4] [After explaining the customary definition of freedom as the right to do what does not deprive another of his right, Kant proceeds as follows:] External lawful *freedom* may be defined as follows: it is the authority [*Befugnis*] not to obey any external laws except those which I have consented to.—Likewise, external (lawful) *equality* in a state is the relationship of the citizens according to which no one can obligate another legally without at the same time subjecting himself to the law of being obligated by the other in the same manner. (We do not explain the principle of lawful dependence since this principle is implied in the conception of any kind of constitution.)—The validity of these innate and inalienable rights which are implied in his very humanity is confirmed by the principle of the lawful relations of man to higher beings (in case he believes in them). For he imagines himself, according to these very same principles, as the citizen of a natural world.—For so far as my freedom is concerned, I have no obligation even with regard to the divine laws which I recognize by pure reason except insofar as I have given my own consent (for only in terms of the law of freedom of my own reason can I form a conception of the divine will). [Kant then argues that the principle of equality cannot be similarly confirmed because God has no equals.] Concerning the right of all citizens to be equal in their subjection to the law, the only thing which matters in regard to the question of the admissibility of a hereditary nobility is the following: whether the superior rank of one subject to another precedes merit or the latter the former, it seems obvious that it is most uncertain whether merit (ability and loyalty in one's office) will follow. Hence it

This republican constitution is therefore, as far as law is concerned, the one which underlies every kind of civil constitution, and the question which we are now facing is, whether this is also the only one which can lead to eternal peace.

The answer is that the republican constitution does offer the prospect of the desired purpose, that is to say, eternal peace, and the reason is as follows: If, as is necessarily the case under the constitution, the consent of the citizens is required in order to decide whether there should be war or not, nothing is more natural than that those who would have to decide to undergo all the deprivations of war will very much hesitate to start such an evil game. For the deprivations are many, such as fighting oneself, paying for the cost of the war out of one's own possessions, and repairing the devastation which it costs, and to top all the evils there remains a burden of debts which embitters the peace and can never be paid off on account of approaching new wars. By contrast, under a constitution where the subject is not a citizen and which is therefore not republican, it is the easiest thing in the world to start a war. The head of the state is not a fellow citizen but owner of the state, who loses none of his banquets, hunting parties, pleasure castles, festivities, etc. Hence he will resolve upon war as a kind of amusement on very insignificant grounds and will leave the justification to his diplomats, who are always ready to lend it an air of propriety.

It is important not to confuse the republican constitution with the democratic one as is commonly done. The following may be noted. The forms of a state (*civitas*) may be classified

---

is as if rank were attributed without merit to the most favored (to be commander). Clearly the general will of the people would never adopt such a provision in its original contract, which is the basis of all right, and in short a nobleman [*Edelmann*] is not necessarily a *noble* man [*edler Mann*]. As far as nobility derived from *office* [*Amtsadel*] is concerned, rank in that case does not attach as a position to the person but is connected with the post, and therefore the principle of equality is not violated, for when a man quits his office, he resigns his rank and returns to the people.

according to the difference of the persons who possess the highest authority, or they may be classified according to the method by which the people are governed by their rulers, whoever they may be. The first method is properly called the form of rulership (*forma imperii*).[5] Only three such forms are conceivable; for either *one,* or a *few* associated with each other, or all who together constitute civil society possess the power to rule (*autocracy, aristocracy,* and *democracy*—the power of princes, of the nobility, and of the people).

The second method is the form of government (*forma regiminis*) and relates to the way in which the state employs its sovereign power—the constitution, which is an act of the general will by which a mass becomes a nation. The form of government in this case is either *republican* or *despotic.* Republicanism means the constitutional principle according to which the executive power (the government [*Regierung*]) is separated from the legislative power. *Despotism* exists when the state arbitrarily executes the laws which it has itself made; in other words, where the public will is treated by the prince as if it were his private will.

Among the three forms of state (or rulership), that of *democracy* is necessarily a *despotism* in the specific meaning of the word, because it establishes an executive power where all may decide regarding one and hence against one who does not agree, so that all are nevertheless not all—a situation which implies a contradiction of the general will with itself and with freedom. For all forms of government which are not *representative* are essentially *without form,* because the legislative cannot at the same time and in the same person be the executor of the legislative will; just as the general proposition in logical reasoning cannot at the same time be the specific judgment which

---

[5] [Kant here uses the term *Form der Beherrschung,* which is rulership—but further on down he shifts to *Staatsform* and *Staatsverfassung;* the essential point, however, is the distinction between form of rulership and form of government.—Ed.]

falls under the general rule.[6] The other two forms of rulership [Staatsverfassung] are defective also insofar as they give a chance to this (despotic) form of government. But it is at least possible that they provide a method of governing which is in accord with the *spirit* of representative system. Frederick II *said* at least that he was merely the highest servant of the state—while the democratic system makes this impossible, because all want to be ruler.[7]

It is therefore possible to say that the smallest number of truly representative rulers approximates most closely to the possibility of a republicanism and may be expected to reach it eventually by gradual reforms. Such an evolution is harder in an aristocracy than in a monarchy, while in a democracy it is impossible to achieve this kind of constitution—which is the only constitution perfectly in accord with law and right [Recht]—except through a revolution.[8]

---

[6] [It seems to be clear from Kant's analogy that the "cannot" of this sentence has a strictly logical connotation—i.e., All men have two legs; A is a man; therefore A has two legs.—Ed.]

[7] Many have criticized the high-sounding titles which are often given a ruler, such as "divinely anointed," "executor of God's will on earth," "God's representative," calling them coarse and flattering, but it seems to me without reason. Far from making the prince conceited, they should make him humble, if he has brains (which surely one must assume) and therefore is conscious that he has assumed an office which is too big for a man: to administer man's law, the most sacred thing that God has on earth, to hurt this prized possession of God in any way must surely worry any man.

[8] Mallet du Pan claims in his profound-sounding, yet hollow and empty language that after many years' experience he had come to accept the truth of Pope's well-known saying: "O'er forms of government let fools contest; that which is best administered is best." If that is to mean that the best-led government is the best led, then, to use a phrase of Swift, he has cracked a nut which rewarded him with a worm. If it is to mean that the best-led government is the best form of government, i.e. constitution, then it is very false; examples of good governing do not prove anything about the form of government. Who has governed better than a *Titus* or a *Marcus Aurelius*? Yet the one was succeeded by a *Domitian*, the other by a *Commodus*. This would have been impossible under

The people are very much more concerned with the form of government in this sense than with the form of rulership [*Staatsform*], although a good deal depends upon the latter's adequacy to realize the former's end. But if the form of government is to be appropriate to the idea of law and right, it requires the representative system. For only in this system is a republican form of government possible. Without it the form of government is despotic and violent, whatever the constitution may be.

None of the ancient, so-called republics knew this representative system, and hence they were bound to dissolve into despotism, which is the more bearable under the rule of a single man.[9]

Second Definitive Article of the Eternal Peace

The law of nations (Völkerrecht) should be based upon a *federalism* of free states.

Nations may be considered like individual men which hurt each other in the state of nature, when they are not subject to laws, by their very propinquity. Therefore each, for the sake of security, may demand and should demand of the other to enter with him into a constitution similar to the civil one where the right of each may be secured. This would be a *union of nations* [*Völkerbund*] which would not necessarily have to be a *state of nations* [*Völkerstaat*]. A state of nations contains a contradiction, for every state involves the relation of a superior (legislature) to a subordinate (the subject people), and many nations would, in a single state, constitute only one nation, which is contradictory since we are here considering the right of nations toward each other as long as they constitute different states and are not joined together into one.

---

a good constitution, since their incapacity to govern was known soon enough.

[9] [It is readily seen that these rather involved thoughts are a restatement of the Aristotelian doctrine that all "good" forms of government are governments according to law and right—the quintessence of constitutional theory. But the ancients did not develop any "constitutional safeguards" for this "rule of law."—Ed.]

We look with deep aversion upon the way primitive peoples are attached to their lawless liberty—a liberty which enables them to fight incessantly rather than subject themselves to the restraint of the law to be established by themselves; in short, to prefer wild freedom to a reasonable one. We look upon such an attitude as raw, uncivilized, and an animalic degradation of humanity. Therefore, one should think, civilized peoples (each united in a state) would hasten to get away from such a depraved state as soon as possible. Instead, each *state* insists upon seeing the essence of its majesty (for popular majesty[10] is a paradox) in this, that it is not subject to any external coercion. The luster of its ruler consists in this, that many thousands are at his disposal to be sacrificed for a cause which is of no concern to them, while he himself is not exposed to any danger. Thus a Bulgarian Prince answered the Emperor who good naturedly wanted to settle their quarrel by a duel: "A smith who has prongs won't get the hot iron out of the fire with his bare hands." The difference between the European savages and those in America is primarily this, that while some of the latter eat their enemies, the former know how better to employ their defeated foe than to feast on them—the Europeans rather increase the number of subjects, that is, the number of tools for more extended wars.

In view of the evil nature of man, which can be observed clearly in the free relation between nations (while in a civil and legal state it is covered by governmental coercion), it is surprising that the word *law* [*Recht*] has not been entirely banned from the politics of war as pedantic, and that no state has been bold enough to declare itself publicly as of this opinion. For people in *justifying* an aggressive war still cite HUGO

---

10 [The German word *Majestät,* like the Latin *majestas,* was a term roughly equivalent to sovereignty; it was becoming obsolete in Kant's time—and yet, one ought not to translate it with *sovereignty* here, because the parenthesis becomes dubious then. It is worth notice, however, that Kant leans toward the idea of *state sovereignty.*—Ed.]

GROTIUS, PUFENDORF, VATTEL and others (all of them miserable consolers). This is done, although their code of norms, whether stated philosophically or juristically, does not have the least *legal* force; nor can it have such force, since states as such are not subject to a common external coercion. There is not a single case known in which a state has been persuaded by arguments reinforced by the testimony of such weighty men to desist from its aggressive design.

This homage which every state renders the concept of law (at least in words) seems to prove that there exists in man a greater moral quality (although at present a dormant one), to try and master the evil element in him (which he cannot deny), and to hope for this in others. Otherwise the words *law* and *right* would never occur to states which intend to fight with each other, unless it were for the purpose of mocking them, like the Gallic prince who declared: "It is the advantage which nature has given the stronger over the weaker that the latter ought to obey the former."

In short, the manner in which states seek their rights can never be a suit before a court, but only war. However, war and its successful conclusion, *victory,* does not decide what is law and what right. A *peace treaty* puts an end to a particular war, but not to the state of war which consists in finding ever new pretexts for starting a new one. Nor can this be declared strictly unjust because in this condition each is the judge in his own cause. Yet it cannot be maintained that states under the law of nations are subject to the same rule that is valid for individual men in the lawless state of nature: "that they ought to leave this state." For states have internally a legal constitution and hence [their citizens] have outgrown the coercion of others who might desire to put them under a broadened legal constitution conceived in terms of their own legal norms. Nevertheless, reason speaking from the throne of the highest legislative power condemns war as a method of finding what is right. Reason makes [the achievement of] the state of peace a direct duty, and such a state of peace cannot be established or maintained without a treaty of the nations among themselves. Therefore there must exist a union of a particular kind which we may call the *pacific union* (*foedus pacificum*) which would be distinguished from a *peace treaty* (*pactum pacis*) by the fact that the latter tries to end merely *one* war, while the former tries to end *all* wars forever. This union is not directed toward the securing of some additional power of the state, but merely toward maintaining and making secure the *freedom* of each state by and for itself and at the same time of the other states thus allied with each other. And yet, these states will not subject themselves (as do men in the state of nature) to laws and to the enforcement of such laws.

It can be demonstrated that this idea of *federalization* possesses objective reality, that it can be realized by a gradual extension to all states, leading to eternal peace. For if good fortune brings it to pass that a powerful and enlightened people develops a republican form of government which by nature is inclined toward peace, then such a republic will provide the central core for the federal union of other states. For they can join this republic and can thus make secure among themselves the state of peace according to the idea of a law of nations, and can gradually extend themselves by additional connections of this sort.

It is possible to imagine that a people says: "There shall be no war amongst us; for we want to form a state, i.e., to establish for ourselves a highest legislative, executive, and juridical power which peacefully settles our conflicts." But if this state says: "There shall be no war between myself and other states, although I do not recognize a highest legislative authority which secures my right for me and for which I secure its right," it is not easy to comprehend upon what ground I should place my confidence in my right, unless it be a substitute [*Surrogat*] for the civil social contracts, namely, a free federation. Reason must necessarily connect such a federation with the concept of a law of nations, if authority is to be conceived in such terms.

On the other hand, a concept of the law of nations as a right *to make* war is meaningless; for it is supposed to be a right to determine what is right not according to external laws limiting the freedom of each individual, but by force and according to one-sided maxims, unless we are ready to accept this meaning: that it serves people who have such views quite right if they exhaust each other and thus find eternal peace in the wide grave which covers all the atrocities of violence together with its perpetrators. For states in their relation to each other there cannot, according to reason, be any other way to get away from the lawless state which contains nothing but war than to give up (just like individual men) their wild and lawless freedom, to accept public and enforceable laws, and thus to form a constantly growing world *state of all nations* (*civitas gentium*) which finally would comprise all nations. But states do not want this, as not in keeping with their idea of a law of nations, and thus they reject in fact what is true in theory.[11] Therefore, unless all is to be lost, the positive idea of a *world republic* must be replaced by the negative substitute of a *union* of nations which maintains itself, prevents wars, and steadily expands. Only such a union may under existing conditions stem the tide

---

11 After the end of a war, at the conclusion of a peace, it would not be improper for a people to set a day of atonement after the day of thanks so as to pray to heaven asking forgiveness for the heavy guilt which mankind is under, because it will not adapt itself to a legal constitution in its relation to other nations. Proud of its independence, each nation will rather employ the barbaric means of war by which that which is being sought, namely the right of each state, cannot be discovered. The celebrations of victory, the hymns which in good Old Testament style are sung to the Lord of Hosts, contrast equally sharply with the moral idea of the father of mankind; because besides the indifference concerning the manner in which people seek their mutual right, which is lamentable enough, they rejoice over having destroyed many people and their happiness.

of the law-evading, bellicose propensities in man, but unfortunately subject to the constant danger of their eruption (*furor impius intus—fremit horridus ore cruento.* VIRGIL).

THIRD DEFINITIVE ARTICLE OF THE ETERNAL PEACE

"The Cosmopolitan or World Law shall be limited to conditions of universal hospitality."

We are speaking in this as well as in the other articles not of philanthropy, but of *law.* Therefore *hospitality* (good neighborliness) means the right of a foreigner not to be treated with hostility when he arrives upon the soil of another. The native may reject the foreigner if it can be done without his perishing, but as long as he stays peaceful, he must not treat him hostilely. It is not the right of becoming a permanent guest [*Gastrecht*] which the foreigner may request, for a special beneficial treaty would be required to make him a fellow inhabitant [*Hausgenosse*] for a certain period. But it is the right to visit [*Besuchsrecht*] which belongs to all men—the right belonging to all men to offer their society on account of the common possession of the surface of the earth. Since it is a globe, they cannot disperse infinitely, but must tolerate each other. No man has a greater fundamental right to occupy a particular spot than any other.

Uninhabitable parts of the earth's surface, the oceans and deserts, divide this community. But *ship* or *camel* (the ship of the desert) enable men to approach each other across these no-man's regions, and thus to use the right of the common *surface* which belongs to all men together, as a basis of possible intercourse. The inhospitable ways of coastal regions, such as the Barbary Coast, where they rob ships in adjoining seas or make stranded seamen into slaves, is contrary to natural law, as are the similarly inhospitable ways of the deserts and their Bedouins who look upon the approach (of a foreigner) as giving them a right to plunder him. But the right of hospitality, the right, that is, of foreign guests, does not extend further than to the condi-

tions which enable them to attempt the developing of intercourse with the old inhabitants.

In this way, remote parts of the world can enter into relationships which eventually become public and legal and thereby
may bring mankind ever nearer to an eventual world constitution.

If one compares with this requirement the *inhospitable* conduct of the civilized, especially of the trading nations of our
continent, the injustice which they display in their *visits* to
foreign countries and peoples goes terribly far. They simply
identify visiting with *conquest*. America, the lands of the Ne-
groes, the Spice Islands, the Cape of South Africa, etc., were
countries that belonged to nobody, for the inhabitants counted
for nothing. In East India (Hindustan) they brought in foreign mercenaries, under the pretense of merely establishing
trading ports. These mercenary troops brought suppression of
the natives, inciting the several states of India to extended wars
against each other. They brought famine, sedition, treason and
the rest of the evils which weigh down mankind.

China[12] and Japan, who had made an attempt to get along
with such guests, have wisely allowed only contact, but not
settlement—and Japan has further wisely restricted this privilege
to the Dutch only, whom they exclude, like prisoners, from
community with the natives. The worst (or viewed from the
standpoint of a moral judge the best) is that the European nations are not even able to enjoy this violence. All these trading
companies are on the point of an approaching collapse; the
sugar islands, which are the seat of the most cruel and systematic
slavery, do not produce a yield—except in the form of raising
recruits for navies; thus they in turn serve the conduct of war—
wars of powers which make much ado about their piety and
who want themselves to be considered among the morally elect,

---

12 [I am omitting a lengthy and obsolete footnote on the origin of the
word *China,* in spite of its interest in showing Kant's keen personal
delight in concrete historical detail.—Ed.]

while in fact they consume [the fruits of] injustice like water.

The narrower or wider community of all nations on earth has in fact progressed so far that a violation of law and right in one place is felt in *all* others. Hence the idea of a cosmopolitan or world law is not a fantastic and utopian way of looking at law, but a necessary completion of the unwritten code of constitutional and international law to make it a public law of mankind. Only under this condition can we flatter ourselves that we are continually approaching eternal peace.

FIRST ADDITION

On the Guarantee of Eternal Peace

No one less than the great artist *nature* (*natura daedala rerum*) offers such a *guarantee*. Nature's mechanical course evidently reveals a teleology: to produce harmony from the very disharmony of men even against their will. If this teleology and the laws that effect it is believed to be like an unknown cause compelling us, it is called *fate*. But if it is considered in the light of its usefulness for the evolution of the world, it will be called *providence*—a cause which, responding to a deep wisdom, is directed toward a higher goal, the objective final end [*Endzweck*] of mankind which predetermines this evolution.[13] We do not really *observe* this providence in the artifices of nature, nor can we *deduce* it from them. But we can and must *add this thought* (as in all relations of the form of things to ends in general), in order to form any kind of conception of its possibility. We do this in analogy to human artifices.[14] The relation and integration of these factors into the end (the moral one)

---

[13] [In a lengthy footnote at this point, Kant discusses the concept of *providence* as something necessary to explain the basic "form" of events in their totality. He rejects the idea as illogical, when applied to specific events, but allows it as a general founding, governing, and directing providence. The discussion follows the treatment in the *Critique of Practical Reason.*—Ed.]

[14] [Where the end shapes the means and tools.—Ed.]

which reason directly prescribes is very sublime in *theory*, but is axiomatic and well-founded in practice, e.g., in regard to the concept of a duty toward eternal peace which that mechanism promotes.

When one is dealing as at present with theory (and not with religion), the use of the word *nature* is more appropriate in view of the limits of human reason which must stay within the limits of possible experience as far as the relation of effects to their causes is concerned. It is also *more modest* than the expression *providence*, especially a providence understandable to us; for by talking of providence we are arrogantly putting the wings of Icarus on our shoulders as if to get closer to the secret of its unfathomable purpose.

But before we ascertain more specifically how the guarantee is worked out, it is necessary to explore the situation which nature has created for those who are actors upon its great stage, and which in the last analysis necessitates its guarantee of peace. Only after that can we see how nature provides this guarantee.

Nature's provisional arrangement consists in the following: (1) she has seen to it that human beings can live in all the regions where they are settled; (2) she has by war driven them everywhere, even into the most inhospitable regions, in order to populate them; (3) she has forced them by war to enter into more or less legal relationships. It is marvelous to notice that in the cold wastes of the Arctic Sea some mosses grow which the *Reindeer* scratches out of the snow thus being enabled to serve as food or as a draft animal for the Samoyeds. Such ends become even more apparent when one discovers that furred animals on the shores of the Arctic Sea, walruses and whales provide food through their meat and heat through their fat for the inhabitants. But nature's care causes the greatest admiration when we find that drift wood, the origin of which is not well known, is carried to these regions, since without this material the inhabitants could neither build boats and weapons, nor huts in which to dwell. In that situation they seem to be sufficiently occupied with war against the animals to live peacefully with each other.

But it was probably war which *drove* the inhabitants to these places. The first *instrument of warfare* among all the animals which man during the time of populating the earth learned to tame and to domesticate was the *horse;* for the elephant belongs to a later time, when established states made greater luxury possible. The same is true of the culture of certain kinds of grasses, now called *grain,* the original form of which we no longer know, as well as of multiplying and refining of fruit trees by transplanting and grafting—in Europe perhaps only two species, the wild apples and wild pears. Such achievements could take place only in established states with fixed property in real estate. Before this men had progressed from the lawless freedom of *hunting,*[15] fishing and sheepherding to cultivating the land. After that *salt* and *iron* were discovered, perhaps the first articles of trade between nations which were in demand everywhere, through which they were first brought into a *peaceful relationship* with each other. This in turn brought them into understanding, community, and peaceful relations with the more remote nations.

Nature, by providing that men *can* live everywhere on earth, has at the same time despotically wanted that they *should* live everywhere, even against their inclination. This "should"

---

[15] Among all the ways of living the hunting life is unquestionably most at variance with a civilized constitution: because the families which are separated from each other soon become alien, and soon thereafter, dispersed in extended forests, hostile to each other, since each requires much room for its feeding and clothing. The Mosaic law forbidding the eating of blood, Genesis 9:4-6, appears to have been originally nothing else but an attempt to forbid people to live as hunters; because in this life there often occur situations where meat must be eaten raw, and hence to forbid the eating of blood means forbidding a hunting life. This law, several times reenacted, was later, with a quite different purpose, imposed by the Jewish Christians as a condition upon the newly accepted heathen Christians.

does not presuppose a duty which obliged them to do it by a moral law. Instead, nature chose war to bring this about.

We observe peoples which by their common language reveal their common ancestry, such as the *Samoyeds* on the Arctic Sea and a people of similar language, about two hundred miles away, in the Altaic Mountains. Between those two a Mongolian, horse-riding and hence belligerent, tribe have wedged themselves in, driving one part of these people far away, and the rest into the most inhospitable regions of ice and snow, where they surely would not have gone by choice.[16]

In the same manner the Finns in the northernmost part of Europe, called the Lapps, were separated from the Hungarians to whom they are related in their language by intruding Gothic and Sarmatian tribes. And what could have driven the Eskimos in the North, and the Pescheras in the South of America as far as it did, except war which nature uses everywhere as a means for populating the earth? War itself does not require a special motivation, since it appears to be grafted upon human nature. It is even considered something noble for which man is inspired by the love of honor, without selfish motives. This martial courage is judged by American savages, and European ones in feudal times, to be of great intrinsic value not only *when* there is a *war* (which is equitable), but also so *that* there may be war. Consequently war is started merely to show martial courage, and war itself invested with an inner *dignity*. Even philosophers will praise war as enobling mankind, forgetting the Greek who said: "War is bad in that it begets more evil

---

[16] Someone might ask: if nature did not intend these icy shores to remain uninhabited, what will happen to their inhabitants when no more driftwood comes to them (as may be expected)? For it may be assumed that the inhabitants of the more temperate regions will, as culture progresses, utilize their wood better, and will not allow it to drop into the river and drift into the sea. I answer: the inhabitants of those regions, of the Ob, the Yenisei, the Lena, etc., will barter for it the products of animal life which the sea provides so plentifully in the Arctic—when nature has forced the establishment of peace among them.

people than it kills." This much about what nature does in pursuit of its own purpose in regard to mankind as a species of animal.

Now we face the question which concerns the essential point in accomplishing eternal peace: what does nature do in relation to the end which man's reason imposes as a duty, in order to favor thus his *moral intent?* In other words: how does nature guarantee that what man ought to do according to the laws of freedom, but does not do, will be made secure regardless of this freedom by a compulsion of nature which forces him to do it? The question presents itself in all three relations: *constitutional* law, *international* law, and cosmopolitan or world law.—And if I say of nature: she wants this or that to take place, it does not mean that she imposes a *duty* to do it—for that only the non-compulsory practical reason can do—but it means that nature itself does it, whether we want it or not (*fata volentem ducunt, nolentem trahunt*).

1. If internal conflicts did not compel a people to submit itself to the compulsion of public laws, external wars would do it. According to the previously mentioned arrangement of nature, a people discovers a neighboring people who are pushing it, against which it must form itself into a *state* in order to be prepared as a *power* against its enemy. Now the *republican* constitution is the only one which is fully adequate to the right of man, but it is also the hardest to establish, and even harder to maintain. Therefore many insist that it would have to be a state of angels, because men with their selfish propensities are incapable of so sublime a constitution. But now nature comes to the aid of this revered, but practically ineffectual general will which is founded in reason. It does this by the selfish propensities themselves, so that it is only necessary to organize the state well (which is indeed within the ability of man), and to direct these forces against each other in such wise that one balances the other in its devastating effect, or even suspends it. Consequently the result for reason is as if both selfish forces

were nonexistent. Thus man, although not a morally good man, is compelled to be a good citizen. The problem of establishing a state is solvable even for a people of devils, if only they have intelligence, though this may sound harsh. The problem may be stated thus: "To organize a group of rational beings who demand general laws for their survival, but of whom each inclines toward exempting himself, and to establish their constitution in such a way that, in spite of the fact that their private attitudes are opposed, these private attitudes mutually impede each other in such a manner that the public behavior [of the rational beings] is the same as if they did not have such evil attitudes." Such a problem *must* be solvable. For it is not the moral perfection of mankind, but merely the mechanism of nature, which this task seeks to know how to use in order to arrange the conflict of unpacific attitudes in a given people in such a way that they impel each other to submit themselves to compulsory laws and thus bring about the state of peace in which such laws are enforced. It is possible to observe this in the actually existing, although imperfectly organized states. They approach in external conduct closely to what the idea of law prescribes, although an inner morality is certainly not the cause of it (just as we should not expect good constitution from such morality, but rather from such a constitution the good moral development of a people). These existing states show that the mechanism of [human] nature, with its selfish propensities which naturally counteract each other, can be employed by reason as a means. Thus reason's real purpose may be realized, namely, to provide a field for the operation of legal rules whereby to make secure internal and external peace, as far as the state is concerned.—In short, we can say that nature *wants* irresistibly that law achieve superior force. If one neglects to do this, it will be accomplished anyhow, albeit with much inconvenience. "If you bend the stick too much, it breaks; and he who wants too much, wants nothing" (Bouterwek).

2. The idea of a law of nations presupposes the separate

existence of many states which are independent of each other. Such a situation constitutes in and by itself a state of war, unless a federative union of these states prevents the outbreak of hostilities. Yet such a situation is from the standpoint of reason better than the complete merging of all these states in one of them which overpowers them and is thereby in turn transformed into a universal monarchy. This is so, because the laws lose more and more of their effectiveness as the government increases in size, and the resulting soulless despotism is plunged into anarchy after having exterminated all the germs of good [in man]. Still, it is the desire of every state (or of its ruler) to enter into a permanent state of peace by ruling if possible the entire world. But *nature* has decreed differently.—Nature employs two means to keep peoples from being mixed and to differentiate them, the difference of *language* and of *religion*.[17] These differences occasion the inclination toward mutual hatred and the excuse for war; yet at the same time they lead, as culture increases and men gradually come closer together, toward a greater agreement on principles for peace and understanding. Such peace and understanding is not brought about and made secure by the weakening of all other forces (as it would be under the aforementioned despotism and its graveyard of freedom), but by balancing these forces in a lively competition.

3. Just as nature wisely separates the nations which the will of each state would like to unite under its sway either by cunning or by force, and even in keeping with the reasoning of the law of nations, so also nature unites nations which the concept of a cosmopolitan or world law would not have protected from

---

[17] *Difference of religion:* a strange expression! as if one were to speak of different *morals.* There may be different *kinds of faith* which are historical and which hence belong to history and not to religion and are part of the means in the field of learning. Likewise there may be different *religious books* (Zendavesta, Vedam, Koran, etc.). But there can only be one *religion* valid for all men and for all times. Those other matters are nothing but a vehicle of religion, accidental and different according to the difference of time and place.

violence and war, and it does this by mutual self-interest. It is the *spirit of commerce* which cannot coexist with war, and which sooner or later takes hold of every nation. For, since the money power is perhaps the most reliable among all the powers subordinate to the state's power, states find themselves impelled (though hardly by moral compulsion) to promote the noble peace and to try to avert war by mediation whenever it threatens to break out anywhere in the world. It is as if states were constantly leagued for this purpose; for great leagues *for* the purpose of making war can only come about very rarely and can succeed even more rarely.—In this way nature guarantees lasting peace by the mechanism of human inclinations; however the certainty [that this will come to pass] is not sufficient to *predict* such a future (theoretically). But for practical purposes the certainty suffices and makes it one's duty to work toward this (not simply chimerical) state.

SECOND ADDITION

A Secret Article Concerning Eternal Peace

A secret article in negotiations pertaining to *public* law is a con- tradiction objectively, i.e., as regards its substance or content; subjectively, however, i.e., as regards the quality of the person which formulates the article, secrecy may occur when such a person hesitates to declare himself publicly as the author thereof.

The sole article of this kind [in the treaty on eternal peace] is contained in the following sentence: *The maxims of the philosophers concerning the conditions of the possibility of public peace shall be consulted by the states which are ready to go to war.* Perhaps it would seem like belittling the legislative authority of a state to which one should attribute the greatest wisdom to suggest that it should seek instruction regarding the principles of its conduct from its *subjects* (the philosophers); nevertheless this is highly advisable. Hence the state will *solicit* the latter *silently* (by making it a secret) which means that it will *let them talk* freely and publicly about the general maxims of the conduct of war and the establishment of peace (for they will do it of their own accord, if only they are not forbidden to do so). The agreement of the states among themselves regarding this point does not require any special stipulation but is founded upon an obligation posited by general morality legislating for human reason. This does not mean that the state must concede that the principles of the philosopher have priority over the rulings of the jurist (the representative of governmental power); it only means that the philosopher be *given a hearing*. The jurist who has made the *scales* of law and right his symbol, as well as *he *sword* of justice, commonly employs the sword not only to ward off all outside influence from the scales, but also to put it into one of the scales if it will not go down (*vae victis*). A jurist who is not at the same time a philosopher (morally speaking) has the greatest temptation to do this, because it is only his job to apply existing laws, and not to inquire whether these laws need improvement. In fact he counts this lower order of his faculty to be the higher, simply because it is the concomitant of power (as is also the case of the other two faculties).—The philosophical faculty occupies a low place when confronted by all this power. Thus, for example, it is said of philosophy that she is the *handmaiden* of theology (and something like that is said regarding the other two). It is not very clear however "whether she carries the torch in front of her gracious lady or the train of her dress behind."

It is not to be expected that kings philosophize or that philosophers become kings, nor is it to be desired because the possession of power corrupts the free judgment of reason inevitably. But kings or self-governing nations will not allow the class of philosophers to disappear or to become silent, but will let them speak publicly, because this is indispensable for both in order to clarify their business. And since this class of people are by their very nature incapable of forming gangs or clubs they need not be suspected of carrying on *propaganda*.

On the Disagreement Between Morals and Politics in Relation To Eternal Peace

Morals, when conceived as the totality of absolutely binding laws according to which we *ought* to act, is in itself practice in an objective sense. It is therefore an apparent paradox to say that one *cannot* do [what one ought to do] once the authoritativeness of this concept of duty is acknowledged. For in that case this concept [of duty] would be eliminated from morals since *ultra posse nemo obligatur*. Hence there cannot occur any conflict between politics as an applied doctrine of right [*Rechtslehre*] and law [doctrine of right and law]. Hence there can be no conflict between theory and practice, unless theory were taken to mean a general *doctrine of expediency* [*Klugheitslehre*], that is to say a theory of the maxims as to how to choose the most appropriate means for the realization of self-interested purposes; in other words, altogether to deny that morals exist.

Politics says: "Be ye therefore wise as serpents"; but morals adds as a limiting condition: "and innocent as doves." If the two cannot coexist in one commandment, there would be a conflict of politics with morals. But if the two are to be combined, the idea of a contrast is absurd, and it is not even possible to present as a task the problem as to how to resolve the conflict. Although the sentence *Honesty is the best policy* contains a theory which practice unfortunately (!) often contradicts, yet the equally theoretical sentence *Honesty is better than all politics* is completely above all objections; indeed, it is the inescapable condition of all politics. The god who guards the boundaries of morals does not yield to Jove who guards the boundaries of force; for the latter is yet subject to destiny. That is to say, reason is not sufficiently inspired to comprehend the range of predetermining causes which would permit it to predict with certainty and in accordance with the mechanism of nature the happy or bad result of the doings or omissions of men (although it may well hope for a result according with what is intended). But what needs to be done in order to remain within the groove of duty according to the rules of wisdom, and thus our final end reason, shows us quite clearly enough.

The practical man to whom morals is mere theory bases his cheerless rejection of our kind-hearted hope upon the notion that we never *want* to do what is necessary in order to realize the end leading to eternal peace, even when he concedes both that we *ought* and that we *can* do [what we should]. Of course the will of *all individual* men to live under a lawful constitution in accordance with the principles of liberty (which constitutes the *distributive* unity of the will of *all*) is not sufficient for this end. In addition it is necessary that *all jointly* will this state (which constitutes the *collective* unity of the united [general] will) which is the solution of a difficult problem. Only thus can the totality of a civil society be created. Since therefore there must come into existence, over and above the variety of the particular will of all, such a uniting cause of a civil society in order to bring forth a common will—something which no one of all of them can do—the *execution* of the idea [of an eternal peace] in practice and the beginning of a lawful state cannot be counted upon except by *force* upon the compulsion of which the public law is afterwards based. This fact would lead one to expect beforehand in practical experience great deviations from the original idea of the theory, since one can count little anyway upon the moral conviction of the legislator so that he would after he has united a wild multitude into a people leave it to them to establish a lawful constitution by their common will.

Therefore it is said: "He who has the power in his hands, will not let the people prescribe laws for himself. A state which is in possession of [the power of] not being subject to any external laws will not make itself dependent upon their judgments as far as concerns the manner of its seeking its right against such other states. Even a continent if it feels itself superior to another one, which may not actually be in its way, will not leave unutilized the opportunity of increasing its power by plundering or even dominating the other. Thus all theoretical plans for constitutional, international, and world-wide law dissolve into empty, unworkable ideals, whereas a practice which is based upon the empirical principles of human nature may hope to find a secure foundation for its structure of political prudence, inasmuch as such a practice does not consider it too mean to derive instruction for its maxims from the way in which the world is actually run."

Admittedly, if there exists no freedom and hence no moral law based upon it, and if everything which happens or may happen is simply part of the mechanism of nature, then politics as the art to use [the mechanism of nature] for the governing of men is the complete content of practical prudence, and the concept of right and law is an empty phrase. But should one find it absolutely necessary to combine the concept of law and right with politics, indeed to make it a limiting condition of politics, then the compatibility of the two must be conceded. I can imagine a *moral politician*—that is, a man who employs the principles of political prudence in such a way that they can coexist with morals—but I cannot imagine a *political moralist,* who would concoct a system of morals such as the advantage of the statesman may find convenient.

The moral politician will adopt the principle that if defects appear in the constitution or in the relations with other states which could not be prevented then it is one's duty, especially for the heads of states, to seek to remedy them as soon as possible; that is to say, to make such a constitution once again commensurate with the law of nature as it is presented to us as a model in the idea of reason. He will do this even though it cost him sacrifices of selfish interests. It would be unreasonable to demand that such a defect be eliminated immediately and with impetuosity, since the tearing apart of a [constitutional] bond of national or world-wide community, before a better constitution is available to take its place, is contrary to all morals, which in this respect agrees with political prudence. But we may properly demand that the necessity of such a change be intimately appreciated by those in power so that they may continue to approach the final end of a constitution which is best in accordance with right and law. A state may be *governed* as a republic even while it possesses despotic *power to rule* [*Herrschermacht*] according to the existing constitution, until gradually the people become capable of realizing the influence of the mere idea of the authority of law (as if it possessed physical force) and thus are found able to legislate for themselves.[18] But should the violence of a *revolution* which was caused by a bad constitution have achieved illegitimately a more lawful one, then it should not be held permissible to bring the people back to the old one, even though during such a revolution everyone who got himself involved by acts of violence or intrigue would rightfully be subject to the penalties of a seditionist. As far as the external relation between states is concerned, it cannot be demanded of a state that it divest itself of its despotic constitution (which is after all the stronger in dealing with external enemies) as long as it runs the risk of being devoured by other states; thus even in this respect the delaying of the execution must be permitted until a better opportunity presents itself.[19]

---

[18] [The last phrase is qualified by a parenthesis which reads "(welche ursprünglich auf Recht gegründet ist)." This phrase is somewhat obscure, but probably means to suggest once more that legislation in the sense of true law is founded upon (natural) law and right in any system—an ancient doctrine of all natural-law thought.—Ed.]

[19] These are permissive laws of reason which allow a state of public law which is affected by injustice to continue until everything is ready for

It may well be true that despotic moralists who make mistakes in executing their ideas violate political prudence in many ways by prematurely adopting or advocating various measures, yet experience will necessarily, in case of such offenses against nature, by and by get them into a better track. On the other hand, moralizing politicians *make* progress *impossible* and perpetuate the violation of right by glossing over political principles which are contrary to right by pretending that human nature is not *capable* of the Good according to the idea which reason prescribes.

Instead of the practice on which these clever politicos pride themselves they employ *tricks* in that they are only intent upon sacrificing the people and even the whole world by flattering the established powers in order not to miss their private profit. In this they follow the manner of true lawyers—of the trade, not legislators—when they get into politics. For since it is not their business to argue, themselves, concerning legislation, but rather to carry out the present commands of the law of the land [*Landrecht*], therefore any presently existing legal constitution must seem the best to them; or should this one be changed by the "higher authorities," then the one following will seem the best. Thus all is right and proper in a formal order. But if this skill of being fit for any task gives such lawyers the illusion of being able to judge the principles of a basic constitution in accordance with concepts of law and right—that is, *a priori* and not empirically—they cannot make this transition except in a spirit of trickery. Likewise, if they boast of their knowledge of

a complete revolution or has been made ripe for it by peaceful means: since a *legal*, even though only to a small degree lawful, constitution is better than none, and a premature change would lead to anarchy. Political prudence will therefore, in the state in which things are at the present time, make it its duty to effect reforms which are in keeping with the ideals of public law and right. At the same time it will utilize revolutions where nature produces them of itself, not for the purpose of camouflaging an even greater suppression, but rather consider it a call of nature to bring about by thorough reforms a legal constitution which is based upon the principles of freedom and therefore the only lasting one.

men (which may be expected, since they have plenty of dealings with them) without knowing *man* and what may be
made of him (for which a higher standpoint of anthropological
observation is required), and if they then, equipped with such
principles, approach constitutional and international law as prescribed by reason, they cannot make that transition either, except in a spirit of trickery. For they follow their usual method
[of reasoning according to] despotically adopted compulsory laws
even where the concepts of reason will permit only a compulsion which is lawful within the principles of freedom, since
only such compulsion will make possible a constitution according to right and law. The pretended practitioner believes he
can solve this problem empirically—from experience, that is—
with hitherto existing, largely unlawful constitutions which
have worked best, while by-passing the basic idea [of basic
principles of freedom]. The maxims which he employs for this
purpose (though he does not pronounce them) are roughly
the following sophistical ones:

1. *Fac et excusa.* Seize every favorable opportunity for
arbitrary appropriation of a right of the government [state]
over its people, or over a neighboring nation. The justification
will be formulated and the use of violence glossed over much
more easily and more decoratively *after the accomplished deed*
than if one tried first to think up convincing reasons and await
the counter reasons. This is especially true in the first of these
cases where the higher authority becomes at once the legislative authority which must be obeyed without arguing. Such
boldness itself produces a certain appearance of inner conviction
of the righteousness of the deed, and the God *bonus eventus* is
afterwards the best legal representative.

2. *Si fecisti, nega.* Whatever [evil] you have committed—
for example driving your own people to despair and into sedition—that you must deny and declare not to be your guilt. Instead you insist that what is to blame is the unruliness of the
subjects. Or if it is a case of seizing a neighboring people, then

blame it on human nature, since one can count with certainty upon being seized [by one's neighbor] if one does not forestall him in the use of force.

3. *Divide et impera.* This means: if there are certain privileged persons among your people who have merely elected you as their head as *primus inter pares,* then disunite them among themselves and set them at variance with the people; if then you will support the latter by pretending to favor greater liberties for them, all will depend upon your absolute will. Or, if it is a situation involving foreign countries, the creation of dissension among them is a relatively certain means to subject one after the other on the pretense of protecting the weaker.

No one is deceived by these political maxims, for they all are generally known. Nor is it a case of being too embarrassed, as if the injustice were too apparent. Great powers never worry about the judgment of the common crowd, but only about each other, and hence what embarrasses them is not that these principles become public, but merely that they *failed to work,* since they are all agreed among themselves on the morality of the maxims. What remains is the *political honor* which they can count upon, namely the *enlarging of their power* by whatever means are available.[20]

---

[20] If there may still be some doubt concerning the wickedness of *men* who live together in a state as rooted in human nature, and if instead the shortcomings of an as yet not sufficiently advanced culture may be cited as the cause of the lawless aspects of their frame of mind, this wickedness becomes quite obviously and unmistakably apparent in the external relation of *states* with each other. At home in each state it is veiled by the compulsion of the civil laws, because a greater power, namely that of the government, strongly counteracts the inclination of the citizens to employ force against each other. This not only gives to the whole a moral lacquer (*causae non causae*), but by putting a stop to the outbreak of lawless proclivities provides a real alleviation for the development of the moral predisposition for directly respecting right and law.—For everyone now believes of himself that he would honor and obey the concept of right and law if only he could expect the same from everyone else, and this latter the government secures for him to some extent; thus a great step (though not a moral step yet) is taken toward

From all these serpentine turnings of an amoral prudential doctrine which seeks to derive the condition of peace among men from the warlike state of nature, one thing at least becomes clear: human beings cannot escape from the concept of right and law either in their private or in their public affairs, and they do not dare to base politics merely upon the manipulations of prudence and thus reject all obedience to a concept of public law—something which is particularly surprising in regard to the concept of a law of nations. Instead they show it all the honor that is due it, even if they think up a hundred excuses and camouflages in order to evade this concept in practice and to impute to a crafty force the genuine authority of being the origin and bond of all right and law.

In order to end this sophistry (although by no means the injustice which this sophistry glosses over) and to bring the deceitful *representatives* of the mighty of this world to confess that it is not right and law but force which they defend (and the tone of which they adopt as if they themselves had something to command in this connection), it will be well to uncover the fraud with which such persons deceive themselves and others, to discover the highest principle from which the purpose of eternal peace is derived and to show that all the evil which stands in the way of eternal peace results from the fact that the political moralist starts where the moral politician equitably ends. In short, the political moralist subordinates his principles to the end, i.e., puts the wagon before the horse, and

---

a morality when this concept of duty is accepted for its own sake and without regard to reciprocity.—Since everyone in spite of his good opinion of himself presupposes a bad character in all others, men mutually pronounce judgment upon themselves to the effect that they all as a matter of *fact* are not worth much (why this is so, considering that the *nature* of man, as a free being, cannot be blamed for it, we will leave undiscussed). But since the respect for the concept of right and law which man cannot abandon most solemnly sanctions the theory of an ability to measure to such a concept, every one can see for himself that he must act in accordance with right and law, whatever others may do.

thereby thwarts his own purpose of bringing politics into agreement with morals.

In order to harmonize practical philosophy within itself, it is necessary first to decide the question whether in tasks of practical reason we should start from its *material* [i.e., substantive] principle, from its end (as object of the will), or from its *formal* one, i.e., from the principle which relates to freedom in one's relation to the outside world which states: act in such a way that you could want your maxim to become a general law (whatever its purpose may be). Without a doubt, the latter principle must take precedence; for as a principle of right it possesses absolute necessity, whereas the material principle is compelling only on condition that the empirical conditions for its realization exist. Thus even if this purpose (e.g., eternal peace) were a duty, this latter would have had to be deduced from the formal principle of the maxims of external action.

The first principle, that of the *political moralist* (the problem of constitutional, international, and world law), is a mere *technical task* (*problema technicum*); the second, which is the principle of the *moral politician,* as an *ethical task* (*problema morale*) is therefore vastly different in its procedure for bringing about the eternal peace which is now desired not only as a mere physical good, but also as a condition resulting from the recognition of duty.

Much knowledge of nature is required for the solution of the first problem of political prudence, in order to utilize its mechanism for this purpose, and yet it is all rather uncertain as far as the result, eternal peace, is concerned, whichever of the sections of the public one considers. It is quite uncertain whether the people can better be kept in obedience and at the same time in prosperity for any length of time by severity or by flattery, whether by a single ruler or by several, or by an aristocracy which devotes itself to the public service, or by popular government. History offers examples of the opposite happening under all forms of government, excepting the one truly republican form which, however, can only occur to a moral politician. Even more uncertain is an *international law* based upon a statute drafted by several ministries which is merely a word without a reality corresponding to it [*ein Wort ohne Sache*], since it would rest upon treaties which contain in the very act of their conclusion the secret reservation of being violated.

By contrast, the solution of the second *problem of political wisdom* readily presents itself, is evident to everyone, confounds all artifices, and leads directly to its end; yet with the remainder of prudence not to force it precipitately, but to approach it steadily as favorable opportunities offer.

Therefore it is said: "Seek ye first the kingdom of pure practical reason and of its *righteousness,* and your end (the well-being of eternal peace) will be added unto you." [21] For that is the peculiar feature of morals concerning its principles of public law and hence concerning a politics which is *a priori* knowable, that it harmonizes the more with an intended objective, a physical or moral advantage sought, the less it allows its behavior to depend upon it. The reason for this is that the *a priori* given general will (within a nation or in the relation between nations) alone determines what is right amongst men. At the same time this union of the will of all, if only the execution of it is carried out consistently, can be the cause within the mechanism of nature which produces the intended effect and thus effectuates the idea of law.

Thus it is a principle of moral politics that a people should unite into a state solely according to the natural-law concepts of

---

[21] [This obvious paraphrase of a famous sentence of Jesus has a somewhat different flavor in German, because Luther speaks of *Gerechtigkeit* or justice, which is indeed nearer to the Greek original *dikaiosyne.* Those who are learned in the precise wording of Biblical texts will also note that Kant speaks of "its," that is the kingdom's righteousness, whereas the King James version has "his." In this case, the English translation is closer to the Greek *autou;* however, Luther no doubt intended the same with *seiner,* but unfortunately this may also be related to the kingdom and it is thus that Kant interprets the passage.—Ed.]

freedom and equality. This principle is based upon duty, and not upon prudence. Political moralists may argue ever so much concerning the natural mechanism of a mass of people entering into society which (according to them) invalidates those principles and prevents their purpose from being realized. They may likewise try to prove their contention against those principles by giving examples of badly organized constitutions of old and new times (e.g., of democracies with a system of representation). They do not deserve to be listened to—the less so, since such a pernicious doctrine may even cause the evil which it predicts. For man is thereby put into the same class with the other living machines, and man then needs only to possess the conscious knowledge that he is not a free being to make him in his own judgment the most miserable of all creatures.

Fiat justitia, pereat mundus is a proverbial saying which sounds a bit pompous, yet it is true, and it means in simple language: "Justice shall prevail, even though all the rascals in the world should perish as a result." This is a sound principle of right and law which cuts off all the crooked paths of cunning and violence. However, care must be taken not to misunderstand this sentence as a permission to claim one's own right with the greatest severity, for that would conflict with one's ethical duty. Rather should it be understood to mean an obligation of those who have the power not to refuse or to infringe someone's right out of ill will or sympathy for others. [In order to achieve this result] there is required first of all an internal constitution of the state which is organized according to the pure principles of right and law, but then also the union of such a state with other states, either neighboring or more remote, for the purpose of settling their controversies legally (in analogy to what a universal state might do).

This sentence really does not intend to say anything more than that political maxims must not proceed from considering the welfare and happiness to be expected from their being followed, that is to say they must not proceed from the end which each of these maxims makes its object, nor from the will as the highest (but empirical) principle of political prudence. Rather such maxims must be derived from the pure principle of duty under natural law (from the Ought the principle of which is given *a priori* by pure reason) regardless of what might be the physical consequences thereof. The world will not perish because there are fewer bad men. The morally bad has a quality which is inseparable from its nature: it is self-contradictory and self-destructive in its purposes, especially in its relation to others who are like-minded. Therefore it yields to the moral principle of the good, though in a slow progression.

No conflict exists *objectively* (in theory) between morals and politics. Only *subjectively*, in the selfish disposition of men—which need not be called practice, however, since it is not based upon maxims of reason—such a conflict may remain [which is all right] since it serves as a whetstone for virtue. Virtue's true courage as expressed in the maxim *tu ne cede malis, sed contra audentior ito* consists in the present case not so much in standing up firmly against the evils and sacrifices which must be borne, but in facing the evil principle in ourselves and defeating its cunning. This principle is much more dangerous because it is deceitful and treacherous in arguing the weakness of human nature as a justification for all transgressions.

Indeed, the political moralist may say: ruler and people, or people and people are not doing *each other* an injustice when they fight each other with violence or cunning, even though they are committing an injustice by denying all respect to right and law. For while one violates his duty toward the other, who is just as lawless in his view toward him, it serves them both right if they exhaust themselves, as long as there remains enough of this species to continue this game till very distant times, so that a later generation may take them as a warning example. Providence [so they say] is justified in thus arranging the course of events; for the moral principle in man never is extinguished, and reason, which is capable pragmatically of executing the ideas of natural law according to this principle, is steadily on the increase because of the progress in culture; but so also is the guilt of such transgressions. It seems impossible to justify by any kind of theodicy the creation of such a species of corrupted beings upon this earth, if we are to assume that mankind never will be in a better state. But this standpoint of judging things is much too lofty for us—as if we could theoretically impute our notions (of wisdom) to the most supreme, inscrutable power.

We are inevitably pushed to such desperate consequences if we do not assume that the pure principles of right and law have objective reality in the sense that they can be realized, and hence that the people within the state and the states toward each other must act accordingly, whatever may be the objections of an empirical politics. True politics cannot take a single step without first paying homage to morals, and while politics by itself is a difficult art, its combination with morals is no art at all; for morals cuts the Gordian knot which politics cannot solve as soon as the two are in conflict.

The (natural) right of men must be held sacred, regardless of how much sacrifice is required of the powers that be. It is impossible to figure out a middle road, such as a pragmatically conditional right, between right and utility. All politics must bend its knee before the (natural) rights of men, but may hope in return to arrive, though slowly, on the level where it may continually shine.

II

On the Agreement between Politics and Morals According to the Transcendental Idea of Public Right and Law

If I abstract right and law from all the *substance* [*Materie*] of public law (as it exists in keeping with the various empirically given relations of men within the state or the relations between states, and as it is customarily considered by jurists) there remains the *formal quality of publicity*. For each law and rightful claim [*Rechtsanspruch*] carries with it the possibility of such publicity, since without publicity there cannot be justice (which can only be thought of as capable of being *made public*) and hence also no right, since that is only attributed by justice.

This capacity of publicity every law and rightful claim [*Rechtsanspruch*] must have. Therefore this quality provides a criterion which is easily applied and *a priori* discoverable through reason, because it is quite easy to determine whether it is present in a given case, i.e., whether it can be combined with the principles of him who is acting or not. If not, we can recognize the falsity (unlawfulness) [*Rechtswidrigkeit*] of the pretended claim (*praetensio juris*) quite readily and as by an experiment of pure reason.

After thus abstracting from all the empirical [substance] which the idea of constitutional and international law includes (of this order is the evil in human nature which necessitates coercion), it is possible to call the following statement the *transcendental formula* of public law: "All actions which relate to the right of other men are contrary to right and law, the maxim of which does not permit publicity." This principle should not only be considered as *ethically* relevant (belonging to the theory of virtue or ethics), but also as *juridically* relevant (concerning the right of men). For a maxim which I cannot permit to become *known* without at the same time defeating my own purpose, which must be *kept secret* in order to succeed, and which I cannot *profess publicly* without inevitably arousing the resistance of all against my purpose, such a maxim cannot have acquired this necessary and universal, and hence *a priori* recognizable, opposition of all from any other quality than its injustice, with which it threatens everyone.

Furthermore, this [standard] is merely *negative,* that is, it only serves to recognize what is *not right* toward others. Like any

axiom it is unprovably certain and easy to apply, as may be seen
from the following examples of public law.

1. A question occurs in *constitutional law* (*jus civitatis*)
which many believe to be difficult to answer, but which the
transcendental principle of publicity easily resolves: "Is rebellion
a right and lawful means for a people to overthrow the oppres-
sive power of a so-called tyrant (*non titulo, sed exercitio talis*)?"
The rights of the people are violated, and no injustice (*Unrecht*) is done to the tyrant by the deposition; there can be no
doubt of that. In spite of that, it is nevertheless in the highest
degree contrary to right and law (*unrecht*) to seek their right in
this manner, and they cannot complain of injustice if after being defeated in such a conflict they have to submit to the most
severe punishment.

Much can be argued both pro and contra in this matter, if
one tries to settle the matter by a dogmatic deduction of the reasons in right and law [*Rechtsgründe*]; only the transcendental
principle of the publicity of all public right and law can save
itself this prolixity. According to this principle, the people ask
themselves before the establishment of the civic contract
whether they dare make public the maxim of allowing an occasional rebellion. It is easy to see that if one were to make it a
condition of the establishment of a constitution to use force
against the head of the government [*Oberhaupt*] in certain cases,
the people would have to claim a right and lawful power over
the head of the government. In that case the head would not be
the head, or, if both [his being a head and the exercise of force
against him] were to be made conditions of the establishment
of the state, such establishment would not be possible, which
was after all the objective of the people. The unrightfulness
[*Unrecht*] of rebellion becomes evident by the fact that its
maxim would vitiate its own purpose, if one *professed it publicly*.
One would have to keep it secret.

Such secrecy would not be necessary for the head of the

government. He could openly declare that he would punish every rebellion with the death of its ringleaders, even though these believe that he had violated the fundamental law first. For if the head of the government is convinced that he possesses the *irresistible* superior force (which must be assumed to be the case even under every civic constitution, because he who does not have enough power to protect each one among the people against the others, does not have the right to command them either), then he does not need to worry about vitiating his own purpose by letting his maxim become public. This conclusion is connected with another, namely, that in case of a successful rebellion such a head of government would return to the status of a subject, and hence he must not begin a rebellion to get himself restored, nor would he have to fear that he would be brought to account for his previous conduct of government.

2. *Concerning international law.* Only if we assume some kind of lawful state (i.e., the kind of external condition under which a man can secure his right), can there be talk of international law, because as a public law it contains in its very concept the publication of a general will which determines for each man what is his own. Such a *status juridicus* must result from some kind of treaty which cannot (like the one establishing a state) be based upon compulsory laws, but at most can be a state of *continuous free* association, like the above-mentioned one of a federalism of different states. For without some kind of *lawful state* which actively links the various physical and moral persons (i.e., in the state of nature) there can only be a private law [and rights of individual persons]. In these cases [of international law] a conflict between politics and morals (morals in this case meaning theory of law or jurisprudence) occurs again, but the criterion of publicity of the maxims [of prospective actions] likewise is easily applied [to resolve it]. There is this restriction, however, that a treaty binds the states only as concerns their intent of maintaining peace among them-

selves and toward other states, but not for the purpose of making conquests.

The following instances [which we shall outline] of an antinomy between politics and morals may present themselves, together with their solution. (a) "If one of these states has promised something to another, whether it be assistance or the cession of a certain territory, or subsidies, etc., it may be asked whether such a state can free itself of keeping its word in a case where the state's safety depends upon it by [its head] declaring that he must be considered as a dual person, namely first as a *sovereign* who is not responsible to anyone in his state, and second merely as the highest *servant of the state* (*Staatsbeamte*) who must give an account to his state: wherefrom it is concluded that he is absolved in his second capacity from what he has promised in his first." But if a state (or its head) were to make public such a maxim, every other state would avoid it, or would unite with others in order to resist such pretensions. This proves that politics, with all its cunning, would upon such a footing [of candor] vitiate its own purpose; hence such a maxim must be contrary to right [*unrecht*].

(b) "If a neighboring power having grown to tremendous size (*potentia tremenda*) causes anxiety, may one assume that such a power will *want* to oppress, because she *can* do it, and does that give the less powerful a right to make a united attack upon such a power, even without preceding insult?" A state which would publicize such a maxim affirmatively would merely bring about the evil more certainly and rapidly. For the greater power would forestall the smaller ones, and as for the uniting of the latter, this would prove a weak reed against him who knows how to use the *divide et impera*. This maxim of political prudence, if publicly declared, vitiates its own purpose and is therefore contrary to justice [*ungerecht*].

(c) "If a smaller state, by its location, divides the territory of a larger one which this larger one requires for its security, is the

larger one justified in subjecting the smaller one and incorpo-
rating it into its territory?" It is easily seen that the larger should
certainly not publicize such a maxim; for either the smaller ones
would soon unite, or other powerful ones would fight over this
prize. Therefore such publicizing is inadvisable, which is a sign
that the maxim is contrary to justice and may be so in a very
high degree. For a small object of injustice does not prevent
the injustice from being very large.

3. As concerns the *world* law. I pass it over with silence: because its analogy with international law makes it easy to state
and appreciate its corresponding maxims.

The fact that the maxims of international law are not compatible in principle with publicity constitutes a good sign that
politics and morals (as jurisprudence) *do not agree*. But one
needs to be informed which is the condition under which its
maxims agree with the law of nations. For it is not possible to
conclude the reverse: that those maxims which permit publicity
are for that reason alone also just, simply because he who has
the decided superiority need not conceal his maxims. For the
basic condition of the possibility of a [true] law of nations is that
there should exist a *lawful state*. For [as we have pointed out]
without such a state there can be no public law, rather all law
and right [*Recht*] which one can imagine outside such a state
(in the state of the nature, that is) is merely private right. We
have seen above that a federative state among the states which
has merely the purpose of eliminating war is the only *lawful*
[*rechtliche*] state which can be combined with the *freedom* of
these states. Therefore the agreement of politics with morals is
possible only within a federative union (which therefore is according to principles of law and right *a priori* given and necessary). All political prudence has only one lawful ground upon
which to proceed, namely to establish such a union upon the
most comprehensive basis possible. Without this purpose, all its
arguments are unwisdom and camouflaged injustice.

This sort of false politics has its own *casuistry* in spite of the best teaching of the Jesuit [*sic*]. There is first the *reservatio mentalis*: to word public treaties in such terms as may be interpreted in one's interest as one sees fit, e.g., the distinction between the *status quo de fait* and the *status quo de droit*; secondly, there is guessing at *probabilities* [*Probabilismus*]: to think up evil intentions of others, or to make the probability of their possible predominance the legal ground for undermining other peaceful states, finally there is the *peccatum philosophicum* (*pecatillum, bagatelle*): the absorption of a *small* state, if by that a much *larger* one gains in the pretended interest of the world at large.

This argument is favored by the duplicity of politics in regard to morals, and its use of one branch of morals or another for its own purposes. Both charity for other men [*Menschenliebe*] and respect for the *right* of others is a duty. But charity is only a *conditional* duty, whereas respect for the right of others is an *unconditional*, and hence absolutely commanding duty. He who wishes to enjoy the sweet sense of being a benefactor must first make sure that he has not transgressed this duty. With morals in the first sense (as ethics) politics is readily agreed, in order to sacrifice the rights of men to their superiors. But with morals in the second sense (as a theory of right and law or jurisprudence [*Rechtslehre*], to which politics should bend its knee) politics prefers not to have any dealings at all, and prefers to deny it all reality and to interpret all its duties as mere charities.[22] This cunning device of a secretive politics could easily be thwarted by philosophy through publicizing its maxims, if only politics would dare allow the philosopher to publicize his own maxims.

To this end I propose another transcendental and affirmative principle of public law the formula of which would be this:

---

[22] [This is presumably a sharp attack upon all utilitarian approaches to government and law, as expounded by Hume, Bentham, and others.— Ed.]

"All maxims which *require* publicity in order not to miss their purpose agree with right, law, and politics."

For if they can only achieve their purpose by such publicity, they must be in accord with the general purpose of the public, namely happiness, and it is the essential task of politics to agree with this—that is, to make the public satisfied with its state. But if this purpose can *only* be achieved by publicity—that is, by removing all mistrust of its maxims—such maxims must be in accord with the rights of such a public; for only in this right can the purposes of all be united. I must, however, leave the further elaboration and discussion of this principle to another occasion. But it is recognizable that this principle is a transcendental formula, [since it can be stated] by abstracting from all empirical conditions of happiness [*Glückseligkeitslehre*] as affecting the substance of law, and by merely taking into account the form of universal legality [*Gesetzmässigkeit*].

If it is a duty, and if at the same time there is well-founded hope that we make real a state of public law, even if only in an infinitely gradual approximation, then the *eternal peace* which will take the place of the peacemakings, falsely so-called because really just truces, is no empty idea, but a task which, gradually solved, steadily approaches its end, since it is to be hoped that the periods within which equal progress is achieved will become shorter and shorter.